PRACTICAL HANDBOOKS FOR COLLECTORS

OLD CLOCKS

OLD CLOCKS

By

H. ALAN LLOYD

FOURTH EDITION

LONDON · ERNEST BENN LIMITED
NEW YORK · DOVER PUBLICATIONS INC

First edition 1951
Second edition (revised and reset) 1958
Third edition (revised) 1964
Second impression 1965
Fourth edition (revised and enlarged) 1970

Published by Ernest Benn Limited
Bouverie House · Fleet Street · London · EC4
& Dover Publications Inc
180 Varick Street · New York 100 14 · N Y

Distributed in Canada by
The General Publishing Company Limited · Toronto
© Dondi Horological Limited 1970
Printed in Great Britain
ISBN 0-510-05301-7
ISBN 0-486-22662-X (U.S.A.)

Note to Fourth Edition

Although the preparation of the new material now incorporated was undertaken by the author, the actual production, and therefore proof reading and final oversight of details, has been carried out since his death in the summer of 1969.

He had not at that time provided an intended short preface to this fourth revised edition, but it is certain he would have wished to emphasise that he regarded the research for the two appendixes as of sufficient importance to be added to a practical handbook. Their importance and bearing on the early history of clock-making are obvious and will produce a fitting memorial for the author of this book and the pioneers of horology.

Acknowledgements for kind permission for reproduction should be made to the British Museum for *Plate 79c* and to the Royal Society for *Plates 80a, b* and *c*. The reproductions of the Dondi MS are from the Bodleian Library, and all photographs of the reconstruction are the copyright of Dondi Horological Limited.

The publisher is also indebted to Dr. F. A. B. Ward for his final reading of the proofs of the new material.

January 1970

Preface to Third Edition

The resetting for this edition has provided the opportunity to make a number of corrections and additions. Thanks are due to the many readers who have written and for their continued expression of interest.

1964

Preface to First Edition

THE past few years have been very active in horological research and many interesting items have been brought to light, thus rendering the Author's book in the 'Chats' Series out of date in many respects.

The present book has a much wider range, including as it does Continental examples, especially in that early period of clock-making, the fourteenth, fifteenth and early sixteenth centuries, where there are abundant examples of very interesting work, whilst we, here in England have little or nothing to show. We have the oldest surviving mechanical clocks at Salisbury and Wells, but these, while made in this country, cannot be proved to have been the work of an Englishman. The bishop who ordered them had been recently translated from the Continent and may well have imported a Continental clockmaker; we have many records of Continental public clocks from the beginning of the fourteenth century. What we do know, thanks to the researches of Mr. Howgrave-Graham, is that judging from decorative resemblances, in all probability these two clocks were the work of one man and this probability is supported by the fact that the bishop in question was translated from Salisbury to Wells just at this same period. Richard of Wallingford is the only Englishman of whom we have record in these early days.

A chapter on American Clocks is included and in the preparation of this the Author acknowledges, with many thanks, the considerable assistance he has received from Mr. Walter M. Roberts, President of the National Association of Watch and Clock Collectors.

As before, no attempt will be made to describe in detail any complicated clocks, these, when occasionally introduced, are so done to illustrate a particular feature incorporated. Those interested in complicated clocks are referred to the author's *Some Outstanding Clocks Over 700 Years, 1250–1950*, recently published.

1

This book will remain discursive rather than scientific. In a way the author has followed the lead of the first author of a book on clocks in English, John Smith, most gloriously English of English names. This little book published in 1674, entitled *Horological Dialogues*, takes the form of an imaginary conversation between a clock-owner and a clockmaker and deals with the current problems of setting up and maintaining clocks.

In the present book the author asks his reader to imagine that all the clocks illustrated form his collection, which he has divided into types and periods for the convenience of display and dissertation. ('Heaven forbid,' ejaculates my wife, 'that we should own all those clocks. We have quite enough; we live in a house, not in a museum.' And she is quite right.) The author is taking the reader round and explaining how evolution and design progressed through the ages.

When we come to a particularly interesting piece which has historical connexions, or is by a particularly famous maker, we shall pause on our tour and deal with that point; there will be no stern chairman to rap the table with his gavel and say: 'Gentlemen, the point before the meeting is . . .' But these temporary digressions will not displace any of the clocks on the shelves, and we shall pick up our narrative of evolution and design just where we left off to traverse the bypaths.

Of course, in spite of a generous allowance of plates and many pages of text, there are many omissions both of examples of clocks and in biographical and historical matter. One may criticise and say that there is a big gap in the series here, or that this or that type has been omitted entirely; or another that there should be more biographical notes or a fuller glossary of horological terms, etc. All too true, but, in the words of the second-hand-clothes dealer who, when his customer brought back a coat and complained that it was full of moth, replied, 'Vot do you expect for thirty shillings?—'umming birds?' The author always feels that illustrations are the heart and soul of books of this nature and he has sacrificed some things to achieve greater completeness in this direction. He hopes that the reader will agree.

The reader also will find a certain amount of repetition in the text; this has been done rather than have too many references back.

Where known, measurements are given; these are only given as a rough guide, since all photographs have been scaled down to uniformly sized blocks. In many instances they have been scaled off from the photographs; where only one dimension, such as that of the dial, has been known they are therefore only approximate.

The most usual questions put by the beginner about an old clock he has inherited or acquired are, 'How old is it?' and 'How much is it worth?' Old clocks do not differ from other *objets d'art*, nor do their owners differ from other human beings; or do they? (The sister of a famous collector, on being introduced to my wife and myself, turned to my wife and said, '*You* are normal, aren't you?') Most owners think that their geese are swans, so the answer is generally, 'Not half as old as you think' and 'Nothing like as much as you hope.' In this matter we generally have to join up with the Irishman, who when asked, after he had killed his pig, what it weighed replied, 'Not as much as I expected; I never thought it would.' Most really fine pieces have been rediscovered during the last fifty years and now the urge to hold something more than paper-money has brought so many into the market who have no real interest in or knowledge of it, that prices are out of all proportion and the real connoisseur is left sadly to look on.

There are, however, still occasional finds to be made. One of the fine early pieces illustrated in this book was bought, just before the war, for £3. Further, there are many fine pieces by the lesser well-known makers, which horologically are just as interesting as some of the less elaborate pieces by the great makers.

The question of dating examples has always been difficult. We get a certain trend in design but, unless we have some documentary evidence, dates must always be approximate. The author states in advance that he will not be drawn into any controversy on this point. Further, it is often difficult to convince those ignorant of the subject that their ideas are quite wrong. The author had the greatest difficulty once in persuading a friend, who claimed descent from an Elizabethan clockmaker, of the same name, that a clock he owned did not date from that period, because someone who had little or no knowledge had told him so, and he liked to believe it. The type of

clock could not have been earlier than Charles II, and it was
in fact a George III piece.

Obviously, the earlier the clock the greater its interest and
value as a general rule; but there are many exceptions, mainly
those pieces which incorporate the first use of later developments in the craft and which are the work of those later masters,
who, not content with the results already achieved by others,
have gone on to devise those later improvements.

But the interest in any subject, and clocks in particular, does
not lie in acquiring the rare and expensive, which are usually,
but not always, also beautiful both in design and manner of
execution. Such possessions are of necessity limited to the very
few by reason of the fact that very few genuine examples exist;
prices have reached such levels that a book dealing only with
the 'aristocrats' of the clock world would have a practical
interest for very few.

No, the vast majority of owners of old clocks have inherited
them from their ancestors and this gives them a personal value
that cannot be appraised in the sale room. It is to these owners
of clocks, in the main, that this book is addressed in the hope
that, by studying the different points brought out, such as the
progress in design of cases, hands, spandrels, dials, etc., they
may be able with reasonably certainty to date their own possessions, and, with these as a nucleus, start a collection based on
some specific idea.

Clocks by makers residing in a particular locality, clocks of a
shape particularly admired, such as basket or balloon, etc.,
clocks showing the evolution of design over a chosen period;
all these could form the basis of a collection. Just to acquire
anything because it happens to be old is not, in the author's
opinion, collecting; it is merely performing the functions of a
dealer who has to keep a large stock to satisfy a catholicity of
tastes; a collector should be strong-minded enough to dis-
criminate between what fits into his plan and what does not.

In writing a book of this sort the author is dependent on
many people for help, especially in the matter of illustrations,
and thanks are due to the following for the items enumerated:

Thureau-Dangin: The Sumerian numeration. Biographical
details of John Shelton: Mr. T. W. Robinson, late Librarian
Royal Society. Details of the travels of Shelton's clock: Pro-

fessor Cope of Philadelphia University. The Librarian of the Royal Society for access to their shelves.

Fig. 8 is from Ungerer's *Horloges Astronomiques*. Hessisches Landesmuseum, Frontispiece, *Plate 45c, d, 46a*; Mrs. Oakden Fig. 10, *Plate 24d*; Bodleian Library *Plate 1b*; Musee des Arts decoratifs, Paris *Plate 2a, b*; Dr. E. Gschwind *Plate 2c, d*; British Museum *Plate 3*; Herzog Anton-Ulrich Museum, Brunswick *Plate 4a, 5, 6, 12*; Dr. H. von Bertele *Plate 4b, c and d, 19a*; The Ilbert Collection *Plate 7, 9a, 14b, 26c, 39c, 40a, b, 46b, 47*; Banff Museum *Plate 8*; Rosenborg Museum, Copenhagen *Plate 9b*; the late Captain H. Vivian *Plate 9d*; Science Museum, London *Plate 10a, 21*; Dr. E. Morpurgo *Plate 10b, c, d*; Bavarian National Museum *Plate 13*; Germanisches Museum, Nuremberg *Plate 14a, 45a, b*; Mr. E. Brooks *Plate 14c, d, 19d*; Dr. Newland *Plate 15b*; Mr. John Huddleston *Plate 15c*; Zwinger Museum, Dresden *Plate 15d*; Mr. P. Dawson *Plate 12c, d*; Fitzwilliam Museum, Cambridge *Plate 17b*; Mr. W. Stopher *Plate 18a, 43c*; the late W. Iden *Plate 17d, 22b, c, 23c, 35c, d, 37a, 38a*; Lord Harris *Plate 17a, 18b, c, d, 20b, 22a, 37b, 43a, d, 44a*; Mr. G. F. Hutchinson *Plate 17c, 24a*; the late Earl of Leicester *Plate 19c*; The President, Queens' College, Cambridge *Plate 20a, 37d*; the Rev. Dinsdale *Plate 20c, 41c, d*; the late J. C. Hirst *Plate 22d, 26b, 39d*; by gracious permission of Her Majesty, the Queen *Plate 25a, c, d, 38c*; the Master of Trinity College, Cambridge *Plate 25b, 39b*; Mr. James Oakes *Plate 26a*; Vienna Clock Museum *Plate 27d*; Mr. L. H. Cooper *Plate 28c, 44c*; The Mond Nickel Co. Ltd. *Plate 29c, 44d*; the Hon. Mrs. B. Ionides *Plate 30, 33b*; Mr. B. Partridge *Plate 31a, 40d*; Mr. C. E. Thornton *Plate 32b, c, 41b*; Mr. A. Greenwood *Plate 33a*; Mr. W. Gibson *Plate 34d*; Mrs. van Zwanenberg *Plate 33c, 41a*; The Royal Society *Plate 35a, b*; Dr. Solbeck-Stojaneck *Plate 36b*; Mr. C. W. Glossop *Plate 42a*; the late A. K. Marples *Plate 42b*; Mr. Ernest Watkins *Plate 43b*; Mr. M. Dineley *Plate 44b*.

From the author's collection *Plate 1d, 9c, 11, 15a, 16a, b, 19b, 23a, b, 24b, 28d, 31c, 37c, 38b, d, 39a, 40c, 42c, d, 46c, d*.

American Philosophical Society and Geo. H. Eckhardt *Plate 48*; George H. Eckhardt *Plate 49b*; Old Stourbridge Village *Plate 49a, d*; C. A. Currier, M.D. *Plate 49c*; J. Cheney Wells Collection, Courtesy Mr. Barney *Plate 50a, b*; D. K. Packhard *Plate 51a, b, c, d*; W. M. Roberts *Plate 52c, d*; *Plate 52b, 53c, d*,

F. Mudge Selchow; *Plate 53a, 54a, b*, R. C. Morrell, Bristol Clock Museum; *Plate 54c, d*, Dr. A. G. Cossidente.

All the other Plates not enumerated are acknowledged, with much gratitude to the late Malcolm Webster, who gave me free run of his extensive stock and let me choose the examples needed; he also gave me valuable advice. Fig. 9 is from a drawing by Mr. F. Janca.

Limpsfield 1958

Contents

Illustrations

9

39   William Osborne, Dial, *c.* 1705 : Richard Street, Dial, *c.* 1708 :
     Daniel Quare, Dial, *c.* 1710 : George Graham, Dial, *c.* 1720

40   Quare Equation Movement, *c.* 1710; Back view : William
     Tomlinson, Dial, *c.* 1735 : Thomas Budgen, Dial, *c.* 1740

41   Finney, Dial : John Benson, Dial, *c.* 1775 : Helm, Dial,
     c. 1785; Perpetual Calendar

42   Thomas Lister, Dial, *c.* 1805 : William Bothamley, Dial,
     c. 1785 : Edward East, Back Plate, *c.* 1660 : John Hilder-
     son, Back Plate, *c.* 1665

43   Joseph Knibb, Back Plate, *c.* 1685 : Henry Jones, Back
     Plate *c.* 1680 : Samuel Watson, Back Plate, *c.* 1690 :
     Daniel Quare, Back Plate, *c.* 1695

44   Claude du Chesne, Back Plate, *c.* 1715 : George Graham,
     Back Plate, *c.* 1725 : Justin Valliamy, Back Plate, *c.* 1775 :
     Back Plate, *c.* 1820

45   Monastic Night Alarm Clock, *c.* 1400; Behind the Dial :
     J. P. Treffle Night Clock, *c.* 1675; Back view

46   Dial and below movement Pendulum in 45 *c.* : Italian
     Night Clock, *c.* 1680 : Joseph Knibb, Night Clock, *c.* 1685

47   P. T. Campani, Night Clock, 1683; Movement : Three
     Early Nineteenth-century Night Clocks

48   Rittenhouse Clock, 1769 and Dial

49   Simon Willard, Tall Clock, *c.* 1785 : R. Shearman, Tall
     Clock, *c.* 1800 : John Osgood, Corner Tall Clock,
     c. 1797 : Joshua Wilder, Grandmother Clock, *c.* 1800

50   Simon Willard, Wall Clock, *c.* 1770 : Movement of Wall
     Clock : Simon Willard, Banjo Clock, *c.* 1810 : Move-
     ment of Banjo Clock

51   Anon. Banjo Lyre Clock, *c.* 1825 : Anon. Lyre Clock, *c.* 1830 :
     Benjamin Morrill, Mirror Wall Clock, *c.* 1820; Movement

52   David Wood, Shelf Clock, *c.* 1800 : Simon Willard, Light-
     house Clock, *c.* 1822 : Eli Terry, Shelf Clock, *c.* 1816;
     Wooden Strap Movement

53   Atkins & Downs, Mirror Shelf Clock, *c.* 1831; Wooden
     Movement : Joseph Ives, Wagon Spring Clock,
     c. 1825; Movement

APPENDIX II

CHAPTER ONE

Early Methods and Mechanical Development

How and when primitive man came to take cognisance of the passing of time can only be surmised. Not being nocturnal in habit, he would rise with the sun and retire at dusk. How did the recording of Time begin? Who made, and how were they made, those first efforts in numeration in order that some record might be kept of the motion of the heavenly bodies; for undoubtedly these inspired the earliest efforts at mathematics and astronomy.

We are now nearing the completion of the second millenium of the Christian era; the birth of Jesus seems incredibly remote and the civilisation and knowledge of those days we look upon as very primitive, except so far as moral precepts are concerned. Yet we have to double this period and then add it to our present reckonings, bringing us to 4000 B.C. in order to arrive at the time that it is estimated that the Sumerian civilisation began; when the Sumerians first started counting on their 10 fingers and thumbs.

Finding 10 not easily divisible, they introduced a unit of 6, which is divisible by 2 and by 3, and formed a system based on a combination of 10 and 6. They then took 60 as another unit and, based on this, they arrived at $2 \times 60 = 120$, $3 \times 60 = 180$, up to $10 \times 60 = 600$. This, again, was taken as a further unit and we get $2 \times 600 = 1200$, $3 \times 600 = 1800$, up to $6 \times 600 = 3600$ or 60^2. This was taken as finality and the word for it was Sar, or a circle, whole, totality. Later they increased their reckoning up to 60^3, 216,000.

This has frequently been accepted as the origin of the circle of 60 degrees of 60 minutes each, but this is not so. The division of the circle originated in space measurements in the celestial sphere, which were eventually converted into time measurements. The division of the day into two periods of 12 hours each is generally credited to the Babylonians.

In the twentieth chapter of the Second Book of Kings, verse eleven, we read, 'And Isaiah the prophet cried unto the Lord: and he brought the shadow ten degrees backward, by which it had gone down in the dial of Ahaz.' This is again recorded in the thirty-eighth chapter of Isaiah, verse eight, reading, 'Behold, I will bring again the shadow of the degrees, which is gone down in the sun dial of Ahaz, ten degrees backward. So the sun returned ten degrees, by which degrees it was gone down.' These passages have sometimes been taken to indicate that sundials, as we know them, were in use in early biblical times; but the marginal notes in the Authorised Version give the alternate translation of the Hebrew rendered 'dial' as degrees, and the Revised Version gives the rendering steps. The Rev. J. R. Dommelow in his *One Volume Bible Commentary* writes, 'Probably a platform surrounded by steps and surmounted by a pillar, the shadow of which fell upon a smaller or larger number of steps according as the sun mounted or declined in the sky.'

It is not within the scope of this book to trace these early efforts to record time. Let it suffice to say that one of the earliest known surviving time-measuring instruments is an Egyptian shadow clock of the tenth or eighth centuries b.c., of which a copy is in the Science Museum, in London; the original is (or was) in Berlin. This was not, as might be supposed, a vertical erection, but a horizontal T-shaped piece, the cross-bar being slightly higher than the tail. As the sun made its daily apparent motion from east to west, rising and declining in the heavens, the shadow of the cross-bar would be thrown on the tailpiece, gradually shortening towards midday and lengthening again as the shadow travelled down the scale in the afternoon.

There are three kinds of day, two natural and one artificial, viz. the sidereal day, the solar day and the mean day. Astronomers have at all times used the sidereal day, that is the time taken by the earth to revolve once, so that any given fixed star again passes the observer's meridian. This period is fixed at 23 hours 56 minutes 4 seconds mean solar time. The mean solar day is longer, because it is measured by the passing of the sun across the observer's meridian, and while the earth has been completing its daily revolution it has been also completing a day's travel in its annual orbit around the sun, which adds, on an average, 3 minutes 56 seconds to the sidereal day. The stars are so far distant compared with the distance between the sun and the earth that this error is negligible in estimating sidereal time. The sun, which is approximately 93,000,000 miles away from the earth, is really only a very near star.

It will be noted that the expression *mean solar day* has been used; the length of the apparent solar day as shown on a sundial varies each day. Because the earth's orbit around the sun is elliptical, owing to the effect of gravity, the daily travel of the earth in its orbit varies. In January, when the earth is nearest the sun, it travels its fastest, whereas in July the earth is at the farthest point in its elliptical course and, therefore, travels at its slowest speed. When farthest from the sun the earth is said to be in its apogee, and when nearest in its perigee.

Another factor is that the sun's apparent motion is not along the celestial equator, but in a plane inclined to it at an angle of approximately $23\frac{1}{2}°$; this causes a daily varying effect. Sometimes these two causes operate together, that is, both tend to increase or diminish the length of the day, and sometimes they operate against each other, the one tending to increase the length of the day and the other to shorten it, or vice versa. The combination of these two causes is a daily variation between mean time as shown by the clock and apparent time as shown on a sundial. This is known as the equation of time, and will be dealt with when we consider equation clocks.

But while astronomers have always known the variation between sidereal and solar time, and divided the day into twenty-four equal parts between the passing of the meridian of any given star, they were, until the general standard was raised by the resurgence of education at the period of the Restoration, a category apart. For the masses there was no standard; in some places, such as Nuremberg and district, the so-called Nuremberg hours of light and darkness were kept. These were equal in duration but varied in number with the season. The twenty-four hours were divided between eight hours of darkness and sixteen of daylight at mid-summer and eight hours of daylight and sixteen of darkness in the middle of the winter. In between, public notices decreed on what dates an hour should be added to or subtracted from the daylight period. Clock dials were often painted, partly light blue and partly dark blue, representing day and night; movable shutters then indicated the proportion of daylight to darkness for the month in question. This system was abandoned early in the seventeenth century. According to Albrecht, in *Die Raeder Uhr*, there is in the Germanisches Museum in Nuremberg a wooden clock with its original dial of date 1630 having a simple twelve-hours dial. Presumably this clock is by a Nuremberg maker, but this is not stated. In the near-by town of Rothenberg the old method of reckoning carried on until early in the nineteenth century.

In Egypt and in the Middle East the time was divided into an equal number of periods, usually six, of light and dark, the length of each period would, therefore, vary daily with the seasons. This method of reckoning time was practised in Japan until 1873; they used clocks with foliot balance, a type which will be described later, having two escapements and two foliots, the one for daylight hours and the other for the night hours; the former would cut out at dusk and set in motion the latter. Every month the clockmaker would call and adjust the weights of each foliot, lengthening the period of the daylight hour and shortening that of the night, or vice versa.

We have, however, wandered somewhat from the theme of very early time-recording methods. As the reader has been warned in the Preface, this is a discursive book, and it will at times wander off into branch discussions. Besides shadow clocks, which were useful only in sunshine – here we must remember that early civilisation started in the Middle East, Egypt and the Mediterranean countries, where there is usually plenty of sun-shine – the Greeks and Egyptians developed water clocks, or *Clypsedræ*, as they were called by the Greeks. These usually worked on the principle of the filling or the emptying of a vessel at a controlled speed, and they had the advantage of being useful at night or in cloudy weather.

The burning of graduated candles or of oil contained in a marked glass vessel was another rough-and-ready method of telling the passing of the hours. These methods were later sup-planted by the sand-glass, which gave more accurate results (see *Plate 1a*). This shows a series of four glasses of the Renais-sance period, so filled to empty in $\frac{1}{4}$, $\frac{1}{2}$, $\frac{3}{4}$ and 1 hour respectively. As will be seen from the illustration, these early glasses were cast in two pieces and joined together in the middle by bands. Up to the eighteenth century, and even in some country parishes into the nineteenth century, these sand-glasses were used in church pulpits to remind the preacher of the passing of time and, if need be, to restrain his eloquence. In the parish church of Titsey, Surrey, near where the author lives, there is still a stand of four sand-glasses on the wall by the pulpit; but as the church has a quarter chiming clock, the sand-glasses have largely lost their usefulness.

With present-day sermons of ten, fifteen, or twenty minutes as the rule, it is difficult to realise the patience with which our forebears sat listening to sermons of two hours' duration or more, and twice a day at that very often, if we are to accept the evidence of the habits of the times as given to us by Samuel Pepys.

We can imagine the Presbyterian, Dr. Bates, using such a glass when preaching his farewell sermon at St. Dunstan's on August 17th, 1662; this being the last Sunday before the application of the Act of Uniformity. Samuel Pepys writing in his *Diary* says:

'17th (Lord's Day). Up very early, this being the last day that the Presbyterians are to preach, unless they read the new Common Prayer and renounce the Covenant, and so had a mind to hear Dr. Bates' farewell sermon, and walked thither ... to St. Dunstan's, where it not being seven o'clock yet, the doors were not yet open. . . . At eight o'clock I went and crowded in at a back door among others, the church being half full almost before any doors were open publicly . . . and so got into the gallery beside the pulpit and heard very well. His text was "Now to the God of Peace" the last Hebrews and the 20th verse: he making a very good sermon. . . . Besides the sermon, I was very pleased with the sight of a fine lady that I have often seen walk in Graye's Inn Walk, and it was my chance to meet her again at the door going out, and very pretty and sprightly she is. . . . After dinner to St. Dunstan's again; and the church quite crowded before I came, which was just at one o'clock; but I got into the gallery again, but stood in a crowd and did exceedingly sweat all the time. . . .'

Sermons were so long that it was possible to visit several churches on a Sunday sampling the sermons at each. Another entry, for November 9th, 1662, reads:

'9th (Lord's Day). . . . Then up, and after being ready

walked to my brother's where my wife is, calling at many churches, and then to the Temple, hearing a bit there too. . . .'

We can imagine the parson, at the end of the first hour, taking the sand-glass and turning it over on its central pivot, taking a deep breath and preparing for the second hour.

Just when clocks, as we know them with trains of wheels, came into use it is impossible to say. They were first used for monastic purposes at a time when the life of the whole community was regulated by the canonical hours. Unfortunately the monks did not consider posterity. They used the same word, horologium, to denote anything that recorded the passing of time whether it be a sundial, water-clock, or any other type, or a mechanical, weight-driven clock as we know it today. Thus there is no guide to the exact date of the change over to weight-driven clocks. It would, of course, be gradual, spreading outwards from the place of its origin.

It would seem correct to suppose that turret clocks were the first to be made. They would be installed in the monastery tower, at first without any dial visible from the outside, and the sexton would strike the necessary number of strokes on the bell. Even if they had had dials very few of the general populace could have read them.

A great deal of controversy has raged over the exact location of the first turret clocks. Some say they started in Italy, some that South Germany was their place of origin. Mr. R. P. Howgrave-Graham, who has perhaps done more to elucidate this problem than anyone – at any rate as regards England – considers the earliest English clock, of which anything has survived to come down to us, to be the old Salisbury Cathedral clock recently discovered by Mr. T. R. Robinson, of date about 1386, being just older than the more widely known clock at Wells Cathedral dating about 1392. He has recently discovered evidence that these two clocks were by the same maker.

The clock from Dover Castle, now in the Science Museum in London, was long thought to be one of the oldest surviving in England, but recent research has shown that this clock is probably of mid-seventeenth-century origin. Turning to the Continent, in 1277 has produced the *Liber del Saber Astronomico Alfonso X de Castille*. This was a book containing the collected writings of Hispano-Moorish authors of the day; it also repeated, probably, the writings of earlier centuries from Arabia and the Near East. In this is depicted a Mercury clock not unlike the seventeenth-century water clocks we sometimes see in which the drum is divided into compartments by radial pierced plates, the water or mercury percolating through the small holes and acting against a weight, giving to the drum a slow but continuous motion, unbroken by any escapement. Since the Court of Alfonso X was the centre of learning at that time, it may be fairly well assumed that the mechanical clock, as we now know it, had not yet been invented.

Opposed to this, Giovanni de Dondi of Padua, about 1350 constructed a weight-driven-balance clock as the motive force for his famous astronomical clock. (*Plate 1b.*) In his detailed description of this clock he says that the ordinary clockwork part is only shown diagrammatically since it is a common clock, of which several types are known. It would seem, therefore, that in the 75 years between 1277 and 1350 the mechanical clock had been invented and become quite common.

Dante makes reference to a clock in his *Paradiso*, which would appear to be a mechanical clock; the *Paradiso* was written around 1320. A clock is also reputed to have been made in Padua by Dondi's father in 1344. Those interested in this aspect of horology are referred to Drummond Robertson's *The Evolution of Clockwork*, perhaps the most exhaustive work on the subject, at any rate in English.

Strasburg Cathedral has been the location of three famous clocks, the first, by an unknown maker, being finished about 1354. This was succeeded by the second, constructed between the years 1571 and 1574 by the famous brothers Isaac and Joseph Habrecht, members of a famous family of clockmakers, from the designs of Conrad Dasypodius, Professor of Mathematics at Strasburg University.

This clock, after many years of inactivity, was replaced by the present clock by Schwilgué, which was finished in 1842. This is one of the marvels of the present time. In its astronomical recordings it even takes in the precession of the equinox, the gearing of which, according to Ungerer, has a ratio of 1 : 9,451,512.

When constructing the second clock in 1574 Habrecht used an automaton in the form of a cock, which crowed and flapped its wings when the clock struck. This cock was part of the original clock of 1354, and was in sufficiently good order to be used again two hundred years later; it is today preserved in the museum at Strasburg. The device of a crowing cock is often incorporated in early clocks to record the hours and probably derives from Our Lord's warning to Peter, that he should deny Him before the cock crew.

Thus we see that, if by 1350 clocks had attained such a degree of perfection that automata capable of functioning over several hundred years were incorporated in them, they must have attained a considerable degree of refinement by that date. The location of this clock at Strasburg favours the South German school of thought as the origin of turret clocks. As we have seen independent thought was active contemporaneously in Italy.

In his *Origin de l'Horologe à Poids* the late M. Charles Frémont illustrated automata which are dated around 1250, but these were not applied to clocks.

The easiest form of motive power which would appeal to the early investigator would be the falling weight. Indeed, today, this is still an ideal method as it gives an even and steady pull. How to control this force was the problem; who solved it no one knows, and no one, probably, ever will. Whatever his name, he was, in the author's opinion, a perfect genius; he had no antecedent work to guide him.

Recently Drs. Joseph Needham and Derek Price have discovered a chinese manuscript of 1088 which describes a water clock where a stream of water flows into a cup at the end of an adjustable steelyard which tips when the requisite weight of water has been introduced. This unlocks a train allowing it to go forward one step and then locks it again as the empty cup returns to its original position, each interval being ¼ hour. Regulation was by adjusting the weight of water necessary to tip the steelyard, by altering the position of the counterpoise. A tube sighted on to a selected star gave the sidereal day as the time standard for regulation. Here we have a definite escapement, functioning at a constant interval to unlock and relock a train of wheels.

The inventor of the verge escapement in all probability had no knowledge of this Chinese clock so that we can credit him, as well as his Chinese predecessor, as being a man of genius.

The invention is known as an escapement because it allows one tooth of the crown wheel to escape at a time, thus enabling it to make a fractional turn before locking the wheel again. The word verge is probably derived from the Latin *verga* a wand or staff. This root appears in the word verger, he who precedes the church procession with his wand or staff of office.

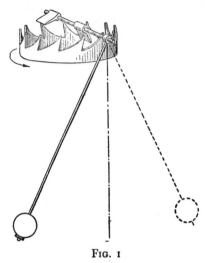

FIG. 1

Fig. 1 shows the form of the verge escapement as later adapted to the pendulum; it consists of a wheel with an uneven number of saw-like teeth, known as the crown wheel – a very apt description. Across this is positioned a staff or arbor, as it is termed in horology, with two pallets set in it at right angles to each other. As the foliot, seen in *Plate 1c*, swings in one direction, one pallet on the arbor releases a tooth of the crown wheel, but the second pallet has now become locked on the crown wheel, causing a check to the swing of the foliot and setting it swinging in the opposite direction.

The term foliot is possibly derived from the old French *esprit follet*, a goblin associated with Puck and represented by the ceaseless to-and-fro motion. This raises the query, was the inventor a Frenchman? In the absence of any more substantial proof of early activity in France, this does not seem likely. The clock in the Palais de Justice in Paris, originally constructed by Henri de Vic, and of which all parts have at different times been renewed once or more times, was for a long time accepted as one of the earliest clocks, if not the earliest. According to Drummond Robertson the real name of the maker was Heinrich von Wiek, and he came from the upper reaches of the Rhine or Lorraine in 1362 to start the work. These details do not lend much support to the theory of a French invention of the verge escapement, which Dondi says was widely known in 1350.

An illustration of a very early foliot-balance clock is given in *Plate 1c*. This is an example of a very early chamber clock without alarm or strike, and dates from the middle of the fifteenth century. Final regulation was effected by the alteration of the position of the weights on the crossbar; in the picture the upper pallet is free and the lower one is engaging one of the teeth of the crown wheel. The driving weight and rope are not shown; the rope would pass over the grooved wheel to the left of the bottom, or great wheel, in the illustration. It will be noted that the foliot balance and pallet arbor are suspended by a thread which allowed a free swing. This gave a further means of regulation; by altering the position of the thread on the notched arm the angle of incidence of the pallet to the crown wheel is changed, longer contact giving a slower release of each tooth and vice versa.

The use of silk for suspending pendulums actuated by a crutch was maintained on the Continent two hundred years later for the suspension of the pendulum after its invention in 1657, but it was not employed in England.

The clock will hang on a hook driven into the wall and passing through the upper ring at the back, a vertical position being maintained by the two lower distance pieces. It will be seen that the arbor of the great wheel passes through the front plate and engages with the toothed periphery of the dial, thus revolving the dial so that each hour in turn passes before a stationary pointer or hand, not visible in the photograph, instead of the hand revolving in front of a stationary dial, as is the custom today.

We have already remarked that, probably, the earliest clocks were used for monastic purposes; they were simple alarm clocks which let off every hour. This served to call the attention of the sexton and, if necessary, to awaken him. He then proceeded to strike the necessary number of hours on the monastery bell, which would be quite independent of the clock. 'Old Time, the clock setter, that bald Sexton Time,' says Shakespeare in *King John*.

These early clocks had to serve the sexton day and night. We therefore often find knobs set into the dial enabling the time to be ascertained by touch, with a double knob set at the 12 or 24, according as the dial was made to record 12 or 24 hours. The use of raised indicators on clock and watch dials is still in use today in what are known as blind men's watches. The Italians reckoned the time in twenty-four equal hours starting at sunset; the South Germans, twice times twelve, starting at midnight. As we have already seen, in Nuremberg and district they had their own method of calculating time.

The question of precedence between the balance and foliot is quite uncertain, nor can we attribute either one or the other to any definite locality. An example of a balance is seen in *Plates 1b and 9a*. The balance wheel has the same reciprocating action as the foliot balance, but regulation was by means of the driving weight. A cylindrical copper sheath would be nearly filled with lead, leaving a space at the top into which more or fewer lead shot could be placed, until the necessary degree of accuracy of going was achieved. One such early weight is seen in *Plate 9c*. The crown wheel in these clocks still remained vertical.

Up to this time clocks and their housings were constructed entirely of metal, the movements of iron and the housings either of iron or, in the case of the finer products, of gilded brass. Fig. 2 shows an illustration from Jost Aman's *Book of Trades* showing 'The Clockmakers'. It was published in Nuremberg in 1658 and brings this point out. The narrow strip plates were riveted or wedged. It was the second half of the sixteenth century before wood was used for the making of cases on the Continent; in England a century later.

Turret clocks were, from the earliest days, made entirely of wrought iron and of the cage type (*Plate 21*). The modern 'bench' type, i.e. a cast-iron horizontal bed with the various trains positioned side by side, was not adopted until later. The earliest found by the author is in the church of Notre-Dame at Versailles dated 1763, but this type was not generally adopted until Big Ben was designed by Lord Grimthorpe, then Edmund Beckett Denison, in the eighteen-fifties.

c

Confector horologij.   Vrmacher.

FIG. 2

The earliest domestic clocks were also all of wrought iron, both movements and housings, as we see in *Plate 1d*. In the sixteenth century, on the Continent, housings began to be made of brass, as mentioned above, and often elaborately engraved and gilded. In England, with a few exceptions at the end of the sixteenth century, this change did not take place until after the turn of the seventeenth century. A transitional clock with iron frame and brass dial and side plates is seen in *Plate 9a*.

Great strides were made on the Continent during the sixteenth century, in Italy, South Germany at Augsburg and Nuremberg, and also in Strasburg, where the noted family of Habrecht were living. The famous Strasburg clock, already referred to, showed the hour, the day, the month, all the festivals of the Church, the motion of the sun, the moon and the celestial globe, as well as the daily passage of the stars across the heavens. It also embodied various automata which performed at the hours as well as the cock already referred to. This clock was about fifty-five feet in height.

The museums and private collections of Europe contain many examples of elaborate astronomical chamber clocks of this period, varying in height from six to about twenty inches. Many of these show minutes as well as hours and often have each minute engraved on the dial.

As we shall see in the chapter on early Continental clocks, Jobst Burgi's cross-beat escapement allowed a very high degree of accuracy for a time standard uncontrolled by a pendulum, and it is thought that Tycho Brahe's and Kepler's accuracy of observation was, at any rate in part, due to the improved accuracy of Burgi's clocks.

England was right behind during the sixteenth century, only turret clocks being made; with few exceptions domestic clocks were not made in this country until the seventeenth century, and the minute hand not really adopted until after the introduction of the pendulum in 1658. From a practical point of view this was of little importance, since the degree of time-keeping was so poor that a single-handed clock showing the quarters was as effective as anything else.

The use of brass for housings was followed by the adoption of this alloy for the trains in the first quarter of the seventeenth century. This statement must be qualified to the extent that brass is never used on to brass. The wheels of the movements would be of brass engaging into steel pinions mounted on steel arbors. Strange as it may seem, it is the steel pinion that wears quicker than the brass wheel. It is thought that grains of dust or dirt embed themselves in the softer brass and have an abrasive action on the harder steel. In dealing with wheels and pinions, we should remember that while wheels have 'teeth', pinions have 'leaves'.

Since wrought iron or steel was the principal medium for the construction of these early clocks, it is quite natural that clockmakers belonged to either the Blacksmiths' or Locksmiths' Guild, according to the size of clock that they were making.

In 1657, Salomon Coster of The Hague made a clock for the celebrated mathematician Christiaan Huygens, which incorporated a pendulum. This was an invention of as great importance to the craft as any, and should be ranked with the verge escapement, the anchor escapement and the fusee – to which reference will be made later. The name pendulum is derived from the Latin *pendulus*, hanging down. Huygens' clock was spring-driven.

To whom belongs the honour of the invention of the pendulum has been the subject of dispute, at times very acrimonious,

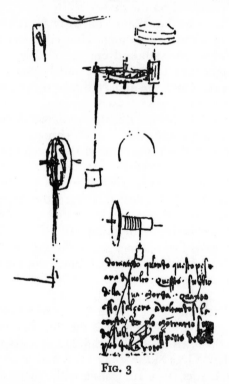

Fig. 3

especially between the contemporary claimants. There is no doubt that a pendulum driven by a weight was invented by Galileo; Tycho Brahe, the famous Danish astronomer, is also reputed to have used a form of pendulum, but in both these cases it is considered that an observer had to count the beats and that they were not geared into a clock as we know it today. As we have just read, it is probable that Tycho Brahe used Burgi's cross-beat escapement. There can be no doubt that several different brains were at work independently at different times. Leonardo da Vinci, that incomparable genius, centuries before his time, had sketches of the pendulum in his note-book[1] at the end of the fifteenth century (Fig. 3), and certainly Galileo's model was working before 1657; but, as stated before, these pendulums were in all probability only accurate oscillants, the number of vibrations to be counted by an observer, a very tedious and uncertain business. The writer is satisfied that Huygens did first apply the pendulum to clockwork and that his work was independent of Galileo's. Further reference will be made to the invention of the pendulum later.

The spring as a motive force came into use about the middle of the fifteenth century. There is in the Musee des Beaux Arts in Antwerp a portrait of a man in the costume of about 1450 in the background of which is shown a clock suspended from the wall by a chain and having no weights. It would appear to be definitely spring driven. The invention of the fusee as an equaliser to the declining force of a spring has long been credited to Leonardo da Vinci on the strength of drawings in his notebooks, but Professor Zinner, of Bamberg, has recently found in the Stuttgart Museum a manuscript by Paulus Alemanus (Paul the German), written in Rome about 1477 in which at least seven clocks with fusees are deleniated, showing clearly that at that date the fusee was in common use. Leonardo's sketch books date about 1485–90. A spring, when fully wound up, exerts a greater pull than when it is nearly run down, so that an uncontrolled spring-driven clock would go too fast when fully wound and too slowly when nearing the end of its time. To counteract this a fusee is used.

The term *fusee* is derived, according to the *Century Dictionary*, from the old French *fusee*, a thread. In medieval Latin, *fusata* was a spindle full of thread or yarn, an expression derived from the word *fusus*, a spindle. Since the first fusees were wound with catgut, the likeness to a spindle full of thread is very obvious.

The principle of the fusee (Fig 4) is that of the lever: when the spring is fully wound the pull is on the smallest diameter; as the spring uncoils, the extra leverage due to the increased diameter equalises the force transmitted to the train. The invention of the fusee will be referred to in the next chapter. The fusee is an invention of the first importance, it is still in

[1] Leonardo always wrote backwards. These copies of his sketches have been laterally inverted to allow the writing to be read without a mirror.

use in high grade clocks after five hundred years. We can appreciate its age better if we relate it to contemporary events, the Wars of the Roses and Jack Cade's rebellion.

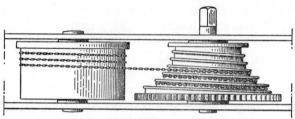

FIG. 4

It has in the past been generally accepted that spring clocks carried on the person were first made by Peter Henlein of Nuremberg about 1510; but we may have to accord that honour now to Italy. Professor Morpurgo, of Amsterdam and Rome, has found old manuscripts dated 1488, originating from Milan, that refer to an 'orologio' to be carried on the person in conjunction with a costly habit.

The fusee, equalising the pull of a spring encased in a barrel does not appear to have been adopted by the early German makers; these adopted a device known as the 'stackfreed' (Fig. 5). This consists of a stiff spring carrying at the end a

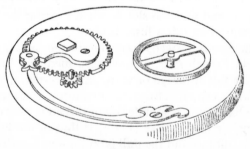

FIG. 5

small roller which bears against a shaped cam mounted on a toothed wheel, not fully cut. A pinion on the mainspring arbor strikes the stop on the wheel after a few turns, thus utilising only those turns of the spring that are most nearly equal in force and then obliging the owner to rewind. At the same time the lessening distance of the edge of the cam from the centre of revolution, decreases the resistance from the roller on the end of the spring, and so counteracting the decreasing force of the spring during these first few turns.

Just what the derivation of the word *stackfreed* is the author has failed to ascertain; even that monument of erudition the *Oxford Dictionary* fails to help us in this case, merely giving a mid-eighteenth-century French writer as the first to employ the word and stating that it is probably a corruption from the low German or Dutch.

A mid-sixteenth-century clock from the author's collection is illustrated in *Plate 1d*. The wheelwork is wholly of iron and, in this case, the housing framework as well. It is weight-driven, and one of the grooved wheels to take the cord can be seen at the back in the lower part of the going train The foliot balance with the notches for the regulating weights can clearly be seen, but the vertical pallet arbor, whose pallets engage the teeth of the vertical crown wheel, is hidden by the foremost corner pillar. Outside the framework at the back is the 'locking plate' or 'count wheel' of the striking train, and above it the 'fly' or air brake that revolves at high speed and acts as a governor to the speed of the falling weight during the actual period of striking. This type of striking arrangement is the earliest known. Like the verge escapement, it was a flash of genius on the part of its inventor, the air brake being a particularly bright idea. This method is still used today, mainly in turret clocks, but also, in France, for domestic clocks.

A pin lifts the locking arm, which can be seen locked in a notch, and allows it to fall again after each stroke of the hammer; while the clock is striking, the count wheel is turning, and the intervals between the notches is so graduated that the locking arm can fall on the rim of the locking plate one less than the necessary number of blows to record the hour. At the last blow it falls into the next notch and stops the locking plate from turning further, thus stopping the striking train until the next hour is reached, when a pin will again lift the locking arm allowing the striking train again to function. In the illustration ten has struck. Revolving anti-clockwise there are spaces for eleven and twelve, when come the small notches for the early hours.

It will be noticed that the whole construction is held together with wedges or rivets; metal screws had not yet appeared in horology.

We left the development of the pendulum to follow the history of the fusee; we must now return to the pendulum, its effect on contemporary horology and the improvements brought to it. Once invented, its considerably enhanced time-keeping caused the owners of foliot or balance-wheel clocks to have them converted. This was quite an easy thing to do. It involved changing the position of the crown wheel from the vertical to the horizontal, so that it would have a horizontal pallet arbor to the end of which would be fixed the pendulum rod, at first a direct and rigid connexion, not suspended on a silk thread and moved by a crutch as was the early Continental practice already referred to.

As a result of this easy possibility of conversion, it is today very difficult to find any clocks that have their original foliots or balance wheels. Many old clocks which had been converted from balance wheel to pendulum have of recent years been restored to their original form, but this must always leave its traces in the matter of empty or filled-in holes in the top and back plates, since, as already explained, the lay-out of the crown wheel had to be changed from vertical to horizontal and then back again to vertical. Care should be taken to make inquiries on this point of restoration when acquiring any clock with a foliot or balance.

Having made the great forward step of the introduction of the pendulum, the next move was to improve the type of escapement. The ideal pendulum swings entirely freely of any outside interference; but, of course, such a pendulum would soon come to rest through air resistance if it had no impelling force. This is provided by the motive force of a weight or spring through the wheels, or train as it is called in horology, of the clock.

The nearest to the ideal is that escapement which leaves the pendulum free for the greatest length of time. Although we acknowledge the inventor of the verge escapement as one of the greatest geniuses of his day, we are forced to admit that his invention is the worst possible escapement in that it never leaves the pendulum free. The teeth travel up the whole length of the pallet and as soon as one pallet is free of one of the teeth of the crown wheel the other pallet engages.

The modifications of escapements are legion, some very good, some not so good. For our purpose we shall deal only with two more, the anchor and the dead beat. They, or slight variations of them, are used in the vast bulk of clocks of interest to the average collector.

First in order of time was the anchor escapement, so called because the curved arm and the two pallets resemble the base and flukes of an anchor (Fig. 6). This type of escapement allowed the teeth of the escape wheel to escape with a much smaller arc of swing of the pendulum, 4° or 5° as compared with 35° to 40° required for the verge escapement.

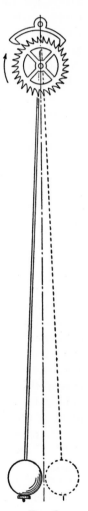

With the wide arc of swing of the verge escapement, pendulum lengths had to be kept very short, and they rarely exceeded the approximate ten inches necessary to give a half-second beat. This new type of pendulum, which was not directly connected to the pallet arbor, but suspended from a cock at the back of the clock by a thin flexible spring strip, allowed a much longer pendulum to be used without its swing becoming unwieldy. This fact, combined with the better time-keeping inherent in the anchor escapement, led rapidly to the adoption of the approximately thirty-nine-inch pendulum, beating one second as the standard. This enabled the second hand to be introduced. The term *second* was originally called the *second minute*, showing that it was the second division of the hour by sixty. John Wilkins, Bishop of Chester, writes in 1650: 'Four flames of an equal magnitude will be kept alive the space of sixteen second minutes.'

Just as many clocks were 'modernised' by the conversion from the balance wheel to verge when the pendulum was first introduced, so those who had not already converted their balances, and many who had either converted balance clocks or had verge lantern clocks, had them converted to anchor escapement with 'Royal'

FIG. 6

pendulums, as they came to be called, since it was considered that this was an appropriate name for these 'more richer kinds of pendulum'. Whether these converted clocks beat exactly one second or some odd fraction of a second would, of course, depend on the train of the clock converted; but since the clocks were not provided with second hands, this would not matter.

The invention of the anchor escapement has been frequently attributed to Robert Hooke, a most versatile genius of the seventeenth century, who from 1662 till his death in 1705 was Curator of Experiments with the then newly formed Royal Society. His industry was prodigious and he was always producing before the Society his ideas on many subjects, many of which were only the first conception of an idea and never developed or perfected.

For years writers have made this attribution, one copying from another until it has become almost legendary, but the writer, who admittedly at first 'followed the crowd', has failed to find any evidence to substantiate the claim. Indeed such scanty contemporary evidence as is available is to the contrary and distinctly favours the rival claimant, William Clement.

The earliest writer in England on horological subjects was John Smith. We could scarcely find a more ordinary and utterly English name. In 1675 he published his *Horological Disquisitions*, a little volume of 120 pages 16mo, detailing an imaginary conversation between a craftsman and a layman concerning the care and use of clocks. In this there are only very brief allusions to the thirty-nine-inch one-second pendulum. On page 34, in answer to a query as to the right method of setting up a long-case clock, he writes: 'In setting up long swing Pendulums, after you have taken them from the coffin, open it, and make free all things that are fastened, etc.' The author, by the way, deprecates this connexion of clocks with coffins; he prefers to think of them as living things. On pages 47 and 48 there are further references to the long pendulum:

'Q. Have you nothing more to deliver concerning Pendulums?

'A. Nothing more concerning these ordinary ones, I confess; something more might be delivered concerning the richer kinds. . . .

'Q. Is the long pendulum subject to variation as the short one is?

'A. No; being once brought to a true time it alwaies keeps it, for it moveth in so small an arch, that it is unpossible for it to move less without standing. . . .'

No mention is made of any inventor of the long pendulum or any controversy on this point, but that the anchor escapement is clearly meant is shown by the reference to the small 'arch' of swing; also it is quite evident that by 1675 the long seconds pendulum had become well established in use.

In 1694 Smith published his second book, *Horological Dialogues*. When writing this he was apparently aware of the rival claims made for the invention, for he writes on pages 2, 3 and 4:

'At length, in *Holland*, an Ingenious and Learned Gentleman, Mr. *Christiaan Huygens*, by Name, found out the Way to regulate the uncertainty of its Motion by the Vibration of a Pendulum.

'From *Holland*, the fame of this invention soon past over into *England*, where several eminent and ingenious Workmen applyed themselves to rectify some Defects which as yet was found therein; among which that eminent and well-known Artist Mr. *William Clement*, had at last the good Fortune to give it the finishing Stroke, he being indeed the real Contriver of that curious kind of long Pendulum, which is at this Day so universally in use among us.

'An invention that exceeds all others yet known, as to the Exactness and Steadiness of its Motion, which proceeds from Two Properties, peculiar to this Pendulum: The one is the weightiness of its Bob, and the other the little compass in which it plays: The first of these makes it less apt to be commanded by those accidental differences of Strength that may sometimes happen in the Draught of Wheels, and the other renders the Vibrations more equal and exact, as not being capable of altering so much in the distance of its Swinge, as those other kind of Pendulums are, who fetch a larger, and, by consequence, a less constant Compas.

'For Pendulums that swing or vibrate very far out, as all Crown-Wheel Pendulums do, are apt, by reason of many Accidents that happen to vary much in the Distance they swing, and that's the reason they do not always go or move the same Pace, a larger Vibration taking up more Time to be performed in, than lesser ones do: But the Vibrations of this Pendulum of Mr. *Clement's* contrivance is so very exact and steady, that, when 'tis well in Order, and the Air of the same Consistence, it shall in Five hundred or a Thousand Revolutions of its Index, keep so equal a Time, that no Human Art can discover the least considerable Difference in any of its Revolutions, an excellence to which no other known Motion can as yet pretend, and for which, I think, it will not be improper now, at last, to call it the *Royal Pendulum*.'

Here we have a very emphatic contemporary opinion that William Clement was the *real* contriver of the anchor escapement, written by a man who fully realised the importance of the discovery and the desirability of giving honour where honour was due.

Two years later William Derham, a parson, at one time a Canon of Windsor, wrote his *Artificial Clockmaker*. On page 96 of this book he also attributes the invention to Clement, writing: 'For several years this way of Mr. Zulichem's was the only method, *viz*. Crown-Wheel Pendulums, to play between two cycloidal cheeks, etc. But afterwards Mr. *W. Clement*, a *London* Clockmaker, contrived them (as Mr. *Smith* saith) to go with less weight, an heavier Ball (if you please) and to vibrate but a small compass. Which is now the universal method of the Royal Pendulum. But Dr. *Hook* denies Mr. *Clement* to have invented this; and says that it was his Invention, and that he caused a piece of this nature to be made, which he shewed before the *R. Society*, soon after the Fire of *London*.'

It will be noted that here is another contemporary writer agreeing that Clement was the inventor; Derham in a marginal note refers to Smith's attribution on page 3 of his *Horological Disquisitions* given above.

The recording by Derham of Hooke's claim is the only piece of written contemporary evidence that has so far been discovered to support the attribution to Hooke, and this is very definitely negative in character. A careful search through the records of the Royal Society papers, both those published and the unpublished Hooke manuscripts, has not revealed any evidence that Hooke ever produced anything approaching the principle of the anchor escapement before the Royal Society.

In view of Derham's statement, particular attention was paid to the period at the end of 1666, shortly after the Great Fire. Already before the Fire, on June 13th, 1666, there is the entry: 'Mr. Hooke exhibited a new contrivance of a circular pendulum, applicable to a watch, and moving without any noise and in continued and even motion without any jerks.'

It should be noted that at this period the going train of a clock was designated the watch part and the striking train the clock part, from the Latin *clocca*, a bell; it was some forty or fifty years later that the pocket watch, at first so designated, became generally known as a watch, and that the term was dropped in connexion with clocks.

On August 8th and again on August 22nd, 1666, Hooke was urged to produce his circular pendulum; the Great Fire intervened in September and we have no further entry until October 31st, 1666, when 'Mr. Hooke produced an inclining pendulum, which, though short, should perform the office of a long perpendicular one, the several degrees answering to the several dimensions of length.'

Here it should be noted that the wide arc of swing of the verge escapement made long pendulums impracticable unless there was ample space; Huygens did at one time make a clock with a verge escapement having a seconds pendulum, reducing the amplitude by an intermediate gearing.

On November 21st, 1666, Hooke presented a paper dealing with the ratio of the times of swing of a pendulum through the various portions of its arc and related these to the motions of a circular pendulum, but there is no mention of any form of escapement to lessen the arc of swing of the pendulum. On the same day 'Mr. Hooke shewed the society another kind of pendulum, which being perpendicular and short, by counterpoising performed the part of a long one.' Here again we have an effort to get a longer period of swing combined with a small arc.

'December 12th, 1666. Mr. Hooke produced a new sort of pendulum made after the manner of a beam, and so contrived, that by placing the beam nearer or farther below the centre of motion, the pendulum may perform its vibrations in any time assigned. . . .' Here we have the basis of the metronome of today, the bugbear of the author's childish and ineffectual efforts on the piano.

On January 1st, 1666–7, February 14th, 1666–7, January

2nd, 1667–8, May 6th, 1669, and October 28th, 1669, there are references to the circular pendulum, pendulums without any check at all, and 14-feet pendulums beating two seconds with an arc of swing of half an inch, which was less than 1°. None of these can be connected with the anchor escapement.

Nevertheless, as we can conclude from the above quotations, Hooke seems to have been fully alive to the desirability of combining a small arc of swing with a long period to improve time-keeping; what today is known as 'circular error'. He has been given the reputation of trying to appropriate, on occasion, the inventions of others; but here we may well have a case of 'I realised years ago that it was necessary to reduce the arc of swing of the pendulum and was working on this problem before the Fire of London', leading, after Clement had solved the problem, in 1671, as we shall see later, to the claim 'That's nothing new; *I* had that idea years ago'.

Gunter, in his *Early Science at Oxford*, volume one, page 232, makes the bare statement that Hooke invented the anchor escapement about 1675, but he makes no attempt to support this statement from any source whatever. This assertion is clearly wrong, as we have seen from Smith's book of 1675 that the long pendulum with its small arc of swing was already well established by that date.

As opposed to the negative evidence in favour of Hooke, we have, besides the positive statements of Smith and Derham, further positive evidence in favour of Clement in the shape of a turret clock, now in the Science Museum in London, signed and dated 'Guiliemus Clement Londini, Fecit 1671' (see *Plate 21*).

This has always had a recoil escapement and the date has been fully authenticated. A full description of the clock appears later.

If Clement had merely applied Hooke's invention of the anchor we should have expected frequent communications between the two men during the early years of application, but Hooke, in his diary which starts on March 10th, 1671–2, only once mentions Clement, on August 30th, 1672, and then only in connexion with the supply of a bell clapper for a turret clock. Clement was at this time still a member of the Blacksmiths' Guild.

The author is somewhat shy at introducing this rather technical passage into a book of a popular nature; but the invention of the anchor escapement was as great a step forward in horological science as that of the verge escapement; and, like it, it embraced entirely new principles which were the inventor's idea. It led the way to the dead beat escapement and many other variants and improvements both in escapements and pendulums, which would have been quite impossible of application to the verge escapement.

Let us give honour where honour is due.

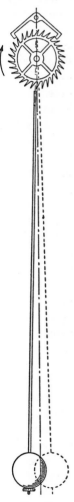

The next stage in escapement development, made possible by Clement's invention, was an important one which held the field for about two and a quarter centuries. If you watch the second hand of the average old long-case clock you will notice after each 'tick' or 'tock' a slight shudder, or recoil as it is termed, due to the jarring when each pallet of the anchor engages a tooth of the escape wheel. Although considerably less than the interference with the pendulum in the verge escapement, it is very definite interference and effects the time-keeping quite considerably, in spite of Mr. Smith's eulogies 'that when 'tis well in order and the air of the same consistence, it shall in Five hundred or a Thousand revolutions of its Index, keep so equal a Time, that no Human Art can discover the least considerable Difference in any of its revolutions. . . .'

About 1715 George Graham invented the dead beat escapement. In this escapement the pallet beds 'dead' on to the escape wheel tooth; there is no jar or recoil (Fig. 7). This escapement is more expensive to make. It is still used in better quality domestic clocks, but its principal use was in connexion with regulators, i.e. clocks sufficiently accurate to be used for astronomical observations and as master-clocks, and remained the most usually adopted escapement for time-keeping of the highest

FIG. 7

accuracy until the end of the nineteenth century, when a German, named Riefler, introduced a different type. With this we shall not deal here, since it was only used in observatory clocks and did not have any general application. Let it suffice to say that Riefler did not entirely supplant Graham; many observatories retained their dead beat clocks.

Besides improvements in the design of escapements, clock-makers also sought to improve the pendulum. We have already seen the great stride forward made by the adoption of the Royal pendulum beating one second. In its first stages this consisted of an ordinary iron wire, suspended by a piece of flat spring, which is slipped through a narrow slit in the cock fixed to the back plate of the clock. The bob is a leaden lenticular mass, faced with brass. Regulation is made by screwing up or letting down a 'rating' nut, which travels on the threaded finial of the pendulum rod.

In the early bob pendulums used with verge escapements, which were usually pear-shaped, although some early makers, such as East, often used more ball-shaped bobs, it was not possible to tap the thread in the interior of the hole drilled through the bob to receive the pendulum rod. The hole was plugged with wood, which in turn was drilled the exact size of the pendulum rod and which then took up the fine threads cut in the pendulum rod itself; allowing an adjustment to be made by turning the whole bob.

These simple pendulum rods made no allowance, or compensation as it is called, for expansion or contraction owing to heat or cold. Graham made some experiments in 1715 with the expansion of metals, but did not pursue them. In 1721, in the course of some other experiments, he noticed the extraordinary high rate of expansion of mercury (quicksilver). He therefore made a bob for his pendulum of a glass jar containing mercury suspended in a brass frame attached to a brass pendulum rod (*Plate 26c*). By trial and error he ascertained the exact amount of mercury necessary in the jar, so that its upward expansion in heat would raise the centre of oscillation of the pendulum to the same extent as the expansion of the brass rod lowered it, with, of course, the converse in cold weather. (Note. The centre of oscillation of a pendulum is not quite the same as its centre of gravity, but we need not deal with that difference here.) Graham mercury pendulums are still in use today in high-grade clocks.

About the same time as Graham was experimenting with the differential expansion of metals in London, the brothers John and James Harrison, sons of a Yorkshire carpenter were making similar experiments which resulted in the invention of the grid-iron pendulum (*Plate 35*). This invention has always been credited to John Harrison, but it would now seem more likely that it was the work of the younger brother, James. John Harrison came to London in 1728 bringing the grid-iron pendulum with him. The brothers had found out that the expansion of brass to steel was approximately in the ratio of 3 : 2. He saw, therefore, if he had a brass rod 6 feet long and a steel one 9 feet long and joined them together at their lower ends, the upper ends would remain 3 feet apart whatever the variation of temperature. However, 9 feet was too long for convenience in a pendulum, so they devised the method of cutting his rods into lengths, three of steel and two of brass. In the illustration it will be noted that there are nine rods; in order to avoid distortion the four outer on one side are duplicated on the other side; we have therefore steel, brass, brass, steel fixed to the outer grid, and steel, brass, steel, brass, steel in the central grid, which is free to move within the guide plates.

This type of pendulum, again, is still in use in high-grade clocks today. John Harrison's life-work was to devise a time-piece which would go sufficiently accurately to enable the determination of the longitude of a ship at sea. After many years of effort, and possibly as many spent in wrangling with his adjudicators, and after the personal intervention of King George III, who was very interested in clocks and watches, he was finally awarded the whole of the £20,000 prize offered in Queen Anne's time for the solution of this problem, which had been the bane of navigation from time immemorial. Latitudinal position was easy to determine from the stars or sun, but to determine one's longitude necessitated very accurate time-keeping, from which could be calculated the number of degrees traversed to the east or west from a known starting-point. Harrison first used his grid-iron in compensating the balance of his first timepiece in 1735.

There was another application of this differential of expansion adopted by John Ellicott in 1752. In this the expansion of the rod downwards raises the bob by means of levers within the bob, and vice versa. It was never widely adopted; we shall therefore not go further into a detailed description of its working.

Thus we have outlined the early efforts at time-recording, at the control of clocks and the main improvements that the ordinary collector or others interested are likely to encounter. In the following chapters we shall deal with the different specimens of clocks illustrated and follow their progression through the years, seeing the effect of inventions on their design, the modifications due to social and economic causes, the influence of design and fashion on them until, finally, we come to the period where machinery and mass production, if only on a limited scale, rob the craft of individuality and interest from a student's point of view. The interest shifts to that of the engineer and workshop specialist.

CHAPTER TWO

Some Early Continental Clocks 1350-1650

IN this period the Continent was far ahead of England. Our early examples of clocks made in England, Salisbury and Wells cathedral clocks, were in all probability made by a foreigner invited to England for this purpose. It is due to the researches of Mr. R. P. Howgrave Graham that we know that the Bishop of Salisbury in 1386 was one Erghum, who came from Bruges to England on appointment to the See. We also know that this same bishop was translated to Wells and was there in 1392 when that clock was made. Mr. Howgrave Graham has also ascertained that the two clocks are, in all probability, by the same craftsman, since they both carry similar decorative or maker's marks. Now we know that there are many records of public turret clocks on the continent from the early days of the fourteenth century; also as we shall see later, in 1350 clocks were considered so common that no particular description of them was deemed necessary. What more likely than a desire by Bishop Erghum, who had been used to having clocks in his churches and cathedrals, that he should send for his clockmaker and commission clocks first in Salisbury and then in Wells.

The only Englishman of whom we have any record is Richard of Wallingford, who about 1340 is said to have constructed an elaborate astronomical clock. All trace of this has disappeared, all we know is that about two hundred years later, Leyland saw it, and from his description, it was apparently still in going order. Some have contended that this machine was the same as Wallingford's 'Albion' (all by one), which appears to have been a type of Equatorium, but the fact that Leyland refers to the clock showing the ebbing and flowing of the sea, infers to the author's mind, a mechanical astronomical clock.

During the years 1348-62, Giovanni de Dondi was working on his famous astronomical clock, which showed with a great degree of accuracy, the motions of the sun, moon and the five

45

planets, as well as the nodes. It also had a perpetual calendar for the fixed feasts of the church and a perpetual calendar for the movable feasts, a feat not since achieved until Schwilgué, in 1842, made the third Strasbourg clock. By this time the Gregorian calendar was in use and the feat was much more complicated. This book is not dealing with complicated astronomical clocks, but the ordinary weight-driven verge escapement mechanical clock, which formed the motive force for all the astronomical dials, as is seen in *Plate 1b*. It will be noticed that Dondi uses a balance. Now this is the earliest depiction of a mechanical timepiece known to us, so it will be seen that the question of priority as between balance and foliot is an open question. It will also be noticed that Dondi only indicates the general lay-out; no details of pivots, bearings or plates are given. Dondi left the fullest possible description of just how he made the astronomical parts of his clock and for this the horological world owes him a great debt. In this he says that (and remember that we are dealing with a man writing in the middle of the fourteenth century), as clocks are quite common, and as there are several types quite well known, it would be a waste of time for him to give further details of this clock, for if he who is studying the manuscript, with a view to making a reproduction, cannot complete this clock by himself, he is wasting his time in contemplating any further work. Now as we have seen in 1277 the mechanical clock was not known. Its spread after its invention must have been very rapid. A notable feature of Dondi's clock is that it is made entirely of brass; in the two hundred pages of manuscript iron is not mentioned.[1]

In *Plate 2* are seen two early spring driven clocks with fusees. The small one has a date 1504 engraved on the little door. If this date be genuine it would make it the earliest surviving example of the fusee. At all events it is very early and is included here to show the very pointed type of fusee employed at the outset. The little door opens to show to what extent the fusee has run down. The clock is in the Musée des Arts Decoratifs, in Paris. The other illustration shows a mid-sixteenth-century clock with its travelling case of tooled morocco leather. It shows the hours of the day and night and has an astrolabe dial that would allow for the rising and setting of certain named stars

[1] See Appendix I.

to be ascertained as well as the temporal hours of the night.
From the revolution of the ecliptic circle the times of the rising
and setting of the sun could be ascertained. In both cases the
movements are all of iron; especial notice should be taken of
the very fine balance of large diameter in the larger clock. The
smaller has a foliot. The travelling clock is engraved for the
latitude of Toledo, and is presumably of German make for
export.

Another interesting piece made for the latitude of London and
dated 1560 is seen in *Plate 3*. The maker's mark, a form of 'M'
is not identifiable, but since the inscriptions are in French, presumably it was made in France. It is not intended in this book
to enter into detailed descriptions of complicated astronomical
dials, this aspect of horology is fully dealt with in the author's
Some Outstanding Clocks over 700 Years 1250–1950, recently published. The object of the inclusion of this example is to give an
illustration of how astrology, which entered so intimately into
all details of daily life, was often introduced into horology. The
signs of the Zodiac are engraved around the base of the drum
containing the movement, and each sign has its legendary
figure engraved upon it:

Aquarius (The Water-carrier)		Virgo (The Virgin)	August
	January	Libra (The Balance)	September
Pisces (The Fishes)	February	Scorpio (The Scorpion)	
Aries (The Ram)	March		October
Taurus (The Bull)	April	Sagittarius (The Archer)	
Gemini (The Twins)	May		November
Cancer (The Crab)	June	Capricornus (The Goat)	
Leo (The Lion)	July		December

The concentric circles on the top of the drum represent the
different celestial spheres. First come air and fire that were
supposed to surround the earth, then the seven spheres of the
sun, moon and five planets, followed by that of the Firmament,
or the fixed stars. Beyond that a sphere representing the
Chrystalineum or the year of $365\frac{1}{4}$ days and finally the sphere of
the *Primum mobile*, to account for a slow motion independent and
in the opposite direction to the others which was later identified
with the precession of the equinoxes.

The front dial will indicate sidereal time and will show the
hour, position of the sun in the ecliptic, rising and setting of the

sun and the principle stars, phases of the moon, &c. The back dial is for direct observation of the sun; the rectangular engraving is for the measuring of vertical and horizontal heights.

Reverting to the twelve signs: often under each sign is engraved the word *Bonum*, *Medium*, or *Malum*, preceded by the initial letter of the sign in question. In the Middle Ages, and even up to the end of the seventeenth century or after, astrology

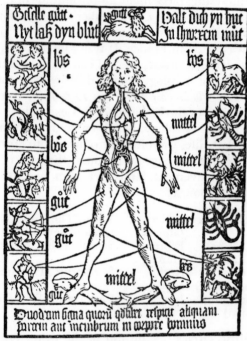

FIG. 8

played a great part in the life of the people; the influence of the stars and planets was good, fair, or bad, according to the month of happening. Surgical operations were supposed to be influenced by the month of their operation. Fig 8 shows a diagram which was originally on the first Strasburg clock, indicating in which months certain organs should be operated on.

Incidentally the ancient Greek and Roman philosophers considered that every hour of the day was under the influence of one of the seven planets then known to them. It must be remembered that the earth was considered fixed and the sun was thought to be a planet like the others, viz., the Moon, Mercury, Venus, the Sun, Mars, Jupiter and Saturn, giving them in order of their distance from the earth. As previously mentioned, the sun is really only a very near fixed star.

Each day of the week was allotted to the god represented by that planet which was supposed to influence the earth at the hour of midday to one p.m. on that day, each succeeding hour being influenced by the planet next distant from the earth. Starting with the moon as influencing the period midday to one P.M. on 'Monday' we get:

Saturn	Jupiter	Mars	Sun	Venus	Mercury	Moon
						1
2	3	4	5	6	7	8
9	10	11	12	13	14	15
16	17	18	19	20	21	22
23	24	1	2	etc.		

giving Mars (French: *mardi*) as the deity for the second day. Following this round, we get Mercury for the third day (Fr. *mercredi*); Jupiter – Jove – for the fourth (Fr. *jeudi*); Venus for the fifth (Fr. *vendredi*); Saturn for the sixth (Fr. *samedi*); and the Sun for the seventh (Fr. *dimanche*), being derived from Dies Dominico, or The Lord's Day. English and German names of the days of the week are derived from their own gods, but, according to the Oxford Dictionary, these gods are identified with the Greco-Roman gods. Tuesday comes from the fem. gen. of O.E. Tiw, the name of an ancient Teutonic god identified with Mars. Wednesday is Woden's day; Woden was the god of eloquence and also had the facility for rapid movement from place to place, the same attributes as Mercury. Thursday, Thor's day, the god of thunder, as was Jove. Friday, according to these experts, does not come from Freyja, but from the goddess Frig, wife of Odin. The name is the feminine of the old Teutonic adjective *frijo*, beloved, loving; here we have our link with Venus.

On the pillar of this clock are marked nine columns, of which seven are for each day of the week, the remaining two being marked '*Heures du jour*' and '*Heures de la nuit*'. The former has roman numerals I to XII and continuing with I and II, the latter runs from III to XII, with the last four spaces blank. In the planetary columns, the last four signs are repeated at the top of the next column, to preserve continuity.

Clocks rolling slowly down an inclined plane, with gravity as the motive force have generally been attributed to the latter half of the eighteenth century, but in the Museum at Brunswick is to be found the clock illustrated in *Plate 4a*, made by Isaac Habrecht of Strasburg, who died in 1620. It will be recalled that Habrecht, with his brother, Josias, was the maker of the second Strasburg clock, to the designs of Conrad Dasypodius.

During 24 hours the clock travels slowly down its inclined plane, which is about three feet long. It has then to be lifted up and placed again at the top of the incline, a very simple method of winding. The hand is fixed and is read against the revolving chapter ring.

Another discovery of the last few years, made by Dr. H. Von Bertele, partly from researches in his native Vienna and partly from visits to other Continental museums, is that of Jobst Burgi's Cross-Beat escapement. This discovery has thrown light on certain, hitherto inexplicable, reference to manuscripts of the mid-seventeenth century which referred to a *libramentum duplice*, or double escapement. Within about 60 years of its invention it was superseded by that of the pendulum. The cross-beat was for some years a closely guarded secret and was only practised by Burgi and a few of his pupils, mainly in northern European plain. With this invention Burgi achieved a very greatly improved time standard over the standard verge escapement, the only other then known alternative. In the early models the very fine teeth on large escape wheels and their precise adjustment to the two pallets of the cross arms, allowed for accurate adjustment, but in his latest designs, each pallet could be adjusted separately.

Plate 4c and *d* shows a delightful little clock, about 6¼ in. high. At the top, in front can be seen the two arms of the cross-beat escapement, which, geared together, oscillate in opposite directions. In this case they are not separately adjustable and regulation is by means of setting up or letting down the mainspring. In the view of the back-plate it will be noted that the key has to be inserted into a square hole in the winding arbor, instead of the arbor protruding and fitting into the winding key. W is the winding arbour and S is for adjusting the setting of the mainspring, the degree to which this is altered is shown by a scale engraved on the spring barrel, and seen through the heart-shaped opening T. R is a lever to slacken the mainspring tension. The clock is by Fransisco Swartz of Brussels and dates about 1630. It is an early example of the introduction of the minute hand.

The remaining illustration in *Plate 4* is one of the religious type of clock that became popular in Roman Catholic countries in the 'Counter Reformation' period. It shows Christ roped to a pillar for the flagellation. The date is about 1610. The hours are shown on a revolving band around the sphere on the top of the column, the quarters being indicated on the small horizontal dial on the base of the clock. A fusee chain is used instead of gut.

As previously mentioned, Burgi's cross-beat escapement was not generally known and others assayed to find a better time standard than the verge escapement. In several cases this took the form of a rolling ball, really a development of the idea of the inclined plane clock that we have just been considering. These ball clocks were often of complicated design, the path of the ball was often tortuous and the method of restoration of the ball various, in fact many of the designs seen on paper would have very little hope of mechanical performance. A Monsieur Grollier de Sevière, who died aged 90 in 1680, designed or collected many examples of rolling-ball clocks and these were set out in book form by his grandson, of the same name in 1719.

The clock of this type illustrated in *Plates 5* and *6* was made in 1601 by Christoph Rohr of Leipzig. The date has been fixed by documentary evidence. A steel ball is released at the top of the run, when it reaches the bottom it falls into a trap and is directed inwards. In its inward passage it strikes the curved trigger seen in *Plate 5b* and more clearly in the enlarged section *Plate 6a*. The ball rolls into a cup attached to the linked chain running in a groove in the side of the vertical tube. The trigger releases the spring drive to the wheel driving the chain, which goes at once into motion and carries the ball to the top in such a time as will make the descent and ascent combined, one

minute. There is only one ball; a second cup, which will descend
to be ready in position when the ball again reaches the end of
its travel can just be seen, upside down catching the highlight
in the centre of the dark shadow under the top plate in *Plate 5b*.
The other long chain serves to drive the carousel on the top.
Every three hours the knights and foot soldiers parade before
the turbaned Turk, who vigorously beats the drum in front of
him with a hammer in each hand. The clock shows the hour,
quarter, date and day of the week.

Before leaving this chapter on early Continental clocks it will
be interesting to include an example which shows that, in the
opinion of some at any rate, old ideas are best. It will be recalled
that one of the earliest subsidiary methods of regulation of a
weight-driven verge escapement clock was to alter the position
of the thread suspending the pallet arbor and so to alter the
angle of incidence between the pallet and the crown wheel. A
most interesting development of this idea applied to a spring-
driven clock is seen in *Plate 7*, a clock by Hans Kiening of Fuessen in Bavaria, of date about 1590.

The clock takes the form of a book, the inner hand indicates
the hour, one revolution in 24 hours, and the longer hand
indicated the quarters, with subsidiary marks for every five
minutes and seven and a half minutes, or half quarters. Above
is a dial indicating the extent to which the spring has run down,
a very early example of the 'up and down'. The shutters
indicate the number of hours of day and night, the Nuremberg
hours, incidentally they also indicate the times of sunrise and
sunset. From the illustrations it will be seen that this clock
combines the stackfreed principle of a shaped cam fixed to a
toothed wheel driven by a pinion on the mainspring arbor and
the adjustable pallet. Fig. 9 shows the functioning quite clearly.
The cam is concealed under the pierced cock, bottom left, and
is shaped with a 'stop' projection which replaces the uncut
portion of the cam-carring wheel in the stackfreed. (See p. 53.)
As the cam revolves it causes the pinion on the bottom of the
arbor carried by the curved arm to engage with the rack connected with the pallet arbor, decreasing the angle of incidence
of the upper pallet and to a certain degree, that of the lower
pallet also, in this way shortening the period of contact,
resulting in a shorter period of oscillation as the force of the un-

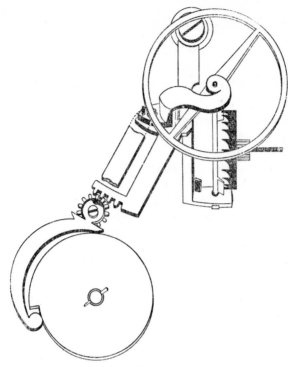

FIG. 9

coiling spring decreases, giving an equalising effect to the power transmitted to the train, as in the case of the fusee. Top right in *Plate 7b* is a dial for the months of the year, each month being represented by its zodiacal sign.

CHAPTER THREE

Lantern and Bracket or Mantel Clocks 1600-1735

T HIS period has been chosen for the first stage in the description of both portable clocks, i.e. bracket or mantel clocks, and long-case or grandfather clocks, because during these years were made all those important inventions which have influenced the clocks we are considering, viz. domestic clocks. They were: the pendulum in 1657; the anchor escapement in 1671; the rack and snail striking method in 1676, which in its turn made repeating clocks possible; the illuminated night clock, first made about 1670–80; the equation clock in 1695; the dead-beat escapement in 1715; the mercury pendulum and the grid-iron pendulum about 1726.[1]

All changes in the design of domestic clock movements after this were modifications of existing ideas; nothing fundamental was introduced. The inventions introducing fundamental changes took place in the design of chronometers and precision time-keepers with which we are not here concerned. It would be interesting to carry this study further and to embrace all methods of time-keeping, but limitations of space do not allow.

The early clocks we have seen illustrated in Chapters I and II were either designed for hanging on the wall or for placing on a table. On the Continent the table clock gained considerably in favour during the early part of the seventeenth century, while in England we were only just beginning to think of making anything but heavy turret clocks.

In the latter years of the sixteenth century a few, very few, makers were working in England, such as Bartholomew Newsam and Nicholas Vallin; some of them appear to have made watches only, at least only their watches have survived to come down to us. The names of Michael Nowen, Randolf Bull and David Ramsay come to mind. This last was clockmaker to James I, who came to London and was to become the first Master of the Clockmakers' Company in 1631.

[1] See Appendix II.

Very few examples exist of the productions of these early workers in London, either British born or of foreign origin. One which the author found a few years ago is seen in *Plate 8*. It is a table clock signed by N. Vallin, whose name we have just mentioned and dates about 1600. It was found and still is in the Museum in Banff, Scotland, in a section devoted to the work and memory of James Ferguson, the eminent eighteenth-century astronomer and horologist, who started life as a humble shepherd lad in the district, and whose name will be seen engraved on the base cover.

Mr. C. B. Drover has made an extensive research into the biography of Nicholas Vallin, who was the son of John Vallin, a Fleming who emigrated to London about 1580. John died in 1603, perhaps of the plague and Nicholas also died of the plague a few months later. That he helped his father is shown by the passage in John's will which indicates that he makes bequests to his son Nicholas in consideration of the way he helped him to earn his living.

This clock is probably one of the most untouched pieces of Vallin's work extant; we see from the back plate that the ratchet wheel for setting up the mainspring is missing, as is also under the top plate a pinion of eight leaves that should engage with a wheel of sixty-four teeth which carrying the hour hand. This combined with the sixteen turns on the fusee, would give two revolutions to the hand every twenty-four hours.

The balluster pillars, used in their logical position are interesting; we shall see later how, when clocks were made to stand up vertically, in the early examples the pillars are still of the balluster type with the base pinned through the back plate although their position is now horizontal and their shape has lost all functional meaning.

The pinion carried on the hand arbor, seen on the top of *Plate 8b* gears in a 2:1 ratio with the wheel carrying the globe, giving a 24-hour period of rotation. This pinion is undoubtedly original and proves that the clock was always intended to carry a globe. Was this an early attempt to 'find the longitude'? The present globe and the engraving of its dial are both about 1830, but the fact that the clock carried a rotating globe seems to have interested the restoration savant John Desagulier, a well-known figure in the Royal Society at that time; he appears to have acquired it in 1719. The scientific interest in the clock is further indicated by its passing to Benjamin Franklin in 1757, thirteen years after Desaugliers died. Benjamin Franklin and James Ferguson are known to have been friends; as Franklin is known to have been in London in 1766, it is presumed that he gave the clock to Ferguson in that year. Kenneth McCulloch was Ferguson's assistant. Who G. W. was we do not know. Henderson, in his *Life of Ferguson*, writes that Andrew Reid, a close friend of Ferguson's, shortly before his (Reid's) death, gave a curious clock to McCulloch, which showed the motion of the earth by the rotation of a globe. We can, therefore, assume that the clock had a globe at that time. Ferguson died in 1776 and McCulloch apparently had the clock in 1774. If the clock did not always have a globe, there would be nothing to distinguish it from many other table clocks of the period, and it would not have had this particular interest to its many scientific possessors. The dial for the globe is engraved I to XII twice over, once clockwise and once anti-clockwise, so that readings were given both east and west of the meridian.

Prior to the seventeenth century, when the English evolved their own style known as the lantern clock, sometimes miscalled the Cromwellian clock, very few domestic clocks were made in England. These 'Cromwellian' clocks were first made in the reign of James I and continued to be made until the reign of Queen Anne, and even later in the provinces.

In the previous chapter it was mentioned that the early clockmakers were either blacksmiths or locksmiths as long as they were working entirely in wrought iron; but when brass was introduced this involved a different technique, that of casting at temperatures considerably lower than that of iron. Just how the change came about is not recorded, but we know that in 1628–29 there were a sufficient number of clockmakers, working in or within ten miles of London, to seek affiliation with the blacksmiths as a separate craft, but without success, and the following year on February 23rd, 1629–30, between fifty and sixty clockmakers petitioned King Charles I for incorporation as a Company, which was granted in 1631.

Plate 9a shows an early English 'transitional' clock of date about 1600–10. The wrought-iron decorated corner posts and the iron top and bottom plates remain, but front and back are faced with brass sheet, on to the former of which is engraved the hour circle, a fairly narrow ring, with 'dumpy' numerals. This is a sign of early work. The side plates have not yet appeared. The wheels are already of brass and the pinions of wrought iron; their different colours can be distinguished in the photograph. The crown wheel is also of brass, the pallet arbor and the pallets will be of wrought iron. The balance wheel is clearly seen under the bell, which is supported by four arms, at the end of each of which is a small pin, which is in turn sprung into a hole drilled in the finial to receive it.

Metal screws were already in use in clocks on the Continent about 1500; they are here making their appearance in England; in the top plate, just above the shield with the monogram, which in turn is seen above the XII, can be seen the square-headed top of an early screw; the finials and feet too are screwed into the pillars, keeping the top and bottom plates in place.

The going train is in front, the striking train behind; the locking plate or count wheel can faintly be seen among the shadows concealing the back plate.

The hand should be noted, a somewhat clumsy, wrought-iron hand with an 'arrow-head' point, heavy central boss and a medium-length tail; the word tail is used here because, with the general heavy construction of the clock, a counterpoise to the hand would not be of any practical use. In later years, when clock movements become works of exact precision, second and minute hands do have a counterpoise, or else the wheels driving them are cut out to provide a true balance in all positions. It will be noticed that there is an absence of the frets in the front and sides which will appear on later models.

The general shape and lay-out became standardised and was practically the only shape of clock made in England for sixty years. Square, going train in front, striking train behind. The similarity to lantern design of the period is shown by the second illustration on *Plate 9*, which is of a silver lantern, taken by King Christian IV of Denmark on his journey to the North Cape late in the sixteenth century. This is now in the Rosenborg Castle Museum near Copenhagen. English country lanterns of this period also bear the same general shape, if less ornate in design.

Plate 9 shows two more examples of lantern clocks, *9c* being

by William Selwood, who worked at 'Ye Marmade' in Loth-
bury. The side door has been removed for the purpose of
photography. The date of this clock is about 1620; the somewhat heavy chapter ring, an early indication, is still there; the
hand is still of wrought iron, but the 'curls' each side of the
arrow-head show signs of rather better finish than that of the
preceding example. The hour numerals are still 'dumpy'. By
the way, the term *chapter ring* or *hour ring*, which is so often used,
comes, no doubt, from the monastic chapters or offices which
took place at each hour of the day and night.

The centre of the dial is engraved all over, a style that persisted in lantern clocks so long as they were made. Sometimes
the maker's name and address were included, but very often,
as in the Selwood clock, they were engraved at the bottom of
the fret placed over the dial. This detail in the photograph has
been lost in reproduction. Regulation was effected by increasing
or decreasing the going train weight by adding or removing lead
shot. An original weight, sheathed in copper, with a cup on top
for the lead, is seen in the illustration.

There is a definite progression in the design of the frets. The
type illustrated, an heraldic shape, is early in the progression;
the arms of the original owner have been roughly scratched on
it. Later crossed dolphins were adopted (*Plate 11a*) passing
eventually to a more nondescript design (*Plate 9d*).

The chapter ring has a circle divided into quarter-hours and
the marks are enclosed, as are the hour numerals, in a narrow
double circle. Later clocks have only a single circle. The half-
hour mark, a star at the end of a line, is also seen in the preceding example. If these half-hour marks be followed, it will be
noticed that they tend to become more elaborate, developing
into a fleur-de-lis *motif* and then gradually reverting to simplicity, until they eventually disappear, together with all other
markings on the dial, except for the bare numerals. It took
nearly a hundred years after the establishment of the minute
hand as a general practice for all quarter-hour, half-hour and
other intermediary marks to disappear as useless, so hard does
habit and tradition die.

The long slender feet with sharp-edged decorative 'ridges'
seen in *9c*, as opposed to the more rounded 'bosses' of *11a*, are
indicative of Charles I's time. The bell, as before, is supported

by four arms, each having a pin at its terminal for springing into the finials. There is a semi-circular suspension hoop for passing over a hook on the wall, as well as two distance pieces which project from the back plate. *Plate 9d* shows a rather later example of lantern clock, dating about 1715. Here we have a slightly wider chapter ring, the hour numerals somewhat larger, but still only one hand and only quarter-hour divisions marked; no minute hand yet. The half-hour marks are the diamond shape usually associated with clocks made by George Graham, as indeed this one is. This example is interesting in as much as it shows the habit of taking one's one and only clock with one on journeys. Very possibly this clock belonged to some wealthy man who had town and country residences, and the clock went with him, back and forth. From the stout nature of the oak travelling case and its somewhat coarse construction, one would judge that this was made at the country seat of the owner. The slot in the upper frame holding the driving and alarm weights, to take the finial surmounting the bell is interesting, indicating that Graham did not make this especially as a travelling clock, or he would surely have omitted this unnecessary decoration. The hollowing out of places to receive the loops of the weights, the forward curve of the bell and the boss of the hand arbor indicate the care taken to prevent all movement during transit. The fret is a very late type, indeed this clock is a very late London example, but it cannot be before 1713, as Graham only succeeded Tompion in that year. Before that date he would have no right to put his name on any clock without that of Tompion as well.

Here we will introduce an Italian clock in the English lantern style by Camerini and dated 1656 (*Plate 10a*). It will be noted that it is fitted with a pendulum and that the date is a year earlier than Huygens' invention. This clock, which was bought by the Science Museum, London, at the Webster sale in 1954, has been the subject of much controversy as to whether the pendulum is original or a conversion. The top plate does not contain any filled or unused holes that would have been necessary for a balance or foliot used in connexion with a vertical crown wheel; if any conversion from balance to pendulum has been made, then the whole top plate would have had to be renewed. A recent close examination of the clock at the Science

Museum resulted in the opinion being expressed that the top plate was original.

Professor Morpurgo has recently made extensive researches into early Italian horology and in his recently published *L'Orologio e il Penduolo* he shows two more Camerini clocks with pendulums, one dated 1652 and the other undated. He also shows sketches of pendulums and escapements taken from manuscripts of the sixteenth and early seventeenth centuries. He has kindly allowed the author to choose one or two for inclusion in this book (*Plate 10*). Fig 3 shows one of Leonardo's sketches for a pendulum and verge escapement, about 1485; probably designed as a storer of energy. *Plate 10b* shows a drawing which contains the germ of the idea of the anchor escapement. This is from a MS dated about 1524 by Benevuto della Volpasia, who was the son of a Florentine friend of Leonardo.

The other two drawings appear in a MS *Questo Benedetto Pendolo* of the early seventeenth century. The one seems somewhat far-fetched in its idea, but the other is a verge escapement with a reversed crown wheel, just as one finds the only two known signed pieces of Johann Treffler (one is in the Museum at Kassel), and who is reputed to have made a pendulum clock for Archduke Ferdinand II of Tuscany in the 1650's before the Huygens invention, and who also is said to have had knowledge of Galileo's pendulum.

While there is no evidence that these sketches were of pendulums actually applied to clocks, we must concede that Italian thought had been very active with the idea of pendulum control, so that the genuineness of Camerini's clocks now appears much more probable than was the case, say, ten years ago. Had Camerini any idea that the pendulum achieved isochronism? There is no indication in the documents that this was so. This property had been noted, but not broadcast, by Galileo, but it still remained for Huygens to provide the theoretical proof.

After the pendulum had been invented, lantern clocks continued to be made in large numbers fitted with a pendulum hanging down the back, the going train in front and the striking train behind, as before, square in shape, although there was now no necessity for this since we have no longer to accommodate a circular balance wheel. Clocks could be, and were, made 'flat' in shape, as we shall soon see.

The next two illustrations (*Plate 11*) show a passing fancy in lantern clock design which lasted only ten or twenty years in the last quarter of the seventeenth century. These are no exception to our generalisation that the going train is in front and the striking train behind, but the pendulum is placed between the two trains. This prevented a pear-shaped bob being used; it would have taken up too much depth. The pendulum bob is made, therefore, from a piece of sheet brass and takes the form of an anchor, the flukes of which appear in the wings as the pendulum swings from side to side. Not many of these clocks survive today. The date of our example is 1675–80; it is an alarm clock, and the disk for the setting of the alarm is seen in the middle of the dial. The chapter ring is still wider and protrudes still further beyond the corner pillars, so much so that it has to be flattened out top and bottom to fit between the top and bottom plates. This overlap of the chapter ring gets still more pronounced later, these clocks getting the name 'sheeps-head', though why one cannot imagine, unless it be the supposed likeness to a sheep's curved horns on each side of a narrow face.

But to return to our particular specimen. The hand is getting progressively lighter in design, the spade head is developing and the shank is much thinner, and it is still fixed by a simple pin through a hole in the hour-hand arbor; tightening washers, or collets, are not yet used, although they are already common in better-quality clocks of this date. The fleur-de-lis *motif* for the half-hour mark is becoming more pronounced and there is only a single circle surrounding the hour numerals. The frets are of the dolphin type.

What we have said about frets is only a very rough guide to dates. These frets varied very much and early styles were often copied in later years. The chapter ring, style of engraving of the hour numerals and the details of the intermediate marks, also the design of the hand, provided that it is original, are surer guides to the date of these lantern clocks.

Lantern clocks were *always* weight-driven and consequently had to hang on the wall; they are one of the most popular types for modern reproductions. These, normally, have a dirty

'stale mustardy' colour achieved in the attempt to make
modern brass look old; the hands are invariably stamped from
a sheet, and they always have minute hands, as it is not much
use making a modern clock without; whereas genuine lantern
clocks would not be made originally with two hands. The
engraving, as a rule, is crude and heavy and they are *always*
spring-driven. Sometimes one gets a genuine old housing containing a modern movement. In this case there will be two
hands and the winding holes for the spring movement will have
been cut in the dial of the clock. The novice should look out
for these points; he should also remember that clocks with
their original balance wheel or foliot are very rare indeed, and
while it is not impossible that he find one, the odds are very
much against him.

In England the lantern clock was the forerunner of both the
long-case and mantel or bracket clock. (These latter two terms
are used indiscriminately.) On the Continent the long-case
clock made its first appearance about the same time as the
lantern clock in England, as we shall see later.

The table clock was a very usual style on the Continent for
domestic clocks in the sixteenth and seventeenth centuries; it
took many forms: square, rectangular, round; sometimes embellished with figures or animals that performed at the striking
of the hour. Its basic construction was a top plate and a bottom
plate; the distance pillars holding them together were usually
shaped and often ornate. Continental practice tended to a
greater degree of ornamentation than English. Actually table
clocks by English makers are very rare.

The dial plate is placed over the top plate of the movement,
and since these all have to be spring-driven, as they stand on
the table, the spring barrel often offers another surface for
decoration with engraving. A German table clock of the latter
half of the seventeenth century is shown in *Plate 11c*. This is of
gilded brass, finely chased, with figures of Venus and Cupid on
the dial. The bell was placed either under the movement, as in
the example illustrated, or above it, in which case the dial and
hand were placed above the bell, which would be in a domed
housing. The thought and care put into the whole clock, the
elaborate engraving on the cock protecting the balance wheel,
the engraved hammer-head shaped like an eagle's, make one

sigh for the times when men worked for the glory of their craft. The maker is Christian Caroli of Koenigsberg.

The year spring-driven clock made by Tompion in the late 1690's for King William III and now in Lord Mostyn's possession, is well known. It has, however, a forerunner, a clock in the Brunswick Museum made by Johannes Buschmann of Augsburg in 1651–2. This is illustrated in *Plate 12*. This early pre-pendulum clock shows the hours on the main dial and the quarters on a subsidiary dial below. The phases of the moon are shown by a revolving globe and its age in days on the small horizontal dial just below it. The master mainspring (*Plate 12c*) is housed in the base, on the one side of which is a dial divided into 365 days, the numbering being at intervals of 5 days up to 100, starting again 5, 10, etc. up to 200 and again starting at 300 to 365 (*Plate 12b*). On the other side of the case at the base is another annular calendar dial with the days of the year and indicating the fixed feasts of the church. At the back in the upper part is a day of the week dial with deities.

Once a day the rack seen in *Plate 12c* is released and governed by the four-bladed fly; it winds up a subsidiary spring in the upper part of the movement. This principle of the remontoire had already been practised by Jobst Burgi about 1595. The force transmitted to the train from the secondary spring wound daily, would be much more even than that that could be transmitted from the big year spring. The chain attached to the housing of the subsidiary spring can be seen in *Plate 12d*.

While Buschmann aimed at a going period of one year, it is understood that he did not quite attain his objective; here Tompion, half a century later, had better success.

We have already seen one example of pre-pendulum effort at accurate time-keeping, the cross-beat escapement. *Plate 13* shows a clock which embodies both this and a falling ball. The latter, in this case, is only decorative and has nothing to do with the driving mechanism of the clock; it was merely designed to give an impression of perpetual motion.

This clock is by Johann Georg Meyer of Munich, date about 1660. It has dials on all four sides, those for the fourth side being held by runners passing into the slots seen at the top and bottom of the inside left of the case (*Plate 13d*.) The case is tortoiseshell veneered, with embossed silver mounts. It shows about everything that it is possible to embody in a single piece. The dial on the right *Plate 13a* shows the hour and minute (it is pre-pendulum but its cross-beat escapement makes it worthwhile to have a minute hand), the phases of the moon and its age. The dial on the left in this view is seen enlarged in *Plate 13c*. In the picture showing the other two dials, that on the right gives the hour, minute, day of the week only. The dial on the left gives the hour and minute, the minute hand is scarcely visible, a thin blued steel hand almost coinciding with the gilt hand with the sun's effigy. The minutes are all individually marked on the bevelled ring immediately outside the roman numerals. The position of the sun and moon in the ecliptic can be read off this dial; where the sun and moon hands cross the circle of the zodiac as it revolves once a year around the inner space of the hour circle, show this. There is also an annual calendar dial. The four subsidiary dials probably give the Italian hours starting at sunset and the Babylonian starting at sunrise and possibly golden number and solar cycle.

Taking the view into the movement (*Plate 13d*) top right, can seen a locking plate for grande sonnerie striking, there being four notches for each hour, the quarters would be struck on another train with its own locking plate. The position of this locking plate is indicated on the 'Back Plate Dial' (*Plate 13c*), top left, the indicating hand is missing. There would also seem to be a switch over to 'dutch striking', where the hour is repeated or anticipated at the half-hour on a different toned bell. The dial for this, complete with hand, is seen below that of the grand sonnerie. The dial on the right may be a minute hand connected with the minute hand on the opposite dial; it will be noted that it is travelling anti-clockwise.

The original cross-beats with cherubs heads painted on them are still there, but the clock has been converted to pendulum with verge escapement, the crutch for the pendulum is seen right at the top. The gilt hour hand with the effigy of the sun and the steel minute hand are to be read off an hour ring engraved on the glass of the door. In the centre is an alarm setting disk. As already mentioned, the ball rolling down the spiral is purely decorative, as is the armillary sphere on the top.

The relationship between the English lantern clock and the Continental Gothic clock is seen in the example illustrated in

Plate 14 which shows a clock of mid-sixteenth-century date indicating the hours, quarters and phases and age of the moon. This influence on design persisted for some time as is evidenced by the late seventeenth-century Italian example of a weight-driven wall clock by Jo. Baptiste Albertis, dated 1685. These examples all have metal cases, indeed all English lantern clocks have metal cases, wood was not introduced for cases in England till after the invention of the pendulum in 1657. Wood was, however, used for cases on the Continent a century earlier. *Plate 4b* shows a wooden base housing the movement for a 'Flagellation' clock of the early seventeenth century. In the Kuensthistorisches Museum in Vienna there is a clock with a painted wooden case as early as 1560–70.

In considering lantern clocks, we have passed from the period of the balance wheel to that of the early days of the pendulum, which, as already stated, has enabled 'flat' instead of 'square' clocks to be made. We will now embark on a series of spring-driven pendulum clocks and follow their progression from the early efforts up to, in this part, the first third of the eighteenth century, during which period all the main improvements had been invented. After this all efforts were concentrated on 'finding the longitude', on improving escapements and the development of chronometers, on finding the means to simplify their construction and consequently their cost, and at the same time on bringing their construction within the capability of a greater number of makers.

In this connexion Arnold, Earnshaw, Mudge and Dent stand out, Earnshaw's work having, perhaps, the most lasting influence; but their efforts are not of a nature to be included in a popular non-technical book.

Since the pendulum came from Holland we go to Holland for our first examples. *Plate 14c* shows a most delightful small clock of early Dutch design known as 'Haagsche Klokjes', or Hague clocks, since they were first made by Salomon Coster of The Hague, who was the original licensee of Huygens. The date would be about 1660. It is quite small, made to hang on the wall, the bevelled edge of the door being veneered in tortoise, shell, following very closely the lines of wall mirrors of the period of the Restoration. Taking first the dial – the word dial, by the way, is derived from the Latin *dies*, a day, medieval

Latin *dialis*. A *diale* was as much land as could be ploughed in a day, according to the *New Century Dictionary*. The term dial was used in early times to denote a watch as well as a sundial:

> 'And then he drew a dial from his poke [pocket];
> And looking at it with lack-lustre eye,
> Says very wisely, "It's ten o'clock;
> Thus we may see," quoth he, "how the world wags."'
> *As You Like It*
> 'Then my dial goes not true.'
> *All's Well that Ends Well*

Just in what order Shakespeare wrote his plays is not known. Many have tried to set them out in chronological order and have failed, but for our purpose the period 1590–1610 covers the years of issue of the bulk of his plays. Although at the end of the sixteenth century and the beginning of the seventeenth century England was lagging behind in clockmaking and many of her efforts were crude and clumsy, there were working in London watchmakers who, judging from specimens of their work to be seen in the British Museum, the Museum of the Clockmakers' Company, and other collections, were producing watches that were equal in craftsmanship and decorative design to anything that contemporary makers on the Continent could produce. The names of David Ramsay, Michael Nowen, Thomas Nixon, Richard Masterton, Isaac Symms, Samson Shelton, Edward East, John Willow, and Nicholas Walter all appear on English watches of this period.

To return, however, to our quotations, the expression 'how the world wags' would seem to indicate a reference to the balance wheel of a watch, and 'my dial goes not true' can scarcely refer to a sundial which, once fixed, always records truly. A pocket sundial would only record incorrectly if incorrectly held by the owner and the expression 'goes' would scarcely have been used. We can conclude therefore that Shakespeare was alluding to watches and not to sundials.

It was the reference to the dial of our early Dutch clock that betrayed us into transgressing into the dissertation on the word *dial*; let us now return to the clock. The dial plate, as was customary at that period on the Continent, is covered with velvet, usually black, but sometimes, as in this instance, plum-coloured. The chapter ring is of solid silver, the hand gilded brass and finely engraved. The small silver shield hanging below the dial bears the maker's name, *J. Bernard van Stryp, fecit Anvers*. This shield can be lifted up and the pendulum bob reached with the finger through a hole covered by the shield to set it in motion, if need be.

Since there is only one hand, the quarter-hours are marked on the inner edge of the chapter ring, and there is an ingenious and rather unique method of approximating the minutes by engraving on the outer edge of the chapter ring six inverted Vs between each hour, the distance between their apexes indicating ten-minute intervals.

The illustration (*Plate 14d*) shows the movement of this interesting and charming little clock. This type of box housing, with the whole movement swinging forward, was very generally adopted in Holland, even when clock cases were designed to stand on the mantel and not to hang on the wall as in this case.

It will be recalled that we dealt with the build-up of the table clock, and this and some of the following examples show how conservatism in design remains when the function of the design has eased. The early type of baluster pillar would be quite natural and functional if the movement were turned over to the left in a horizontal position instead of vertical, as would be the case with a table clock, but it is some years before the baluster pillar disappears and a pillar with a centrally turned boss appears. In conformity with table-clock construction, the pillars are neatly riveted into the front plate of this clock, which would be the visible bottom plate in a table clock, and protrude through the back plate, and are there pinned, an untidy finish, which in a table clock would have been hidden under the dial. As we shall see, makers gradually awoke to this point after some years of somnolence, and the pillars become neatly riveted into the back plates and are pinned behind the front plates.

This little clock is only a timepiece; hence there is only one winding hole. The pendulum is suspended by a silken thread, the usual Continental practice, and is actuated by a crutch affixed to the end of the pallet arbor.

Bearing down on each side of the pendulum suspension will be noted two curved arms. Huygens discovered that a pendulum, in order to beat truly, should not swing the exact arc of a circle, but in what he termed a cycloidal curve – i.e. the line traced by a point on the circumference of a circle which is rolling along a straight line. This gives a slightly more U-shaped line than the pure arc of a circle. He therefore tried to give the pendulum this more upward swing at the end of its traverse by guiding it by these specially designed curves; this was possible since he adopted the silk-thread suspension. The trouble was that the correction introduced more errors than it overcame, and so had to be abandoned some few years later. The rectification came with the anchor escapement, with its small arc of swing as compared with the verge (Figs 6 and 1). By limiting the swing to a few degrees the cycloidal curve and the true arc of a circle are practically the same. It is remarkable that Huygens never adopted the anchor escapement in any of his experimental clocks, although it was invented nearly a quarter of a century before his death.

This clock is probably one of the oldest pendulum clocks in existence today.

Three of the clocks shown on *Plate 15* are English, and of about the same date as the two Dutch clocks, around 1660, but before we go into the details of the clock let us consider what we know about their maker, Edward East.

There has been a good deal of confusion as to his life-span. This was brought about by a claim made by a Dr. Williamson, in a book entitled *Behind my Library Door*, to identify a Quaker named Edward East with the clockmaker. This Edward East was buried in 1701, having died 'of age'; but he was only eighty-four at the time of his death, which would have made the year of his birth 1617. Yet East the clockmaker was elected in 1631 an original member of the Court of Assistants of the Clockmakers' Company, which in modern language would be termed the Council or Board of the Company – manifestly impossible for a boy of fourteen. Thus Britten and Baillie have been led to surmise that there may have been two men of the same name working during the period 1631 to 1693 when Edward East was still alive and associated with the Company, as its records show.

The recent discovery (by the author) of Edward East's will shows the claim for the Quaker buried in 1701 to be false. East made his will in 1688 and it was proved in February 1696 -7, so that he was ninety-four when he died, records in the parish of Southill in Bedfordshire showing his baptism on August 22nd, 1602. It is a strange coincidence that he should have been born within three miles of Northill, Bedfordshire, where thirty-six years later Tompion was born, and it is an interesting speculation whether the success of East had any influence on the young Tompion in deciding him to come up to London to establish himself.

In his will he describes himself as 'Watchmaker, Citizen and Goldsmith of London'. The Goldsmiths' Company records show that he was the son of John East, of Southill, Beds, and that he was apprenticed to Richard Rogers on March 27th, 1618, at the age of sixteen years; for a period of eight years, being made free of the Company in 1627. Thus he had been a master-goldsmith for four years when he was elected, at the age of twenty-nine, the junior member of the Court of Assistants of the Clockmakers' Company. He was Warden of the Company in 1638 and 1639, and Master in 1645 and 1652.

He was watchmaker to King Charles I and, according to Atkins and Overall in their *History of the Clockmakers' Company*, Charles II, when Prince of Wales, would play tennis, the stakes being an 'Edwardus East' – i.e. a watch by East. The Prince must have been quite a boy when he did this, as he was born only in 1630 and was sent to the Scilly Isles in 1646 and later that year to Paris. He remained abroad then until after his father's execution, and when he did return he, of course, did not come to London. East would appear to have held his Court appointment until King Charles' execution. Sir Thomas Herbert's memoirs of the last two years of the reign refer to an incident when he, Herbert, oversleeping, failed to call the King in time, upon which the King remarked, 'Herbert, you have not observed the command I gave you last night. Well, I will order you for the future; you shall have a gold alarm watch, which as there may be cause shall awake you; write to the Earl of Pembroke to send me such a one presently.' The Earl immediately sent to Mr. East, his watchmaker in Fleet Street, about it.

In 1671, when the clockmakers were applying for a coat of arms, the application was made in the names of the Master, the Wardens and several named Assistants, and 'also Edward East, the only person now living of those mentioned in the said Letters Patent of Incorporation'.

In 1654 Henry Jones, who was probably then fourteen years of age, was apprenticed to him. When Jones was Master in 1692 we have the following entries in the records of the Company: '1692, October 20. Mr. Henry Jones, the present Master this day acquainted the Court that Mr. Edward East formerly Master was pleased to give £100 now in his lifetime to this Company for the benefit of the poor. And Mr. Jones after the charitable example of his said Master having promised to give one hundred pounds more for the benefit of the poor likewise in such manner as shall be hereafter appointed and declared by the said Mr. East and Mr Jones. . . .'

'1693 June 20th. Mr. Edward East gave the £100.'

'1693 July 18. Mr. Henry Jones did give the £100 promised.'

It is thus clear that the one and the same Edward East was referred to up to this date, and according to our reckoning he must have been ninety, and wishing 'to make a gift in his lifetime'.

Having thus dealt with our Master's life-history, let us return to these examples of his craft. The delicate little clock (*Plate 15a*) is probably one of the earliest departures from lantern clock tradition in England and to be put in a wooden case. Dealing first with the case, this is of ebony veneered on oak, and takes the classic 'portico' type so much favoured by the early masters in the third quarter of the seventeenth century. The two three-quarter Corinthian columns and the two quarter columns at the back have beautifully built-up capitals of acanthus leaves, brass gilt. The little glass-fronted side door (on the side not seen in the photograph) is hinged to open with a little key. The object of this is not very clear. It might be to allow access to the pendulum bob at the back if the clock stopped, but this clock is unusual inasmuch as the movement fits so tightly in the case that it cannot be withdrawn through the door, either front or back. The whole of the top pediment lifts off and the clock is withdrawn upwards. When the top is removed it is easy to touch the pendulum rod with the finger and to set it in motion. Possibly, being a very early case, it was designed for the side door to open as was usual in lantern clock practice, it only being asertained later that it was necessary to have a movable top.

The movement extends inside the case only to the bottom

of the front door; in order to maintain a balanced design, the casemaker has been obliged to introduce a deep base; this contains a drawer for keeping the key, one of the prettiest pieces of cabinet-work imaginable. The early gilded claw-and-ball feet are interesting. The door at the back is of solid wood and the back plate plain; glass back doors and engraved back plates came later.

Dealing with the dial, we have a change from the engraved dials of the lantern clocks we have so far been considering and from the Dutch velvet-covered dial. In England the plain gilt dial found favour in the early clocks. This is matted all over, an art that seems to have been entirely lost; it is finely gilt. In some of the very early clocks a Tudor rose or similar design is engraved around the central hole through which the hand arbor passes. The corner decorations or 'spandrels', have not yet appeared. Spandrel is an architectural term used to denote the three-cornered space with one flat and two curved sides to be found between the apexes of a series of archways in a colonnade.

The chapter ring is of solid silver and slightly chamfered towards the centre, giving a nice effect of delicacy. The methods of depositing silver from its salts on to brass was not yet practised. The quarter-hours are marked on the inside of the chapter ring, although since there is a minute hand this is no longer necessary, but custom and tradition die hard, as we shall see in several cases. Quarter-hour marks continued, in some cases, up to 1740–50, although minute hands were usual from 1660 onwards. While some early clocks with minute hands have every minute numbered (*Plate 17a*), this particular example has the numbering every five minutes, the figures being placed within the minute circle. If these numberings are followed, it will be found that the figures get progressively larger, first within the minute circle, and later on the outside.

The hour hand is now a very delicate development from the crude arrow-head that we had on our early lantern clocks and the true 'spade' hand has appeared; the minute hand has good proportions and is stout enough to fulfil its functions. The minute hand has, perhaps, to stand more handling than any other part of a clock. The hands 'fit' the dial exactly, each one terminating at its respective marking, hour or minute. When the hands do not fit they are usually later replacements. The hands are still fixed with a simple pin through the arbor. Lantern clock practice is still found in this clock, inasmuch as when the dial is removed the motion work between the dial and front plate falls away. Later practice was to keep this in position by means of a bridge screwed to the front plate.

The winding squares, placed in a high, very high, location, between the x and II, is an early sign. These winding squares gradually get lower as times goes on, till they reach VIII and IIII, when they rise again to IX and III, at which position they appear to stabilise during the last quarter of the eighteenth century. Both trains of this clock wind left-handed. Right-handed winding had not yet become standardised. Later, if a clock winds left-handed it is usually a sign that it is a month movement.

In *Plate 37a* is seen a dial with the squares very low. This is an exceptional piece in which the positioning is for reasons connected with the case. The winding is effected through idler wheels.

Another indication that the clock (*Plate 15a*) is a very early departure from standard lantern clock practice is that the fusees have only fourteen grooves instead of sixteen; thus the going period is exactly seven days. The advantage of the extra day's going had not yet been appreciated. Sunday after lunch is clock-winding time at home, and this one has to be 'caught' before two o'clock or else the hour hand covers one winding square and the clock stops before it is clear. Prior to this date lantern clocks were, almost without exception, made to go for thirty hours only; indeed some very early ones, such as the Selwood shown in *Plate 9c* go only twelve hours for a six-foot drop.

The back plate, as is consonant with a solid door, is quite plain, except for the maker's name and the slight decoration on the pendulum cock and locking plate (*Plate 42c*). The flowing style in which the name is engraved is very pleasing. It will be noted that the baluster pillars and the pinning of the pillars behind the back plate, table clock practice, still persist.

Two other clocks (*Plate 15*), are other examples of the work of Edward East. In one we have again the 'architectural' type of case, ebony veneered on oak. The centre of the dial is now matted, but the corners are plain and spandrels have appeared.

This form of cherub head is one of the earliest. The chapter ring is still narrow and the hour figures 'dumpy'. The five-minute notation remains small within the minute ring. The hour hand remains the same but the minute hand is becoming more ornate – bayonet-shaped. A collet has now appeared; this is rather earlier than one would expect. On the other hand, the minute hand is of a style rather later than the rest of the clock. Possibly about two hundred and fifty years ago the minute hand was broken, and a 'modern' one of the time fitted and the collet added at the same time. The winding squares are a little lower and a calendar wheel has been added. The door at the back of this clock is also of solid wood and the back plate plain.

The third clock by Edward East, illustrated, has an interesting history. It belongs to the Huddleston family of Hutton John, near Penrith, Cumberland, and is reputed to have been given to an ancestor, Father Huddleston, who was at the Court of Catherine of Braganza, by James II. Father Huddleston is reputed to have brought Charles II into the Roman Faith on his deathbed. The clock, which is 2 feet high, is probably a little earlier than that we have just been considering. Originally it wound from the back, the change having been made when it was converted to anchor escapement and the bell replaced by a gong. The engraving on the dial is by the same hand as that on the dial of the Hilderson clock shortly to be described. As with the clock (*Plate 15a*), the going period is exactly seven days.

The fourth clock (*Plate 15*) has been introduced to illustrate the anticipation on the Continent, both of the use of wood for cases and their design. It shows a clock by Jobst Burgi, made in Prague in the first decade of the seventeenth century.

Plate 16 shows another clock of very similar design, which most people at first sight would attribute to Edward East, but, as a matter of fact, it is made by a certain John Hilderson. We find no record of his entry into the Clockmakers' Company, but we find records of apprentices bound to him. His name is sometimes spelt Hillersden. The plain severity of the lines of this case, again ebony on oak, are most pleasing. The dial is held against the front of the case by two small wooden pegs that have to be inserted, behind the dial plate, into two holes drilled into the top of the framework of the case, a most awkward proceeding. But the main features of the clock are its striking arrangement and the engraving of the dial; this is illustrated again in the section on dials (*Plate 37c*).

It will be noted that the chapter ring is widening and that the minute ring and the numerals within it are, proportionately, a little wider. The chapter ring is no longer solid silver, but consists of a thin silver plate sweated on to a thicker brass backing. Solid silver was often used, after the deposition of silver had been practised, in very high-class clocks; also silver spandrels and case decorations, as we shall see later.

Reverting to the striking arrangement, to which reference has already been made, this is quite unique; the clock has what is termed 'Dutch striking'. In the early days of clocks they were very expensive and could be afforded only by the very wealthy. They were usually placed in the rooms of large mansions where it was not easy to read the time across the room. For this reason quarter-striking and quarter-chiming clocks had already been made, especially on the Continent, for a hundred years or so already. But this system did not indicate to the listener the hour, only that it was one, two, or three quarters past an uncertain hour. A system of repeating the hour at the half-hour was introduced by the Dutch – presumably since it is so called – but the author has not been able to ascertain just when this system was first used.

The general rule was to have two bells and two hammers. When the hour had struck, during the next half-hour, the striking mechanism was transferred, or 'pumped' as it is termed, over to the hammer acting upon the smaller, higher-pitched bell, which is struck at the half-hour, and back again for the striking of the hour on the bigger bell. Thus we have two bells and two hammers; but in the clock in question we have the two bells, but only one hammer. The actuating mechanism is seen in *Plate 16b*. The minute-hand wheel is geared into another having the same number of teeth, and which therefore revolves once an hour with the minute hand. On to this second wheel are fixed two humps, one on each side of the wheel and 180° distant. The bells (the smaller is hidden behind the larger but can be seen in the illustration of the back plate, *Plate 42d*) are mounted on to the left hand of the two upright columns, the right-hand one being merely to provide the upper pivot. Attached to the lower end of the bell-supporting column is a bent arm forked at the end and straddling the wheel carrying the two humps; in the illustration one of the humps can be seen entering the fork. As the wheel turns, the hump presses the forked arm outwards to the left and turns the bell-supporting column to the right, bringing the larger bell in front of the hammer. Conversely, as the wheel with the hump turns round 180°, the hump on the other side turns the bell column to the left and brings the smaller bell before the hammer.

In Dutch, German, Swedish and some other languages the quarters of the hour are expressed in terms of the next coming hour; thus while we say a quarter-past six, half-past six and a quarter to seven, in these languages they say a quarter seven, half seven and three-quarters seven, and the clock can be set to strike either the number of the hour just past or that of the next succeeding hour, according to the custom of the country.

The disadvantage of Dutch striking is that it needs more power as, during an eight-day going period, there are 2496 hammer blows to be made against 1298 for a clock striking the hours only, or 1440 for a clock striking only one at the half-hour. Later, to overcome this difficulty of telling the exact hour in a large and often poorly lit apartment, a full system of striking was introduced, when the hour was repeated at each quarter together with one, two, or three blows on a higher-pitched bell to indicate the quarter. This required a great deal of power, was expensive to produce and appears only in the most exceptional clocks, mostly made for royalty. One of the earliest was given by Charles II to one of his mistresses, Barbara Villiers, Countess of Castlemain. She was the mother of the first Duke of Grafton and the case and dial are still in the Grafton family, though the movement was taken out by B. L. Vulliamy. In his time he did irreparable damage to many valuable clocks by putting movements of his own design behind their dials. He considered his movements superior to those of any other maker and had a complete disregard for tradition or history, a fact we much lament today. The movement is in possession of the Institute of Civil Engineers, to whom Vulliamy presented it.

Reverting to our Hilderson clock, we still have the table clock design persisting in the baluster pillars neatly riveted into

F

the front plate and pinned behind the back plate (*Plates 16b* and *42d*). Incidentally, the two trains wind inwards; that is, the going train on the right winds to the left and the striking train on the left winds to the right. Standardisation has not yet come.

Our next stage in the progression of design is a lovely clock by William Knottesford in an olive-wood case (*Plate 16c*). The use of cross-sections of branches to produce the 'oyster-shell' effect should be noted. The pediment top to the case has disappeared and a flat top takes its place, later to pass into the dome-shaped 'basket' type. We also get in this clock the twisted 'barley-sugar' columns, still with the fine acanthus-leaf capitals of the Corinthian column. The door at the back is glazed, although the decorated back plate has not yet appeared. In the top of the case is a little drawer to hold the key; in this position this is quite an unusual feature.

The matting in the centre of the dial is very fine, the corners remaining plain under the early cherub-head spandrels. The hour ring remains relatively narrow, but the minute spaces are deeper and the half-hour marks are becoming bolder. The hands, which are similar to the last example, are fixed under a collet. There is a seconds dial, an unusual feature in a spring-driven bracket clock, because the pendulum rarely beats a simple fraction of a second; thus although the second hand may revolve once a minute, the hand will not indicate one second at each advance. The winding squares are covered, which indicates that the clock has maintaining power; that is, on opening the shutters an auxiliary pressure is brought to bear on the train which causes it to continue its forward motion for the short period during which winding nullifies the force of the spring. Actually, winding only takes a few seconds, but it is usual for the maintaining power to operate for two or three minutes. When the period of maintaining is finished, the shutters automatically drop again into position, so that the clock cannot be wound again until the maintaining power has been brought into operation. While the idea was good in theory, in practice it was a useless elaboration in a verge clock, since the errors in time-keeping inherent in the design of these clocks was far more than the few seconds lost while winding. By the time this clock was made the anchor escapement with the seconds pendulum and dial had made its appearance, and it is probable that the maker, or possibly the man who ordered the clock, wanted all the latest details incorporated in his clock, irrespective of whether they were really effective or no. The clock has also a calendar dial, showing the day of the month through the aperture in the bottom of the dial. This would have to be adjusted by hand at the end of the short months.

When we turn to the back of this clock we notice that the distance pillars have now a turned central boss as well as turned bosses at each end and that they are neatly riveted into the back plate and pinned into the front plate. We have left the table clock practice, never to return to it. The signature has passed from the back plate to the bottom of the front plate. Later it will rise to within the dial itself. The movement is held in position on the seat board by two small swivelling hooks catching each corner; this is not found in later cases.

The illustrations on *Plate 17* show the stage next in progression, known as the 'basket top'. This description will be better appreciated if the succeeding illustrations with their decorative metal plaques or entirely metal baskets are consulted. In the earliest form, here illustrated, the basket is relatively flat, and in point of overall height above the door very little different from the William Knottesford clock we have just been considering. A fret, better to allow the escape of the sound of the bells, has appeared in front, but not yet at the sides. The case, as was still the fashion of the time, is ebony veneered on oak. On each side of the door frame are modifications of the cherub spandrel design. It will be noted that, while that on the right is fixed with a pin top and bottom, that on the left slides in a groove at the bottom and swivels about the pin at the top, thus exposing the keyhole of the door. This is a feature employed exclusively by Joseph Knibb, the maker of this clock. The reader should also note that a handle has appeared. Clocks were expensive; there would be only one in the house and this would be carried from room to room, hence the handle. Handles were a regular feature until the third quarter of the eighteenth century, when clocks became sufficiently inexpensive to have several in the house.

Turning to the maker of this clock, there were several members of the Knibb family who were clockmakers. Samuel would seem to have been of one generation. He was born, according to

Dr. Beeson to whom I am indebted for many of the details of the Knibb family given here, at Claydon in Oxfordshire, coming later to London in 1663. He died in 1674. There is a clock by him in the Guildhall Museum, of which the dial is engraved by the same hand as that which executed the dial of the Hilderson clock we have just considered (*Plate 37c*). The date would be around 1665–70, and therefore during the period when Samuel Knibb was working in London.

Joseph, who was the most renowned member of the family, was also born at Claydon; he was a cousin of Samuel. He started working in Oxford, as is shown by examples of his work signed Joseph Knibb, Oxon, *fecit*. In 1670 he entered the Clockmakers' Company and remained in London until 1697, when he retired to Hanslope in Oxfordshire. Here he seems to have done a little work, as occasionally examples signed Joseph Knibb, Hanslope appear. He was buried at Newport Pagnell in Buckinghamshire, about five miles distant, on December 14th, 1711.

Joseph's brother John worked with him while he was in Oxford, and seems to have continued a fairly close collaboration after Joseph came to London, the one helping the other out if they were short of a particular type of movement at any given time. John remained in Oxford and acquired local eminence, having been Mayor of the city in 1698 and again in 1710. Joseph would have been a small boy when King Charles set up his government in Oxford in 1644–46.

There are two members of a younger generation, according to the records of the Clockmakers' Company. Peter was apprenticed to Joseph Knibb about 1670 and was made free of the Company on November 5th, 1677. Edward Knibb was apprenticed on December 5th, 1693, also to Joseph Knibb, and young Joseph, who was the son of John, was apprenticed to Martin Jackson on June 5th, 1710. Neither of these two last appear to have proceeded to acquire the Freedom of the Company. When a son is apprenticed to his father it is usual for this fact to be recorded. We have no evidence that Edward was the son of Joseph. Peter was George's son,

Joseph is, however, the outstanding member of the family. His best work can compare with that of Tompion and Quare, but he had not the creative ability of Tompion. He devised a quarter-striking Grande Sonnerie on a locking plate, but the size of the clock limited the striking up to six, when it recommenced at one (*Plate 43a*). (The size of Georg Meyer's clock, (*Plate 13d*), enabled him to have this system striking for the full twelve hours.) He also introduced into this country what is known as 'Roman Striking'. In order to save power by reducing the number of blows of the hammer necessary during one winding, he caused the hours to be struck on two bells, one deeper toned than the other. The deeper-toned bell represented the v in the roman numeral system, four being represented as IV on the dial, instead of IIII as is usual in chapter rings (*Plate 18c*). I, II and III were struck on the high-pitched bell, IV, one high one deep, IX, one high two deep, XII was two deep and two high. This meant only 60 blows a day instead of 156, or 480 for an eight-day movement instead of 1248. This system did not find general adoption and only a few of Knibb's clocks with it have survived; they are consequently much sought after by collectors.

It is thought that Knibb specially developed a connexion with Italy. Good Knibb clocks have been found there, and the Roman Striking is another indication. Further, Knibb may well have got the idea of night clocks from Italy, where they were reasonably common in the latter part of the seventeenth century. Not many night clocks of this period have survived, but whereas three or four are known to the author by Knibb, he knows only one each by one of the Fromanteels, East and Henry Jones. These were all examples made in the last years of their respective careers. More about these clocks will be found in the chapter on night clocks.

Returning to the clock illustrated, the dial is very fine and unusual inasmuch as it is a skeleton. Joseph Knibb, and occasionally other makers, made some of their better clocks with this type of dial. It must have been a good deal more expensive to produce as the matting of the dial alone covers an area nearly twice as large as with an ordinary full chapter ring, to which must be added the cost of cutting out the numerals, quarter-hour and minute rings, a very delicate operation. Each minute is numbered, as previously mentioned, an early indication. Special attention should be paid to the hands, how the hour hand is of relatively heavy metal, yet, through chamfering, given a delightful appearance of lightness. Even the collet securing the hands is decorated. The clock is a repeating movement.

Our next illustration is an elaboration of the basket type due to the insertion of frets between the basket proper and the case. It is an alarm clock, the disk for setting the alarm being in the centre and the winding square for the alarm top right. The maker, Thomas Tompion, did not intend that his client should oversleep by reason of not hearing the alarm, for not only have frets appeared at the side of the case at the top, but the side panels are openwork and lined with silk. It is only a timepiece – that is, it does not strike the hours. We see this as there is only one winding square for the going train. Tompion towards the middle of his career numbered his clocks and watches. This clock is early in the clock series of numbers, No. 15, date about 1685.

As is always the case with Tompion, the finish of every detail is exquisite; all the frets are cast, hand-finished and chased. Tompion usually favoured simplicity both in dial and case, and the gilt frets in this case are, therefore, somewhat unusual. The clear-cut lines of the dial should be noted, the hour hand is a typical 'Tompion' hand, the half-hour marks are simple and clear. Here we have the five-minute numbers, still small, appearing outside the minute ring.

Of Tompion there has been more written than of any other clockmaker. He was, without doubt, the leading craftsman of his day and did more than any other to raise the standard of English clockmaking at the end of the seventeenth century. Biographical details have been flogged to death in these past few years, probably because Tompion is a name to be conjured with in the auction room in these post-war years, where his clocks are so often being bought up for fabulous sums by those who are wealthy but are without any knowledge or appreciation of their possessions. They simply buy a Tompion as they would buy a Reynolds or a Rembrandt, not that they could distinguish the style of one painter from that of the other, but as a means of capital investment. So writing up Tompion is 'good business' today, and if it creates a still greater demand for his clocks and Mr. X's clock goes up in value, the appreciation is all tax-free in these days of heavy taxation. As far as Mr. X is concerned, he would not have minded if his money had been employed in buying anything, as long as he could see an equal appreciation in capital values. These particular gentry are making the market impossible for the genuine clock-lover, who knows and appreciates what he is acquiring.

Tompion, who never married, was the son of a Bedfordshire blacksmith, and his father was churchwarden at the local church. Statements have been made that he was a Quaker, but Dr. Raistrick, in his book *Quakers in Science and Industry*, admits that Tompion's name does not appear in their records and that there is no evidence on this point. When he came to London is not known, but he is assumed to have trained as a black-smith and to have been apprenticed to that trade outside London. He did not enter the Clockmakers' Company till 1671, when he was thirty-one, at which time he was admitted as a brother – that is to say, as a fully qualified craftsman. He is described as a maker of 'Grete Clocks' – i.e. turret clocks. He must have rapidly established himself as a worker in brass, for about 1674-75 he made a fine astronomical clock, the only one known by him and now in the Fitzwilliam Museum in Cambridge, and in 1676 he was commissioned by Sir Jonas Moore to make two clocks for the use of the first Astronomer Royal, John Flamsteed, in Greenwich Observatory. These two were year movements, and the author inclines to the view that they were the first year movements ever to be made in England. They also had two seconds pendulums approximately 14 feet in length; here again they were probably the first of their kind to be made.

It has always been supposed that the pendulums of these two clocks hung down in the stair-well under the floor behind the clocks.[1] Now that the Observatory has left, the Ministry of Works is restoring the original buildings and the 'Octagon Room' to the state in which they were when first built, in John Flamsteed's day. A replica of one of Tompion's clocks has been made and put in position. In doing this it was discovered that the floor mentioned was intact and had never been disturbed. On the other hand, the beams above the clock position had been hollowed out to allow for a pendulum rod and the passage of a weight suspended above the clock. Thus it is seen that Tompion took advantage of Hooke's experiment of 1669, when

[1] See Appendix II.

he demonstrated that a freely suspended pendulum of 14 feet beating two seconds, with a heavy bob, could be kept in motion by a pin fixed on to the rim of a watch balance.

All Tompion's work is of excellent finish, but the movements and cases of some of his finest examples are superb. He was Master of the Clockmakers' Company in 1704; he died in 1713 and was buried in Westminster Abbey; and therefore could not have been a Quaker at the time of his death. If indeed he joined the movement only to secede, he could not have been a very good Quaker.

Tompion was an exquisite craftsman and an ingenious designer of complicated clocks but, except in so far as better timekeeping is inherent in good workmanship, Tompion made no contribution to the improvement of timekeeping as did Graham, Harrison, Earnshaw and others whose inventions and improvements are still in use today in high-grade clocks; whereas Tompion's products are merely collector's pieces. This cult for a name has had the regrettable result that we have recently lost to the States one of the finest examples of Tompion's clocks and cases. A few years ago we were gratified to learn that this clock had been bought back from the States, but this importation put the clock in a category which did not need a special export licence, and it has now returned to the States at a very much enhanced figure, to the great regret of all except those directly concerned in the transaction.

Plate 17c shows a metallic basket clock and from this illustration the description is better understood. In this case we are fortunate in having a clock with silver mountings, from the hallmark on which we can get the exact date of this specimen, 1698. The maker is Joseph Windmills, a maker of repute, who was Master of the Company in 1702. In this dial we still have the early cherub-head spandrels; these were retained much later in bracket clocks than in long-case clocks, since, as we shall see when dealing with this type later, the dials of the latter gradually became larger and consequently required larger spandrels, which were too big for bracket clocks of the same years.

The chapter ring has become much wider and the five-minute figures are much larger and have appeared outside the minute ring. The half-hour marks are more ornate and in addition to the inner circle for the quarter-hours there have appeared little +'s for the half-quarters between the five-minute marks. The winding holes are ringed, a fashion more usual in long-case clocks for a few years than in bracket clocks. The hands, both hour and minute, have become more ornate. A slot in which swings a false bob has also appeared, enabling the clock to be started without tipping or having to turn it round and open the back. In the photograph the pendulum is fixed in its carrying hook and the false bob is just seen on the extreme left of the slot. Another clock on *Plate 17* illustrates a somewhat excessive exuberance in decoration and is known as a double basket. With the exception of the design of the hour hand, the two dials are very similar. The coming of finials on the corners of the case should be noted. The maker is John Shaw of Holborne. Here again the pendulum has been fixed in its carrying hook, in this case to leave clear the back plate of the slot carrying the maker's name. The false bob here is on the extreme right.

Plate 18 shows a rather elaborate basket clock by Samuel Watson; its plain wooden basket-top tones down the somewhat heavy ornamentation of the sides and the ornate side panels. Particular attention should be paid to the fine handle. The back plate of this clock is shown in *Plate 43c*. The faceted bob as a means of more exact regulation should be noted.

Samuel Watson is a maker who in the past has not received sufficient attention or recognition from horological writers since our early friends, Smith and Derham, who were loud in his praises. They record a famous astronomical clock made by him to the order of King Charles II, who however died before it was finished in 1690, when Queen Mary II honoured her uncle's order and took delivery of the clock for £1000. No description of it had appeared in any standard horological work until the author rediscovered it in 1942 in Windsor Castle and described it fully in the *Horological Journal* for December of that year. Watson was the leading astronomical clockmaker of his day, in this branch surpassing Tompion, who is only known to have made one astronomical clock. The clock we have just referred to was ordered by King Charles II after he had already taken delivery of a more simple one in 1682 for which he paid £215. Watson also made two astronomical clocks for Sir Isaac Newton. One is constructed on the Ptolemaic principle – that is, with the earth fixed and the sun and planets revolving around it. This is in the possession of the Clockmakers' Company. Another, in the possession of the author, made about 1695 – i.e. after the publication of the *Principia* – is on the Newtonian (Copernican) principle of the fixed sun, with the universe revolving around it. This latter clock is probably the first to be made in England embodying Newton's principles. This book is not the place for the illustration and discussion of complicated astronomical clocks; the author hopes one day to write another book dealing with the more unusual phases of seventeenth- and eighteenth-century horology, if he can find a publisher who thinks that there are sufficient readers interested in the subject. The purpose of the present comments is to bring Watson's name more fully into the position it deserves in the horological world.

We will stop our chronological progression for a moment and take a step a year or two backwards to examine three clocks included for the specific points they illustrate. It will be noted that all three have the five-minute numbers within the minute ring and that they are therefore, presumably, a little earlier than the last example considered. *Plate 18b* shows a clock by Knibb where he has attempted to have the *grande sonnerie* striking referred to earlier – i.e. striking the full hour and the quarter each quarter of an hour. There are three trains: going, hour-striking and quarter-striking. To strike the hour four times an hour instead of once requires 5192 blows of the hammer in 8 days instead of 1248. The spring driving the hour strike has to be much stronger to provide the necessary power. Knibb did not feel quite equal to this at this time, so he only provides for the hour to be repeated up to six, dividing the day into four parts of six hours as far as striking is concerned. He left it to the listener to decide in which quarter of the day he is by 'the Hexercisin' 'hof 'is brain – that is, assumin' that 'e's got any,' as our friend Private Willis in *Iolanthe* ruminated in Palace Yard as he watched the M.P.s pass into the House while he stood as sentry at the entrance gates. In this way Knibb 'gets away' with 384 blows a week instead of the 1248 required for a normal clock to strike the hours only. He can therefore do with much less power in his modified *grande sonnerie* than in an ordinary striking clock and yet tell the exact hour every

quarter to the listener, who has only to make a very simple
mental effort during two six-hour periods, in one of which he
will almost certainly be asleep. The back plate of this clock is
seen in *Plate 43a*. From this it will be seen that it would not be
easy to incorporate the much larger locking plate necessary to
provide for *grande sonnerie* striking over the twelve hours.

In *Plate 18c* we have another Knibb idea to reduce the power
needed for striking – the Roman striking already referred to on
page 79. It will be noted that the four is shown as IV and not
IIII. The clean Knibb hands should be noted; otherwise there
is little to comment on this clock, beyond the remarks already
made in connexion with previous clocks. The fourth clock on
this page shows one of the many attempts to get good time-
keeping at sea. The clock is suspended from a ball-and-socket
joint, and under the base is a ring to which a cord could be
attached to limit movement.

'Finding the longitude' was a problem which beset all
mariners, and the English in particular as a maritime nation,
from the earliest times until the last quarter of the eighteenth
century, when as already mentioned it was solved by John
Harrison and later brought into the realm of economic possibility by Earnshaw and Arnold. At the time we are considering,
watches did not have the isochronous balance spring; it was
only just being invented, let alone perfected, so that they were
far inferior to clocks in time-keeping.

Some travelling clocks were made with balance-wheel movements at this time, but they were for land travellers whose
determination of their whereabouts did not depend on the
accuracy of their timepieces. The most accurate clocks of the
day were weight-driven pendulum clocks. The weight is an
ideal driving force; it is constant in application and needs no
adjustment. Many were the varied efforts made to find a
suitable method of keeping time at sea with pendulum clocks.
All failed, of course, because the solution of the problem did not
lie in that direction; but it was to take many years of weary
searching to discover this.

In examining this clock we find that the chapter ring is much
broader in proportion to its diameter than in the other examples, giving a much heavier appearance to the dial; the
hands, while good, are not so well finished as Knibbs'. The

decoration of the day of the month aperture, an early appearance of this feature, makes it too heavy in relation to the small matted surface of the centre of the dial. The back plate of this clock is seen on *Plate 43d.*

The maker of this clock is Daniel Quare. He was one of the leading makers of the latter half of the seventeenth century and the first half of the eighteenth. He entered the Clockmakers' Company as a brother in 1671 and was Master in 1708. He was a Quaker and a stout defender of his religious beliefs, several times fined or punished for non-compliance with different ordinances that conflicted with his conscience. He was clockmaker to King William III and, as will be seen later, he appears to have moved in the diplomatic circle of his time, which probably accounts for the relatively frequent appearance of his clocks on the Continent. The *Friends' Quarterly Examiner* of 1900 gives full details of Quare's career. He was one of the petitioners to James II in 1686 for liberty of conscience, which petitions of Nonconformists James tried, a couple of years later to bring in, to cover, under the guise of general religious freedom, the emancipation for his Roman co-religionists, which he knew he could not get by direct appeals.

Quare's progress in the social circle can be followed by the ascending degree of those attending the marriages of his various children. In 1705 Anne Quare married John Falconer, and the envoys of Venice, Florence, Hanover, Portugal, Sweden, Prussia and Denmark were present. In 1712 both a son and a daughter were married, the guests including the Earl of Orrery, the Duke of Argyll, the Venetian Ambassador, the Compte de Briançon, etc. But in 1715 when his daughter Elizabeth married Silvanus Bevan, besides the Countess of Brocklinborough, the Count and Countess of Guicord, Francis de Fleurs and many others, Sarah, Duchess of Marlborough, was present. The Prince and Princess of Wales and all the 'High Quality' were only prevented from attending the wedding by an Act of Parliament which forbade the attendance at dissenting places of worship. The Princess of Wales attended the reception.

Quare refused a pension of £300 a year as watchmaker to King George I, because his conscience forbade him to take the oath; nevertheless he was given access to the palace.

Quare also invented the repeating watch, but he had a rival

claimant, Dr. Barlow, who about 1676 invented the rack-and-snail system of striking for clocks and so made repeating clocks possible. According to William Derham, about 1687 (towards the end of King James' reign), the two rivals submitted their claims to the King in Council, the King giving the award to Quare, whose watch repeated the hour and quarter with one push of a lever, whereas Barlow's needed two separate levers for hour and quarter.

Plate 19 introduces a maker well worthy of being, if not put into the front rank, at any rate being placed at the top of the second flight, Peter Garon. The clock in a tortoiseshell veneer basket case was recently found on the Continent; it is *grande sonnerie*. The date is the first decade of the eighteenth century; it will be noted that the decoration around the calendar date has spread to the lower winding hole and the false bob aperture, also that the other two winding holes are ringed. Garon may have been a good clockmaker, but he does not seem to have been a good man of business, for Baillie records that he was adjudged bankrupt in 1709 and the final record of him in the Company's records is that he was insolvent.

The illustration (*Plate 19b*) shows a reversion to the plain wooden basket. The clock is by Tompion and is one of his more 'ordinary' productions. Nevertheless it has elegance of proportion, simple and clean-cut lines, and altogether is a very pleasing piece. The reader is immediately struck by an innovation in the design by the introduction of the two subsidiary dials at the top. That on the right is a simple lever which prevents the striking train from functioning (now that we have the rack-and-snail, described below, we can shut the strike off at will without upsetting the sequence) and so renders the clock silent during the night hours if so desired. It is a repeating clock, and so we can imagine its original owner taking it up by the handle and carrying it up to his bedroom, divesting himself of his full-bottomed periwig, full-skirted coat, flowered silken waistcoat, knee-breeches and red-heeled shoes, putting on his nightshirt and drawing on his nightcap. He then places the clock on a table beside his bed where he can easily reach the repeat pull cord by passing his hand through the bed curtains. He snuffs the light and pulls the curtains of the four-poster and settles down to sleep, only to be told by his wife in the morning that his snoring was far worse than any hourly striking of the clock could have been. The repeating cord, for which he sleepily groped during the night, is clearly seen in the picture. As will be seen from *Plate 44b*, these clocks were generally so arranged that the repeat could be actuated from either side.

We have heretofore only considered the locking-plate type of striking, where the count wheel, independent of the hour-hand arbor, is released each hour and continued to turn, allowing the clock to strike the necessary number of hours, after which an arm falls into a groove and locks the plate until it is released by the lifting of the arm just prior to the next hour. In this way, only a continuous sequence of the hours can be struck (*Plates 42c* and *d* and *43a*). About 1676, according to Wm. Derham, a Dr. Barlow invented the striking system known as the rack-and-snail. In this case a stepped wheel is fixed to the hour-hand arbor, the hour hand being only a tight friction fitted on the arbor, so that for adjustment it can be moved around the arbor without setting the going train in motion. As the hour wheel turns once in each twelve hours, each step, which comprises one-twelfth of the circumference at that point, remains in position to receive the rack tail in the same position for the whole of that hour. This regulates the number of teeth that the gathering pallet can collect, and so the number of blows that can be struck before the striking cuts out. Thus, however often the repeat cord is pulled during any hour, the same number of blows is achieved.

Thus with the locking plate you have to set the plate to the hour by releasing the detent of the striking train with the finger until the number of blows struck corresponds to the hour on the dial, but with the rack-and-snail, if the strike gets out, and this is very rarely so, the hour hand can be pushed round until stroke and dial agree.

The function of the strike-silent dial led us into this dissertation on repeating and striking mechanisms. Reverting to the clock being described, the subsidiary dial on the left is what is generally referred to as the 'rise and fall' regulator; it is for altering the length of the pendulum. We have seen how on the Continent the earliest pendulums were supported independently by a silken cord from a cock on the back plate and were actuated by a crutch fixed to the escape pallet arbor, while in

England the pendulum rod was affixed direct to the escape pallet arbor.

As related in Chapter One, the anchor escapement, actuated by a crutch with its pendulum carrying the heavy lenticular bob, suspended by a thin spring strip passing through a cock on the back plate, came into use in the early sixteen-seventies. Towards the end of the decade Tompion appears to have combined anchor-escapement practice with verge movements; that is to say, he suspended his verge-movement pendulums from a spring and actuated them through a crutch. This necessitated a heavier bob, which would take up much too much depth if made ball- or pear-shaped as have been the bobs we have heretofore seen; so a flat lenticular bob had to be used as with the anchor escapement. This introduced a complication; the bob had to swing parallel with the back plate so that any adjustment could not be less than one half-turn of 180 degrees. But this might be too much, so the bob was made a loose sliding fit on the rod, the bottom of which was threaded to take a 'rating' nut placed underneath, which could be screwed round any desired amount and so raise or lower the bob as in an ordinary grandfather clock. This again had the inconvenience that the whole clock had to be turned round and the back door opened to get at the rating nut, so Tompion introduced the rack-and-lever principle of regulation from the front. The central arbor of the left-hand dial carries a toothed rack which gears into the end of a lever from which the pendulum is suspended (*Plate 44b*), the steel spring suspension being free to move through the cheeks of the cock. Thus very fine adjustments could be made to the pendulum length with the minimum of effort. It may here be noted that although the anchor escapement was readily and generally recognised as much superior to the verge in time-keeping properties, verge escapements were general for all mantel or bracket clocks until the latter half of the eighteenth century, because the clocks were carried from room to room and the verge escapement did not need anything like the same exact levelling that is required by the anchor. Thus, until clocks were cheap enough to have several in the house and there was no longer any necessity to move them from room to room, the anchor escapement did not become popular for this type of clock.

Reverting to our Tompion clock, it will be noticed that the cherub spandrels and all elaborations of them have gone and we now have a female head as the central point of a more or less indefinite design. Tompion's escutcheons are different from those of Knibb. The signature has now appeared above the chapter ring, between the two subsidiary dials. This was adopted by Tompion and his successor Graham, but was not very much used by other makers. The hour hand should be compared with that of *Plate 17b*; it will be seen that both are elaborations of the plain spade *motif* of *Plate 15*, but this hand has developed the design still further than in *Plate 17b*.

Following on this Tompion, we have a real bracket clock – i.e. a clock standing on the original bracket made for it – a product of the hands of George Graham (*Plate 19c*). In pursuance of our custom, since we are dealing with another of the great clockmakers of his day, we will give a few biographical notes on this maker before considering in detail the clock he has made.

For the past seventy-five years George Graham, the horologist, has been identified with a child, George, born on July 20th, 1673, and registered by the Society of Friends as being the son of George Graham, of Rigg, in Cumberland.

The author finds, however, that the Grahams of Rigg also registered the births of Hannah in 1677, another George in 1708, and six more children between 1715 and 1724. The burial registers mention Elizabeth, wife of George in 1708. Surely this indicates that by 1707 George of 1673 has succeeded his father and married. His wife dies soon after his own first-born, George, is born; he marries again and raises a second family.

Clearly this George Graham never came to London.

The Apprenticeship Indentures of Graham to Henry Aske, July 2nd, 1688, read: 'George Graham, sonne of George Graham, late of ffordlande in the County of Cumberland, Husbandman, deceased'. Here we have Graham's own declaration of his origin, and the Friends burial registers confirm the burial of George Graham, of Foordlands, on October 20th, 1679.

The horologist was buried in Westminster Abbey, beside Tompion, and the Abbey burial records give his age as seventy-eight in 1751, which makes him born in 1673, so that he was fourteen or fifteen when apprenticed.

There is no record in the Society of Friends books that Graham ever attended any London Meeting House. He was not apprenticed to a Quaker. When made Free in 1695, he was free to affirm; but there is no record that he did not take the oath. He did not marry a Quakeress. He entered Tompion's employ in 1696 and later married his niece. Burial in Westminster Abbey would not be open to a Quaker. Thus we have no evidence that he practised the Quaker faith after the age of five or six years. Indeed all the evidence goes to show that he did not.

But Quaker or no Quaker, a man whose reputation has come down the ages as 'Honest George Graham' must have been a fine character.

He was Warden of the Clockmakers' Company 1719-21 and Master in 1722. On Tompion's death in 1713, he succeeded to his business.

Graham is best remembered in horology for his two inventions which are today still widely employed, viz. the dead-beat escapement and the mercury pendulum (Fig. 7 and *Plate 26c*).

He was also a maker of astronomical instruments for Greenwich and other observatories and the inventor of the cylinder escapement for watches. He was a Fellow of the Royal Society and communicated several important papers to it.

Reverting to our illustration, we see that the basket has had an addition on top, giving what is termed the 'inverted-bell'-shaped case. Still ebony veneered on oak, the bracket repeats the *motif* in a reversed form. The bracket contains a drawer to hold the key.

In the main the dial is very little different from the Tompion we have just been discussing, except that the half-hour *motif* based on a fleur-de-lis is gone and a diamond has taken its place. Graham favoured this mark, others used it also, but not often to denote the half-hours. The marking of the eighth-hours between the five-minute marks has also gone. The spandrels, while still based on a female head, are becoming less elaborate in design; the hour hand, while remaining on the basic spade design, is becoming more pointed.

Also on this plate we have an interesting clock by Joseph Antram, who was Clockmaker to King George I. Its date must be before 1723, for in that year Antram died. In this case the arch has been used to accommodate a calendar dial showing the day of the month, the month of the year and the day of the week. The two subsidiary dials are, left for rise and fall pendulum regulation and on the right a strike/silent arrangement which allows for the clock to strike the hour only, hours and quarters on one bell, or to chime the quarters on six bells or to cut out the striking altogether. The clock has very historical associations. George I married, as Prince of Brunswick-Luneberg, Sophia Dorothea of Celle. It was a marriage of convenience and suited neither party. George neglected his wife and she sought consolation elsewhere, although there is no evidence that she was actually unfaithful. In the event she was divorced and sent to the castle of Ahlden and known henceforth as the Duchess of Ahlden. There she was kept prisoner till her death in 1727. She never came to England and was a queen who was never crowned. The clock we are illustrating would seem to have belonged to her; on the front plate is scratched 'Sophie Dorothea geb. 15.9.1666 zu Celle gest. 13.11.1726 zu Ahlden. vermaehlte 21.11.1682 mit Georg Ludwig, spaeter Georg I von England. geb. 7.6.1660 gest . . . 21/22.6.1727.' rest of inscription illegible. (Note: some of the days of the month given do not tally exactly with English histories.) Translated: Sophie Dorothea born 15.9.1666 at Celle, died 13.11.1726 at Ahlen. married 21.11.1682 to George Lewis, later George I of England. born 7.6.1660 died 21/22.6.1727. George I died in his coach on his way to Osnabruck, in Germany.

CHAPTER FOUR

Long-Case Clocks 1660–1735

WE will now leave for a while the bracket clock and follow the development of the long-case clock. This, in England, only started after the invention and the adoption of the pendulum. Concurrently with the early long-case clocks which stand on the ground, there was a limited movement to have wooden-cased clocks hanging on the wall. One such clock is illustrated in *Plate 20b*. It is a very fine eight-day striking movement by Edward East and is a good example of the change-over from 'square' to 'flat' clocks mentioned in the last chapter. It is in an ebony-veneered case with the hood sliding up along grooves in the back board, as was common practice in the early long-case clocks. These were short by later standards, only six feet to six feet six inches high. As the clocks got taller they were too tall conveniently to have the hood sliding up, so the hoods were made to slide forward and to come off instead of sliding up, and finally they were fitted with an opening door, as in a bracket clock.

Except for the two pineapple pendants, which are believed to be later additions, and the apron concealing the lock to the hood, the overall design follows very closely mantel-clock practice of the period. The three flaming-urn decorations on top are the start of a vogue for the decoration of the top of long-case clocks that was to persist for nearly two hundred years. The columns, it will be noted, are only three-quarter columns, being let into the framework of the hood; the Corinthian capitals should be compared with those on the early East mantel clock shown in *Plate 15a*. The date of this clock is a little later than the mantel clock; engraved spandrels have appeared, the hands are slightly more elaborate, it has maintaining power and a calendar dial. The winding squares are here in the 'low' early position as compared with those in the 'high' position in *Plate 15a*. As with lantern clocks, there is no back door to reveal a back plate. The clock is therefore signed on the front plate, in this case outside the chapter ring, the words Edward East appearing between VIII and VII, and London between V and IV. The weights, as is always the case with weights of this period, are brass-encased.

The clock illustrated (*Plate 20a*) is an example of a short pendulum movement originally made to stand on a bracket hanging on the wall. It was later encased, either to exclude dust, or more likely because Mistress James, the wife of the President of Queens' College, Cambridge, from 1675–1717, to which college this clock was presented by the maker Edward East in 1664, wanted something more in keeping with the fashions of the time. At that time, anchor escapement, to which system this clock has been converted, and long-case clocks were becoming 'all the rage', and Mistress James did not want to be left behind in the race. It would seem that the job was given to a local joiner, about 1685–90, who had no knowledge of contemporary clock-case design, and he just boxed it in in oak to harmonise with the panelling of the room in which it stood. The minute hand was probably added at the time when the conversion to a seconds pendulum anchor escapement was made – perhaps about 1685–90. The 'bar' across the dial is an engraved plate reading *To Queenes Colledg Cambridg The Guift of Edward East Clockmaker to King Charles the second 1664.* This plate was evidently originally placed on the apron of the bracket supporting the clock, but when it was encased it was riveted on to the top of the beautifully engraved dial, quite spoiling the proportions. It is a great pity that it was not affixed to the door of the hood, or in some other place on the case. The engraving is by the same hand, both as regards lettering and design, as that on the author's clock illustrated in *Plates 37c* and *42d*. The similiarity of design shown in the illustration of the dial of this clock in *Plate 37* and the dial of the author's clock in *Plate 37* should be noted.

It will be recollected that we said earlier that in England the long case only came into use after the invention of the pendulum, but on the Continent there are examples half a century earlier, one of which is illustrated in the Frontispiece. This fine anonymous three-train clock is of date about 1600, stands about 8 feet high, is fitted with automata and is finely painted and gilded.

The overhanging scallop shell supporting the platform for the Jacks to circulate and strike the quarter bells, is most pleasing. Above in the next tier, Christ and Death will appear alternately with the hours, a favourite, if gruesome, reminder of the frailty of life, very popular at the time. Surmounting the whole is a cock that will crow, again a reminder of the frailty of man in recalling St. Peter's denial of Our Lord. This cock will flap its wings and crow, probably every twelve hours, the hours being struck by Jacks on the big bell at the top.

In the arch of the dial we have the phases of the moon and its age (incidentally this arched dial appears nearly a century before it makes its appearance in England, see *Plate 25a*). The hand with the reproduction of the human hand will indicate mean time, the idea was that this was the hand of God controlling men's lives; that with the sun will revolve once a year and will show its position in the zodiac, the symbol for each sign being painted in the twelve 'gothic' shaped divisions in the centre of the dial. Within them in the centre are the numbers 1 to 16 twice over, the tail of the sun hand passes before these to indicate the hours of daylight, and by subtraction from twenty-four, those of darkness for the month in question. The hand with the lunar effigy will revolve once in a lunation and will show the position of the moon in the zodiac at any time. The two subsidiary dials show left, the day of the week and right the quarter-hour. A really fine piece of work.

Plate 20d shows a good example of 'how not to do it'. Here is a very nice clock of the third quarter of the seventeenth century, utterly ruined in an attempt, some two hundred years ago to modernise it. 'Keeping up with the Joneses' is no new idea. The clock, by Henry Jones, has had the very attractive narrow panelled case, following the cabinet practice of the period, utterly spoilt by additions to increase its height. The insert between the hood and pediment and the addition of a double plinth and feet, of a style a hundred years later than the clock, quite ruin its appearance, and proportions.

Our next illustration (*Plate 21*) is of the historic clock ordered by King's College, Cambridge, at Michaelmas 1670 from William Clement. Mr. Saltmarsh, archivist of the college, has kindly supplied me with the following facts from the college records. A clock was evidently in existence before 1670 under the care of one Wardell. During the Michaelmas term of that year, William Clement visited Cambridge to inspect the clock and was paid £1 10s. for his expenses. He evidently recommended a new clock and would naturally be keen to introduce his new invention of the anchor escapement, as being an infinitely better time-keeping proposition than the verge or very possibly foliot balance on the old clock. The college contracted with him to supply a new clock for £40 and eventually paid in all £42. The clock appears to have been finished and installed before Michaelmas 1671, because all payment entries are in the accounts for the year ending on that date, and that date is marked on the clock.

The following are the actual entries in the College Mundum Book:

Custus Ecclesie
Term. Nat. 1670
    Sol. Wardell pro supravisione Horologii pro Anno
        ultime elapso   0.6.8
    Et pro reparando Horologio   0.3.0

Expensae Necessariae
Term. Mic.
    Sol. Gulielmo Clement pro expensis Itineris ad viden-
        dum Horologium   1.10.0

Reparaciones Novi Templi
    Sol. Gulielmo Clement in partem 40ⁱⁱ pro Horologio
        novo secundum Articulos in Manibus Mᵣⁱ Drake
        depositos   5.0.0
    Sol. Gulielmo Clement in plenum pro Horologio novo
        Secundum Articulos   35.0.0
    Et eidem ultra Articulos ex Conssesu Mᵣⁱ Prepositi et
        Seniorum   2.0.0

From which we see that the keeper Wardell was paid 6s. 8d. per annum for maintenance, and in addition, in this year, he was paid 3s. for repairs. Next comes the payment to Clement for his journey expenses to view the old clock and to make his recommendations, during which visit he appears to have contracted to supply a new clock for £40. Who was the Master Drake in whose hands the contract was deposited we do not know. A Mr. Drake was among the original subscribers to the Clockmakers'

Company in 1631, and in 1656 we find John Drake a signatory to a petition to the Lord Mayor and Aldermen in a dispute between the Clockmakers and the Blacksmiths. The researches of Dr. Penfold have disclosed that Clement was an anchor smith in Rotherhithe, south of the Thames, who moved north when he joined the Clockmakers Company in 1670. This discovery strengthens the claim for Clement to be the inventor of the anchor escapement.

Then come the two payments totalling the £40 of the contract and in addition a payment of £2 for some reason unknown.

From the illustration it is seen that the Master has signed his work + GVLIELMVS + + CLEMENT LONDINI + + FECIT 1671 +, and the foregoing history proves that this date is correct. It will be noted that the flukes of the anchor are riveted on to the curved base, a proof that this part of the escapement is original. Had it been replaced a hundred years or so later, the anchor would have been made in one piece.

The present escape wheel and the pendulum with its double suspension spring and wooden rod are later replacements, but the new brass escape wheel would have to follow the pattern of the original one in order to work with the original anchor. One or two of the other wheels in the train are also of brass and therefore not original; these changes may have been made when the clock passed to St. Giles' Church. One thing is certain; the clock has always had a recoil escapement; it has never been converted from a verge.

The little central dial records when the clock passed from King's College, Cambridge, to St. Giles' Church at Cambridge, in 1819.

In this clock we have the Genesis of all long-case clocks, and derived from this clock we have nearly all the regulators and observatory clocks for two and a quarter centuries, and for many of them for a further fifty years. The dead-beat escapement and refinements thereof were only made possible by improvements of the principle demonstrated by Clement in this clock.

In Chapter One we have traced the arguments for and against Clement and Hooke as inventors of the anchor escapement, and the author submits that there is no evidence at all in favour of Hooke. This is gradually finding wider acceptance; there are a few who obstinately cling to the older idea, but none can produce any evidence. That Hooke's experiment with the small arc 14-foot pendulum was due to the anchor escapement, has definitely been exploded.

Ponder on this clock carefully, as it introduced an improvement in time-keeping as important as that of the pendulum itself, and let us give honour to the *real* contriver of the royal pendulum, as Smith says.

Just when the long-case clock started is a matter for conjecture. Some of the earliest known have very narrow trunks, only wide enough to take the weights of clocks with verge escapements and bob pendulums. The author inclines to the view that it was the anchor escapement with its narrow arc of swing that so thoroughly established the long case, but no invention, however revolutionary and improving, sweeps the board at once. Some makers, such as Fromanteel, who introduced the verge escapement with the pendulum into England and who would naturally be predisposed to it, still continued to make verge escapement movements with short pendulum and encase them in the new and rapidly becoming fashionable long case.

If this be true, we do not get any long cases before 1671–72. It has generally been accepted that the desire to see the weights enclosed led to the placing of short bob movements in a long case some time in the sixteen-sixties, but the author knows no real basis for this. Certainly the enclosing of lantern clocks from time to time was, in the writer's opinion, a result of the introduction of the long case and a desire to 'modernise' an existing possession; not, as has sometimes been asserted, a precursor to it.

In *Plate 22* we have four early long-case clocks by Johannes and Ahasuerus Fromanteel, Edward East and Joseph Windmills respectively. The Johannes Fromanteel has a short pendulum with a verge movement, that by Ahasuerus an anchor escapement with seconds pendulum. These early cases follow the mantel-clock tradition of ebony veneered on oak, slide-up hoods, and have 'spoon' locking devices for the door. This is a hinged hook with a broad tail, rather like the handle of a spoon, which, hanging down below the hood inside the case, has the tail pressed backwards when the door is shut, bringing the hook forward to engage the lower framework of the hood and preventing its being raised until the door is again unlocked and opened, thus ensuring no meddling with the hands by unauthorised persons.

The general style of the cases, with their panelled doors, and, in the case of Ahasuerus, panelled base, is in conformity with cabinet-making trends of the period. The higher base, supported on a deeper plinth resulting in a shorter trunk, gives better proportions to the Ahasuerus clock than to the Johannes, and is one of the reasons for dating this clock a little later than the other. A 'swag' or decorative ornament has appeared on each case, one on the top of the door, the other on the pediment. These swags more often appear on early long-case clocks than on mantel clocks and, in any event, disappear about 1690. It will be noted that the moulding at the junction of the hood and the case is convex in form; this style continued until around 1700 when it took a concave shape, which shape has so continued ever since.

Except for the fact that, being a short pendulum movement, it has no seconds dial, there is nothing special about the Johannes Fromanteel clock that has not already been dealt with in the chapter on mantel clocks. For, as has already been stated, at this period, in outward appearance, the long-case clock of the day was simply a mantel clock placed upon a trunk and base; it was quite small, had a dial only about ten inches square and stood about six feet to six feet six inches tall.

The dial of the Ahasuerus Fromanteel is very interesting, and for many years it proved an enigma to experts. It will be noted that there is no XII; a ◇ takes its place. The minute ring is a loose friction fit, as are also the seconds ring and the ring in the lower part of the dial. The dial of this clock is illustrated in *Plate 37b*, and it will be fully discussed in the chapter dealing with dials and back plates. Otherwise the chapter ring, hands, spandrels and matted centre are all true to type of the period.

The other two small long-case clocks with ten-inch dials are approximately six feet high. That on the left is by Edward East and incorporates two interesting innovations. Firstly, the case is veneered in walnut. We are breaking away from the black case only to return to it relatively rarely during the next fifty years, and never thereafter, in spite of the fact that when questioned by her husband, who in 1675 had gone to London to buy a clock, as to whether she would prefer olive wood, walnut-tree wood or ebony, the young wife replies (as quoted by Symonds) : 'My dearest Soule; as for the pandolome case, I think black suits anything.' The second innovation is the 'lantern' or glass aperture let into the door at the level of the pendulum bob so that its motion may be clearly seen through it. The seconds hand is now making its regular appearance but the design of the hands and the width of the chapter ring have not changed much. The other clock shows the next stage of development, the abandonment of the portico top and the adoption of a decorative case, a development more in harmony with the taste for elaborate cabinets at this period. The height is up to six feet six inches, and the hood is now flat-topped. The door is veneered with 'oyster pieces', i.e. cross-sections cut from the boughs of trees, often laburnum, and displays a geometrical design in ebony and holly, offset by an ebony edging to the door. The maker is Joseph Windmills, one of the best makers in the second flight. He entered the Clockmakers' Company in 1671 and was Master in 1702. It will be noted that with the departure of ebony we also have the departure of the gilded capitals.

Plate 23 shows clocks which illustrate the steady trend to increase in size, and since proportions must be maintained, this increase is all round : in height, size of dial, width and depth. On to the flat top of the hood has been added a cresting, to which was added originally, but which has since been lost, a central finial, probably a wooden ball; the socket to receive the peg on which it would be set is still there. The case is veneered with walnut and has inset marquetry panels of flowers, with, in addition on the centre panel, a bird. The general style of this design is reminiscent of the Dutch floral painting of the period and gives credence to the theory that the earliest marquetry panels were imported from Holland. Very little information exists as to the early history of English clock cases; it would seem evident that the earliest cases were the product of the general cabinet-maker's workshop, but as clocks in wooden cases became more universal in production there seems no doubt that clock-case makers established themselves as a separate trade, or at any rate as a specialised branch of cabinet-making. In a list of clockmakers from 1631 to 1732 the name of Richard

Blundell occurs as a case maker. Blundell was admitted as a Brother on July 3rd, 1682 – that is to say that he was already free of some other company, possibly the Woodworkers'. On April 3rd, 1682, Blundell was arraigned for exercising the craft, not having been admitted, and was served with a writ. The result was that on May 1st 'Richard Blundell paid his fine, and promised to take his Freedome the next Quarter Court'. From the date of his admission we gather that he did so.

There is a certain school of thought that maintains that, since no examples of early development efforts in marquetry cases have come down to us, there was not any production in England, and that all these marquetry cases were imported from Holland. On the other hand, there were many foreign craftsmen living and working in London who could have produced these panels locally. The author has not had the opportunity of studying closely case construction and developments, and does not feel qualified in any way to be dogmatic on this subject. He will, therefore, content himself with following the developments in the finished examples rather than delve into the details of origin of production.

Marquetry passed through many stages in English clock cases and was popular from about 1680 to 1720, except with Tompion and Graham, who rarely used it. It will not be possible in this small book to deal with all the phases of marquetry design, but an attempt will be made to show the main developments from which they sprang. We had in *Plate 22d* an example of the early geometrical pattern, which is really inlay instead of marquetry proper. This was followed by a more complicated type of inlay involving flowers, birds and figures (*Plate 23a*). In these designs stained wood and often stained bone or ivory were inlaid. Later came more intricate designs of conventional beasts and scrolls (*Plate 24b*), to be succeeded by what the author describes as Persian carpet designs (not illustrated), and finally in very small arabesque patterns, sometimes known as seaweed marquetry.

Reverting to the clock with the cresting in *Plate 23*, it will be noted that the glass lantern referred to in *Plate 22c* has appeared in the base of the case. This indicates that the clock has an approximately 61-inch pendulum beating 1¼-seconds instead of the usual 1 second. When William Clement, who was the maker of this clock, invented the anchor escapement the vastly superior time-keeping properties achieved with the 39-inch 1-second pendulum were recognised to be due not only to the design of the escapement and greater freedom of the pendulum, but also to the fact that the slower the pendulum motion the less the cumulative effect of any slight error. Clement, therefore, tried out a 1¼-seconds pendulum and was copied by others. Occasionally one finds a genuine 1¼-seconds pendulum clock; on account of their rarity they are much more valuable than a 1-second clock of exactly the same style by the same maker. It is an easy matter for an unscrupulous person to substitute an escape wheel of twenty-four teeth for the standard wheel of thirty teeth and to fit a 1¼-seconds pendulum, but unless the clock was originally designed for a 1¼-seconds beat the seconds ring will have each 5-seconds interval divided into five instead of four. Further, if the case was originally made for a 1-second movement there will be no door in the base of the case, nor will a lantern have been fitted into the door in the base. The provision of a lantern is by no means universal in original 1¼-seconds clocks. After all, the object of the lantern is to allow the swing of the pendulum to be seen, and this cannot be achieved with the lantern in the base unless one stands very far back or else performs contortions close up. If the case be of marquetry or other type of inlay it is almost certain that a lantern cannot be added without impinging on the design employed. In our case we see the marquetry pattern nicely designed around the lantern. In other words, more care should be exercised in the purchase of a 1¼-seconds clock than in the case of an ordinary 1-second clock. The author does not know of any 1¼-seconds clocks later than 1710–20 and can only recollect seeing one dating later than 1700.

The second illustration of this clock shows the clock with the hood removed. This hood, undoubtedly, originally slid up; there are joins in the back board where the original grooves ran. It now pulls forward. In order to obviate the necessity for kneeling on the ground in order to reach a rating nut below the pendulum bob, Clement fits a micrometer screw adjust- ment above the pendulum suspension. He was very fond of this type of adjustment and it is felt that we can claim originality for him although the Ahasuerus Fromanteel clock shown in *Plate*

22a has a similar device. The dial of the Clement clock is shown in *Plate 38d*.

In the other illustration in *Plate 23* we continue our growth upward and as a result the case is slightly wider and deeper. The clock is another 1¼-seconds clock, this time by John Clowes.

It has just been said that, for all practical purposes, 1¼-seconds clocks were not made after 1700, but in the search after better time-keeping efforts were made to minimise the cumulative effect of slight errors by increasing still further the length of the pendulum, thus reducing its frequency. Tompion made two clocks in 1676 for Greenwich Observatory with 14-feet 2-seconds pendulums, each with a year movement, thus practically cutting out losses in accurate time-keeping due to winding, in spite of maintaining devices. These two clocks are thought to be the first year movements he made. Hooke, in 1669, experimented with a 14-feet pendulum with about a 2-seconds beat which he reported to have an 'excursion of half an inch or less' and with its weight of 3 lb. to be 'moved by the sole force of a pocket watch'. This would seem to indicate a light impulse to keep a free pendulum swinging. But the whip of these long pendulums counteracted the advantages gained from their length and they died a natural death. It has recently been discovered that in installing the two one-year clocks at Greenwich, Tompion adopted this method of a free pendulum suspended above the clock with the crutch engaging below the bob. Two-seconds pendulums are now only found in some turret clocks, where a sufficiently stiff pendulum rod can be used.

But to revert to our John Clowes clock, a small flat dome has appeared on the top of the hood; this dome will gradually get higher. The author inclines to the view that the majority of flat-topped square-hooded clocks existing today started life with domes which have been discarded either for reasons of space or taste. The case we are considering is veneered with very nicely figured walnut. The hour hand is becoming more elaborate; it will be noticed that the seconds hand in these early clocks has no tail or counterpose. There are glass panels in the hood, as has been the case with practically all these long-case clocks illustrated so far. One school of thought says that London makers put in these glass side panels and that provincial makers did not. The author has not had sufficient experience of the multitudinous provincial makers of the latter half of the eighteenth century to be dogmatic on this point, but it is interesting and worth putting to the test.

The clock (*Plate 24a*) embodies both earlier and later features; later inasmuch as the dome is higher, it also has had three finials on the top, and the bases for the two side ones remain. The dial has now been increased to twelve inches, at which size it remained for seventy-five years, and the overall height is eight feet four inches. It will be noticed that this is the first example we have had of the arabic five-minute figures appearing outside the minute ring. The cherub-head spandrels are now much more ornate, as is also the hour hand. Winding squares are ringed, and the seconds hand arbor is also heavily ringed, which in the author's opinion is a mistake, because it makes the seconds dial too fussy. The date aperture is decorated. All these are later points than in any long-case clock we have so far discussed. What is jumping back fifteen to twenty years is the inlaid case, which really should precede *Plate 23a*, but, as Bernard Shaw says, 'You never can tell'. The inlay is of coloured woods and stained bone in the form of flowers, with a helmeted warrior's figure, a most unusual *motif*, as the focal point of the design. The whole is on a black ground, probably pear-wood ebonised, which gives it a mournful appearance, quite different from the plain black cases with their gilt mounts that we have seen in the earliest examples. It is not a clock that appeals to the author; it is very nearly top-heavy, if not quite. The maker is Christopher Gould, a maker of renown, who was admitted to the Company in 1682 and died in 1718, but who never occupied the Master's chair.

The William Osborne clock on *Plate 24b* gives a fine specimen of the heyday of English marquetry and illustrates an example of beginner's luck. As an impecunious newly-wed a year or so after the First World War, the author was unable to satisfy his desire for a grandfather clock at the inflated prices for antiques then ruling, but in the early thirties prices had come tumbling down, and having been lent Britten by a friend he proceeded to be somewhat selective in his search. Eventually the clock on the left was selected and, as times were very bad, a price a good deal below the marked price was agreed upon. This figure happened to agree roughly with the yearly income from a small legacy bequeathed by a recently departed aunt and the first year's income was so allocated. Thus 'Aunt Louie's Tombstone' came into the family. Having had the clock about three years, when wandering down Piccadilly one day the author saw Macquoid's *Age of Walnut* open in a shop-window showing a coloured illustration of a clock case in the Victoria and Albert Museum which seemed familiar. The official photograph of this case was procured, from which it was seen that the two cases are 'part' and 'counterpart' of the same marquetry pattern. To find two such cases is very rare indeed, except where a pair of clocks might have been made for some family and have remained in the possession of that family ever since.

When only two woods are used there are just the part and counterpart, but when more woods are used, and in this case about six different woods are in use, there are as many counterparts as there are different woods.

The date of this clock is about 1705-10. The dial is illustrated in *Plate 39a*. The chapter ring is broadening and consequently the hour numerals are elongating. The spandrels have passed into the next stage of progression, and two cherubs are complete instead of heads only, supporting a crown surmounted by a cross. This design was frequently found in the furniture of the day, on the stretchers of chairs or on chair backs. It is also to be found on the door furniture in Hampton Court Palace. The hands are more ornate and very fine, the date aperture is decorated and the winding holes are ringed with slight ringing around the seconds-hand arbor – altogether a very pleasing dial and case.

The third illustration on this plate is a small example of early lacquer-work – a lady's boudoir clock of Queen Anne's time. It is a small thirty-hour timepiece with a six-inch dial. The trunk of the case is only six inches wide and the height six feet. The maker is John Drury of London and the date about 1710. Being a timepiece, it will have only one weight; there would scarcely be room for two in so narrow a case. It has a short-bob verge movement. If the dial be examined closely it will be seen that the hour hand has a slight counterpoise indicating that it originally belonged to a one-handed clock. This is confirmed by the absence of minute markings on the minute ring. The addition of the minute hand was probably made soon

after it was taken into use. Another feature is the late employ-
ment of the early cherub-head spandrel which went out of use
in long-case clocks twenty to twenty-five years earlier, but, as
previously mentioned in Chapter Two, they are found in these
smaller dials because they are much smaller than the actual
spandrels in current use at the time. The lacquer is in the best
Chinese style, the bird of paradise at the top and the weeping
willow towards the bottom of the case being particularly finely
executed. Those interested in lacquer and its method of production should visit the Russell Coates Museum on the East
Cliff at Bournemouth, where there is a very fine series illustrating all the manifold stages in the production of lacquer objects.

These dainty little Queen Anne clocks are very rare and
consequently much sought after; the drawback is that they
have almost invariably thirty-hour movements and this severely
restricts their value. If you have one of these clocks the author's
advice would be to have it in the main living-room of the
house, where it is handy to be wound up each night, as he does
with the little gem illustrated in *Plate 31c*, which is also only
thirty-hour; or else have it in some position that you pass on the
way to bed. Human nature is so naturally lazy that the zeal of
possession soon wears off and it becomes just too much trouble
to go into a room specially to wind a clock every evening, even
if you *do* remember it.

To find clocks in Royal possession that have been there ever
since they were made is not very rare, but to find a clock of the
seventeenth or eighteenth century that is still in the family is
much rarer, and to find that the original invoice has been preserved is much rarer still. Such an example is to be seen in the
last clock illustrated on this Plate. It is an eight-day clock by
George Graham, No. 681, sold in 1728. From the invoice (Fig.
10) it will be seen that the clock cost 16 guineas, packing and
carriage 12 shillings. An accompanying note says that in Mr.
Clay's ledger for 1728 there is an entry for the payment of
£17. 9s. 0d, possibly 1 shilling tip to the carrier included.

The clock does not have Graham's dead-beat escapement,
only an ordinary anchor, it is a walnut case and is about eight
foot overall, including the flaming urn finial. The hands,
unfortunately, have been broken and have been replaced in the
early nineteenth century by a very ordinary pair.

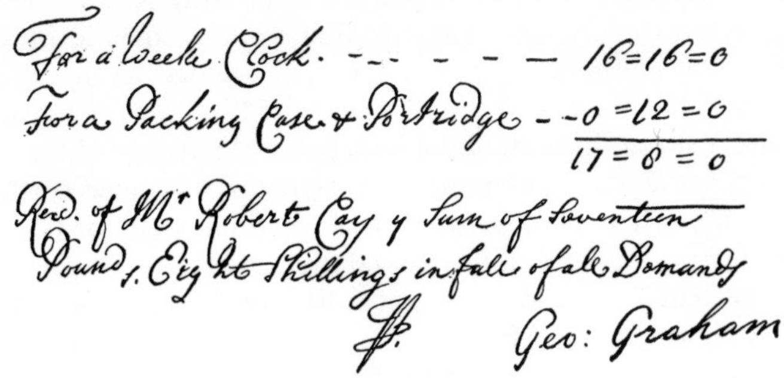

[handwritten receipt]

For a Weeke Clock. -.. - - — 16=16=0
For a Packing Case & Portridge - -0 =12 =0
                                ———————
                                 17 = 0 = 0

Recd. of Mr Robert Cay y Sum of Seventeen
Pound 1. Eig[ht] Shillings in full of all Demands
                    P.   Geo: Graham

FIG. 10

The next two illustrations (*Plate 25*) are interesting inasmuch as they show the 'birth' in England of the arched dial and case so familiar in later clocks from 1715–20 onwards. An example by Tompion, presented by him to the City of Bath in 1710, is frequently cited as the start of arched dials and cases, but the magnificent arched case of the Tompion clock on the left is fifteen years earlier. And as we have seen, the arch appeared on the Continent nearly a century earlier. The second clock is by Richard Street of London and is actually dated 1708, and shows that these early arches were not confined to Tompion, although the author feels that there is some connexion between Tompion and Street that has not yet been discovered. Examples of Street's work are sometimes so 'Tompionesque'.

There is a great deal to say about these two clocks, so let us begin our detailed examination. The Tompion clock is a year equation movement and was made for King William III about 1695. The difference between mean and solar days, giving rise to the equation of time, has been explained in Chapter One. The beautiful lines of the finely figured walnut-veneered case are at once apparent. It will be noticed that the arch has been introduced to show on the annual calendar ring the zodiacal circle indicating the position of the sun in the ecliptic as well as the day of the month and the month of the year; it should be noted that its introduction is purely functional in origin, not decorative. The door of the trunk, which is decorated at the corners with little spandrels, has a Gothic-shaped lantern which is placed lower than in other examples; that is because the escapement – an anchor escapement – is placed below the movement proper. One arm of the anchor can be seen in *Plate 25c*. The winding square, covered by the plate of the maintaining power lever, is situated at the upper XII. The pendulum bob shows so clearly in the photograph because it swings in front of the heavy slab-shaped weight necessary to drive a year movement. As has previously been recorded, Tompion's first year movements were made in 1676 for Greenwich Observatory and had two seconds pendulums, which were not very satisfactory. Here, to get sufficient drop for the weight for a year's running within the compass of a clock eight feet high, Tompion arranges for the hour hand to revolve once in twenty-four hours, and the minute hand once in two hours. The minutes are numbered every five *between* the hour numerals and the minute ring on the fixed dial and outside the minute ring on the mobile minute circle showing the equation. The dial is shown separately in *Plate 38c*. Now, it was explained in Chapter One that for two reasons there was a daily difference between mean and solar time; this difference is irregular both in amount and direction. The variation lies between mean time being about sixteen minutes fast on the sun around November 4th and its being about fourteen minutes slow on the sun around February 12th. But the rate of change is not a simple progression between these two extremes, as the mean and solar days are equal at four irregular times during the year, around April 16th, June 14th, September 1st and December 25th. Further, the variations in the length of the days falling between any two of the four days of equality just cited are themselves irregular, so that any simple circular motion is ruled out. The difference between mean and solar days had been known to astronomers for hundreds of years, but it never entered into the daily lives of the people until the invention of the anchor escapement made time-keeping sufficiently accurate that errors of a minute or so a day became noticeable. Before the pendulum was invented, errors up to half an hour a day were common, and even after its invention, and its use with the verge escapement, its time-recording was not very reliable.

Many efforts were made between 1670 and 1695 to find some way of recording the equation, but they were all based on wheel work and were not successful. The problem was finally solved by the invention of the 'equation kidney' which is seen in *Plate 25d*. This is rotated once a year by the clock's ordinary movement. Bearing against its edge is a compensated rocker arm, clearly visible in the illustration. This rocker arm terminates in a toothed rack, seen on Plate *25c*. As the kidney revolves about its axis, the pin on the rocker arm bearing against its edge will approach towards or recede from the centre of revolution, giving a corresponding backwards or forwards movement to the toothed rack, which in turn engages in the toothed wheel carrying the outer and moving minute circle (*Plate 38c*). The outline of this cam is so calculated that the moving circle advances or recedes the necessary amount each day in relation to the fixed minute ring, thus giving the daily difference, plus or minus, as between mean and solar time. Later a third hand was fitted on to the central arbor instead of the mobile minute ring, thus giving a clear and direct reading (*Plate 38b*).

The first equation table calculated for use in the correction of clocks was probably that made by Christian Huygens, the Dutch mathematician and astronomer, and published in his *Horologium Oscillatorum* in 1673. The date of the calculation is not known, but records show that it must have been before February 15th, 1662, thus very soon after his invention of the pendulum in 1657. These tables were presented before the Royal Society on May 10th, 1669, i.e. before the invention of the anchor escapement, which, by the way, Huygens never used. John Flamsteed, who was later to become the first Astronomer Royal, compiled tables in 1666. In 1668 John Smith, whose writings have already been mentioned, published a little book on the *Unequality of Natural Time* embodying an equation table. Tompion and possibly others had tables printed for them and sometimes stuck them inside the doors of long-case clocks.

All these tables, however, were only a means of enabling a check to be kept by the owner of a clock on the true time-keeping of his clock when compared with a sundial; they did nothing towards the solution of the problem of the direct recording of the equation. Heretofore Joseph Williamson, a London clockmaker, has been regarded as the inventor of the kidney on the strength of a letter written by him in 1719, to the Royal Society, i.e. about a quarter of a century after the event, in which he claims to have made all the equation clocks with equation movements that had been made in England up to that

date, his first being about six years before 1700. He writes:
'So that I think I may justly claim the greatest right to this
contrivance of making clocks to go with Apparent time and I
have never yet heard of any such clock sold in England, but
what was of my own making, though I have made them so
long.' It will be noticed that he does not claim the invention,
only the making. That his claim is not correct is shown by the
Tompion clock here illustrated, which bears the inscription
Tho : Tompion London Inventit, indicating it as a first production
of this type. There are four more Tompion equation clocks
known to the author, and there may possibly be more.

Now Williamson worked for Quare, and all Quare equation
clocks have the equation work quite separate from the clock
movement proper, driving the former by means of a long connecting rod and endless worm. It would be, therefore, quite
feasible for two individuals to have worked on these clocks and
united their work. In all the Tompion equation clocks known
to the author the equation work is integral with the movement
and must have been the work of one man only. The date of the
Tompion clock illustrated is *ca.* 1695. Huygens, in his last
recorded letter, dated March 4th, 1695 (he died in June 1695),
writes to his brother in London: 'You will have spoken to him
[Tompion], I take it, of my newly invented Clock of which I
am going to make a description and demonstration. I have had
it adapted to an old clock with a three-foot pendulum which
also shows the hour without need for the equation of time. . . .
The Barometers of the Quaker [Quare] are in Alance's book,
but perhaps he has made improvements.'

It would seem that Huygens died before he made any description or demonstration; but here we have a definite reference
to a direct recording of the equation coupled with Tompion's
name and with a less direct reference to Quare, in the very
year that the Buckingham Palace clock has been quite independently dated by the late Mr. Percy Webster, the greatest
expert on old English clocks we have ever had.

An equation clock by Huygens was bequeathed to Leyden
University by A. J. Royer, a great-nephew of Huygens, in 1809;
this has since been lost, and Professor Vollgraff, the erudite
editor of the *Œuvres Complètes de Christian Huygens*, takes the
line that this clock was, probably, not an equation clock. He

assumes that Royer had not sufficient horological and astronomical knowledge to know an equation clock when he saw one and was confusing the equation clock with a seconds clock made for Huygens by Thuret of Paris (the French 'Tompion') which is now in the University Museum. The writer submits that since in that same museum there is Huygen's planetarium, or Orrery, which bears an inscription to the effect that Royer restored it with his own hands, Royer certainly would know an equation clock when he saw one; furthermore, by 1809 equation clocks were no longer novelties, they were fairly common. It seems, therefore, to the author that we should accept the evidence recorded by the only man who is known to have seen and handled the missing clock and not brush it aside as a mistake. Vollgraff assumes the new clock referred to by Huygens in his letter of March 1695 to be a clock made by Huygens in 1693 with an isochronous balance, designed to be tested in his efforts to 'find the longitude'; but, however successful this might be from a time-keeping point of view, accurate equation tables would be a necessity, yet Huygens says that his clock has no need for the equation of time, i.e. it records it automatically. Again, Huygens writes that he is going to make a description and demonstration, yet the clock of 1693 is fully described in Huygens' notes. Further, Huygens was a man of prolific inventions; would an invention of 1693, on which he had been working since 1683, still be his new invention of 1695? It would seem probable that Huygens died before even the prototype of his clock was made, hence we have no claim from him to the invention. When Vollgraff made his assumptions the coincidence of the letter from Huygens with the appearance of the first clocks to be made embodying the equation kidney had not been established; this was first done by the author in an article in the *Horological Journal* in December 1943, which, owing to war conditions, would not have had circulation in Holland.

If Williamson were really the inventor it is funny that a man who could make the intricate calculation to establish the shape of the kidney should not have sent his invention into the world under his own name, instead of letting Quare get all the credit, as far as he was concerned. If he were the inventor and had an arrangement with Quare it does not seem very commercial that Quare should agree to pass it on post haste to his chief rival,

Tompion; for Williamson never mentions Tompion in the letter he wrote to the Royal Society.

We have seen from the date of Huygens' equation tables that he had had this problem of the equation before him since soon after the invention of the pendulum. The author submits that he had the type of brain to calculate the kidney and that Tompion, Quare and Williamson were more mechanically than mathematically creative.

Equation clocks by Williamson are known in which he places the equation kidney directly under the pendulum suspension and so modifies the length of the pendulum day by day, with the result that the hands of the clock show 'sun time' directly, and there is no indication of mean time. Such a clock could then be compared directly with a sundial for checking purposes. Clocks of this type have been signed *Joseph Williamson, Inventit*, and the author maintains that this claim to invention, as well as Tompion's already mentioned, refers to the method of applying the kidney and not to the invention of the kidney itself. There are three methods, so far; Quare-Williamson had the equation dial separate from the meantime dial, Tompion integrates it into the dial and Williamson gives a direct reading of the equation.

All this diversion and digression introduced because the case of the clock happened to be the first known with an arched hood! The author hopes that the lay reader has not been too bored with the development of a rather abstruse theory (at any rate he can skip it if he wants to); but it is his weakness to try to delve into the past and elucidate such of the mysteries of early English horology as still remain to be solved and to apportion credit where it is due, although in this case there is no great benefit to horology, as was the case of the anchor escapement. An equation clock is really only a glorified toy, and good equation tables were just as effective.

The second clock on *Plate 25* is another early example of the use of the arched case. It is rather a case of 'arches above them, arches below them, arches all round them,' but it is very historic and deserves inclusion. As mentioned above, it is by Richard Street, who was Junior Warden in the Clockmakers' Company in 1715, and is dated 1708. The clock was presented by Sir Isaac Newton to the Observatory at Trinity College,

Cambridge, where he had spent so many years as a Fellow and where his *Principia* was written. The dial illustrated in *Plate 39b* bears the following inscribed plate: 'Collegio St. Trinitatus Cantab. Isaacus Newton Equis Auratus Dato D.' The term of eulogy *Auratus* was applied to anyone who had attained an outstanding position in his profession or calling – The Gilding of refined Gold. Thus we have the arum lily, believed to be the most perfect of its kind, giving rise to the expression of today of 'gilding the lily' as trying to improve perfection.

In connexion with our particular clock, the following letter among the records of Trinity College is interesting.

Letter from Roger Cotes in Cambridge to his Honoured Uncle, Professor Cotes; dated February 10th, 1708.

'I have lately been in London, I found y^r letter at Cambridge upon my return. The occasion of my going thither was partly to view a large brass sextant of 5 foot radius (y^t had been making for us & is now finished) before it should be sent down. Whilst I was in town Sir Isaac Newton gave order for ye makeing of a Pendulum Clock which he designs as a present to our new Observatory. The sextant will cost the College 150£ & I believe Sr. Isaac's Clock can cost him no less than 50£.'

This is an interesting commentary on the cost of a clock that runs one month between windings.

The lay-out is very like the Tompion. The escapement is below the movement and the winding square high up, just below the xii. In both cases there is maintaining power. The spandrels are of no particular period or fashion; they have evidently been designed especially for this clock. The dial in the upper arch is a dummy to balance that below the dial in which the seconds hand is affixed direct on to the escapement arbor. The calendar is of the ordinary variety and has to be adjusted by hand for the short months. The pendulum rod is tubular and has a heavy cast-iron and gilded bob; this is thought to be a late eighteenth-century alteration; the columns of the hood and the spires are of gilded wood. The case is ebony veneered on oak.

Plate 26 shows two very beautiful examples of burr walnut cases, both the work of the finest masters of their day, Quare and Graham respectively. That on the left is a three-month movement by Daniel Quare, the details of whose history have already been given in Chapter Three. In point of chronological

sequence it is rather earlier than our last illustration of the
Street clock. This Quare clock would date the later half of the
last decade of the seventeenth century; its height, seven feet
six inches, eleven-inch dial, ringed winding holes and later type
of cherub spandrel would all confirm this. Furthermore, the
convex moulding below the hood is a pretty safe indication of
'before 1700'. Just when the change from convex to concave
took place cannot, like all changes of course, be determined with
exactitude; it was probably gradual, but it was more quickly
established than most changes. The cutting of the base panel
veneer into two horizontally is unusual and, in the author's
opinion, detrimental to the overall lines of the clock. It may
well be that this line is more marked in the photograph than is
apparent to the eye; these details are often more pronounced in
photographs, especially when a filter is used.

The other clock on this plate is by George Graham and is of
date 1715–20. It must be after 1713, because Graham did not
succeed Tompion until the latter's death in that year. This
clock, in the author's opinion, comes very near to perfection for
simple and effective design, proportions and legibility; the dial
is separately illustrated in Plate 39d. It probably had some
ornamental finial on top originally, and this is all that is lacking
to complete the harmony. We are progressing in our overall
height, with a twelve-inch dial, and we have an overall height
of just over eight feet. This height is, in part, achieved by the
double plinth.

Especially pleasing is the large diameter and narrow width
of the seconds dial permitting the long and delicate seconds
hand. It will be noticed that the dial is as large as is possible to
fit in between the chapter ring and the hand arbor. The ringed
winding squares have gone, the hour hand is much more
elongated and is establishing a 'Graham' pattern. The quarter-
hour marks on the inside of the chapter ring have given place
to half-hour marks only. The half-hour 'lozenge' has now gone.

All Graham's work is characterised by simplicity of line and
design; you never find a Graham clock in a marquetry or
highly decorated case; this is probably due to the influence of
Tompion; also quite possibly to his Quaker father's influence
during his early formative years, till he was five or six.

We now say good-bye to the square hood and very nearly

to the square-topped door to the trunk that goes with it. For a while square-topped doors were fitted to cases with arched hoods, but it was soon considered that an arched door 'went' better with an arched hood and it was universally adopted. Personally, the writer likes the square door with the arched hood.

One more clock by Graham is shown on this plate (*Plate 26c*), being an early mahogany case; few, very few, cases were made in mahogany prior to 1760 and these are usually of solid mahogany, as is the case with the clock illustrated. Later mahogany cases were almost invariably veneered. The author owns a clock of about the same date as this Graham, which also has a solid mahogany case. The dial of his clock is illustrated in *Plate 40c*. In this Graham clock we have another example of simplicity of design; the door originally had a glass panel, no doubt to show to all and sundry the newly invented mercury pendulum fitted to the clock, for this is a very early type of this pendulum invented by Graham in 1726 and still in use today in high-grade clocks. A later owner has removed the glass door panel and substituted a mahogany panel.

Graham found out, more or less accidentally, in 1721, that mercury had an expansion rate that was exceptional, as explained in Chapter One. He read his paper on his mercury pendulum before the Royal Society in 1726, and the present clock is about 1730. The period of going is one month. The dial is very similar to that in the previous plate. There are still half-hour divisions on the inner edge of the chapter ring, although these will probably get lost in block reproduction, and in both cases the seconds dial is as large as can be accommodated, but now the seconds hand is compensated, which detracts from its delicacy, but which is necessary to help to reduce friction. The longer the going period of a clock, the greater the number of wheels in the train that are needed and the greater the necessity to eliminate all possible causes of friction. The third hand is to show the equation of time. When the first Tompion equation clock was considered it was seen to have a second movable minutes ring mounted on a toothed wheel and actuated by a rack; here Graham has a third hand fitted as a tight friction fit on the main arbor. Thus we get direct visible reading of the equation, the hand bearing the effigy of the sun indicating solar time.

The introduction of a concentric equation hand involves much complicated gearing. As we have seen, when there is a separate dial to record the equation, the difference can be shown by a follower arm on the equation kidney actuating a rack and pinion recording on a separate dial or minute ring; but in the case we are considering, both hands have to record on the same fixed dial. Joseph Williamson was the first to do this, employing a true differential gear such as we find in motor cars today, but he used two dials back to back. In the example we are considering there is a complicated system of epicyclic gearing actuated from the equation kidney to give the effect of the equation to the third hand. Any clock with a concentric equation hand is well worthy of further study and investigation. They are very rare.

Many clocks of this period had year calendar disks on which were engraved, daily or at intervals, the daily difference due to the equation. This clock has such a calendar disk in the arch, which revolves once a year and shows the day, the month, the equation, the position of the sun in the ecliptic and the rising and the setting of the sun. This calendar disk in the clock is not the original. In September 1752 the adjustment from the Julian to the Gregorian calendar was made in England, when the calendar was advanced eleven days, leading to riots among the ignorant, who thought that they were being deprived of eleven days of life and rioted under the slogan, 'Give us back our eleven days!'

This adjustment, of course, put out all previous calendar and astronomical dials, and from the style of the engraving of the present dial it is evident that a new one was made soon after the adjustment mentioned above. At the same time the dial was 'modernised' by the substitution of spandrels of the style in fashion in the middle seventeen-fifties, thus explaining how these relatively late spandrels appear on this early clock. It is only a timepiece; the second winding hole will be for the setting of the equation hand.

The last illustration of clocks in this chapter in *Plate 26d* is of a clock dated about 1735, which is in a dark walnut case, interesting inasmuch as it has a glass mirror panel in the door, which consequently is of quite different construction to that of an ordinary clock-case door. It is of the same type as the door of a bookcase or wardrobe. A similar type of construction is seen in the Graham clock on this plate.

The production of flint or crystal glass was a London speciality in the Restoration period and in the century that followed it. The location of the works was at Vauxhall, on the Surrey bank of the Thames. The Duke of Buckingham is reported to have established a works at Vauxhall about 1670, employing Venetian workmen. The nobility of those days had no less an eye to the main chance than is assumed natural today. Buckingham, no doubt, sought and obtained a monopoly for the production of flint glass, in which the distinguishing feature is the introduction of lead. The relatively large numbers of mirrors of the Restoration period that have survived to come down to us are indicative of their popularity at that time. They are also found in bookcase doors and in bureau doors of the Queen Anne period.

A glass plate with mirror surface three and a half feet long would be quite a technical achievement at the time this clock was made, before the introduction of rolls for the rolling of hot glass. At the bottom of the right-hand corner can be seen the slightly different reflection of the bevelled edge of the panel; all these old original panels when bevelled, and they usually are, can be distinguished by the somewhat irregular edge of the bevel as opposed to the strictly regular edge of the modern machine-cut mirror.

In the *Present State of England*, written in 1683, it is stated that 'flint glass plates for looking glasses and coach windows were made about 1673 in Lambeth by the encouragement of the Duke of Buckingham'. The author also read recently, somewhere, he cannot now recall just where, how My Lady X, driving in her coach, wished to bow to an acquaintance passing in another coach, forgot that she had had her coach windows fitted with the new glass, which was so clear that she pushed her head through it.

The maker of this clock is Anthony Hebert, who entered the Clockmakers' Company in 1725. The arch is purely decorative, the arch of the dial-plate being engraved with a nondescript design centring around a woman's head. The quarter-hour marks are still here, and the ringing of the winding holes and the decoration around the calendar date aperture, which latter will no doubt be lost in reproduction, are late in their appearance. The spandrels are of a type of two cupids supporting a crown surmounted by a cross (*Plate 39a*).

Thus, as was the case with bracket clocks, we come to the close of the period where, horologically interesting, developments have taken place in domestic clocks. From now on, movements are more or less standardised and the main interest assumes a furnishing aspect. In movements the chief development towards the latter part of the eighteenth century was the introduction of more complicated musical mechanisms and often extravagant automata.

CHAPTER FIVE

Bracket or Mantel Clocks 1735-1835

W E are now entering a period of definitely plain clock dials, not that they are any the worse for that. Indeed many, one might almost say most, are very pleasing and very legible at a distance, which is a great asset; after all, that is their chief function. Not so always with the later long-case dials, as we shall see in Chapter Five, which deals with them; some of these are so cluttered up with ornamentation that they become the very height of illegibility.

We are arriving at the time when clockmakers began to make their dials round, instead of square or rectangular; although, as we shall see, the arched dial still persisted for many years, side by side with the round dial. In *Plate 27a*, the door is edged with brass and a brass bezel encircles the glass. The whole front of the clock still opens, although it would only be necessary for the bezel-mounted glass to open; that came later. The dial is silvered and no longer has an applied chapter ring. The quarter-hour divisions have gone, but their erstwhile presence is remembered by a single circle that will persist for many years, until we finally bury this relic of single-handed lantern-clock practice about a hundred and fifty years after it started, and about a hundred years after it ceased to have any meaning. The five-minute numerals are still there and will remain there on and off for some time. The hour hand is becoming plainer and will continue to get more and more simple. The minute hand has the characteristics of the mid-eighteenth century. The winding squares are rising again to the IX and the III, where they will remain stationary, indicating a standardisation in the lay-out of the trains and fusees. We still have a carrying handle and the escapement is still verge. Clocks are not yet cheap enough to have them all over the house.

It will be noted that we have passed to the 'True Bell' style and the top is convex instead of concave. The case is pearwood, ebonised, and the door has not the brass beading around the edge, but against this we have the clock fitted with brass pine-apple finials, a type of decoration which died very hard; in fact for many purposes it has never died; it is used in archi-tectural design still today. It had its origin in the commemora-tion of the introduction of the pineapple into England in Charles II's reign. There is a picture of the gardener at Hampton Court presenting the first pineapple to the King. The movement is a verge, but for the rest the description applied to the clock on the left will apply equally to this clock, except that it has a strike-silent mechanism, the end of the lever operating this can be seen by the forty-five minute mark, conveniently placed so that the door need only be partly opened to silence the strike when the clock was taken upstairs to the bedroom. There is no trace of the maker, George Hodgson, in any London records. It sometimes happened that an apprentice or journeyman would make a clock privately for one of his master's customers and inscribe it with a fictitious name in order to escape detection.

The Plate shows two more English bell-topped clocks; that by Stennet shows at a glance that it is a good movement; the general careful finish is at once apparent. The case is ebonised pearwood. It is rather an enigma. So far the 'going' has been too good for us, everything has proceeded in an orderly chrono-logical fashion, but this comes to 'put a spanner in the works' of all our theories. It should come in the 1780–90 period, but Benjamin Stennet did not become free of the Clockmakers until 1808 and it does not give the impression of a first effort. It is a case of the resuscitation of earlier styles a quarter of a century later (such cases are by no means unheard of), or Stennet may have had it to overhaul at some time or possibly to fit a new movement and at that time replaced the original silvered half-hoop with one bearing his name. This also was by no means an uncommon practice. Probably it is the case of the late appear-ance of an earlier design; at any rate, whatever its history may or may not have been, it is a very fine clock.

It is a reversion to type in another way, the chapter ring being again superimposed and the centre of the dial matted and gilt. It has a seconds dial, most unusual for a bracket clock, and it has a half-seconds dead beat escapement with a wooden pendu-lum rod to minimise the effect of changes of temperature. The reversal of the usual arrangement by placing the subsidiary dials in the base of the case instead of in the arch is interesting. The dial on the left is a calendar dial and that on the right for the strike-silent lever. Just at the right of the xii the light catches the end of the lever for regulation. The spandrels are of the 1770-90 period.

The clock by Metcalfe on this plate is also of ebonised pearwood, with a plain painted dial and verge escapement, a simple straightforward piece. The inner circle below the hour numerals has gone, as have also the five-minute markings. The hands, which are of gilded brass, have become much lighter and are of the openwork pattern favoured in the Regency period. It will be noted that it is signed in French.

The fourth clock on this Plate has been included to illustrate yet another case of Continental anticipation of English clock design. It is a 'true bell' case made by Elias Kreitmeyer of Friedberg about 1710. It was formerly in the Town Hall of Vienna and is now in the Vienna Clock Museum. The case is in the style of Boulle, the famous seventeenth-century cabinet maker, who worked for Louis XIV. It is a three train-clock and it will be noticed that the dial still retains the pre-pendulum habit of recording the quarters with the minutes only marked in a subsidiary manner, both these markings being on the inside of the hour ring. The subsidiary dials are left, the month of the year with its sign of the zodiac and its number of days, and right, the age and phase of the moon and the day of the month.

Here in *Plate 28* we interpose a type of clock that was very popular for forty or fifty years from about 1760, known as 'balloon' clocks. They were made in all sizes and in all kinds of wood, often with a Sheraton type of shell inlaid in the lower part. Not infrequently they had their own wall-brackets. Small balloon clocks up to, say, ten inches in height are very much sought after in these days of small flats. The clock on the right is of an elaborated balloon type showing marked French influence with its black ebonised case, and brass gilt mountings and feet. The dial is an early example of enamelling; the inevitable chips, which sooner or later disfigure all enamel dials, sad to say, can be seen by both winding holes. The hands are of the serpentine type and are correct for the period. It has a recoil escapement and a pull repeater on two bells. Repeating clocks remained in vogue until the invention of friction matches in 1827. The maker is Thomas Brass of Guildford, who was working from some time prior to 1767 up to 1784.

The other balloon clock on this plate is a pure balloon in a mahogany case with narrow brass inlay, the whole having a very warm and pleasing tone. This clock is dated 1796 and is pretty well at the other end of the span of years during which these clocks were made; this is reflected in the style of the dial. The heavy copying in paint of the old superimposed chapter ring as seen in the photo on the right is gone; the dial will compare with those in the later plates of this chapter. The hands are delightful. Unfortunately the clock is anonymous.

In the flat inverted bell clock (*Plate 28c*) we go back a few years to about 1775. The reversion to the inverted bell is interesting. This is a very nice clock by Justin Vulliamy, the first of a long line of noted makers who came to London from Switzerland. This is still a verge movement – the false bob can be seen in the top of the arch – but since it swings above the escapement arbor the shape of the slot is in the inverse to that shown in other clocks (*Plate 17*). This arrangement allows the curved slot to be tucked in very nicely under the arch. The dial is beautifully enamelled, but here again, unfortunately, there there are signs of chipping round the winding holes. The dial is delightfully clear and the hands are most pleasing. Unfortunately the photographer, who in this case happened to be the author, slipped up in not moving the hour hand from in front of the winding square. The subsidiary dials are for pendulum regulation on the left and for strike-silent on the right. The case is ebony on oak. The spandrels, although nicely finished, are of the uninteresting late eighteenth-century type. The back plate of this clock is seen in Plate *44c*.

The fourth clock on this plate introduces another very prolific type of case, the 'arched' case. There are broken arch, shallow broken arch, deep broken arch, broken arch decorated passing to the plain arch, plain arch decorated, etc. All of these will not be illustrated, but a sufficient number will be shown to enable the reader to visualise the remainder.

This clock is another of the author's lucky finds. It is a deep broken-arch type, which is not lacquered but is decorated with coloured and varnished prints of flowers, after the style of

'Vernis Martin'. These prints are interspersed with latticed traceries in gold. It is a real 'lady's' clock, and the author has never seen another quite like it. When the doors, back and front, are opened they are seen to be decorated on the insides as well; more simply, of course. The whole of the inside of the case is also coloured. The maker is Henry Fish of the Royal Exchange, London, a son of Henri Poisson, a Huguenot refugee who worked in London about 1695–1720. Henry Fish died in 1774.

As will be seen from the slit with the false bob and the light pendulum, it is a verge movement. The subsidiary dials are the usual, pendulum regulation and strike-silent. The rise-and-fall arm, which is worked by an eccentric cam, a much cheaper form than the rack-and-pinion, passes behind the dial to fit on to one end of a movable arbor which, passing through the front and back plates, transmits the movement to the second arm fixed to the other end of the arbor, which, in turn, carries the pendulum suspension.

Here again we have a late retention of the matted and gilt dial centre with superimposed silvered chapter ring. All these details are essential to the harmony of the conception of this clock, with its delicate warm tones derived from the colouring of the flowers and the painting of the case. A silvered dial, such as we have just seen, or the new fashioned enamel dial would be quite out of place. Altogether a very pleasing piece.

Plate 29a shows an example of the shallow broken-arch type, of date 1780–1800. The case is ebonised with brass bezel and brass-filled spandrels. This retention of an earlier style leads the eye away from the enamelled dial, which is, however, delightfully clear. Minutes are now represented by dots only, and the hands show an elegance of design combined with sufficient boldness to assure easy reading. The five-minute numerals have disappeared, the hands are Regency and always remind the author of the delicate ironwork of balconies and verandas of this period.

From now on there is no definite style of hands by which a clock can be dated to within a few years, each maker, it seems, having followed his own fancy. The reader will notice that the hands in every clock in the remainder of this chapter are different from all the others.

The carrying handle is still there, although this clock has an

I

anchor recoil escapement and will need much more care when moved from place to place. The handle is probably only a relic of the past and will not be intended for daily use.

This plate shows the coming of the plain arch. A very broad generalisation in handles – and, like all generalisations, directly you have made it you can start to pick holes in it – is that when the arch is broken the handles will be on top, but when you get the plain arch and later chamfer tops which followed it, and the Gothic style lancet clocks, there are two handles, one on each side.

This plain arch clock is by Edward Baker, London, who was working between 1785 and 1821. It is also in a mahogany case with brass inlay and feet. The dial is painted and the hands again different from the previous examples.

The third clock on this plate brings us a further step in our progression; it is a chamfer-top clock in mahogany with brass inlay, it is anonymous, but very pleasing in appearance. Its back plate is shown in *Plate 44d*, from which it will be seen that a coiled-wire gong has been introduced instead of a bell, giving a deeper, richer tone. The case is light mahogany with brass inlay, the hands are particularly attractive; the hour hand is fractionally too long, but there is no doubt that they are original.

Plate 29d illustrates what is known as the lancet-type, Gothic style, in harmony with the newly established Gothic revival. This by Hawkins of Southampton is quite pleasing; it has a cream-painted dial and a milled bezel to the glass instead of the ordinary pressed one. This milled bezel is more expensive and indicates that more than usual care has been put into the clock. The ebony inlay in the mahogany case is very restrained and pleasing. The hands are dainty but not very practical; note how the minute hand gets lost in the III.

And so we come to what may be called the end of ordered progression in clock design. After this date case design, like the hands already referred to, was very much a case of individualism, frequently striving after effect and trying to be different, often with disastrous results. One could illustrate as many variations in bracket clocks between 1830 and 1860 as there are illustrations in this book; but the Victorian era is not renowned for its good taste in artistic design.

Before, however, we finally leave bracket clocks, let us look at a few made towards the end of the eighteenth century for export to China and the Far East. From the very elaborate examples illustrated, it would seem that this was a very lucrative luxury trade. Indeed, from the fact that at the time of the Boxer Rebellion in 1900 there were over six hundred clocks in the Hall of the Imperial Palace alone, it would seem that there was plenty of scope for trade; the only proviso would seem to be the make everything move that can move and to decorate every possible inch of space. Unfortunately most of these pieces are unsigned; the names of James Cox and Francis Maquire are associated with this market, but there must have been many others.

Plate 30a shows a very fine example; it strikes the hour and the quarters and is musical. At each hour the lotus flower in the centre emerges from the square housing and the petals unfold, as in the illustration. When the hour has struck, the lotus flower on the top, seen with petals folded, opens and the petals turn upright and the blossom is open, so that there is always one blossom open and one shut. The lotus flowers are set with paste in various colours. The *appliqué* ornamentation is of gilt brass. The base of the bodywork appears to be plain black steelwork until closely examined, when it is seen that it is very finely engraved all over. Besides the opening and shutting of the lotus flowers, the glass rods in the base turn, giving the impression of a waterfall.

In *Plate 30b* the clock surmounts a large case containing a musical train which is released by the clock at set intervals. Here we have three stages of twisted glass rods that turn at the hour giving the effect of a cascading waterfall. The first tier is supported by palm trees with outspread foliage; surrounding the glass rods is a series of figures, alternately fat and lean, possibly some Chinese lore that escapes the author. The two swans, apparently nesting on the top of two somewhat fantastic palm trees, seem to have followed, or set the fashion of today for the ladies frequent 'hair-do'. The second tier, decorated with figures of children has still fewer glass rods simulating the source of the waterfall. The dial represents a sunflower and is flanked by female figures.

Plate 30c is still more elaborate. It is again a three train musical clock with a centre seconds hand. The minute hand is missing. The whole supported on gilt lions, each with a taper holder on its head. The corner columns are in imitation of lapis lazuli. The *appliqué* ornamentation is gilt brass and all the floral decoration is set with multi-coloured paste. At the hour the glass rods, including the four at the upper corners, turn with the usual waterfall effect, a procession passes through the aperture under the dial and a group revolves in the circular opening in the top tier.

The last illustration (*Plate 30d*) is more restrained and more pleasing to the western taste. Again three train and musical. At the hour the spiral at the top, which is set with red and green paste, opens out and revolves; the 'jewelled' disk below the dial also revolves. The case is decorated in coloured translucent enamel on an ultramarine base. The dial and circle below surrounds are set with red and white paste. The hands are solid gold.

After this digression into oriental splendour, we will leave bracket clocks and return to more sober western styles in the later long-case clocks.

CHAPTER SIX

Long-Case Clocks and Regulators 1735-1835

As was the case with bracket clocks, during the earlier part of this period there were some mechanically interesting pieces, followed later by an increase in the number of musical clocks and those showing mechanical automata; the simplest form of this last was a ship's effigy in the arch of the dial attached to the top of the pendulum rod (rather in the manner of the false bob in the verge escapement), which rocked 'in the waves' as the pendulum swung. This developed later into moving figures, a man or two men sawing, revolving windmills; in fact anything that could be driven by a straightforward wheel motion or cranked from a pin set eccentrically in the wheel surface. None of these automatic figures is illustrated, limitations of space do not permit, but they are all only adjuncts to the prevailing style of clock; they usually appear after 1770–75 and do not call for any departure from the general trend of design which we are now going to discuss.

In *Plate 31a* we have a fine astronomical clock by Thomas Budgen of Croydon. Croydon lies just on the fringe of the ten-mile radius of London to which the jurisdiction of the Clockmakers' Company extended. William Budgen, possibly a son, was made free of the Clockmakers' Company in 1750 and therefore seems to have recognised that the authority of the Company extended to his town; there is no mention of Thomas in the Company's records. Croydon is sufficiently near London for the case to have the clean London lines, and it was probably made in the City and sent out to Croydon. It is of finely figured walnut; in Chapter Four we had examples in these arch-topped doors of the trunk being outlined in a banding of cross-grained veneer. Here we have a fine inlaid line of holly or laburnum or other light-coloured wood within the frame of the door itself and also forming two spandrels on the trunk above the door.

It will be noted that the hour hand goes round only once in twenty-four hours and that the minute hand revolves once an hour; owing to the position of the seconds dial the minutes between four minutes to and four minutes past the hour have to be approximated. The hands, it will be noted, do not fit. They are not of a style of the period of the rest of the clock, but rather belong to the end of the eighteenth century, at which period they were probably renewed.

This clock has a very pleasing arched-type top, unencumbered by any superstructure; probably at one time the arch between the door top and the top of the hood had a fret, but in the course of time this has become broken and the space has been filled in with a piece of plain veneer, cut running with the grain of the wood instead of across it, as is the case with the veneer in the rest of the case. The introduction of a double plinth with the corresponding reduction in the depth of the base panel tends to give a rather squat appearance to the base, but this is probably more noticeable in the photograph than in the original. The dial is illustrated in *Plate 40d* and will be dealt with in the section dealing with dials.

The second clock on this plate, by Charles Coulon, shows another well-proportioned case in walnut veneer; this time the clock has the flat-topped finish to the hood, which very probably was originally surmounted by a dome as in *Plate 26b*. We have again the fine banding in the door and in the spandrels above, giving a pleasing touch of lightness to the case. The dial is clear; it will be seen that the inner markings on the chapter ring for the quarter-hours, or as we have seen in the case of the Graham clock in Plate *26b* the half-hours, have quite disappeared, never to reappear. The most we shall have in future is a simple circle at the base of the hour numerals on painted or enamelled dials, this being the survivor of the inner edge of the applied chapter ring, as seen in the illustration (*Plate 28b*), but very often not even that. After all, why should it be there? It serves no useful purpose. The spandrels are no longer designed around a female head and the dolphins have disappeared from those in the arch. They are now composed of purely conventional design, but are quite interesting. Later in the century they tend to become less full and to give a skimpy appearance. The hands are rather clumsy and really not worthy of the clock. The design is correct, but they could, with advantage, have been more delicately finished. The author suspects an accident and replacement by unskilled hands; they are too much out of harmony with the finish of the rest of the clock. The arch is purely decorative, conforming to fashion, and has a strike-silent lever in it.

Next in chronological order is the clock illustrated in *Plate 31c* which shows the author's largest and smallest long-cast clocks. (He is not the proud owner of a year clock, which would have needed a still higher case against which to make the comparison.) The larger is a fine month-equation movement by Graham's successors, Colley and Preist, housed in a dark walnut-veneered case. The inlaid banding and the spandrels above the door are there, but as they are not in such a contrasting colour they do not show up so well in the photograph.

Graham died in November 1751, aged seventy-eight; this clock has a year calendar disk made out in the new style which was adopted in September 1752. It has a dead beat escapement and has all the signs of Graham's handiwork; it was probably among his stock when he died and was taken over by Colley when succeeding to the business. The dial has that clearness of finish and simplicity that marked Graham's work (*Plates 19c and 26b*). This dial is shown again in Plate *38b*.

That traders often had long to wait for their money in those days is shown by two letters in the author's possession written by Colley to a customer, Mr. Cyrill Wycke of Hockwold, near Brann, in Norfolk, for whom he was making a quarter-chiming musical long-case clock. It was to be a large clock, fourteen inches dial with arch, these larger dials being fashionable in the latter half of the eighteenth century. It was to play 'The Smirking Man', 'Willy's ye lad for me', 'Ally Croaker' and 'The Lass of Patie's Mill'. In the arch were to be two subsidiary dials, one for pendulum regulation and the other for silencing either all strike, chime and music, or the hours and music, or the quarter chimes. There was also a day of the month dial showing through an aperture.

The first letter reads:

SIR,
I have been in hopes of seeing you in London before this and likewise settled yᵉ account of the clock case; I think it and yᵉ packing

case come to fourteen Pounds which is a great deal of Money for a Tradesman to be out of for two Years together and as your coming is so uncertain I shou'd take it as a favour if you would Please to let me have Ten Pounds on Acct. thereof which would greatly oblige Sir,

Your most hum^{ble} Servt,

LONDON, *Sept.* 8, 1759.   THO^s COLLEY.

The outside of the letter is endorsed: *Colley, Watchmaker, Sept. 8, 1759, rec*^{d.} *10th. 4d.*

It is interesting to see that as late as 1759 clockmakers were still being called watchmakers, that a letter took two days to get to Norfolk and that the charge was 4d. The second letter is more satisfactory to Mr. Colley; he gets his £10.

SIR,

I rec^d yours with ye bill enclosed of Ten Pounds which I Receive in part of Payment for your New Clock I am making for you; I have herewith sent you a sketch of ye Dial Plate of ye Clock and I believe 3 weeks hence will do for your determination as I can forward part of ye clock without tho' I am a little afraid I shan't have time to get it completed before you come to Town.

I am S^r
Your most oblig'd hum^{ble} Servt

LONDON, *Octo*^r 6, 1759.   THOS. COLLEY.

The outside is endorsed: *Colley, Watchmaker, Oct. 6, 1759, recd. 8th (4d). D-al Pl-te- Cl-ck. £10 (Pd).*

The other little clock shown on *Plate 31c* is evidently the work of a craftsman making a little piece as a hobby for the love of his craft. It is a little thirty-hour movement with a plain brass dial, dated on the front plate, by means of a punch, June 15th, 1817. It is signed Sanders, Brinkworth. There is a village of that name in Wiltshire, but the author has not yet had time to search local records to find if any entries exist. Just the name Sanders, without any Christian name or even initials, leaves a pretty wide field.

There is another Brinkworth, a small railway junction in South Australia, so presumably a Wiltshireman went out to Australia in years past and founded a settlement named after his native village. However, the object of this book is to discuss clocks, not to give geography lessons, so we will return to the 'Grand-Baby,' or 'Baby' as it is popularly known in the author's household. It is cased in mahogany, with beautifully reeded columns having turned Doric capitals and bases, with quarter columns inset each side of the trunk. The door is edged with laburnum and ebony domino banding, and the base is decorated with two lines of the same. The trunk could, with advantage, have been a little longer and the base correspondingly shorter. Its overall height is two feet eleven inches. All lady visitors 'fall' for this little pet, which stands on its own bracket on the library wall. The library is the family's main living-room, so the author practises what he preaches in having a thirty-hour movement in a place where it is handy for winding each evening before going to bed.

Plate 32 shows two clocks of the 'hollowed pediment' type; this type ran concurrently with the curled pediment 'Chippendale' style seen in this plate, for sixty years or so. While the terms Chippendale, Adam and Sheraton are often applied to clock cases, these really only incorporate some features in the style of one, and frequently more than one, of these cabinet-makers. These were, in fact, cabinet-makers, and the basic structure of the pieces they designed was quite different to that necessary for a clock case; their typical designs would not have been practical. The clock on the left is by George Margetts of London; it is astronomical, a type in which Margetts specialised. This is a very high-grade clock and as a result has a very high-grade case. It is of mahogany, and in fact practically all cases from now onwards will be of mahogany. The use of any other wood was exceptional, although towards 1800 oak was sometimes used, rarely in London, more frequently in the provinces. An innovation which will be maintained from now onwards is the chamfering of the corners of the trunk and the frequent insertion of quarter columns, or their reeding. The plain arch top to the door has now given way to the broken arch; from now onwards makers will let their fancy play with the shape of the door in the trunk. The flaming lamp *motif* of the finials is a revival of a style of a hundred years earlier.

The clock, by John Benson of Whitehaven, in Cumberland, is rather an enigma. It is a very fine clock, yet nothing is known of its maker. Neither Baillie nor Britten list him, and it seems peculiar that nothing else should have survived of a man of such capabilities. The case bears every stamp of being London made; it has open frets at the side of the hood for one thing, and this, if our theory is correct, rules the provinces out. It has such a close resemblance to the other clock illustrated on this plate that the two may well be by the same hand. The name of the maker is on a plate let in behind the main dial plate, immediately below the lunar dial in the arch; this is seen more clearly in the plate showing the dial in detail (*Plate 41b*). It is quite possible that the man who supplied the clock bought it in London and then had his own nameplate inserted. If so, this is a pity. It is a very fine clock with perfect lines, whoever made it, but London-made clocks usually fetch better prices than those made in the country.

It differs from the other clock in this plate in the more elaborate Corinthian columns to the hood, the quarter columns to the trunk and, what is most unusual, quarter columns in the base. The author is never very keen on anything light in colour in the base of a clock, such as the gilded column capitals and bases in this case; they take the eye too easily from the dial, but this, no doubt, is a matter of individual taste. From the three winding holes it will be noted that it is a quarter-chiming and musical clock.

The other two illustrations on this plate are of the 'Chippendale' type of case as portrayed by provincial makers. That in *Plate 32d* is a British-made clock by Philip Lloyd, Bristol (not an ancestor). The proportions are good, but it is a pity that the dial, which reflects a London style of thirty years earlier, is all of brass, a feature often found in provincial clocks but not often in London-made, except in cheap thirty-hour movements. The lack of contrast of a silvered chapter ring makes the dial flat and dull. It could easily have been re-silvered.

In the arch is a lunar dial with two rings of marking, the inner 1 to 29½ giving the age of the moon and the outer from 6.30 to 6.30 twice over. This is a tidal dial, the outer circumference of this dial being marked HIGH WATER AT BRISTOL KEY. At new and full moon high water at Bristol is at approximately 6.30, and this lunar disk, which revolves once in two months, indicates, e.g. 6.30 A.M., high tide at new moon on the first day of a lunation, gradually changing the time daily till at full moon at 14¾ days 6.30 P.M. is reached, and finally at the end of the lunation we come back to 6.30 A.M. The moon's effigy then disappears behind the dial for the second month and a second effigy appears in the upper half of the arch. The dial is only suitable for Bristol. In all the tidal clocks the author has seen made for Bristol the word *quay* is always spelt *key*, nor has he found the word *key* or *quay* on any tidal dials except those made for Bristol, although he has made a special study of this type of dial. The reason may be that Bristol is the only port where shipping came right up the river into the city streets in the centre of the town.

This clock has Corinthian columns with gilded capitals and bases, but these are not carried on in the trunk; the chamfered edge is simply reeded. The trunk door is decorated and has a base panel to match.

The fourth clock on this plate is another mahogany-cased provincial clock, this time with only a lunar dial, since as the maker, Thomas Brown, was in Birmingham there was obviously no need for a tidal dial. The dial is silvered all over and engraved in the centre. Towards the end of the eighteenth century engraved dials were fairly frequent, but in the majority of cases this engraving only had the effect of making the dial less legible. There are two subsidiary dials, seconds the upper and calendar dial the lower. Instead of having only a small aperture, through which only one date could be seen, the fashion arose for a semicircular opening as seen, the uppermost mark being that of the current day; since only every fifth day was numbered, a smaller diameter disk could be used.

Regarding the case, the quarter columns on the trunk have an ivory inlay at their base, distracting the eye from the dial. The base corners are now chamfered and carved, presumably to add to the importance of the piece, but in the author's view making the case too ornate.

Plate 33a shows a Liverpool clock by Rigby, presumably Henry, who died in 1787. Others, James and Joseph, do not appear in the records till 1813 and 1821, too late for this piece. This has lunar and tidal dial combined, this time for Liverpool, where high tide at new and full moon is about eleven o'clock. In this case the moon's effigy is painted on the same dial as the days of the moon's age and the time of high tide, the whole revolving as one dial; the reading for the day for the lunar dial is taken from the high point. The outer edge of the arch is inscribed *The moon is appointed for Seasons*. Again we have the engraved dial centre. There is a compensated centre seconds hand of the whole diameter of the inside of the chapter ring, also a calendar hand, which in the photo is hidden behind the minute hand; four hands on one dial is too much for easy reading.

The mahogany case has double columns to the hood, and at the trunk the Doric columns have been fashioned in the round, but do not go the full length of the trunk, which is a pity. The panelling at the bottom of the door and the high bases to the columns are an unfortunate experiment.

The quoins on the chamfered base corners seem a Lancastrian detail; the writer has only seen this on Lancastrian-made cases, two by Barker of Wigan, which he has particularly in mind, and another by Coats, illustrated by Ceszinsky and Webster, also a Wigan maker.

Plate 33b shows another clock made to show high tide at Bristol Key, by Thomas Bruton of Bristol. It is a very good quality clock in a finely figured case of kingwood. The radial star parquetry design in the centre of the pillar formation of the case is interesting. Its whole design is reminiscent of the equation clock presented to the City of Bath by Thomas Tompion in 1710. The dial records the usual seconds and date besides the moon's phase and tidal details; it is silvered with an applied and silvered chapter ring. The centre is again embellished with unnecessary engraving; nevertheless a very handsome piece.

The remaining two clocks on *Plate 33* are two types of pedestal clock; *Plate 33c* illustrates a clock in the Adam style made by Finney of Liverpool. It is unusual in that it has a year movement in that very small case; less that six feet high. The dial is interesting and will be described later. The other clock is an anonymous piece in the Empire style, recording quite simply hours and minutes.

These pieces obviously need setting in a room furnished in a corresponding style, when they will harmonise and look very well. It will be noticed that in *Plate 33d* the door of the trunk is hinged on the left as one faces the clock.

Plate 34a and *b* shows two clocks which, towards the end of the eighteenth and in the early nineteenth century, were increasingly made; very plain and simple designs both for dial and case, but with movements made with much more care than had been usual for the average long-case clock up to this time. Almost invariably they will have Graham's dead beat escapement and prove themselves really sound time-keepers. That on the left is a striking movement by Josiah Emery of London, who was noted for the all-round high standard of his movements. It is in a plain oak case; all the money has gone into the movement. The silvered dial is a little late for the retention of the inner line at the base of the hour numerals and the numbered minute ring is in contradiction to the brass openwork hands; nevertheless they are certainly original.

The other timepiece, by Ross & Peckham of London, is essentially simple and utilitarian. In its plain mahogany case and severe dial it seems to say, 'My function is to record time accurately, that's all'. It has Graham's dead beat escapement and a wooden pendulum rod to minimise as far as possible temperature compensation errors; but it has no maintaining power.

Plate 34c and *d* shows two more of the later type of case in vogue towards the turn of the nineteenth century. Both are provincial clocks, that on the left is anonymous and shows the adoption of the Gothic-shaped door. The columns to the hood and down the trunks which are of the multiple perpendicular style, give a link with ecclesiastical architecture. These columns, as in *Plate 33a*, do not extend the whole length of the door, but there is no corresponding panelling at the base of the door, so that these shorter columns do not so much detract from the length of the trunk on the whole design of the case. The heavily carved and scrolled pediment is surmounted by a carved taurus topped by a ball and spire to match the sides. The base should have an octagonal-shaped moulding, but this appears to have been broken off, only the glue marks remaining.

Both these provincial clocks have solid side panels to their hoods, thus maintaining our theory that this is a feature of provincial clocks.

The illustration on the right is of a 'Yorkshire clock'. This type of clock was not confined to Yorkshire, but is found all over the North Midlands. The clock case is broadening, dials are increasing from twelve to fourteen inches, with a corresponding increase in width, but without any increase in height;

indeed clocks are already high enough, seven feet six to eight feet six is tall enough for any clock in domestic use. The particular clock illustrated is about as nice an example of the type as the author has seen; it still retains a degree of elegance. Generally these Yorkshire clocks remind him of Mr. Jorrocks in their relation of width to height. Our clock is the work of an unknown maker at Otley, in Yorkshire, Chippendale's birthplace, and there is a trace of both Chippendale and Sheraton in its design. The case is of richly figured mahogany inlaid with satinwood. The small door is a feature of these Yorkshire clocks; this the author avers is a mistake, as it tends to increase the air of 'stumpiness' they already have by reason of their large width-to-height proportions. The turned hood columns are another feature to be found in country clocks from now on; columns are just columns to the country maker. He has no appreciation of the elegance of the proportions of the classic designs, and turned columns are cheaper to make. The feet are too light, but again this is a fault to be found in nearly all these clocks. The painted dial is, in this case, of exceptionally good finish.

REGULATORS

All the long-case clocks we have so far considered in this chapter have been for domestic use, nearly all being fitted with the ordinary recoil anchor escapement; only one or two have had, exceptionally, Graham's dead beat escapement. In the next two plates will be illustrated some regulators, i.e. clocks made specially for use in observatories for astronomical observations.

The clock illustrated in *Plate 35a* and *b* is very historic. It was made by John Shelton of Shoe Lane, London. Shelton, of whom too little has been heard in the past, was born in Clerkenwell, London, in 1702. He was apprenticed very young, at the age of ten years, to Henry Stanbury in 1712, and was admitted to the Clockmakers' Company in 1720. He was one of the original Liverymen at the creation of the Livery in 1766. He worked for Graham in the making of clocks for astronomical use, and there, no doubt, received the training that made him capable of making high-grade regulators later. There is still at

Greenwich Observatory a regulator, the work of Shelton, which for many years served as their transit clock. Besides this there are three others known to survive: one at Armagh Observatory in Northern Ireland, one in the Museum of the History of Science in Oxford, and one, that illustrated, owned by the Royal Society, London, by whose permission it is reproduced. It has had a most notable history.

In the latter part of the seventeenth century Christian Huygens had perceived that because of the rotation of the earth an object must weigh less at the Equator than at the poles. About the same time, Richer of Paris had shown that a pendulum clock regulated in France ran slow when tested in Cayenne, in French Guiana. Newton also found that 'the variation of gravity in different latitudes depended not only on the centrifugal force, but also upon the figure (shape) of the earth'.

In the latter half of the eighteenth century a great deal of attention was paid to this problem of establishing the earth's shape by sending clocks to different places and noting their different rates of going as compared with the same clock going at Greenwich.

On December 23rd, 1760, the Royal Society paid Shelton £34. 16s. 6d. for the clock we are illustrating. We find that in June 1761 it is in St. Helena, and according to a report dated June 30th, 1761, it had been used for gravitational experiments and also in connexion with the Transit of Venus on June 5th of that year. On November 28th, 1761, it was sent to the Cape of Good Hope for gravity experiments and returned to St. Helena on December 31st of that year. In 1762 it was returned to England and reported working at Greenwich on June 17th, 1762. In 1763 the Commissioners of Longitude were sending an expedition to Barbados to test John Harrison's chronometer; the Royal Society loaned the Shelton clock to them on August 18th, 1763. It was used in experiments in Barbados from November 10th, 1763, to October 8th, 1764. On November 11th, 1764, Maskelyne, then Astronomer Royal, announced that the Royal Society would sponsor the measurement of one degree of latitude in Pennsylvania and that they had offered the use of the clock that had been sent to St. Helena and to Barbados. It was shipped in the good ship *Ellis*, Sam Richardson Egdon, Master. This ship it appears was wrecked, but the clock suffered no damage beyond the breaking of the pendulum suspension. On December 11th, 1766, it was set up in 'Mr. Harland's field' until it was dismantled for return to England on February 28th, 1767, sailing on May 26th of that year.

On November 19th, 1767, it was reported again set up at Greenwich ready for the ensuing Transit of Venus. Later we find it going in the *Endeavour*, Lieutenant James Cook (later the famous Captain Cook), on an expedition to the South Seas. In a report dated September 15th, 1769, from Fort Venus, Royal Bay, King George Island (now Tahiti), details were given of the observation of Venus. In 1774 Maskelyne took the clock to Perthshire, where he measured the deflection of a plumb-line caused by the attraction of the mountain Schiehallion. In 1815 Lieutenant Parry made a voyage to the Arctic. The reports from this expedition stated that the clocks used for the pendulum experiments were the property of the Royal Society, and the same as had accompanied Captain Cook round the world; they were made by Shelton.

The clock was specially prepared for travelling by securing the pendulum at its point of suspension and also by fixing the bob rigidly by means of two pieces of shaped wood encasing it and screwed firmly to the back of the case. In the photograph the holes in the back board necessitated by this proceeding are clearly visible, thus proving this to be the same clock as that of which we have been following the travels. The correct position for the upper edge of the pendulum bob on the pendulum rod to ensure a recorded rate of going at Greenwich was scratched on by Maskelyne before the clock left Greenwich; this mark, made one hundred and ninety years ago, is still there and today records the correct position for the bob.

Plate 35c and *d* shows a regulator made by the famous John Arnold, his No. 1 made for Greenwich. He made two, No. 1 and No. 2. In 1774, £84. 16s. was certified for payment to Arnold, and an inventory dated December 14th, 1774, includes an 'Astronomical clock by Arnold with ruby pallets' in both the Quadrant Room and the Great Room. Greenwich does not seem to have used the Arnold clocks very regularly; the main transit clock was made by Shelton under Graham's observation in 1748 and taken into use in 1750. Presumably the Arnold regulators did not offer any advantage over the clocks then in use. The dial shows the hours through the slot below the centre, the minutes on the main dial, and in the subsidiary dial the seconds.

Arnold, however, did not make his reputation with regulators, his main claim to fame being his work on improved and simplified chronometer escapements after Harrison had primarily solved the problem of 'the longitude'. In 1764, when he was twenty-eight, he made the smallest repeating watch ever attempted. It was set in a finger-ring and was presented by him to King George III, who was so pleased that he gave him 500 guineas for it. This brought him before the public, who were ready to appreciate his extraordinary skill in fine workmanship and finish. The King also gave him £100 to enable him to experiment with the improvements to chronometers.

The heavy compensated grid-iron pendulum, made after Harrison's principles, is clearly seen, as are also the holes in the back of the case where the clock has been bolted to the wall at different times. To ensure accurate time-keeping it is essential that a clock be kept absolutely rigid.

Plate 36a shows one more English regulator by Barwise, London. This may be either John Barwise, who was working in St. Dunstan's Lane 1790–1820, or his successors, Barwise & Sons, in the same road. Again, its direct simplicity proclaims its purpose; the minute hand is compensated; the two slots show one the hour and the other the day of the month. It has a peculiar grid-iron pendulum consisting of three bars only, two of brass and one of steel.

Plate 36b shows a very graceful Vienna Regulator by Glueckstein, about 1830. It is an eight-day, quarter-striking piece with a lunar dial in a fire-gilt case, as opposed to the very severely designed English regulators, which are always only timepieces and destined only for severely practical uses. These decorative domestic pieces were in great favour in Austria in the early part of the nineteenth century, their elegance matching the general elegance of that country at that time. The design shows distinct French influence, the dial especially being reminiscent of Breguet.

The final illustration in this chapter, *Plate 36c*, shows what is popularly known as an 'Act of Parliament Clock'; just how

K

this name became fixed on to this type it is hard to say. In 1797 a tax of five shillings per annum was levied on any clock or watch, whether public or private. In some of Rowlandson's drawings of the period are depicted Tavern scenes showing this type of clock on the wall. It may well be that large dial clocks were exhibited in public places to offset the loss of the watch or clock privately owned, and it has been assumed that these clocks originated for this purpose. The Act was repealed next year as it caused such unemployment in the horological industry, so that many clocks of this type could not have been made during that short period. The fact is that, whilst we have known for a long time that the style dated from at least 1760, there hangs in the Vestry of St. Mary's church, Bury St. Edmunds, a clock of this type made by George Graham. This clock is numbered 575; now Graham was a partner of Tompion until the latter's death in 1713, and the highest known Tompion & Graham number is 556. Graham carried on with the numbering when he succeeded to the business, so that 575 is most likely about 1715, or eighty-two years before the Act of Parliament which is supposed to have given rise to the appellation.

CHAPTER SEVEN

Dials and Back Plates

THE decoration of clock dials, as well as their housings, was always a favourite means for the craftsman to express his love for his handiwork and the degree of veneration in which he held his patron. Some sixteenth-century pieces are housed in structures which are works of art in themselves; worthy housings for the wonderful mechanisms they contained, which were held in awe by the uninitiated masses of that day.

The desire to decorate as a finish to the design and as an expression of the degree of importance of the piece continued when clocks became more general in domestic use; but, as we have seen in perusing the pages of the preceding chapters, decoration gradually gave way to simplicity and functional design, till at the beginning of the nineteenth century all the grace and effect in clock design was the function of line, pure and simple.

The main features of these dials and the progress in design of each have already been described when the clock in question was dealt with in the previous chapters. These descriptions will not be repeated here, but it is hoped that the larger illustrations of the dials here given will help to clarify any points not too clearly brought out in the smaller illustrations. Only the more complicated dials will be dealt with fully in this chapter.

Lantern clock dials were usually engraved, as we have seen in Chapter Three. Sometimes the more important pieces had the side doors engraved as well. When clocks began to be made to go eight days and to be encased, the first tendency was towards very plain dials, as we have seen in *Plates 14c* and *15a*. The next stage was the engraving of a Tudor rose around the hole pierced for the hand arbor; then followed spandrels with, as a rule, a matted centre to the dial plate (*Plate 15b*).

In *Plate 37a* we have a plain dial with the cherub spandrels, but not matted, by Ahasuerus Fromanteel. The engraved central rose just referred to has been replaced by a cast and finely tooled ornament. Today, when with high-powered rolling mills, sheets of brass are turned out many tons an hour, all with a highly polished finish, it is perhaps not fully realised just how difficult it would be to get a smooth and flawless surface as that illustrated. Matting the surface after it had been hammered and scraped reasonably flat would hide any minor surface defects, but in this case we have a piece of flawless brass casting, about one-sixteenth of an inch thick. There were no rolling mills in those days, all larger sheets being beaten out from castings by hammers worked by water-power. Batteries they were called, because there were frequently four or six hammers falling in rotation on to the anvil as the water-wheel turned and, by means of cams, lifted them in turn. The highly placed bell and the long upright hammer rod are typical of Dutch practice in the second half of the seventeenth century. This clock was made by a Dutchman working in London, who probably fled from the Spanish oppression in Holland in the sixteenth and seventeenth centuries.

The dial on *Plate 37b* is one that caused a great deal of speculation for many years. The actual minute ring is a loose friction fit and can be moved in either direction by inserting a peg in any of the little holes pierced midway between each five-minute figure. There is no xii, only a diamond; this is presumably to give an exact point to correspond to the lower point of the smaller diamond in the minute ring. Each minute is subdivided into six ten-second spaces. In the illustration the minute ring is indicating fifty seconds slow on the hour ring. The author's explanation of this peculiar dial is that it is for the purpose of measuring the equation of time before the equation kidney was invented, which invention enabled the equation to be recorded mechanically. According to the equation tables of the time, the minute ring could be set daily, or at any other desired interval, so that the diamond of the minute ring would be fast or slow by the diamond of the hour ring by the amount shown in the tables for the day selected. When opportunity arose to check the clock by the sundial, a direct reading on the minute ring would indicate the same as the sundial, if the clock were keeping good time.

The seconds dial also moves freely; since the minute ring

is only graduated to ten-seconds intervals, the exact seconds adjustment could be made on this dial. The lower subsidiary dial is also loose; the hand slips on to the winding square and has to be removed before the clock is wound; it does not bring into action any type of maintaining power. It revolves with the barrel round which the gut carrying the weight is wound; thus with an eight-day clock the hand would revolve sixteen times, once every twelve hours. It will be noted that the hours are marked anti-clockwise; unless the clock be wound exactly at III, VI, IX, or XII it would be necessary to stop winding the last turn of the drum in such a position as would enable the hand to be replaced on the square at the correct hour. In the photograph this has not been done.

It will be noticed that there is a micrometer screw for adjusting the pendulum length; Clement is usually credited with being the first to use this and it is not thought that the application on this Fromanteel invalidates Clement's claim.

Plate 37c and *d* shows the dials of the clocks illustrated in *Plates 16a* and *20a*. From, or rather conjointly with, the latter part of the period of very plain dials we get a few wholly engraved dials, as seen in this plate. There was one particular engraver who was working at this period, mainly for Edward East, but the author has seen dials by him on a clock by Samuel Knibb, and two anonymous clocks as well as that by John Hilderson, one of the subjects of our illustration. While penning these lines, the author cannot recollect any wholly engraved dial at this period that is not by this particular artist. He is believed to be of Dutch origin and working in London, as his style is quite distinctly in the Dutch genre: a floral pattern always perfectly balanced, flower balancing flower and bird balancing bird, but his designs never symmetrical. He never uses a straight line, and in his earlier work he cannot abide an empty space, every little plain spot being filled in with dots or small circles. These are not so marked in his later work. The author has an idea that he may be John Droeshout, who on January 31st, 1671–2, engraved and signed the brass plate affixed to the cover of the engrossment of the Clockmakers' Company Charter which was presented to the Company by Richard Morgan, but has so far not been able to confirm this. The author would appreciate any further information from those possessing engravings known to be by John Droeshout which would enable him to check his theory.

Plate 38a shows a dial very similar to that shown in *Plate 37a*, but the matted centre has appeared; this is another Edward East dial, delightful in its simplicity and its clarity. The narrow chapter ring and even, proportionately, narrower seconds ring appeal at once to the eye. The ratio of width to diameter is 1 : 12 for the seconds ring and 1 : 8 for the chapter ring. There is a very high degree of elegance and finish in the hands, and the hour hand is nicely chamfered, always the sign of a good hand and a good clock. The additional decoration of the minute hand changes its production from a straight filing job to that of an artist. Also should be noted the J-shape of the 1 in the five-minute numerals; when this shape is used it is always an indication of early work. The clock to which this dial belongs is shown in *Plate 22c*.

The dial below in the same plate is a little later and by William Clement. The chapter ring is getting broader, the ratio of width to diameter being 1 : $5\frac{1}{3}$. All the dials illustrated so far, as well as those illustrated on the next plate, are signed on the bottom of the dial plate below the VI of the chapter ring.

This style of signature is general until about the sixteen-nineties, when as will be seen in *Plate 39a* it is usually placed on the chapter ring itself, although at times it appears upon a special cartouche, or even on a specially affixed plate. The five-minute numerals of this dial are still within the minute ring and the 5 has no curl at the bottom; this is indicative of 'before 1700' as compared with the 5's of *Plates 39c, 39d, 40c, 38d, 41b* and *41c*, which show the progression of the shape of the 5. The hands, although well shaped, have not the rounded finish of the hour hand referred to in the last example.

Plate 38c shows the dial of Tompion's first equation clock illustrated in *Plate 25*. It is a superb piece of workmanship. Starting at the top, we have in the first sector opening an annual dial showing the position of the sun in the ecliptic, indicating the name of the 'Celestial House' or sign of the Zodiac in which the sun is in on that day. The dial is read by carrying the eye up from the small pointer affixed to the dial above the '45'. The next dial is an annual calendar dial indicating February 15th, the sun being 25° of Aquarius – the Water-carrier – in its journey towards Pisces – the Fishes. It will be recollected, as explained in Chapter Four, that it was to enable this dial to be read that Tompion introduced the arch into the hood door, which gave birth to the arched dial and hood with which we are so familiar today. Next comes the moving minute ring showing sun, or apparent time, which moves backwards or forwards in relation to the fixed minute ring, showing mean time, by means of the rack actuating the toothed wheel on to which this moving minute ring is mounted (*Plate 25c*). In the illustration the clock shows the sun approximately 14 minutes 40 seconds slow on mean time; it is around mid-February that mean time has its maximum rate in excess of apparent time. The minute hand revolves once in two hours; this is a year clock, and this disposition enabled Tompion to reduce the number of turns on the barrel round which the gut carrying the weight is wound, and thus reduce the distance the weight has to drop during the year. The upper xii is replaced by a small arabic 12 to allow for the hole for the winding square, covered by the maintaining power shutter which is actuated by releasing the lever at the right-hand side of the dial. The hands are about as perfect as can be conceived, and the delicate tracery of the hour hand and its openwork base are quite exceptional, as is also the hollowing out of the decoration of the minute hand. This has a counterpoise to reduce the amount of power needed to raise it during the upward part of its two-hourly circular journey. The very fine degree of matting of the dial centre should be noted; the spandrels are of the ordinary type of developed cherub's head found on the best-quality clocks made during the period 1695–1700. The signature *Thos. Tompion, London, Inventit*, signifies a first production of this type of equation clock.

Plate 39a shows a typical dial of the first half of the first decade of the eighteenth century. It is from the author's clock illustrated in *Plate 24b*. The chapter ring is broadening, the ratio of width to diameter is now 1 : 4¾, and the seconds ring is broadening too. The ringed winding holes and the decorated calendar aperture have appeared. In the spandrels, the cherubs, poor dears, are no longer regarded as bodiless heads blowing the winds from the four cardinal points. They are allowed bodies, and to earn their keep they have to support a crown and orb. The five-minute numerals have taken up position outside the minute ring and there they will remain. The 5's have not yet developed their final curve and there are marks at seven-and-a-half minute intervals where these do not coincide with a multiple of five. The hands are very finely worked and are a good fit.

Plate 39b shows another early example of the arched dial, this time definitely dated 1708. The history of this clock is related in Chapter Five, and the whole clock illustrated in Plate *25b*. The arching both top and bottom is, in the author's experience, quite unique. The hour hand is very 'Tompionesque' but has not the delicacy of that seen in Plate *38c*. The minute hand is counterpoised, as the period of going is one month. As in the case of the Tompion equation clock, the escapement is below the movement, and the lower arching of the dial is to provide a seconds dial, which Tompion omitted in the Buckingham Palace clock, but this clock was designed for astronomical observations, hence a seconds dial was essential. The dial in the upper arch is a dummy put in to balance. The inscription reads *Collego St.* TRINITATIS *Cantab* ISAACUS NEWTON *Equis Auratus Don. D.*, and the signature *R. Street London 1708.*

Plate 39c shows a Quare year dial, also with equation movement, but, as in the case of all such movements by Quare, the equation portion is quite separate, having been made by Joseph Williamson. In this case the equation dial is situated below the movement and shows through a glass plate in the door of the trunk. This dial is fixed to two bearers coming from the main plates of the movement which are clearly seen (*Plate 40a* and *b*), and the drive is through a rod and endless worm seen in the back view; this, when in position, gears with the wheel carrying the plain calendar hand revolving once a year, on the axis of which is fixed the equation kidney. The follower arm, bearing on this, turns the larger wheel, which in turn gears into a pinion fixed to the arbor of the hand bearing the effigy of the sun, moving it the necessary amount backwards or forwards each day. For the sake of symmetry the inner edge of the upper semicircle is marked fifteen minutes each side, actually the maximum variations are approximately minus fourteen minutes and plus sixteen minutes. It will be seen that the teeth in the upper part of the big wheel have not been finished, since they are never used. A wheel is really unnecessary; a rack segment as in *Plate 25c* is all that is needed; but a wheel gives better balance.

This year clock appears to have been designed for Queen Anne, as it bears the Royal Arms. The dial is not standard in size, hence the specially cast spandrels. The subsidiary dial upper right is for pendulum regulation. The clean and precise design of the hand is very pleasing. It will be noted that the curl of the 5 is developing and that the seven-and-a-half-minute signs are lozenges. The very large eccentrically placed winding square indicates a year movement. A very heavy weight is required to overcome the friction caused by the introduction of two extra trains from the ordinary eight-day movement, i.e. eight-day to month, and month to the thirteen months which is usual for a year movement. This very heavy weight necessitates a thick gut with deep grooves on a long and extra heavy barrel; hence the big winding square.

The dial on *Plate 39d* is by George Graham, the clock being shown on *Plate 26b*. It is one of the finest dials the author knows, plain, simple, dignified and clear. The half-hour marks have now gone from the chapter ring as have the seven-and-a-half-minute marks. The quarter-hour marks on the inner edge of the chapter ring have given way to half-hour marks. The proportions of the width to diameter for the chapter and seconds rings are $1 : 5\frac{1}{3}$ and $1 : 9\frac{1}{3}$ respectively. The lever for the maintaining power is seen on the right; the spandrels have the head of a bearded man wearing a kind of rabbinical turban as the central *motif*; this design was favoured by Graham.

Plate 40c shows a dial of a clock by William Tomlinson dated about 1735. The herring-bone engraving round the edge is late for this kind of decoration; it is usually found before 1700. The spandrels based on a female head and on a dolphin in the arch are correct for the period and are exceptionally well finished. Here we have a reversion to ringed winding holes and quarter-hour divisions on the inner edge of the chapter ring, clear evidence that these minor changes took place slowly and overlapped. The curl of the 5 is developing a little further, as is that of the 3. In the arch is a tidal dial; this is universal – that is to say it can be set for any port desired. The inner ring is a loose friction fit, the little lugs for moving it can be seen at

XII, IIII, and VIII. In the illustration it is set for London Bridge, high tide at III, at new and full moon. By putting the appropriate hour under the 29½ for high tide at new moon for the port in question, the daily time of tide is read off the hand which clicks forward every twelve hours.

The dial of the clock shown in *Plate 40d* is astronomical. Firstly, in the arch is an aperture showing the day of the week and its appropriate deity as described in Chapter One; then come subsidiary dials for, left, the age of the moon, and right, the day of the month. The hour hand revolves once in twenty-four hours and the minute hand once an hour. These hands are thought to be early nineteenth-century replacements, for their style is not contemporary nor do they match the seconds hand; neither do they fit. The minutes between fifty-six and four have to be approximated. Each side of the minute ring are two pairs of shutters which rise and fall once a year. The outer one on the right when fully raised uncovers, as it descends, the appropriate sign of the zodiac, which is indicated by the edge of the shutter as it falls during the first six months. As the shutters rise during the next six months the signs are read off the ascending edge of the left-hand shutter. In the same way the outer pair of shutters descend, and on the right is read off the edge the date of the month from December 29th to June 25th; as they ascend, on the left are read off the days from June 26th to December 28th. This odd division of dates is to agree with the dates on which the sun passes from one sign of the zodiac to another. Against the day of the month, at intervals, are painted how many minutes fast or slow, by the sun, the clock should be. The painted spandrels represent the seasons; this is a very early appearance of this type of decoration, if original; it is thought that when the new hands were fitted the painted spandrels were added; both are of the same period, early nineteenth century.

The inner pair of shutters read off against the hour ring, indicates the time of sunrise and sunset.

Plate 41a shows the dial of the clock on *Plate 33c*. It is a year movement by one of the Finney family of Liverpool. The clock is only a timepiece, the second winding hole is a dummy, put in for symmetry. The hour dial revolves and is read off the numeral that is uppermost, then comes the minute hand and a

centre seconds hand. The other hand protruding from behind
the hour dial, revolves once a year and indicates the day and
month of the year. On the extreme outer edge are marked, at
intervals, the difference of the equation.

This dial contains a curious mixture of ecclesiastical and secular commemorations, the abbreviations for some of which
proved a little puzzling. August 12th. *PWB*, is the Prince of
Wales's birthday. George IV was born August 12th 1764. July
31st. *Do. Beg.* and September 5th, *Do. dae.*, Dog days begin and
end. January 31st. *KCM*, King Charles, Martyr, May 29th.
KCRe, Restoration of Charles II. On June 4th and May 19th
are recorded the birthdays of George III and Queen Charlotte.
C. Day, February 1st. Candlemas Day. April 1st is marked *AF*,
which needs no explanation. Of the Feasts of the Church, only
CSP gave any difficulty, January 15th. Conversion of St. Paul.
Inside the door is written in ink the date 1769 which fits well
with the date recorded for the Prince of Wales's birth.

Plate 41b shows the dial of the clock shown in *Plate 22b*, which,
we have come to the conclusion, was made by a London maker,
Mr. Benson of Whitehaven merely being the supplier to the
final purchaser. It has the odd number of thirteen tunes, thus
the hour at which any tune is played is advanced two hours
daily. The spandrels have become of the nondescript type
belonging to the late eighteenth century. The hour hand is
much lighter in design and the serpentine minute hand has
appeared. These types of hands will persist on practically all
long-case clocks and on many bracket clocks. The hand with
the sun's effigy is not, as might be supposed, an equation hand
but an annual calendar hand, the date being read off the outer
ring, which again bears a curious mixture of ecclesiastical and
secular dates, e.g. *Christmas Dav, Epiphany, St. Paul, Charles I
(Martyr) beheaded, Lady Day, St. George (Martyr), Longest Day,
Visitation of Mary, Dog Days begin, Lammas Day, John the Baptist
beheaded, London Burnt (old style), King George III born, Prince
William Henry born*, appearing amongst other notifications. The
author has not been able to ascertain which of the fifteen children, otherwise unrecorded in history, Prince William Henry
was, but since George III married in 1761, a date of 1770–75
can be assigned to this clock. The third winding hole is for
the musical train.

Plate 41c and *d* shows an ingenious and simple perpetual-calendar movement, made by Helm of Ormskirk, which records not only the short months but also leap year. The slotted wheel revolves once in four years; in four years there are twenty months of less than thirty-one days. When the pin is bearing on the edge of the slotted wheel, as seen in the photograph, the toothed wheel goes forward one tooth at the end of a month, from 31 to 1. When the rocker arm goes into a slot, according to the depth of the slot, the centre toothed wheel will actuate the moving of the calendar dial one, two, or three extra teeth as may be required. In the photograph it is evidently the early days of December; we have just passed the November notch, needing the turning of the calendar dial one extra day. During December and January the rocker arm will be bearing on the circumference, so passing from 31 to 1 at the end of these months; on February 28th it will drop into the deep slot to enable three teeth to be moved forward on the dial. Three scribing lines appear for the three different depths of slot, and it will be noted that all the three long slots in focus in the picture are of the same depth, so that that of middle depth, to allow for two days' shift in leap year, must be that on the far side of the picture.

This rear view of the dial plate is interesting inasmuch as it shows from the edges of the apertures in the plate that this was cast and not rolled, as was explained in the earlier pages of this chapter. Accidental holes sometimes appear when one examines the back of a dial plate, but this one seems to have been so planned, as there are three holes in the plate shown in the photograph. A complaint against these northern provincial makers that the author has is that they must 'mess up' their dials with useless ornamentation thus impairing their clarity; patchwork-quilting is all right on a bed, it has no place on a clock dial. It is a pity hands to fit the dial were not selected.

Plate 42a, shows a painted dial from a large musical clock by Charles Lister of Halifax. There is nothing much to describe in this dial – day of the month, month of the year calendar dial; there are evidently fourteen tunes which can be selected by turning the hand on the subsidiary dial on the left. On the right, pendulum regulation. The photograph is included mainly to show the nesting of the bells in a complicated musical clock. It is a large, spring-driven bracket clock.

The dial (*Plate 42b*) is probably unique. It is a tidal dial made for the little Lincolnshire port of Fosdyke on the Wash. Here at the time that the clock was made there was a very deep estuary and correspondingly long tides. The subsidiary dials are for the day of the month and the age of the moon on each side, and for seconds in the centre. There is no hour hand; the hour is read from the low point of the aperture in the seconds dial. Minutes are read direct off the minute hand, and finally we have the bottom dial around which is written *The Influence of the Moon on the Waters*. This shows the state of the tide at half-hourly intervals and indicates how far it was safe to ride in the estuary or the need to bring cattle in. The inscriptions read:

Full Sea at Fosdike	*Drover's Wash*
Reflux	*Drover's Wash*
Reflux	*Drover's Wash*
Reflux	*Drover's Wash*
Reflux	*Wash just spent at Cross Keys*
Reflux	*Wash ends at Cross Keys*
Wash begins at Fosdike	*Wash just spent at Fosdike*
Good Riding	*Wash ends at Fosdike*
Good Riding	*Flux*
Good Riding	*Flux*
Good Riding	*Flux*

BACK PLATES

In dealing with back plates we have, of course, only to consider bracket clocks; naturally the back plates of long-case clocks were never decorated.

Lantern clocks sometimes had their side doors decorated, but the back plate which went against the wall was, of course, plain, and so when the spring-driven bracket clock came into being it was usual to have a solid wooden door at the back concealing a quite plain plate except for the maker's name and a slight touch of decoration, as seen in *Plate 42c*, which is the back plate of the clock shown in *Plate 15a*. It will be noticed that the decoration of the cock is by the same engraver as that of the dials on *Plate 37c/d*. The design is balanced but is not symmetrical. Another early feature of this clock is the baluster pillars. As already explained, all spring clocks heretofore have been horizontal table clocks standing dial up, with the winding squares protruding through the bottom plate. If we lay this clock movement so that the winding squares face downwards, we get a logical position for the baluster pillars. These are neatly riveted on to the front plate, which would have been the visible bottom plate in a table clock, and they are untidily pinned on to the now visible back plate, which in the table clock would have been the top plate hidden by the dial. Later, as we shall see, the pillars will be neatly riveted into the back plate and pinned on to the front plate; the pillars themselves will take on a straight form with turned feet and a turned central boss. The vertical bell and the high position of the locking plate and its positioning outside are all early features.

The other back plate this plate shows is that of the clock seen in *Plate 16a*. It will be recollected that this clock had a unique system of Dutch striking. This photograph shows the two bells which swivel upon their support to come in front of the hammer at the right time. It will be noticed that the locking plate has twice the number of notches, enabling the clock to repeat the hour at the half-hour. All the remarks regarding early features applied to the East clock on the left apply equally to the Hilderson clock on the right. The early makers were not able to tap a small thread inside the pendulum bob; this was drilled and bushed with a piece of wood, which in turn was drilled with a hole just fractionally smaller than the threaded base of the pendulum rod. The bob then cuts its own thread in the wooden bushing as it is screwed on.

After the plain back plate with the solid wooden door we have glass coming into the back door as well as in the front door, inducing decorated back plates. At first, floral designs were usual; four are illustrated in *Plate 43*. In the top two we have examples of the work of another engraver who was at work at this period; his designs are always symmetrical. Note how the pinned pillars have gone from the back plate.

Plate 43a shows the back plate of the clock illustrated in *Plate 18b*, which, it will be remembered, was the clock in which Knibb made his early effort at *grande sonnerie* striking. The locking plate for quarter-striking is on the right, and when this has struck, the count wheel tips down the cross-bar, the other end of which rises and releases the locking arm of the hour strike. It will be noted that there are four repetitions of each hour up to six, enabling the hour to be repeated each quarter up to six, as explained in Chapter Two. *Plate 43b* shows a plate where the floral design is converging into the conventional and is on a clock by Henry Jones, an apprentice of Edward East. This clock has now rack-and-snail striking which was invented by Edward Barlow in 1675. The setting-up ratchet wheels for the main springs are usually on the front plate, but in some early cases, as in this instance, they are placed on the back plate.

Plate 43c shows another example of the floral type merging into the conventional and also the passing of the floral *motif* and the adoption of the purely conventional; *Plate 43d* is the back plate of the clock shown in *Plate 18d*. The cast cock of the Watson clock represents a fashion of the latter part of the seventeenth century. As is seen in the Quare clock, the size of these cocks became very overdone; in this case the cock is a restoration. The faceted bob of the Watson clock to facilitate regulation is interesting; the author had a similar bob on a clock by William Clement he formerly owned.

Plate 44a shows a clock by Claude du Chesne. The flat disk bob has been adopted, and since this can only be turned a full 180° if the bob is to swing true, some means of lesser regulation had to be found. This takes the form of an eccentric snail, seen upper right, which can be turned by a hand on the dial, so adjusting the essential flexing point in the suspension spring.

Plate 44b shows about the maximum degree of back-plate decoration before the tendency for this to lessen, and finally to disappear, sets in. It is on a clock by George Graham and is on lines very similar to Tompion, which is, of course, not surprising since he worked so many years for him. The winged and crowned semi-angels should be noted. The clock is a repeater and can be pulled from either side, though the pull cords are missing.

Plate 44c is the back plate of the Vulliamy clock illustrated in *Plate 28c*. The degree of decoration is now considerably less.

It is a pull repeater from one side only. Our final illustration shows the back plate of the clock given in *Plate 29c*. Here we have merely a decorated edge. The decoration on the pendulum bob is unusual. Note that a gong, giving a deeper tone, has replaced the bell; this is a feature of the end of the eighteenth century.

CHAPTER EIGHT

Night Clocks

THE earliest record that we have of a clock to record night hours is the biographical tablet of Amenemhe't, Prince and Holder of the Royal Seals, who lived at the beginning of the eighteenth Dynasty, and who was born about 1565 B.C. In his memorial tablet he describes his invention of a water clock to tell the time at night, and the hieroglyphic he uses to describe it is ∇, that is an inverted truncated cone, in common parlance a vessel somewhat like an ordinary flower pot, which corresponds to the shape of all known Egyptian water clocks. That found in the Temple of Karnak, of which a plaster reproduction is to be seen in the Science Museum, London, was made about 1450 B.C. The Egyptians divided the day and night each into twelve equal periods and Amenemhe't states in his tablet that he has taken this into account. His clock formed the model for all subsequent Egyptian water clocks.

To drop an equal amount vertically, in spite of decreasing pressure, during a given period would need a container with a wall of about 77°, all the known Egyptian water clocks have walls of nearer 70°, and Dr. F. Hoepper, in an article in the *Deutsche Kolloid Zeitschrift* for January 1942, related a series of experiments with a container with walls of 70°. He had calculated that with walls of 77° and water subjected to the average fall in temperature for the Egyptian night, errors up to three-quarters of an hour would creep in, an error far too big to pass unnoticed by the proficient Egyptian astronomers. He reduced the temperature of the water in his container thermostatically by the $1\frac{1}{2}$° per hour that he had calculated as the average fall in night temperature in Egypt and found that he succeeded in getting equal falls in level for equal periods of time. The Karnak clock is marked on the inside with a series of vertical dots at unequal intervals, representing the length of the hours of the night during the different months.

This clock, of course, needed an artificial light by which to read it; later we get the appearance of touch knobs. *Plate 45a* shows a clock from the church of St. Sebaldius, in Nuremberg, and now in the Germanusches Museum there. It will be seen that it has sixteen touch knobs, that at the top being longer than the others, as a point of reference. *Plate 45b* shows the under-dial work where a pinion of 3 engages a wheel of 48, a 1 : 16 ratio, thus proving that this clock was designed for use during the night hours, which are at a maximum of sixteen at the winter solstice. Had the clock been intended for day use the touch knobs would not have been needed. In later years the dial has been painted over to mark twelve hours only and all descriptions that the author has seen of this clock assume that there is a pinion of 4 into a wheel of 48, giving a 1 : 12 ratio, but the pinion of 3 has not lost a tooth, it is undoubtedly original.

Now the Egyptian clock required an artificial light and both these clocks call for the proximity of the observer; it is not until the seventeenth century that we get night clocks that can be read at a distance. They are of two kinds, those that were made for use in large salons, which often had striking trains, and could be used as day or night clocks, and those for bedrooms where silence was a primary consideration. Of the latter one of the earliest is in the Museum at Kassel. It is by Johann Philip Treffler and is one of the only two signed pieces by this maker known. Mr. Silvio Bedini, of Salem, Massachussets, has recently published in the Journal of the National Association of Watch and Clock Collectors of the U.S.A. a most exhaustive study of this maker's Life. Treffler was at one time attached to the Court of Archduke Ferdinand II of Tuscany. This clock (*Plate 45c*) is dated about 1675–80. It will be seen that it has an ordinary chapter ring and can be used by day; above is a small hinged plate covering a small transparent glass dial which is marked with the twelve hours. The back view *Plate 45d* reveals a lamp and reflector and chimney. In *Plate 46a* is seen a closer view of the back plate and the glass dial above it. This latter is in duplicate, one sheet is fixed with the hours painted on it whilst that other, bearing the hand, revolves before it once in twelve hours. It will be noted that the pendulum hangs from the bottom of the movement necessitating an inverted crown wheel. This is also found in the other Treffler clock known and was also shown in the sketch of the clock at the Medici Palace sent to Huygens in 1658. It would seem to be an Italian conception (see *Plate 10d*).

Judging from those still to be found in Italy, thirty-hour night clocks were fairly usual at this period; a day and night clock of Italian origin is seen in *Plate 46b*. With the poor illumination available in a large room, it would not be possible to see across to a clock on the other side of the room, so an hour dial, fixed to the arbour of the hour hand and of a larger diameter than the day-hour ring, shows through a slot above the chapter ring. In the illustration the clock is recording 3.15.

In England night clocks of the seventeenth century are known by East, Fromanteel, Knibb, Bartlett, Seignior and possibly others. One by Joseph Knibb *Plate 46c* and *d*, burns each night in the author's bedroom. The main dial revolves once in two hours, on its reverse side it carried 180° apart, two subsidiary dials, one with the even numbers and one with the odd. As these pass the low point a small arm knocks them one place forward. In the illustration it is just 11 o'clock, 10 is disappearing and 11 is coming up. The objection to a verge movement in a bedroom is the noise it makes, but in this clock this disadvantage has been overcome by fixing a piece of very thin spring steel under the pallets and letting it protrude a fraction, so that the spring takes up the impact with the crown wheel. The result is almost complete silence, only in the dead of night can a faint sound be heard. There is a small screw for adjustment of the depthing.

In the quest for quietness in the bedroom Peter Thomas Campini invented a pendulum clock that actuated an eccentric balance which had a continuous, instead of an intermittent motion, the result being an entirely silent movement. This is seen in *Plate 47a* and *b*. The clock is signed on the back of the movement *Petrus Thomas Campanus Inventor, Roma 1683*. In *Plate 47b* it will be noted that the pendulum hangs from a curved arm that is connected on one end with a weighted bar, and at the other eccentrically on to a small disk on the hub of the escape wheel, if so we may call it, since that is no escapement proper. This arm is set in motion by the forked piece on the top of the pendulum rod; once in motion the weighted bar continues to give the impetus to the balance wheel. Modern attempts to make the clock function to time have not been very successful, but the idea is ingenious.

An illustration exists of a very ornate French bedroom of about 1725, where an elaboration of Treffler's transparent glass dial is seen in a 'magic lantern' clock projection of the dial on to the wall of the room. This idea of projection was revived about one hundred years later; *Plate 47c* shows two early-nineteenth-century clocks which can be used as ordinary clocks by day and which are fitted with dials for projection by night; yet electric clocks, that on the press of a switch, projected the dial on to the ceiling were hailed as a great novelty some twenty years ago. The third clock on this plate is a very simple idea, a night light is placed on a shelf behind the slotted dial. This type was used in Scandinavia.

This concludes the chapters on European clocks, merely a brief outline; to be exhaustive would need several volumes resulting in a work so expensive that no one would want to buy it. Nevertheless it is hoped that the Reader's interest has been stimulated and that what has been omitted may be the incentive to others to fill the gap.

In our final chapter we shall take a look at those clocks in which our cousins across the Atlantic take an interest and collect.

CHAPTER NINE

American Clocks

A s MENTIONED in the preface, Mr. Walter M. Roberts,
President of the National Association of Watch and Clock
Collectors, has been largely responsible for the gathering
together of the examples illustrated, for the historical details
of their makers and the general evolution of American Clockmaking, the author is duly appreciative of his help.

Little is known of American clockmaking during the early
days of the Colonies. A few English-trained clockmakers
came to America during the period of 1620–1700. It is known
that Boston had a tower clock in 1650 cared for by Richard
Taylor but nothing is known of his clocks. William Davis
worked in Boston in 1683 and Edward Bogardus was active in
New York in 1698. There are no known examples of seventeenth-century American clocks.

During the eighteenth century clockmaking became well
established in Boston, Newport, New York and Philadelphia.
Since the demand for clocks was slight the American clockmakers required other talents to insure an adequate income.
They were usually silversmiths and often gunsmiths, metalmen,
traders, locksmiths and tinkers.

Eli Terry produced the first clocks in large quantities early in
the 1800's. Daniel Burnap and Gideon Roberts used inter-
changeable parts but in no great volume. American clockmaking then developed into big business for the times. Many new
clockmaking shops came into existence in the Bristol, Connecticut area. Along a stream in Bristol there were eleven clock-
manufacturing plants within an eighth-mile.

The introduction of low-cost brass in America made possible
low-priced clocks. Wooden movements disappeared and thousands of brass-movement clocks were produced where hundreds
of wooden-movement clocks had formerly been made. Cases
became styled for price production and markets were enlarged.

Salesmanship as such and mass production can be credited to the American clockmaker. Terry and Jerome were good organisers but themselves poor craftsmen.

Clock work was done under great difficulties. Many makers made all of their tools. Many wheel and pinion cutters were made by hand of rough material yet with accurate results. Communication was difficult; transportation facilities poor, yet the 'Yankee Trader' was born and prospered. He was resourceful and ingenious. He extended his markets on horseback and stagecoach; later on sailing ships.

In this chapter a few types and styles are shown to give an idea of the clocks that were produced and are today respected by the collector of American pieces. There were thousands of styles, many of which can be found in the works to which reference is made later.

The clockmakers in America during the late 1600's and 1700's were, for the most part, English-trained. Their work reflected this training and it was not until the late 1700's that modifications of the traditional type appeared. A few tower clocks were built during this period, but the tall clock accounted for the greater portion of clocks built, each being individually made until possibly Daniel Burnap and certainly Gideon Roberts followed by Eli Terry arranged their shops to make clocks in quantity. This founding of mass production led the way for a strong manufacturing economy in America.

American production can conveniently be divided into three categories: tall clocks, wall clocks and shelf clocks, each variety of which will be examined in turn.

Until the turn of the nineteenth century the bulk of the clocks produced in America were tall clocks made in the Atlantic seaboard states, but many of the surviving pieces from this period bearing American names were, in fact, either imported complete from England or imported as movements and cased in the States.

In the main movements with straightforward going and striking trains, anchor escapement and rack and snail strike were produced, although occasionally a movement with calendar or other simple astronomical indications was made. The most famous maker of these more complicated movements was David Rittenhouse (1732–96) whose name is a household word among American collectors, although the number of pieces from his hand is very limited.

Plate 48 illustrates a clock by Rittenhouse. On its case is a ticket describing it as an astronomical clock, but as there are in fact no astronomical indications, it should be more correctly described as a clock made by Rittenhouse for use in astronomical observations.

It is reputed to have been used by Rittenhouse when observing the transit of Venus on June 3rd, 1769.

This is said to be the most accurate timekeeper made by Rittenhouse, but full details as to the improvements introduced to give it that superiority in timekeeping over his other productions are lacking. Mr. Robert A. Franks who examined the clock some time ago reported that the movement had a Graham dead-beat escapement, but of a most unusual type, the escape wheel being planted behind the back-plate of the movement engaging directly with the upper portion of the pendulum rod which is 'expanded' to encompass the escape wheel and which holds the two pallets, thus eliminating the customary anchor and fork, consequently reducing friction. The perfection of the workmanship is striking, one notes the high number of leaves on the pinions, a refinement that reduces friction and uneven power delivered to the escape wheel. No mention is made of the type of pendulum and the nature of its compensation, which must be assumed if such accurate results are to be achieved.[1]

Plate 49 shows four tall clocks: *a* is by Simon Willard of Roxbury, Massachusetts and is of date about 1785. It is a good example of a mahogany case with Sheraton style inlay, fret top and ball and spire finials. The painted dial indicates seconds and has a calendar opening. In the arch is a lunar dial that will revolve once in two lunar months and carries landscape and seascape scenes. The movement is brass, eight-day and weightdriven.

Plate 49b is a scroll pediment clock by R. Shearman of Philadelphia about 1800. This scroll top followed on after the fret trimmed top and reflects Chippendale styling. The pediment is finished with urn and flame finials in wood with a fluted block below the centre finial. It has free standing columns on the hood, fluted quarter columns on the trunk and base and

[1] The author recently saw a clock by Ellicott with the escape wheel embraced within the expanded pendulum in Lord Harris' collection.

bracket feet. The dial is painted and shows seconds and calendar. It will be noted that the hands have passed from the mid- to late-eighteenth-century style of *a* to the Regency style. The brass movement is eight-day, weight-driven.

Plate 49c is a corner tall clock by John Osgood of Andover, Massachusetts, of about 1797. This is a case of a movement being given to a country carpenter to have the case made; a man who evidently had no idea of introducing style or proportion into the pine case with butternut hood that he made. The hands too would seem to have been adapted from a larger dial. The dial is early nineteenth century but the minute hand is mid-eighteenth century and the hour hand smacks more of the later seventeenth. The hour hand should just touch the inner edge of the hour ring and the minute hand the outer edge, as is seen in examples *a* and *b*. This rule is broken in *d*, but in this case there is no doubt that the hands are original. The movement of *c* is a brass weight-driven timepiece.

Plate 49d is a miniature tall clock or grandmother clock by Joshua Wilder of Hingham, Massachusetts, dated about 1800. In this case the case is mahogany veneer on pine with the fret pediment and urn finials of a quarter century earlier; it has free standing columns with brass mountings on both the hood and trunk. The movement is eight-day, brass, weight-driven with alarm. The illfitting hands are probably due more to the lack of appreciation of the finer points of a dial, rather than to anything else.

Space does not allow a further expansion of our study of tall clocks, we must now pass on to that of wall clocks. These, having short pendulum movements, first appeared around 1760–5. Simon Willard developed a type with a forty-hour hand-made movement of brass with the pendulum rod fixed directly to the anchor, thus saving scarce brass and lessening the time of making. Wall clocks gradually replaced tall clocks and after 1800 were made in increasing numbers following the introduction of the banjo clock. *Plates 50* and *51* illustrate a few of the many types.

Plate 50a shows a Simon Willard wall clock made at Grafton, Massachusetts about 1770. The delicate case is of mahogany with a kidney door opening, fret top and brass finials. There is a lunar dial and a dial and a day of the month calendar. These two indications are on the same dial as the phase of the moon, which makes one turn in two lunar months or fifty-nine days. It is read off the top of the stationary hand fixed above the hour dial. Since the calendar dial will have to be corrected by hand after each short month, the lunar indications will become very approximate after a short while. The painting of the lunar disk and the starry sky is very crude compared with the good finish and engraving of the rest of the dial. The brass movement is seen in *Plate 50b*. There is no striking train, one blow on the bell being given at every hour. This clock is one of fifteen known examples.

Plate 50c is another clock by Simon Willard, made after he had moved to Roxbury in Massachusetts and dates from about 1810. It takes the well-known banjo shape, a style developed in the 1790's and patented in 1802. A glance at the movement *Plate 50d* shows at once that there has been a great improvement in the workmanship employed and this resulted in much better timekeeping, making this type of clock immediately popular. The T-bridge in the movement, the clean lines of the design of the case, as well as the clear dial and graceful hands should be noted.

These banjo clocks were first made of mahogany with inlay at the throat and door. The flat base made this type equally suitable for wall or shelf. Later examples used a bracket base with the entire front gold-leafed, including rope trim on the frames. Glass panels are reverse painted, some being very elaborate. When gold-leafed, the clocks were called 'presentation clocks'. A book on Simon Willard, dealing with his life and work is mentioned in the bibliography given at the end of this book.

Plate 51a shows a Banjo-lyre clock, anonymous, but typical of the work of Sawin, *c.* 1825. This clock has a brass banjo type movement with going, striking trains and alarm. The glass in the carved lyre throat and base is reverse painted and there is the typical bracket base. The feather finial is also characteristic. Here we are losing the light and graceful lines of the true banjo and a heavier type is developing, which is again reflected in *Plate 51b* which illustrates a true Lyre clock, again anonymous, but having a dial and hands as usually employed by Curtis. Its date is about 1830. It is a weight-driven timepiece with alarm.

The use of a shorter pendulum had permitted a redesigning of the base. Aaron Willard Jr. is generally credited with the original design of the lyre clock.

Our last example of a wall clock is seen in *Plate 51c*, a New Hampshire Mirror clock of about 1820 by Benjamin Morrill of Boscawen, New Hampshire. This design is unique to this state and proved very popular at the time. The brass movement seen in *Plate 51d* differs from others in that the pendulum is placed at the side, earning for this type the name of 'side wheeler'. As will be seen there are going and striking trains. Vermont and Massachusetts makers copied the case style but used banjo-type movement.

We now pass to the last of our three categories, shelf clocks. Mass production was responsible for the wide popularity of American shelf clocks. Shortly after 1800 Eli Terry designed and produced a 30-hour wooden movement using oak plates, laurel wood pillars and black cherrywood gears. Since brass held a premium price and these woods were locally available, it was possible to sell wooden-movement clocks at a much cheaper price. It was not until 1839 that brass became available at a low price. After that date the low-priced brass-movement clock became a reality. The variety of styles produced between 1810 and 1910 is almost without limit, seven of these are reproduced here.

Plate 52a illustrates a Massachusetts shelf clock by David Wood of Newburyport, Mass. *c.* 1800, an eight-day timepiece in a nicely inlaid mahogany case, possibly by Pillsbury, who made many cases for Wood. The design here, in the upper portion, follows the English broken-arch type, very popular in England in the latter half of the eighteenth century. Clocks of this type invariably had fine cases, well proportioned, some with kidney dials, others with glass panels or tablets for the door and lower case. Glass-panelled cases often used deeply dished dials. The Willards made many fine case-on-case and shelf clocks.

In *Plate 52b* we see a very rare Willard clock, known as a lighthouse clock. It was made about 1822 by Simon Willard at Roxbury, Massachusetts, but the style did not prove popular and very few were made. Aesthetically one does not wonder at this; nevertheless today, since it is a Willard production and so few are available, they are much sought after. The movement is eight-day, brass, some having strike and alarm.

In *Plates 52c* and *52d* we have two Terry Shelf clocks, that in *Plate 52c* being the pillar and scroll type while *Plate 52d* is the experimental box cased model. Terry was working at Plymouth, Connecticut at this time, about 1816. This pillar and scroll clock was the first of its kind that Terry produced, and was the third model in his series of production. This model has the escapement in front of the dial with the solid plate wooden movement fastened to the dial. The movement is wood throughout with weights compounded and often with drop holes cut in the case bottom to permit operation for a full day. The hands which are very similar in design to those in England at this period were usually of cast pewter with a counterbalance as part of the minute hand.

Plate 52d shows the experimental model having the strap type wooden movement but with brass rack and snail strike control, as a carry over from Terry's tall clock work. The first clocks produced used a nicely engraved label which was changed to a printed label when the outside escapement model was dropped and the design modified to the same style case, but slightly higher, to permit a full thirty hour operation with non-compounded weights of cast iron.

The pendulum bob has been taken off in order not to hide the name paper inside the case. The hour ring of this clock is reverse painted on the glass of the door, which then shuts in front of the hands and movement.

These pillar and scroll shelf clocks are a classic American design and are considered one of the most graceful. Later designs somewhat increased the height of the case and the escapement was moved on to the front plate. Terry's original patents can be seen at The Bristol Clock Museum, Bristol, Conn.

Plate 52a gives a mirror shelf clock by Atkins & Downs for George Mitchell, Bristol, Conn. about 1831. It has an eight-day wooden movement with compounded weights. The case is mahogany veneer on pine with stencilled half columns and top. *Plate 53b* shows a typical clock of this type with the front plate removed revealing the wooden movement with going train, strike and alarm; the double-headed hammer for the latter appearing at the bottom of the illustration where it would fit inside the bell striking it on the inside on both sides, as opposed to the single strike on the outside of the bell for the hour strike. These thirty-hour cheap clocks were sold throughout the world, many being sold in England.

So far we have been dealing exclusively with weight-driven clocks; the production of spring-driven clocks was hampered by the difficulty of getting good homogenous spring steel. To overcome this the ordinary waggon spring was very ingeniously adapted to horology and such a clock is illustrated in *Plate 53c*. It is a waggon-spring clock by Joseph Ives, of Brooklyn, New York about, 1825. As will be seen from *Plate 53d* the movement is brass strapped with an unusual train lay-out, the waggon spring is seen in the base. It has a mahogany Phyfe-type case with a reverse painted glass panel in the door.

The waggon spring was a patent of Joseph Ives; other patents of his were for roller pinions for both wood and metal movements to reduce friction, on the lines of John Harrison's work a century earlier, although it is probable that this was not known to Ives; the printed descriptions of Harrison's work was probably circulated to a scientifically interested few. Ives also made a wall mirror clock with a seconds pendulum with steel and brass movement, roller pinions, square toothed gears. He produced a tin plate movement with squirrel cage escapement for low price production and was responsible for improved methods of brass rolling. Case types were double steeple for thirty-hour and eight-day movements, square and moulded cases for thirty-day shelf clocks and wall clocks housed in octagonal cases. Joseph Ives was a good inventor but a poor man of business; he was associated with many partners through his career.

Plate 54a shows the forerunner of the steeple and beehive designs that became so popular in the mid-nineteenth century. It is a Gothic Ripple shelf clock by Brewster & Ingraham and was designed by Elias Ingraham during a sea voyage in 1845. It has a spring-driven movement with stamped brass plates and wheels, a striking clock with alarm, the setting dial for which can be seen in the centre around the hand arbor. The ripple trim found a certain amount of acceptance about this period. The E. Ingraham Co. is the only American clock company still under family management, being one of the largest producers.

Plate 54b illustrated a sidearm acorn shelf clock by Forestville

Mfg. Co. Bristol, Conn. about 1845, J. C. Brown, owner. Mr. Brown's name always appears on the labels of his clocks together with the firm's name. He designed several unique cases, one of which is shown; the style was never copied. The clock illustrated has an eight-day movement, brass, with spring drive and fusees in the lower part of the case with gut connexions with the winding arbors. The glass panel shows the J. C. Brown residence.

Whilst in the early years of American Clockmaking ideas and designs were copied largely from England, the finishing note of this chapter will be an example where the American Horologist led the world. *Plates 54c* and *d* show a year torsion pendulum clock made and patented by Aaron D. Crane about 1830. Crane's first patent for torsion pendulum clocks was taken out in 1829, just about a century before their appearance in the European market. Crane made 8-day, 30-hour weight driven torsion pendulum clocks and also 400-day spring-fusee clocks. The one illustrated is marked to go for 376 days. The pendulum comprises six weights and revolves about three and a half complete turns in each direction about a stationary figure. Crane clocks are usually in Empire style cases, as in the example illustrated.

The astronomical dial is seen in *Plate 54d*. The calendar dial will revolve once a year and the day and month will be read off the stationary hand. The sun will make one revolution in a mean day and the moon one revolution in the period between two successive southings, i.e. its passing of the meridian, its globe making one complete turn in a lunation. The position of the sun at midday will show its place in the ecliptic and its 'aspect' or angular position in relation to the moon. The hand before the globe will revolve once with the moon hand and will show the state of the tide in 1/6ths at any time. Since there are no age of the moon indications, the clock will have to be set to the time of high or low tide at new or full moon for the port selected and the moon's globe adjusted accordingly. The clock will then register for the selected port. The sliding shutters, which are wrongly adjusted (their tops should be horizontal), show the proportion of the twenty-four hours in daylight and darkness, as judged by the eye. Had the hours been marked on the outer bezel, the times of sunrise and sunset would be indicated. The bottom part of the dial, the plate on which the word 'Astronomical' is engraved, marks those hours of the twenty-four which are dark at all times of the year in the latitude of the locality selected.

There is romance in the history of clock and watch-making in America – the struggle for existence – the success of an idea – the lasting effect on the economy of a country. Craftsmen from abroad became part of a new country, sharing their knowledge and training younger men, thus founding an industry that prospered.

Industry moves ahead constantly. Research on time measurement has made possible the atomic clock such as the ammonia, cesium and maser types with an accuracy of one part in ten billions. Co-operation among scientists, governments and industries makes such accuracy available. The future holds as great a romance as does our past.

Special thanks to those through whom these photographs were made available and whose names appear in the List of Acknowledgments. Also to be thanked are Cartwright F. Lane, Charles Parsons, Edwin Burt, Willard Porter and many other members of The National Association of Watch and Clock Collectors Inc. whose co-operation was given.

For the convenience of those interested in obtaining more and specific information on American clocks and their makers, a Bibliography on the subject is appended.

Bibliography

ALBRECHT, Rudolf   Die Raeder-Uhr, Rothenburg, 1906

BAILLIE, G. H.   Watchmakers and Clockmakers of the World.
                         London, 1947
                         Clocks and Watches, An Historical Biblio-
                         graphy. London, 1951

BASSERMANN-JORDAN,
Ernst von   Die Geschichte der Raederuhr. Frankfurt,
                         1906

BRITTEN, F. J.   Old Clocks and Watches and their Makers.
                         7th Ed. London, 1956

BEESON, Dr. C. F. C.   Clockmaking in Oxfordshire. Antiquarian
                         Horological Society, 1962

CESCINSKY, Herbert   Old English Master Clockmakers. London,
                         1938
CESCINSKY, H. and
WEBSTER, M.   English Domestic Clocks. London, 1913

CHAPUIS, Alfred   L'Horlogerie, Une Tradition Helvétique.
                         Neuchâtel, 1948

CHAPUIS, A. and DROZ,
Ed.   Les Automates. Neuchâtel, 1949

DEFOSSEZ, Leo   Les Savants du 17ème siècle et la Mesure du
                         Temps. Lausanne, 1946

EDWARDES, Ernest L.   The Grandfather Clock, 2nd Ed. Altrin-
                         cham, 1952

GORDON, G. F. C.   Clockmaking Past and Present. (Revised
                         A. V. May). London, 1949

GREEN, F. H.   Old English Clocks. London, 1931

LLOYD, H. Alan   Chats on Old Clocks. London, 1951
                         Some Outstanding Clocks over 700 Years:
                         1250–1950. London, 1958

ROBERTSON, J.
Drummond   The Evolution of Clockwork. London, 1931

SYMONDS, R. W.   A Book of English Clocks. (Penguin.)
                         London, 1951
                         Thomas Tompion: His Life and Work.
                         London, 1951

TARDY   La Pendule française. Paris, 1948–50

ULLYETT, Kenneth   In Quest of Clocks. London, 1950

WARD, Dr. F. A. B.   *Time Measurement*, Pt. I Science Museum,
                      London, 1961; Pt. II, 1966
WENHAM, E.   *Old Clocks for Modern Use.* London, 1951

American Bibliography

ARTHUR, James   *Time and Its Measurement*, 1909
BARNUM, P. T.   *Struggles and Triumphs*, 1872
BARR, Lockwood   *Eli Terry Pillar and Scroll Shelf Clocks*, 1952
BENSON, James W   *Time and Time Tellers*, 1902
BOOTH, M. L.   *New and Complete Clock and Watchmakers Manual*, 1860
BREARLEY, Harry C.   *Time Telling Through the Ages*, 1919
CHAMBERLAIN, Paul M.   *It's About Time*, 1941
CHANDLEE, Edward E.   *Six Quaker Clockmakers*, 1943
DREPPERD, Carl W.   *American Clocks and Clock Makers*, 1947
ECKHARDT, George H.   *Clocks of Pennsylvania and Their Makers*, 1954
HERING, D. W.   *The Lure Of The Clock*, 1932
HOOPES, Penrose R.   *Connecticut Clockmakers of the 18th Century*, 1930
JAMES, Arthur E.   *Chester County Clocks and Their Makers*, 1947
JEROME, Chauncey   *History of the American Clock Business for the Past Sixty Years*, 1860
JONES, Leslie Allen   *Eli Terry, Clockmaker of Connecticut*, 1942
LYONS, Harold   *Atomic Clocks, Scientific American*, Feb. 1957
MILHAM, Willis I.   *Time and Timekeepers*, 1923
MILLER, Edgar G., Jr. *American Antique Furniture*, Vol. 2, 1937
MOORE, N. Hudson   *The Old Clock Book*, 1911
MUSSEY, Barrows   *Young Father Time*, 1950
NEW YORK UNIVERSITY   *Time and Its Mysteries*
NUTTING, Wallace   *The Clock Book*, 1924
NUTTING, Wallace   *Furniture Treasury*, Vol. 3, 1933
PALMER, Brooks   *The Book of American Clocks*, 1950
                       The Romance of Time, 1954
WILLARD, John Ware   *A History of Simon Willard, Inventor and Clockmaker*, 1911

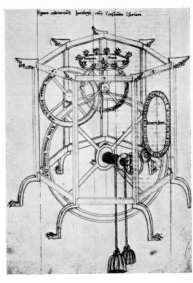

Plate 1

A. ANONYMOUS. Drum clock with fusee, bearing date 1504

B. MOVEMENT OF 2A showing very early type of fusee

Plate 2

D. MOVEMENT OF 2C
Note very large and light balance

C. DRUM CLOCK WITH TRAVELLING CASE, *c.* 1550

A. FRENCH ASTRO-
LOGICAL CLOCK
DATED 1560,
MADE FOR THE
LATITUDE OF
LONDON

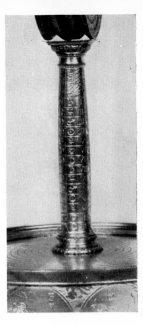

B. PILLAR WITH ENGRAVING
COLLATING A PLANET
WITH EACH OF THE
TWELVE HOURS OF DAY
AND NIGHT

Plate 3

C. FRONT DIAL
The black central tidal dial was added
by the astronomer, James Ferguson, to
whom the clock once belonged, in the
eighteenth century

D. BACK DIAL WITH ALIDADE FOR
SIGHTING THE SUN

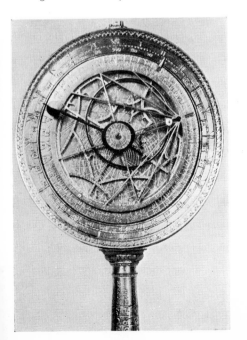

A. INCLINED PLANE CLOCK BY ISAAC HABRECHT OF STRASBURG, *c.* 1600. $3\frac{1}{2}''$ dia.

B. FLAGELLATION CLOCK, *c.* 161(

Plate 4

C. FRANSISCO SCHWARTZ, BRUSSELS. Small clock with cross-beat escapement, *c.* 1630. An early example of a minute hand. *Ht.* $6\frac{1}{4}''$

D. BACK VIEW OF 4C. Showing aperture for calibration marks for the setting up of the mainspring to effect regulation

A. ROLLING BALL CLOCK BY CHRISTOLPH
ROHN, *c.* 1601. Period of ball, 1 minute
including return

B. MECHANISM OF THE BALL CLOCK. Note
the second cup (in the top shadow)
ready to descend. The long chain
drives the carousel

Plate 5

(See also *Plate 6* for details)

A. DETAILS OF THE TRIGGER RELEASE OF THE BALL FOR ITS UPWARD PASSAGE IN THE TUBE

B. THE CAROUSEL WHICH FUNCTIONS ONCE EVERY THREE HOURS

Plate 6

C. THE GOING AND STRIKING TRAINS

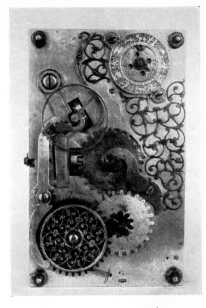

A. BOOK CLOCK BY HANS KIENING OF FUESSEN. With regulation by pallet impact angle, *c.* 1595

B. BOTTOM PLATE OF KIENING'S CLOCK (See also Fig. 9, page 53)

Plate 7

C. MOVEMENT OF KIENING'S CLOCK

D. ANOTHER VIEW OF THE MOVEMENT

A. CLOCK WITH GLOBE ATTACHED BY
NICHOLAS VALLIN, *c.* 1600
Was this an early attempt to 'find
the longitude'?

B. MOVEMENT OF VALLIN'S CLOCK
Note the pinion on top for driving the
globe

Plate 8

C. BOTTOM PLATE WITH VALLIN'S SIGNA-
TURE CLEARLY VISIBLE

D. INSIDE OF THE BOTTOM COVER OF VAL-
LIN'S CLOCK. Showing the record of
its various owners

A. TRANSITIONAL BALANCE-
WHEEL LANTERN CLOCK
Anonymous, 30-hour move-
ment, *c.* 1600–1610. Note decorated wrought-iron pillars

B. SILVER SHIP'S LANTERN
Late sixteenth century

C. LANTERN CLOCK
By Wm. Selwood, London,
12-hour movement, *c.* 1620.
Ht. 1′ 4″. *Dial* 6¼″

Plate 9

D. GEORGE GRAHAM. Travelling lantern alarm
clock with strong oak case, *c.* 1714

A. PENDULUM CLOCK BY CAMERINI
   DATED 1656
   (*Crown copyright*)

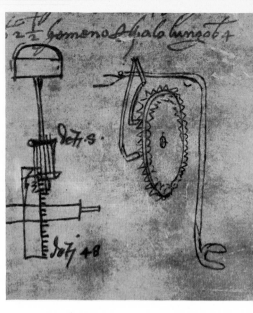

B. A SKETCH SHOWING THE PRINCIPLE OF THE
   ANCHOR ESCAPEMENT FROM AN ITALIAN MANU
   SCRIPT OF ABOUT 1524

Plate 10

C. PENDULUM DESIGN FROM
   Questo Benedetto Pendulo
   Early seventeenth century

D. SKETCH OF PENDULUM WITH IN-
   VERTED CROWN WHEEL
   Early seventeenth century. Com
   pare with B

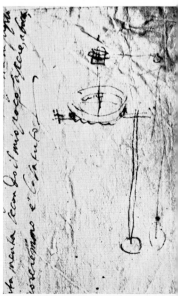

B. **WING LANTERN CLOCK**
By Thos. Wheeler, Neare ye French
Church, 30-hour movement, *c.* 1675–
80. *Ht.* 1′ 4″. *Dial* 6¼″. *Width over
wings* 12″

Plate 11

D. **GERMAN TABLE CLOCK**
By Christian Caroli, Koenigsberg, 30-hour movement, *c.*
1675. *Dial* 4½″ square. *Ht.* 3¼″

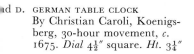

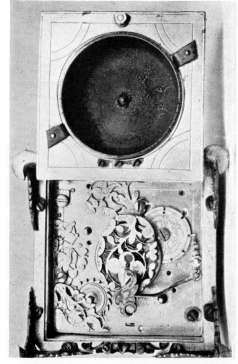

A. HANS BUSCHMANN
Year spring driven clock, *c.*
1651–52. *Ht.* 1′ 11″

B. BACK VIEW OF BUSCHMANN'S
CLOCK WITH DAY OF WEEK
AND YEAR DIALS

Plate 12

C. MAINSPRING DRIVE IN THE BASE
WITH RACK FOR THE REMON-
TOIRE WINDING OF THE SUB-
SIDIARY SPRING

D. MOVEMENT OF BUSCHMANN'S YEAR
CLOCK

A. J. G. MAYER, MUNICH
Complicated clock, *c.* 1660.
Shows two of the dials

B. THE OTHER TWO DIALS OF
MAYER'S CLOCK

Plate 13

C. BACK PLATE OF MAYER'S CLOCK

D. PART OF THE MOVEMENT OF MAYER'S
CLOCK

A. IRON CASED CLOCK OF LANTERN
STYLE, *c.* 1560. German

B. J-B. ALBERTI
Italian lantern style clock. 1685

Plate 14

C. EARLY DUTCH PENDULUM CLOCK
By J. Bernard van Stryp, Antwerp, *c.* 1660.
Dial 6½″ *by* 8¼″

D. MOVEMENT OF VAN STRYP CLOCK
Showing cycloidal cheeks

A.   EARLY WOODEN-CASED PEDIMENT CLOCK
By Edward East, London, 7-day movement, *c.* 1660. *Ht.* 1′ 5″. (See also *Plate
42C*)

B.   PEDIMENT CLOCK
By Edward East, London, 8-day movement, *c.* 1670

Plate 15

C.   EDWARD EAST
Early cased clock, 7-day movement,
c. 1665

D.   JOBST BURGI
Continental anticipation of the
'Architectural' type of case, *c.* 1610

A. PEDIMENT CLOCK
  By John Hilderson, London, 8-day
  movement, *c.* 1665. *Ht.* 1′ 6″

B. MOVEMENT OF HILDERSON CLOCK
  Showing unique striking arrangement. (See also *Plates 37c* and *4*

Plate 16

C. CLOCK. By Wm. Knottesford, London. 8-day
  movement, *c.* 1685

D. BACK VIEW OF KNOTTESFORD CLOC
  Note the drawer for the key

A. WOODEN BASKET CLOCK
   By Joseph Knibb, London, 8-day, quarter-
   striking and repeating movement, c. 1685.
   Ht. 1′ 2″

B. WOODEN BASKET CLOCK
   By Thomas Tompion (No. 15),
   8-day, repeating and alarm
   movement, c. 1685

Plate 17

C. BASKET CLOCK. By Joseph Windmills,
   London, silver mounts, hall marked for
   1698, 8-day movement

D. DOUBLE BASKET CLOCK
   By John Shaw, Holborne, 8-day movement, c. 1695

A. WOODEN BASKET CLOCK
   By Samuel Watson, London, 8-day
   repeating movement, *c.* 1690. (See
   also *Plate 43C*)

B. WOODEN BASKET CLOCK
   By Joseph Knibb, with early attempt at
   Grande Sonnerie striking, 8-day movement,
   c. 1685. *Ht.* 1′ 2″. (See also *Plate 43A*)

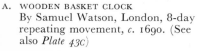

Plate 18

D. WOODEN BASKET CLOCK
   By Daniel Quare, London, made for
   use at sea, 8-day movement, *c.* 1695.
   Ht. incl. hook 1′ 2″. (See also *Plate 43D*

C. WOODEN BASKET CLOCK
   By Joseph Knibb, London, with Roman
   strike, 8-day movement, *c.* 1695. *Ht.* 1′ 2″

A. PETER GARRON
   Three train grande sonnerie clock in tortoiseshell veneered case, *c.* 1705

B. WOODEN BASKET CLOCK
   By Thos. Tompion, London, No. 312, 8-day quarter repeater, *c.* 1705. *Ht.* 1′ 2″

Plate 19

C. INVERTED BELL CLOCK
   By George Graham, London. With original bracket 8-day movement, *c.* 1715. The bracket has a drawer for the key

D. JOSEPH ANTRAM
   Three train clock. Antram was clock maker to George I. This clock belonged to his disowned wife, the Countess of Ahlden, *c.* 1715

A. LANTERN CLOCK
   MOVEMENT. By
   Edward East,
   London, dated
   1664, 30-hour
   movement. En-
   cased about
   1685. (See also
   Plate 37D)

B. HANGING CLOCK
   By Edward East, London, 8-day
   movement, *c.* 1670. *Ht.* 1′ 9″

C. EXAMPLE OF A FINE
   CLOCK SPOILT BY 'MOD-
   ERNISATION' IN PAST
   CENTURIES

Plate 20

A. WILLIAM CLEMENT'S TURRET CLOCK
WITH THE EARLIEST KNOWN ANCHOR
ESCAPEMENT. Made for King's College, Cambridge, dated 1671. From
an exhibit in the Science Museum,
South Kensington. (*Crown Copyright*)

B. BACK VIEW OF WILLIAM CLEMENT'S
TURRET CLOCK. (*Crown Copyright*)

Plate 21

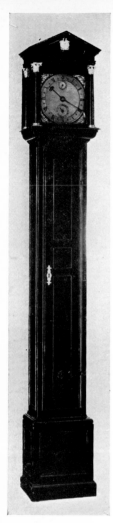

A. AHASUERUS
FROMANTEEL,
LONDON
8-day move-
ment, c. 1680.
Ht. 6′. Dial
8½″. (See also
Plate 37B)

B. JOHANNES
FROMANTEEL,
LONDON
8-day move-
ment, c. 1675.
Ht. 6′. Dial
8½″

C. EDWARD EAST,
LONDON
8-day move-
ment, c. 1685.
Ht. 6′. Dial
10″. (See also
Plate 38A)

D. JOSEPH WINDMILLS,
LONDON
8-day movement, c.
1690. Ht. 6′ 6″.
Dial 10½″

Plate 22

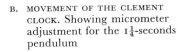

A. WM. CLEMENT, LONDON
c. 1685. *Ht.* 7′ 3″. *Dial*
10″. (See also *Plate*
38D)

C. JOHN CLOWES, LONDON
8-day movement, 1¼-
seconds pendulum, *c.*
1685. *Ht.* 7′ 4″. *Dial* 10″

B. MOVEMENT OF THE CLEMENT
CLOCK. Showing micrometer
adjustment for the 1¼-seconds
pendulum

Plate 23

A. CHRISTOPHER
   GOULD, LONDON.
   8-day movement,
   c. 1690. *Ht. 8′ 4″.*
   Dial 12″

B. WM. OSBORNE,
   LONDON. 8-day
   movement, *c.* 1705.
   Ht. 7′ 3″. Dial 12″.
   (See also *Plate 39A*)

C. JAS. DRURY,
   LONDON. 30-
   hour move-
   ment, *c.* 1710.
   Ht. 6′. *Dial* 5″

D. GEORGE GRAHAM.
   8-day long case
   clock,
   No. 681, *c.* 1728.
   Ht. 8′. *Dial* 12″

Plate 24

A. THOMAS TOMPION, LONDON. Year equation movement, *c.* 1695. *Ht.* 8′. *Dial* 12″. (See also *Plate 38C*)

B. RICHARD STREET, LONDON. 1-month movement, 1708. *Ht.* 10′. *Dial* 1′ 6″ by 2′ 6″. (See also *Plate 39B*)

C. MOVEMENT OF TOMPION'S YEAR CLOCK Fixed dial plate removed to show the engaging of the rocker arm rack with the wheel actuating the moving minute ring. (See also *Plate 38C*)

D. SHOWING EQUATION KIDNEY AND ROCKER ARM, *c.* 1695 (A, C & D are *by gracious permission of Her Majesty The Queen*)

Plate 25

A. DANIEL QUARE, LONDON. 3-month movement, *c.* 1695. *Ht.* 7' 6". *Dial* 11"

B. GEORGE GRAHAM, LONDON. Month movement, *c.* 1720. *Ht.* 8' 3". *Dial* 12". (See also *Plate 39D*)

C. GEORGE GRAHAM, LONDON. Month equa movement with early mercury pendulu *c.* 1730. *Ht.* 7' 6". *Dial* 12"

D. ANTHONY HERBERT, LONDON. Vauxhall plate-glass door, 8-day movement, *c.* 1 *Ht.* 7'. *Dial* 12"

Plate 26

A. TRUE BELL CLOCK. George
Hodgson, London, 8-day movement, *c.* 1760. *Ht.* 1′ 6″

B. TRUE BELL CLOCK. Benjamin
Stennet, London. Half seconds,
dead-beat escapement, 8-day
movement, *c.* 1810. *Ht.* 1′ 9″

Plate 27

C. TRUE BELL CLOCK. G. M. Metcalfe, Londres, 8-day movement, *c.* 1785. *Ht.* 1′ 8″

D. ELIAS KREITMEYER, FRIEDBERG
Continental anticipation of the true
bell case, *c.* 1710

A. BALLOON CLOCK. Anonymous. Recoil escapement, 8-day movement. Dated 1796

B. BALLOON CLOCK. Thomas Brass, Guildford, 8-day movement, pull repeater, *c.* 1780. *Ht.* 1′ 7½″

Plate 28

C. INVERTED BELL CLOCK. Justin Vulliamy, London. Enamelled dial, 8-day movement, pull repeater, *c.* 1775. (See also *Plate 44C*)

D. DEEP BROKEN ARCH CLOCK. In Vernis Martin, Henry Fish, London, 8-day movement, pull repeater, *c.* 1765. *Ht.* 1′ 3″

A. SHALLOW BROKEN ARCH CLOCK
James Thwaites, London, recoil
escapement, 8-day movement,
enamelled dial, *c.* 1795. *Ht.*
1′ 4″

B. PLAIN ARCH CLOCK
Edward Baker, London, recoil
escapement, 8-day movement,
painted dial, *c.* 1815. *Ht.* 1′ 5″

Plate 29

C. CHAMFER TOP CLOCK
Anonymous, painted dial, recoil escapement, *c.* 1820. *Ht.*
1′ 8″. (See also *Plate 44D*)

D. LANCET CLOCK
Hawkins, Southampton, recoil
escapement, 8-day movement,
painted dial, *c.* 1810. *Ht.* 1′ 7″

A. ANONYMOUS. 8-day musical clock with unfolding lotus buds and waterfall, 3rd quarter eighteenth century. *Ht. 2′ 8″*

B. ANONYMOUS. 8-day clock with sunflower dial and cascading waterfalls. Musical train in case on which clock is standing, 3rd quarter eighteenth century

Plate 30

C. ANONYMOUS. 8-day musical clock with automata, waterfalls and procession, 3rd quarter eighteenth century

D. ANONYMOUS. 8-day enamelled musical clock with automata, 3rd quarter eighteenth century

ASTRONOMICAL CLOCK. Thomas Budgen, Croydon, 8-day movement, c. 1740. (See also *Plate 40D*)

CHARLES COULON, LONDON. 8-day movement, c.
1745. *Ht. 7′. Dial 12″*

C. THE AUTHOR'S LARGEST AND SMAL-
LEST LONG CASE CLOCKS. Graham's
Successors Colley & Preist, London. Month movement, c. 1755.
Ht. 8′ 6″. Dial 12″. (See also *Plate
38B.*) Sanders, Brinkworth, dated
15.6.1817, 30-hour movement. *Ht.
2′ 11″. Dial 5″*

Plate 31

A. ASTRONOMICAL CLOCK. George Margetts, London, month movement, *c.* 1780. *Ht.* 9′. *Dial* 14″

B. MUSICAL CLOCK. Benson, Whitehaven, 8-day movement, *c.* 1775. *Ht.* 8′ 6″. *Dial* 12″. (See also *Plate 41B*)

C. THOMAS BROWN, BIRMINGHAM. 8-day movement, *c.* 1785. *Ht.* 7′. *Dial* 12″

D. PHILIP LLOYD, BRISTOL. Tidal dial, 8-day movement, *c.* 1780. *Ht.* 8′ 2″. *Dial* 12″

Plate 32

RIGBY, LIVERPOOL. Tidal dial, 8-day movement, c. 1785

THOMAS BRUTON, BRISTOL. Tidal dial, 8-day movement, c. 1795. *Ht. 8'. Dial 12"*

C. FINNEY, LIVERPOOL. Year clock, 1769. *Ht. abt. 6' 6".* (See also *Plate 41A*)

D. ANONYMOUS. 8-day movement, c. 1800. *Ht. 6' 6". Dial 11"*

Plate 33

A. JOSIAH EMERY, LONDON. 8-day movement, *c.* 1795. *Ht.* 6′ 10″. *Dial* 12″

B. ROSS AND PECKHAM, LONDON. 8-day
   movement, *c.* 1800. *Ht.* 6′ 6″. *Dial* 12″

C. ANONYMOUS, PROVINCIAL. 8-day movement, *c.* 1800. *Ht.* 8′ 6″. *Dial* 1′ 2″

D. ANONYMOUS, OTLEY, YORKS. 8-day
   movement, *c.* 1810. *Ht.* 8′ 3″. *Dial* 1′ 2″

Plate 34

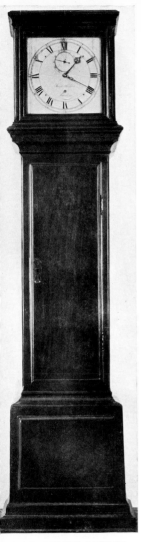

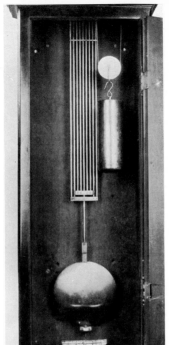

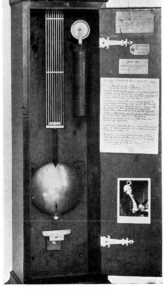

JOHN SHELTON, LONDON
Month movement, 1760.
Ht. 5′ 7″. Dial 12″

GRIDIRON PENDULUM OF
SHELTON'S CLOCK. Show-
ing the holes in the back-
board round the bob used
when clamping the bob
for travelling

D. GRIDIRON PENDULUM OR ARN-
OLD'S CLOCK. In this case the
holes in the back-board are
merely for fastening to the
wall, when the clock is in
position

C. JOHN ARNOLD
Regulator No. 1, month
movement, 1774

Plate 35

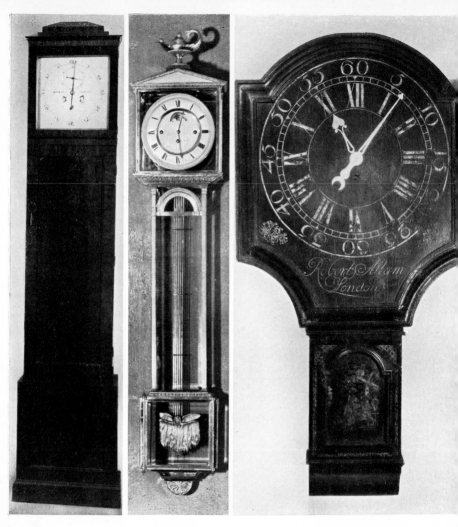

A. BARWISE, LONDON. Regulator, 8-day movement, *c.* 1820. *Ht.* 6' 3". *Dial* 12"

B. GLUECKSSTEIN. Vienna Regulator, 8-day, 3 train with lunar dial in fire-gilt bronze case, *c.* 1830

C. ROBERT ALLAM, LONDON. 'Act of Parliament' Clock, 8-day movement, *c.* 1760. *Ht.* 5'. *Dial* 2' 6"

Plate 36

AHASUERUS FROMANTEEL, LONDON
c. 1660. *Dial* 8¼"

B. EARLY EQUATION DIAL FOR ADJUSTMENT BY
HAND. *c.* 1680. *Dial* 8½". (See also *Plate 22A*)

Plate 37

JOHN HILDERSON, LONDON
c. 1665. (See also *Plates 16A* and *42D*)

D. EDWARD EAST, LONDON, 1664. The minute hand, added later, has to be set independently of the hour hand and is not
correctly set here. (See also *Plate 20A*)

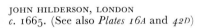

A. EDWARD EAST, LONDON
   c. 1680. *Dial* 10″. (See also *Plate 22C*)

B. GRAHAM'S SUCCESSORS,
   Colley & Preist, London, *c.* 1755.
   Dial 12″ (See also *Plate 31C*)

Plate 38

C. THOMAS TOMPION, LONDON
   c. 1695. *Dial* 12″. (See also *Plates*
   25A, *C*, and *D.*, (*By gracious permission*
   of Her Majesty The Queen)

D. WILLIAM CLEMENT, LONDON
   c. 1685. *Dial* 10″. (See also *Plate 23A*)

A. WM. OSBORNE, LONDON
   c. 1705. *Dial* 12″. (See also *Plate 24B*)

B. RICHARD STREET, LONDON, 1708
   Dial 1′ 6″ by 2′ 6″. (See also *Plate 25B*)

C. DANIEL QUARE, LONDON
   Year movement, c. 1710. *Dial* 14″ by 17″

Plate 39

D. GEORGE GRAHAM, LONDON
   c. 1720. *Dial* 12″. (See also *Plate 26B*)

A. (Front view) QUARE EQUATION MOVEMENT
SEPARATE FROM THE CLOCK MOVEMENT
c. 1710. (See also *Plate 39C*)

B. Back View of A

C. WILLIAM TOMLINSON, LONDON
Universal Tidal Dial, *c.* 1735. *Dial* 12″

D. THOMAS BUDGEN, CROYDON
c. 1740. (See also *Plate 31A*)

Plate 40

DIAL OF FINNEY YEAR CLOCK
(See also *Plate 33C*)

B. JOHN BENSON, WHITEHAVEN
Dial 12″, c. 1775. (See also *Plate 32B*)

Plate 41

C. HELM, ORMSKIRK
Perpetual calendar movement,
c. 1785

D. DETAILS OF PERPETUAL CALENDAR
Note holes in the brass casting
forming the dial plate

A. THOMAS LISTER, HALIFAX
Musical bracket clock, c. 1805

B. WILLIAM BOTHAMLEY, KIRTON
Unique tidal dial, c. 1785

Plate 42

C. EDWARD EAST, LONDON
c. 1660. (See also *Plate 15A*)

D. JOHN HILDERSON, LONDON
c. 1665. (See also *Plates 16A* and *37C*)

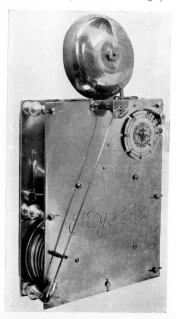

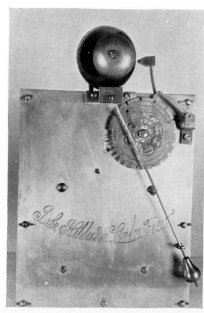

JOSEPH KNIBB, LONDON
Grande Sonnerie movement, c. 1685. (See also *Plate 18B*)

B. HENRY JONES, LONDON
  c. 1680

Plate 43

SAMUEL WATSON, LONDON
c. 1690. Note facetted bob. (See also *Plate 18A*)

D. DANIEL QUARE, LONDON
  c. 1695. (See also *Plate 18D*)

A. CLAUDE DU CHESNE, LONDON
   c. 1715

B. GEORGE GRAHAM, LONDON
   c. 1725

Plate 44

C. JUSTIN VULLIAMY, LONDON
   c. 1775. (See also *Plate 28C*)

D. ANONYMOUS
   c. 1820. (See also *Plate 29D*)

EARLY MONASTIC NIGHT ALARM CLOCK FROM ST. SEBALDIUS CHURCH, NUREMBERG. 16-hour movement, *c.* 1400

B. BEHIND THE DIAL OF 45A
Showing pinion of 3 meshing with wheel of 48

J. P. TREFFLER, NIGHT CLOCK
c. 1675

Plate 45

D. BACK VIEW OF TREFFLER'S CLOCK

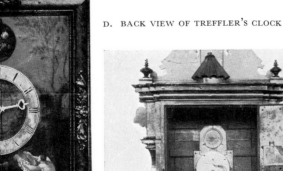

A. DETAIL OF NIGHT DIAL AND BELOW
MOVEMENT PENDULUM IN TREFFLER'S
CLOCK. (See also *Plate 45D*)

Plate 46

B. ANONYMOUS
Italian Day and Night Clock, *c.* 1

C. & D. JOSEPH KNIBB, LONDON
Night Clock, *c.* 1685.
Ht. 1′ 8″

B. DETAILS OF CAMPANI'S SILENT MOVEMENT

P. T. CAMPANI'S SILENT NIGHT
CLOCK, 1683

Plate 47

THREE EARLY NINETEENTH-CENTURY NIGHT CLOCKS

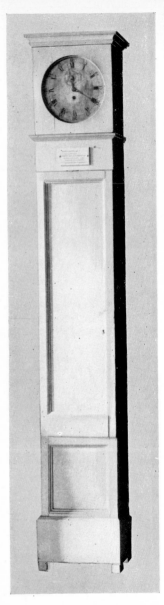

B.   DIAL OF A

A.   DAVID RITTENHOUSE USED
     FOR HIS OBSERVATIONS OF
     THE TRANSIT OF VENUS IN
     1769

Plate 48

A. TALL CLOCK BY
   SIMON WILLARD,
   ROXBURY, MASS.
   c. 1785

B. TALL CLOCK BY R.
   SHEARMAN,
   PHILADELPHIA
   c. 1800

C. CORNER TALL CLOCK
   BY JOHN OSGOOD,
   ANDOVER, MASS.
   c. 1797

D. GRANDMOTHER
   CLOCK BY JOSHUA
   WILDER, HINGHAM,
   MASS., *c.* 1800

Plate 49

P

A. WALL CLOCK BY SIMON
WILLARD GRAFTON, MASS.
c. 1770

B. MOVEMENT OF 50A

Plate 50

C. BANJO CLOCK BY SIMON
WILLARD ROXBURY,
MASS., *c.* 1810

D. MOVEMENT OF 50C

A. ANONYMOUS BANJO
   LYRE CLOCK, *c.* 1825

B. ANONYMOUS LYRE
   CLOCK, *c.* 1830

C. MIRROR WALL CLOCK BY BENJ.
   MORRILL, BOSCAWEN, NEW
   HAMPSHIRE, *c.* 1820

D. MOVEMENT OF 51C
   'A side Wheeler'

Plate 51

A. SHELF CLOCK BY DAVID
   WOOD, NEWBURYPORT,
   MASS., *c.* 1800

B. SIMON WILLARD, ROX-
   BURY, LIGHTHOUSE
   CLOCK, *c.* 1822

Plate 52

C. SHELF CLOCK BY ELI TERRY, PLY-
   MOUTH, CONN., *c.* 1816

D. TERRY SHELF CLOCK. WOODEN STRAP
   TYPE

A. MIRROR SHELF CLOCK BY
    ATKINS AND DOWNS FOR GEO.
    MITCHELL, BRISTOL, CONN.
    c. 1831

B. TYPICAL WOODEN MOVEMENT FOR
    53A

Plate 53

C. WAGON SPRING CLOCK BY
    JOSEPH IVES, BROOKLYN, N.Y.
    c. 1825

D. MOVEMENT OF 53C

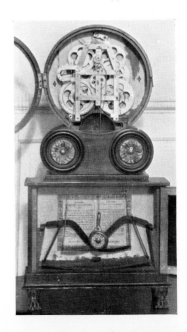

A. SHELF CLOCK BY BREWSTER AND
    INGRAHAM, *c.* 1845

B. SHELF CLOCK BY FORESTVILLE MF
    COY., BRISTOL, CONN., 1845

Plate 54

C. YEAR ASTRONOMICAL TORSION PEN-
    DULUM CLOCK BY AARON D. CRANE
    c. 1830

D. DETAIL OF ASTRONOMICAL DIAL OF
    CRANE CLOCK

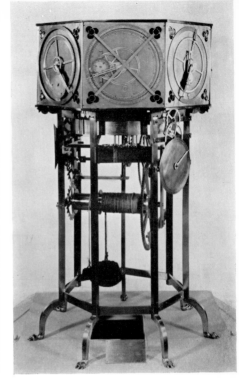

Plate 55

A. THE RECONSTRUCTED CLOCK
   Meantime dial with sunrise and
   sunset wings, dial of Mars *left*, Venus
   right

B. The dial of Mercury with the
   Perpetual Calendar for Easter below,
   dial of Venus *left*, Moon *right*

C. The dial of Jupiter with dials of
   Saturn *left* and Mars *right*

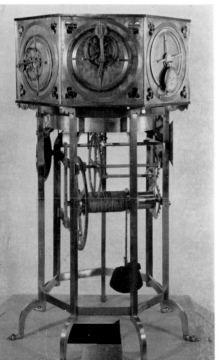

Plate 56

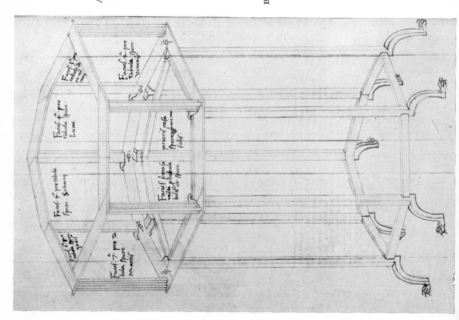

A. DONDI'S SKETCH OF THE
   FRAMEWORK

B. THE RECONSTRUCTION

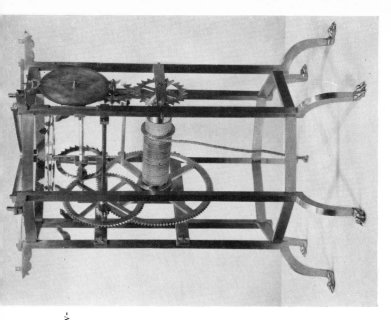

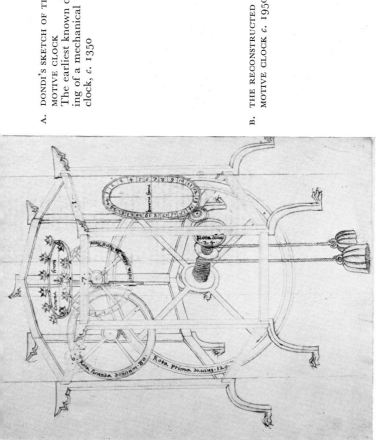

A. DONDI'S SKETCH OF THE
MOTIVE CLOCK
The earliest known draw-
ing of a mechanical
clock, c. 1350

B. THE RECONSTRUCTED
MOTIVE CLOCK c. 1950

Plate 57

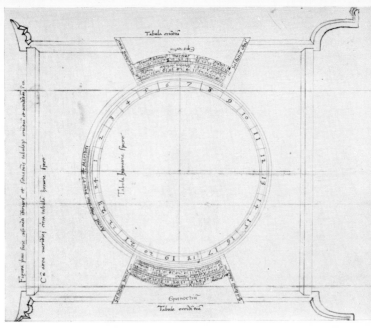

A. THE MEANTIME DIAL
with the wings for the rising and setting of the sun

Plate 58

B. THE RECONSTRUCTED DIAL
showing part of the train for the conversion of mean to sideral time

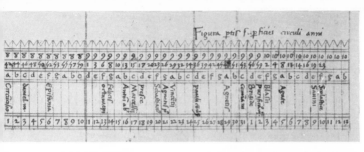

Figura ptis f. p̃ficei circuli anni

Plate 59

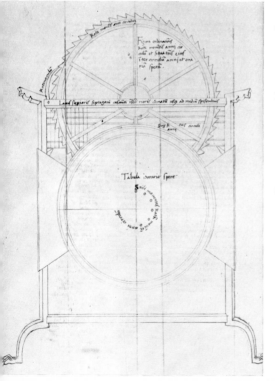

A. DONDI'S
   DETAIL OF
   THE ANNUAL
   CALENDAR
   WHEEL

B. The recon-
   structed wheel
   with one of the
   the racks for
   actuating the
   Calendar on
   the inside

C. The method of
   communicating
   the daily
   motion to the
   Annual
   Calendar
   wheel

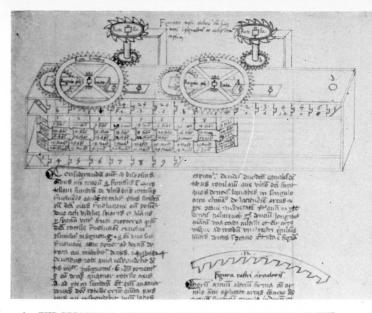

A. THE PERPETUAL CALENDAR FOR THE MOVABLE FEASTS OF THE CHURCH

showing the rack to be fitted inside the annual Calendar wheel

Plate 60

B. THE RECONSTRUCTED PERPETUAL CALENDAR

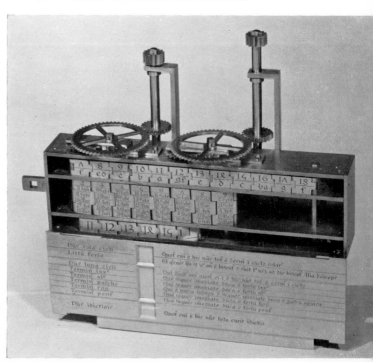

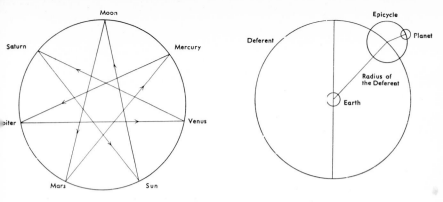

. Diagram showing the derivation of the names of the days of the week
. The first concept of planetary motion

Plate 61

. The second concept of planetary motion
. The third concept of planetary motion

B. THE RECONSTRUCTED DIAL
of the *Primum Mobile*

Plate 62

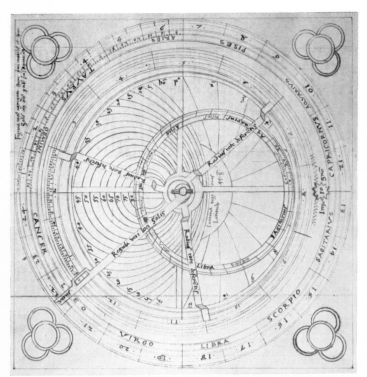

A. THE DIAL OF THE *Primum Mobile*
sideral time

C. THE RECONSTRUCTION

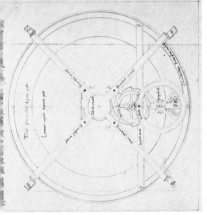

B. DONDI'S METHOD OF TURNING THE RETE
of the *Primum Mobile*

Plate 63

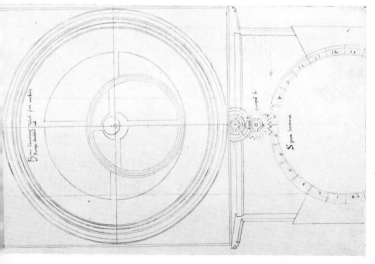

A. DONDI'S METHOD OF CONVERSION
from mean to sideral time (for
reconstruction see *Plate 58B*)

Plate 64

B. THE RECONSTRUCTION

Note the small window in which appears the Saints' day of the year

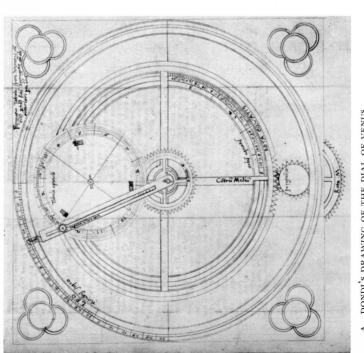

A. DONDI'S DRAWING OF THE DIAL OF VENUS

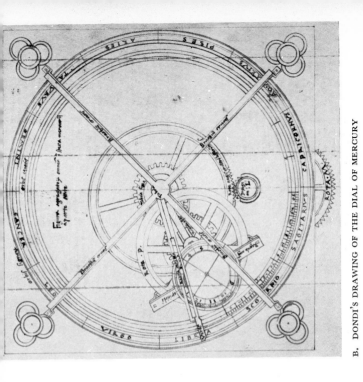

B. DONDI'S DRAWING OF THE DIAL OF MERCURY

Plate 65

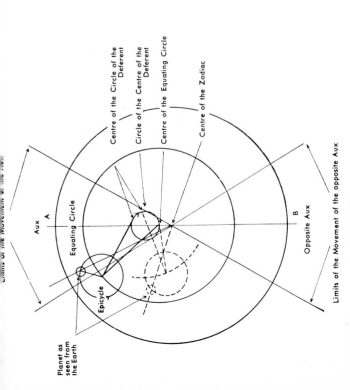

A. THE CONTEMPORARY CONCEPT
of the motions of Mercury

Aux

A

Equating Circle

Planet as
seen from
the Earth

Epicycle

Centre of the Circle of the
Deferent

Circle of the Centre of the
Deferent

Centre of the Equating Circle

Centre of the Zodiac

B

Opposite Aux

Limits of the Movement of the opposite Aux

A. RECONSTRUCTION OF
THE DIAL OF
MERCURY
below, the Perpetual
Calendar for Easter
in position

[The next clock with a
perpetual calendar for
Easter was the third
Strasburg clock by
Schwilqué in 1842]

Plate 66

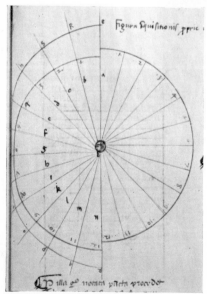

B. DONDI'S DIAGRAM FOR MAKING
THE OVAL WHEELS
to achieve the believed motion
of Mercury

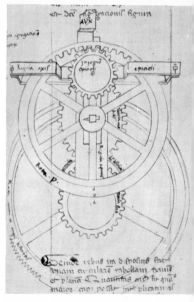

C. UNDER DIAL WORK FOR MERCURY
Note the wheel with internally
cut teeth, this may well be a
first application

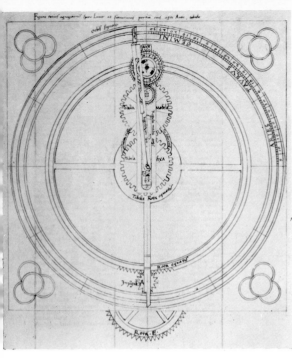

A. DONDI'S DRAWING OF
   THE LUNAR DIAL
   Note the upper oval
   wheel with an unequal
   number of teeth in
   equally sized sectors

Plate 67

B. THE RECONSTRUCTED
   LUNAR DIAL

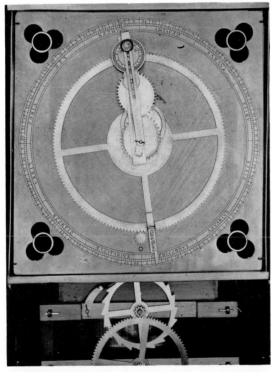

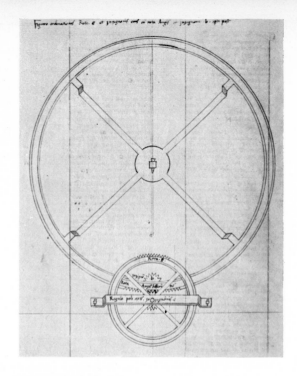

Plate 68

B. DONDI'S SKETCH OF THE DRIVE FOR THE MOON
off the *Primum Mobile*. On a seven-sided frame this
involves a skew gear, again possibly a first appearance

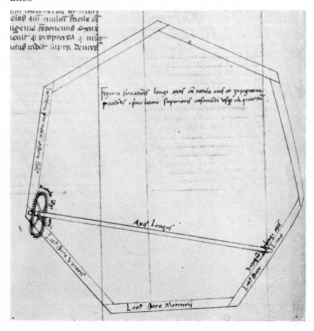

Plate 69

THE RECONSTRUCTION OF THE SKEW GEAR DRIVE
and interior view of the clock, with dials of Jupiter and
Saturn removed

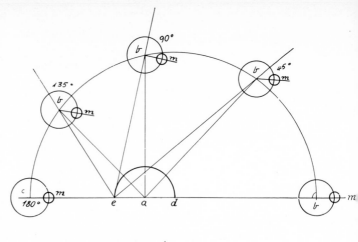

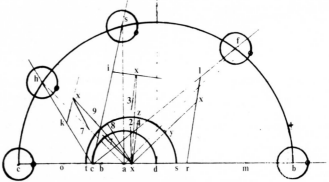

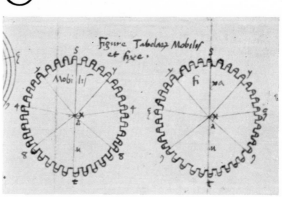

A. DIAGRAM TO SHOW THE MOON'S PROGRESSION
   through equal angles in equal periods of time over unequal arcs

[The next clock to provide for the Moon's eliptical orbit was made by Thomas Mudge nearly 400 years later *c.* 1755–60]

B. DIAGRAM FOR THE OVAL WHEELS
   needed for the lunar dial (*modern lettering added*)

C. THE WHEELS
   resulting from the reconstruction of 70B

Plate 70

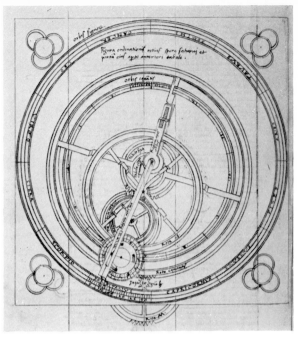

Plate 71

A. DONDI'S DRAWING OF THE DIAL OF SATURN

B. THE RECONSTRUCTED DIAL OF SATURN

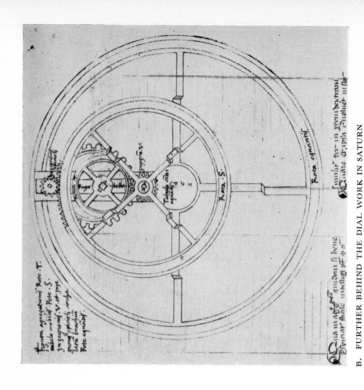

B. FURTHER BEHIND THE DIAL WORK IN SATURN

Plate 72

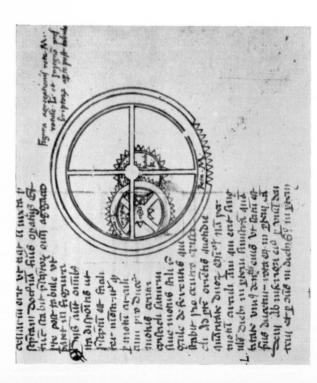

A. BEHIND THE DIAL WORK IN SATURN
to attain the long period of revolution

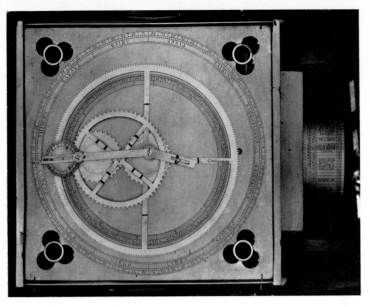

B. THE RECONSTRUCTED DIAL OF JUPITER

Plate 73

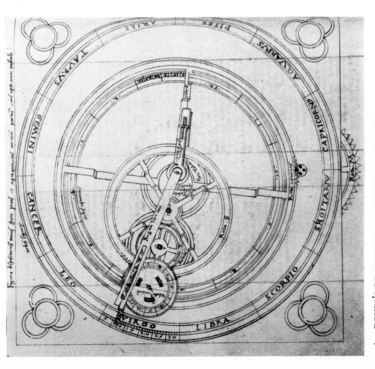

A. DONDI'S DRAWING OF THE DIAL OF JUPITER
This is driven by the only stub pinion in the clock

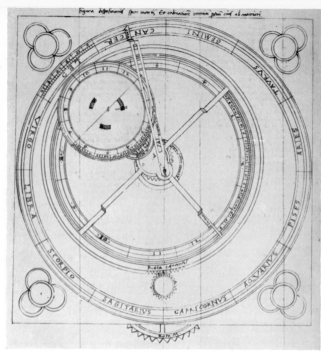

A. DONDI'S DRAWING OF THE DIAL OF MARS

Plate 74

B. THE RECONSTRUCTED DIAL OF MARS

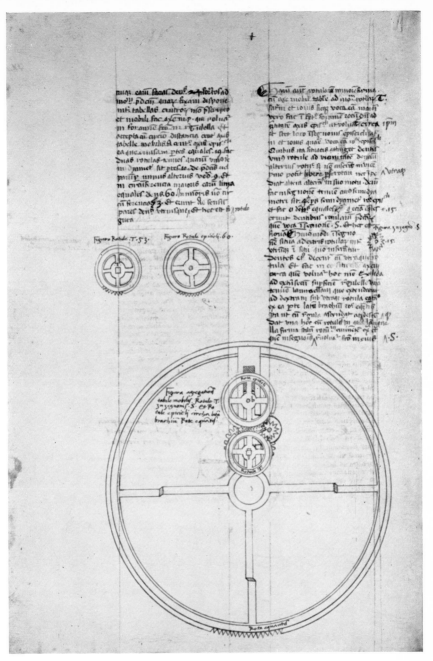

Plate 75

UNDER DIAL WORK FOR MARS
This also serves to show how appearance of the actual MS. taken from the
Bodleian copy (reduced by half)

B. THE RECONSTRUCTED NODAL DIAL
which is driven off the Lunar dial

Plate 76

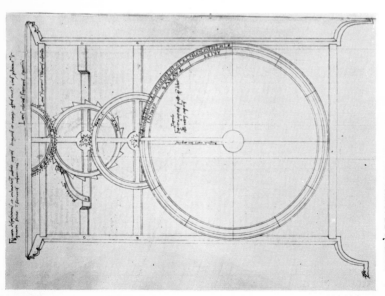

A. DONDI'S DRAWING FOR THE NODES
Period of revolution of the hand approximately
28 years

Plate 77

PROSPECTUS INTRA CAMERAM STELLATAM

The Octagon Room at Greenwich *c.* 1680 in Flamsteed's time, showing the two 'Great Clocks' and a long telescope in use

APPENDIX II

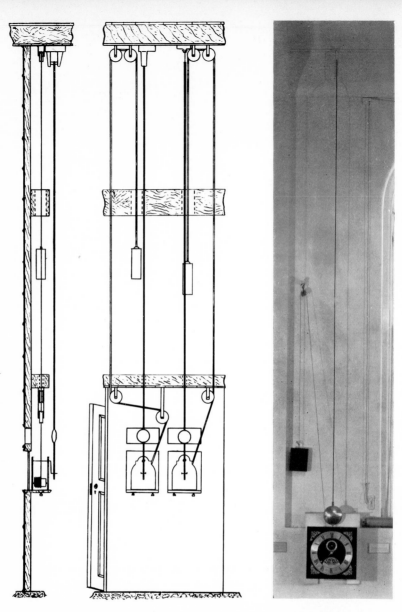

A. Possible lay-out of the two clocks presented by Sir Jonas Moore with their 14ft pendulums suspended above the movements and the pendulum bobs showing through the small windows

B. The reproduction clock with pendulum suspended above, in a temporary position at Greenwich

Plate 78

A. The reproduction of Tompion's original clock now in the British Museum

B. Connection between escapement and pendulum in the reproduction clock

c. One of Tompion's original clocks now in the British Museum

Plate 79

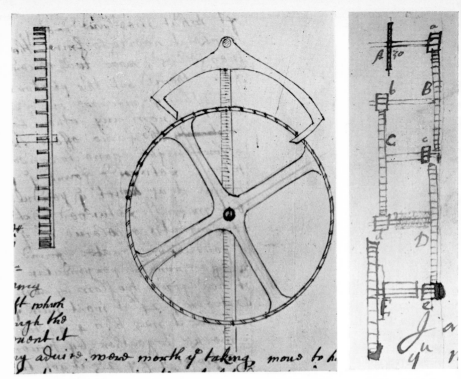

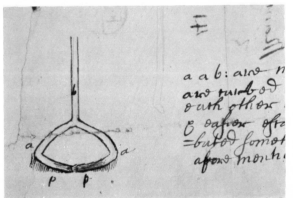

A. Tompion's sketch of his
escapement taken from
a clock in Sir Jonas
Moore's dining-room;
a semi dead-beat.
From Flamsteed's
letter of Dec. 11, 1675
to Richard Towneley

B. Flamsteed's description of the trains of Flamsteed's Greenwich Clocks given to
Towneley in a letter Feb. 15, 1678

C. Tompion's pin pallet escapement described in his letter to Towneley, Feb. 9, 1678

Plate 80

Giovanni de Dondi's Horological Masterpiece 1364

This Appendix is based on a description of the Dondi Clock written
by the Author which appeared in the *Suisse Horlogère* in July 1955.
The line drawings are from the copy of the MS in the Bodleian
Library, Oxford, Laud MS 620.

THE DOCUMENT that we are about to consider is probably the most
important that is ever likely to be found in connexion with the early
history and development of mechanical clocks. It is just about six
hundred years old and details, to the minutest degree, the construction of an astronomical clock, the like of which had probably never
before been attempted, and which was many centuries before its
time. It adds very appreciably to our knowledge of the state of
horological understanding at that time. In the first place it portrays
the earliest construction of a mechanical clock that has come down
to us; for this reason alone it is worthy of record; and indeed has
been so recorded by Drummond Robertson and Baillie.[1]

That this was regarded as an exceptional document is shown by
the fact that the original MS, or the earliest surviving copy, if it be
not the original, that which is preserved in the library of St. Mark's,
Venice, and is ascribed to the fourteenth century, has been copied at
least five times within the next two centuries. There are two copies
in the Ambrosia library, Milan, one in the library in Padua, one in
Eton College library and one in the Bodleian. Thorndike[2] states that
the two copies in Milan belonged to V. Pinelli (1531–1601). One is
in a gothic fourteenth-century hand the other, not so good or nearly
complete, is a fifteenth-century MS. The Eton College copy states
that it was copied from one dated 1397. The Bodleian copy was done
by two people, the text by John of Leyd (?Leyden) and the titling of
the chapters, the diagrams and their explanatory notes by Jacomo

---

[1] *The Evolution of Clockwork*, Robertson, 1931. *Clocks and Watches*, Baillie, 1951.
[2] Lynn Thorndike in *Archeion*, 1936, pp. 308–19. *Isis*, Vol. 10, 1928. *History of
Magic*, Vol. III, p. 740.

Politus, who describes the termination of his labours very exactly as on the 8th day of November 1461 at the 4th hour, which we must remember would be, in Italy, the fourth hour after sunset. Another MS, probably also a copy, is in Cracow University, 577 (DO. III. 28); it is of sixteenth-century date and is entitled 'Johannes de Dondi, Fabrica horarii magistralis'.

The clock itself was the subject of a description by Philip de Mézières in his 'Le Songe du vieux Pèlerin', c. 1389, and also by Giovanni Manzini, Podestà of Pisa, in 1405. These two records show that the clock actually existed, and was not merely a design.

Coming to later years, the Bibliographie Universelle, published in Paris in 1814 (Vol. II), contains a short article on the work of Giovanni de Dondi and his father, Jacopo. In 1896, the Royal Institute of Venice for Science, Letters and Art, published an article by Andreas Gloria, running into 61 pages, on the 'Two marvellous clocks invented by Jacopo and Giovanni Dondi.'[1] The Biographie Universelle says that the son wrote a description of the father's clock, which led to his being identified with the work; but the MS is, in the writer's opinion, certainly the work of the actual maker of the clock.

According to Thorndike, Jacopo, the father, was born in Padua in 1293, and was appointed municipal physician of Chioggia in 1313. He was recalled to Padua in 1342, and made a clock which was placed in the Carrace Tower in 1344. This earned for him the title of 'Dell'Orologio', which his son and later descendants inherited. The son, Giovanni, has usually been credited as being the first recipient of the title. This clock was probably just a simple mechanical clock, which at that time was in itself considered an achievement, especially if it embodied a simple lunar dial. Gloria illustrates the memorial tablet to Jacopo in the Baptistry of the cathedral at Chioggia, in which his achievements are catalogued. This uses the words 'horas inventum', which, he assumes, indicate something more than a simple clock. In any event, we see that the son had some introduction to horology through the efforts of the father, who is also reputed to have computed some astronomical trains.

The inscription, which is in medieval ecclesiastical Latin, has been translated as follows: 'I Jacobus was born in Padua and having crept back to earth whence I came, this confined urn conceals my cold ashes. My work was useful enough to my country and known to many a city. My art was medicine, and to know the sky and the stars, whither I now proceed, released from the prison of my body. And

---

[1] *Atti del Real Istituto Venito di Scienze, Lettere, Arti,* Series 7, Vol. 7, 1896, pp. 675–736.

truly each art remains, adorned with my books. Yet indeed, dear Reader, know it is my invention that, from afar, shows at the top of the lofty tower the time and the changing hours that you count. And pray in silence for my peace and pardon.'[1]

Since a clock striking the hours is mentioned as being in the church of Beata Virgina in Milan in 1335[2] it is more probable that this reference is to a clock dial, the date of the invention of which has never been established.

Sarton[3] states that Giovanni was born in 1318; in 1349 he was appointed personal physician to the Emperor Charles IV (1347–78). In 1350 he was lecturing in astronomy at Padua; in 1367–70 he was lecturing in medicine at Florence, and from 1379–88 he was again connected with the University at Padua. He died at Genoa in 1389.

All these references deal either with the lives of the father and son biographically, or with the MS as a MS; none of them attempts to treat it from the horological point of view. This was first done by the late G. H. Baillie. From the Venice MS he had made a translation, which has generously been put at my disposal by its present owner, Mr. Charles Drover; but although, as is clear from the very able way in which the translation is edited, Baillie evidently studied the whole matter very carefully, he never published any full description, a brief report in the *Horological Journal* for 1934 being his only record. This description has been left, after all these centuries, for the present author to do, working from the translation above referred to for the text and for the illustrations from the Bodleian copy, which are much clearer, and better for reproduction. The two correspond very well, both contain the same number of chapters, but their headings do not always occur in the same places.

The drawings and diagrams are faithfully reproduced, even to errors noted by Baillie.

In the present description an attempt will be made to record all the various dials in order that a due appreciation may be shown of the immensity of the genius of this fourteenth-century savant, and the extremely complicated trains he devised in order to portray accurately, not only the exact motions of the then-known planets, but also for the layman and cleric, all the feasts of the Church, both fixed and movable. Nothing comparable in complexity is known to the writer until we come to the mid-sixteenth century, when a somewhat similar clock was made by Baldewin, in Kassel, from thence to Samuel Watson's clock of 1690. In 1769, David A. Cajetano of

---

[1] *Mechanical Universe*, Bedini and Maddison. Am. Philosophical Soc. Phila., Oct. 1966, p. 18.

[2] Britten, 7th ed. p. 6.

[3] *Introduction to the History of Science*, Baltimore, 1948.

Vienna made a clock incorporating differential gearing. There is also at this period the work of Aureliano, whose masterpiece is in the National Museum, Munich, and that of Father Philip Matthaeus Hahn, c. 1780, in Vienna. All these are some 200 to 400 years later than Dondi, during which time the sciences of horology and astronomy had made vast strides.

While giving details of the train of the timepiece portion of his clock, Dondi gives no details as to how this should be fixed within the framework of the clock. The clock has the usual revolving 24-hour dial of the period, registering before a fixed pointer; this he states is an ordinary common clock, of which several varieties are known. Its function is confined to the demarcation of the 24 hours of the day through the regular revolution of its wheels. He adds that if the student is not capable of devising for himself the general layout of this part, he had better not attempt to make the parts that follow.

This raises the point, how long must mechanical clocks have been in general use, in this part of Italy at any rate, for them to need no description as to how they should be made? For the planetary dials Dondi gives the most detailed instructions how to make the most simple parts, such as cocks and bridges, just where to drill holes for bearings, the thickness of the sheets to be employed, the length of studs, etc. The standards of measurement taken by Dondi are interesting: a thumb's breadth, two fingers' thickness, the size of a goose quill, as big as a cock's quill, a knife's or half a knife's thickness, etc. Another interesting point is that iron is never mentioned. Terms translated as bronze, brass and copper are occasionally used for the materials for the framework and dials, but no mention is ever made of the material employed in the trains. Philip de Mézières, who was Chancellor to the King of Cyprus, says that the clock was made entirely of brass and copper, and that its construction took Dondi sixteen years.

But to revert to the query concerning the earliest mechanical clocks. We must remember that about this time, 1350, the first of the famous series of clocks in Strasbourg cathedral was being constructed. Little is known as to the details of this; according to Ungerer[1] it probably contained an annual calendar dial, an astrolabe, and possibly a lunar dial. The upper portions would be occupied with figures moving at the hours or their subdivisions, doing obeisance to the Virgin and the infant Christ, etc. The whole was surmounted by a cock which, at the hours of mid-day and midnight crowed and flapped its wings, in commemoration of St. Peter's denial of Our Lord. This was a monumental clock, many feet high

[1] *Les horloges astronomiques et monumentales etc.* Strasbourg, 1931.

and was the much cruder blacksmith's work when compared with Dondi's, which was more of the nature of work by a locksmith, goldsmith, or precision instrument maker. The Strasbourg clock would, no doubt, make a greater impression on the devout and credulous, with its moving and bowing figures, than would Dondi's, with the movements of its dials imperceptible to the eye.

Here then we have in Italy and in South Germany, in the middle of the fourteenth century two clocks of great complexity, in which a 24-hour timepiece is incorporated as a prime mover.

THE FRAMEWORK OF DONDI'S CLOCK

This consists of a heptagonal frame in two parts, *Plate 56*, the lower, which should not be less than about two feet high, contained the clock dial proper, the annual calendar dial showing the fixed feasts, the dial giving the dates of Easter and the movable feasts dependent upon it, and the dial of the Nodes. The other three frames in this part were presumably blank. In the upper frames, which were about one foot square, were the dials of the *Primum Mobile*, Venus, Mercury, the Moon, Saturn, Jupiter and Mars.

MEAN TIME MOVEMENT AND 24-HOUR DIAL (PLATE 57)

Dondi details his train, 144 teeth on the revolving hour circle, meshing with a pinion of 12, which carries a wheel of 20 meshing with a wheel of 24 fitted to the winding drum. Thus for every revolution of the dial in 24 hours, the winding drum revolves 10 times. This drum carries the great wheel of 120 teeth, meshing with a pinion of 12, which in turn carries the second wheel of 80 teeth. This second wheel therefore revolves 100 times a day. It meshes with a pinion of 10 carrying the escape wheel of 27 teeth. This latter, therefore, makes 800 revolutions a day. Each revolution of the escape wheel calls for 54 oscillations of the balance wheel, giving a total of 43,200 oscillations a day, or 1,800 per hour. That is a 2-second beat. This Dondi describes as the usual rate of beat in his day. The pinion of 12 meshing with the hour circle was made to slide out, so that adjustments could be made easily as and when required. It should be remembered that the Italian hours were calculated 1–24, starting at sunset, which would mean daily adjustment. Dondi remarks later in the manuscript that it is more convenient to use the clock in the astronomical method, starting the day at midday.

It will be noticed that there is a balance wheel and not a foliot with adjustable weights. Regulation was by means of adjusting the driving weight if the clock were slow, but, as will be seen later, if the clock were fast, small weights were to be fixed to the balance.

We have then, here, a common clock, 'of which there exist many varieties', with a 2-second beat which is the 'usual rate'. How many years would it have taken with the comparatively slow spread of knowledge of those days, combined with the small number of horological craftsmen and their known secrecy, for such knowledge to be considered 'general' and not worthy of detailed description? The writer suggests that Alfonso X, the Learned, who died in 1284, would certainly have known of a weight-driven clock had it existed; so that a date around 1290–1300 is not an unreasonable guess as that of the first mechanical clock.

As we have seen, of the material used in the construction little is said, but iron is not mentioned at all. Words translated: brass, bronze and copper are used very occasionally. We can assume that, in the main, the clock was made of brass for the trains and dials and bronze for the frame, although in one case a dial is referred to as being made of bronze sheet and in another as of copper. There is nothing to guide us as to whether the standard practice of brass wheels and iron pinions had been adopted at this date. The process of annealing is also mentioned. These details may, therefore, possibly modify the view, very generally held, that all the earliest mechanical domestic clocks were made of iron. The writer is tending to the view that brass was, possibly, more usual in Italy and that iron was more generally applied in that other cradle of horology, South Germany.

It is also to be noted that although Dondi sketches all his pinions showing the number of their leaves, not once is a lantern pinion shown, and only once a 4-studded pinion in the drive of the dial of Jupiter, *Plate 73*.

We can now pass to the indications given in the other panels of the lower framework.

The first of these is, naturally, the 24-hour dial with which we have already dealt. On each side of this were set the scales by which the rising and setting of the sun could be determined for every day of the year, *Plate 58*. Dondi gives very lengthy details for the construction of these scales. The figures indicate the hours starting in each case at the dividing line on the left, as the dial rotates anti-clockwise.

If the clock is set at sunset, so that the line between 24 and 1 is just registering with the date, then (*a*) treating the date as the fixed pointer, the clock will continue to indicate hours since sunset; and (*b*) treating the meridian mark as the fixed pointer, it will indicate hours since noon. In either case, when the division between 24 and

1 reaches the same date over on the right, it will be sunrise, and similarly for sunset on the scale on the left.

In considering this clock throughout it must also be remembered that it is constructed for the latitude of Padua, 45° N, where the length of the day at summer solstice is 15 hrs. 33 mins., while here in England we are used to considering clocks made for London, $51\frac{1}{2}°$ N., with the length of the day at summer solstice 16 hrs. 45 mins. At the time this clock was made the dates of the solstices were June 13th and December 13th; by 1582 when the Gregorian calendar was introduced, a further two days had been lost, making the solstices June 11th and December 11th.

THE ANNUAL CALENDAR DIAL WITH THE FIXED FESTIVALS

Dondi's next care is the annual wheel, which is to show the fixed feasts of the year and to drive the various planetary dials. He makes a large and broad band wheel of as large a diameter as will be accommodated within the framework. Midway in depth inside the band is a stiffening circle with six radial arms terminating in a central plate carrying a vertical upward-pointing arbor. The wheel is supported by brackets fixed to the uprights of the frame and the upper pivot for the arbor revolves in a central plate carried by radial arms fixed to the seven corners of the base of the upper framework. The supporting brackets are so fixed that the teeth of the wheel are level with the top of the lower part of the framework.

Its broad and now vertical flange is divided into the 365 days of the year, *Plate 59*. To get his 365 divisions, Dondi divides the circumference first into six parts one of which he subdivides into three, and this 1/18th part he subdivides again by four, giving a 1/72nd part. He then takes the remaining 71/72nds and divides this similarly into 72 parts. He thus gets 73 virtually equal parts, which he again subdivides by five, giving him his necessary 365 divisions.

On the upper edge of this wheel are then cut 365 teeth to correspond with the days of the year. On the vertical surface of the wheel are inscribed, first the length of each day of the year in hours and minutes, next the dominical letter, then the name of the Saint commemorated on that day, and finally the date of the month, the actual name of the month not appearing. In the diagram the band starts at January 1st, the Feast of the Circumcision, dominical letter *a*, length of daylight 8 hrs. 42 mins. in Padua.

The frame of this dial is covered with a plate in which is cut a slot just wide enough for a single day to appear, *Plate 64b*. The alternate months were to have been gilded and silvered, with the engraved letters and numbers alternately in red and blue enamel.

He communicates motion to the annual calendar wheel from the time train in the following way: A pinion of 10 has its bearing in the inner side of the upper bearer of the lower No. 1 frame, i.e., that carrying the 24-hour dial, and at such a distance that it can mesh with the 365 teeth of the annual calendar wheel. This pinion has to be capable of easy removal so as to allow for any adjustment of the annual calendar dial. This pinion is then affixed behind the large wheel having 60 saw-like teeth and which is let into the thickness of the cross bearer of the frame. This wheel in turn is engaged by 6 studs set in the rear of the 24-hour dial wheel. These 6 studs will therefore turn the large wheel 1/10th of a turn a day, which is one tooth of the pinion of 10, which will turn the annual wheel 1 tooth or 1 day. When not actually in engagement with the studs, the large wheel is steadied by a detent, *Plate 59c.*

Dondi points out that if the whole of the seven dials for the planetary motions he is considering, as well as the annual dials for the fixed and movable feasts, are to be driven from the annual calendar wheel via the 6 studs mentioned, there will be a heavy strain on the train during the night, when the studs are in engagement, consequently the clock will go slower at night than by day. To overcome this he adopts the following measures. An auxiliary weight, seen end-on in *Plate 69* has a click bearing into the teeth of the annual calendar wheel and is just insufficient to turn the wheel when it is loaded with all the dials. When the pins behind the meantime dial, *Plate, 59c* come into action and begin to take up the drive of the annual calendar wheel, they have practically no work to do as the necessary power has been provided by the auxiliary weight.

CALENDAR OF THE MOVABLE FEASTS

In the third section of the lower frame was shown the table of the movable feasts, and this is a most ingenious conception. From the dominical letter can be ascertained on which day of the week any particular calendar date will fall. January 1st is *a*, and the next succeeding six letters, *b–g*, are used for the dates, January 2nd to January 7th, the dominical letter being that in the sequence on which the first Sunday in January falls. The days of the month fall on the same sequence of days of the week once every solar cycle of 28 years. The same dominical letter is kept throughout the year, except in leap years, when the first preceding letter is taken up to leap year day and the next preceding letter for the rest of the year. Incidentally Dondi gives February 24th, the feast of St. Matthew, as

leap year day. As will be seen later, Dondi intended to stop the
clock for a day on February 24th in leap year.

February 24th was the sext of March in the Roman Calendar and
its repetition gave rise to the term bis-sextile year.

The cycle starts with the dominical letter f (i.e., a year in which
January 6th is the first Sunday of the year) and the letters are taken
in the reverse order, thus the letter for the second year of the cycle is
e, that of the third year d, and that of the fourth up to leap year day c,
and b for the rest of the year. The 28th year of the cycle, also a leap
year, will then end with the two letters a and g, leaving the cycle to
recommence with the letter f.

Of the five movable feasts, two, Septuagesima and Quinquage-
sima, are seven and five Sundays before Easter, and Rogation
and Whitsun five and seven Sundays after. Once therefore Easter
Day is fixed, these other feasts all hold fixed positions in relation
to it. In order to find Easter it is necessary to know the dominical
letter.

Dondi takes Easter as the first Sunday after the 14th day of the
1st lunation, i.e., the 1st full moon, after March 7th. The beginning
of the critical lunation varies each year, but the Greek astronomer,
Meton, discovered that the days of full moon fall on the same days
of the month every 19 years. This is called the lunar cycle. The
Greeks considered this discovery so wonderful, that they caused it to
be carved in stone in letters of gold, hence the numbers of this cycle,
1–19, are known as the Golden Number. In the first year of this
cycle the new Paschal moon was, in Dondi's day, on March 23rd,
resulting in Easter Sunday being in April 5th, and in the 19th, or
last year of the cycle, on April 17th. *Plate 60* shows how Dondi met
this problem.

He makes a series of hinged linked chains; the top one has 28
links, marked on top with the 28 years of the solar cycle, and below
the corresponding dominical letter, with two letters every fourth, or
leap year. The central and broad chain has 19 links, corresponding
to the lunar cycle, each link being engraved with the dates of the five
movable feasts, that of Easter being in the middle. The bottom chain
has 15 links, and deals with the period of the Indiction which will be
discussed later.

Each chain runs in a separate compartment of the box enclosing
the whole on three sides, and there are two separate drives. That on
the left drives the chains of the solar and lunar cycles and that on the
right, the chain for the Indiction.

The two wheels with 20 teeth placed on the outer surface of the
box carry on their arbors pentagon pinions, each side of which

corresponds to the length of one link of the chains. These wheels of 20 mesh with pinions of 10, which carry the larger wheels of 60 teeth. These, in turn, mesh with pinions of 24, which carry vertical arbors supporting wheels having 12 saw-like teeth.

Thus for every turn of the saw-tooth wheels the large wheel is turned 24 teeth, i.e. 2/5ths of a turn. This causes the pinion of 10 to turn through 4 teeth, turning the wheel of 20 through 4 teeth correspondingly, or 1/5th of a turn. Thus the pentagon pinion will make a 1/5th turn, advancing the chains one link.

The Indiction is a period used in Roman law and was frequently applied to leases and other contracts, but it started on September 1st not on January 1st. Dondi had, therefore, to provide for the annual changes of his chains at different times. In order to do this he does not gear his chain drives direct into the teeth of the annual calendar wheel, but he affixes to the inner surfaces of this two rake-like shoulders, each having 12 teeth, and so places them that they finish their engagement with the saw-tooth wheel on January 1st and September 1st, respectively. One of these racks can be seen on the inside of the annual calendar wheel (*Plate 59b*).

Before considering the remainder of the dials, it will be as well to recall the state of astronomical knowledge at that time. Also to be considered is astrology, since it had played an important part in the lives of all men from time immemorial. How often do we not find it recorded in the Bible that the King sent for his astrologers, magicians and soothsayers? This belief in the influence of the planets on the daily, or even hourly, progress of one's life was still commonplace until about the end of the seventeenth century; after which the science of astronomy began to replace that of astrology in the daily life of the people. We owe, however, the names of our days of the week to the astrological superstitions of our ancestors. They believed that every hour of the day was influenced in turn by the planets, in succession, in their order of distance from the earth. Thus, if we take 1 a.m. Monday as our start, we have 24 hours to be divided by the seven planets, which gives each planet its influence three times during the day, with three hours over. *Plate 61a* will show that this leads to Mars being the planet to influence the first hour of the next day, Tuesday, in French mardi, then Mercury, Wednesday (mercredi), and so on throughout the week.

The serious attention paid in those days to astrology is illustrated by a remark Dondi makes. He says that there are very few people who are capable of understanding astronomy or the reading of his clock. He ascribes the capacity of the few to the fact that they were born when the stars were propitious.

Dondi summarises the knowledge of those he calls the ancients substantially as follows:

In their observations they had noted that besides the fixed stars there were seven stars that wandered, i.e., the planets, which in those days included the sun and the moon. The fixed stars were only fixed in their relative positions, while they continued in an unceasing motion in one direction in what they termed the firmament. They noticed that the sun and moon followed this same motion; they therefore attributed the same motion to the other five planets.

However certain differences were observed between the apparent motions of the fixed stars and those of the planets; the ancients therefore thought that beyond the firmament and all the stars there was another sphere, which they called the *Primum Mobile* because it was a law unto itself. This sphere, having the swiftest motion of all, carried round all orbs and spheres and stars and influenced them. Another name for this was simple or rational motion, since it was uniform in time; it was also sometimes called the diurnal motion, because its movements were repeated every 24 hours.

Two immovable points were accepted, about which the sphere of the *Primum Mobile* turned, and which they called the poles of the world, one in the north, which they called arctic after Arctus, or Ursa, which is near it, and the other in the south, antarctic, because it was diametrically opposed to the arctic.

The measure of motion of the planets was taken along an imaginary circle midway between these points the equator, it being the more pronounced in this plane. They noted that the seven planets made the whole passage of the firmament in unequal periods of time and with motions proper to themselves. Therefore, other spheres than those of the *Primum Mobile* and the firmament of the fixed stars had to be taken into account.

It was considered that these planets had their motions about other poles, since their distances from the poles and the equator varied. It was also observed that the planets never proceeded outside a band of a certain depth in the heavens. They therefore imagined a band of this breadth, the 'Zodiac' on the surface of the *Primum Mobile*, and crossing the circle of the equator at two opposing points, one passing from the north and the other from the south at an angle of about 24° in relation to the equator. They also discovered a proper motion to the firmament and the fixed stars (this was the precession of the equinoxes; Dondi states that as this motion is so slow, he ignores it in his clock. It amounts to about 1° in 100 years). They noticed that this motion rotated in the inverse direction to that of the *Primum Mobile*; they consequently called it the eighth sphere. It was the

orderly and harmonious movements of these spheres that later gave
rise to the expression 'the music of the spheres'.

It was noted that none of the planets preserved a fixed rule
in its course, but each traversed unequal distances of the zodiac
in equal spaces of time, and that their distances in the firmament
and from the earth varied. The five planets, other than the sun
and moon, were observed to have not only irregular forward motions,
but also at times to be stationary and even to have retrograde
motions.

Having made these postulates, the astronomers of the day had to
devise a means of the representation by circular motions, as such
only were considered suitable for celestial bodies in those days.
The variety of the motions of the stars led to the postulation
of the plurality of the spheres and the irregularity of the planetary
courses, the theory of epicycles[1] and of other eccentric circles.
(*Plate 61b.*)

However, it was found that the motions of the planets did not
conform exactly to the theory of perfectly circular motion, consequently the centre of the circle of the deferent was considered as a
point outside the earth, *Plate 61c*. The irregularities of the eccentric
motions were further corrected by equating circles. The centre of
the epicycle was taken to revolve with a variable speed around the
deferent circle, but with a constant speed, its *mean motus*, from the
centre of the equating circle, that is to say it moved with constant
angular velocity. *Plate 61d*.

This was the state of knowledge in Dondi's time, and it so remained until the coming of Copernicus, in the sixteenth century,
who recognised the Sun as the centre of the universe, and so founded
the heliocentric theories of today.

Dondi's lengthy exposition of the state of astronomical knowledge
of his time, of which the foregoing is a very brief summary, concludes
with the expression of his wish to make a work that should show
the motions of the stars, as they have been taught by the authorities on the subject; so that at any time of the day, the correct position
of any of the planets could be seen at a glance, just as if their positions
at that moment had been worked out laboriously from tables.
He also hoped to induce 'the vulgar' to have more respect for
astronomy.

With this brief description of the state of the astronomical thought

---

[1] An epicycle is the circular motion of a planet, the centre of which circle travels
round the earth in a circle the radius of which springs from the centre of the earth,
and which circle is called the deferent.

of the time before us, we can better appreciate the construction of the dials of the *Primum Mobile* and the several planets.

THE DIAL OF THE PRIMUM MOBILE

In the upper frame, above the 24-hour dial, was placed the dial of the *Primum Mobile, Plate 62*. On the extreme outside we have the sidereal 24-hour circle, superimposed upon the square basis plate and divided into 10-minute intervals. Within this lies the circle of the zodiac, marked off into the twelve signs, each subdivided into 30°. Dondi divides the radius of this circle into 26 parts, and strikes a centre 1/26th up from the centre of the zodiacal circle. This point will be the centre of the deferent of the sun, which will be a circle of radius from this point to the inner edge of the zodiacal circle. The dial of the sun's deferent is the next circle, divided into twelve and subdivided into 30 for each of the twelve divisions. This is carried round by the three arms marked 'Radius rotae deferentis', its centre being, as explained above, eccentric to the extent of 1/26th part of the radius of the circle of the zodiac.

Fixed behind the dials is a four-armed bracket carrying the central plate, which carries the arcs of circles called almucantars or parallels of altitude in the upper half, and in the lower half the semi-circle is divided into 15° of arc to represent, between 6 a.m. and 6 p.m., temporal or unequal hours used in monastic life; these are calculated for the latitude of Padua, i.e. 45° N.

The ring of the sun's deferent carrying with it the circle of the ecliptic, is now free to revolve across the plate of the temporal hours, as in the case of an astrolabe.

Dondi communicates the correct movement of the dial of the *Primum Mobile* from the 24-hour dial in the following way. He takes a wheel of the same diameter as the outer circle of the zodiac and in it he cuts 365 teeth. Into this he gears a wheel of 61, *A* in *Plate 63c*, meshing with a pinion of 24 *b*, *Plate 63a*, which communicates the drive from the 24-hour ring of 144 teeth. Both *A* and *b* carry on their arbors wheels of equal diameter, each of 60 teeth. Thus during the 24 hours the pinion *b* is turned 6 times and, through the two wheels of 60, turns *A* 6 times or through 366 teeth of the hour wheel of the sidereal hour dial. Thus this makes one revolution plus one tooth each day, so that it will complete the 366 sidereal days during the period of 365 mean days.

He recognised that the true ratio was $366\frac{1}{4}$ to $365\frac{1}{4}$, corresponding to a daily difference of 59' 8" of arc, or 3 m. 56 secs. each day. To correct this he stops the clock on leap year day.

Dondi's next care is to record the eccentric motion of the sun's deferent (what we should today call the eccentricity of the sun's apparent orbit). The outer edge of the ring of the sun's deferent is divided into 183 parts, first by dividing into 60, then dividing 59/60ths again into 60, thus obtaining 61 very nearly equal divisions These are again subdivided into 3, giving the 183 required. Into this wheel of 183 he meshes a pinion of 10, not seen in *Plate 63b*, which is on the same arbor as the wheel *E* of 20 teeth, *Plate 63b*. This meshes with a pinion of 15 *f*, *Plate 63b*, which carries the wheel *g*, of 60 teeth. This in turn meshes with a pinion of 8 which carries a wheel having 8 'humps'. As the wheel of the *Primum Mobile* revolves once a sidereal day, it carries this train with it so that the humps come into contact with the 4 studs on the bracket (in the sketch the diameter of the hump wheel is too small). Thus this wheel of 8 humps makes half a revolution a day, which equals 4 teeth of the pinion of 8, that is 4 teeth or 1/15th of the wheel *g*, equals 1 tooth of the pinion *f*, turning the wheel *E* 1 tooth, i.e., 1/20th turn, communicating 1/20th turn or ½ tooth to the invisible pinion of 10, which is driving the dial of the sun's deferent. Thus the deferent dial advances 1 tooth every 2 days; 2 × 183 teeth equals the 366 days of the sidereal year. The hump wheel is provided with a detent to steady it when not in engagement, and the pinion of 10 can be slipped out, to allow for adjusting the dial.

The circle of the deferent carries a pin, not shown in *Plate 62a*, that engages in the slot in the arm marked 'Verus' which is twice the length of the eccentricity of the sun's deferent. This arm is keyed to the arbor of the centre dial, so that as the deferent dial makes its eccentric turn, the pin in the slot, which should carry the effigy of the sun, *Plate 62b*, will show the true position of the sun, hence the inscription 'Verus'. It was intended that the constellations of the zodiac should be gilded and silvered alternately, and the engraving thereon be filled with red and blue enamel, as before.

Next we have to consider the six planetary dials, that of the sun being incorporated in the dial of the *Primum Mobile*, as we have seen.

THE DIAL OF VENUS

For the Venus, *Plate 64a*, Dondi takes the *Aux*[1] as in the same position as that of the sun, in the beginning of Cancer, and the *motus* of the centre of her epicycle as exactly equal to that of the sun in its eccentric deferent, i.e., 59' 8" of arc a day; the argument of Venus i.e. its movement around the circumference of the epicycle, measured from the line of the *Aux*, he takes at 36' 59" of arc a

[1] The *Aux* is the point on the Zodiac struck by a line from the earth through the centre of the epicycle, when this latter is farthest from the earth.

day. He therefore arranges to show these motions. For this dial the material used is translated as bronze.

The vertical radius of the zodiacal band is divided into 54 parts, and the centre of the equating circle is 1/54th part above the centre of the zodiac. Basing his calculations on Ptolemy, the centre of the deferent is halfway between these two points, its radius being 30/54ths of the radius of the zodiac. From the point of intersection of the vertical radius of the zodiac by the deferent circle, the epicyclic circle is described with a radius of $21\frac{7}{12}$/54ths of the zodiacal radius (we must remember that at this time the decimal notation for fractions did not exist). The equating circle is divided into 12, beginning at the *opposite Aux* and running anti-clockwise. These 12 are again divided into 30 to give the 360° of the equating circle.

The wheel at the bottom, M, has 60 teeth meshing into the 365 teeth of the annual calendar wheel and carries a pinion of 24 meshing with the 146 teeth of the equating wheel of Venus. Thus with a daily motion of 1 tooth of the annual wheel, in 5 days it turns M through 1/12th of a turn, i.e. 2 leaves of the pinion of 24, which corresponds to 2 teeth of the equating wheel every 5 days or 1/73rd of a mean year. Thus in 365 mean days the equating wheel turns through 2×73, i.e 146 teeth, one complete revolution.

On the arbor of the equating circle is fixed the wheel E of 45 teeth. Behind the dial of the epicycle is the wheel of the epicycle of 72 teeth. The teeth of wheel E should be unevenly cut to the maximum extent that will allow them to mesh. The teeth should be wider (or larger) on the side opposite to the *Aux* than on the side of the *Aux*. This method can be used for Venus because the distance between the centres of the equating circle and the deferent is small. Other steps will be taken for the other planets.

During the 365 days forming one rotation of the equating wheel, the wheel E of 45 teeth turns the wheel of the epicycle, not visible in *Plate 64*, through 45 of its 72 teeth, i.e. 5/8ths of a turn of 360°, or 225°, which is equivalent to $7\frac{1}{2}$ signs of the zodiac. By calculation Dondi gives the actual motion of Venus as 36′ 59″ 32‴ daily for the 365 days of a non-leap year, to this he adds 9′ 15″ for the odd 6 hours, calculating that his dial is out by about 11 minutes of arc a year.

THE DIAL OF MERCURY

For this dial, which, with that of the moon, is the most complicated, Dondi gives three motions; the first eastwards, equal to that of the sun in its eccentric, viz. 59′ 8″ almost daily. This motion is not uniform over the circle of the deferent or across the zodiac, but is uniform around the equating circle, and a straight line running through the centre of the epicycle will describe equal angles at the centre of the equating circle in equal periods of time. The second is the motion of the centre of the deferent. With Venus the motion of the planet was depicted by its travel around its epicycle, of which the centre travelled around the deferent, as modified by the equating circle. The centre of the deferent was fixed at a point eccentric to the centre of the zodiac; but with Mercury the centre of the deferent is taken to be in motion, moving in a circle in the contrary sense to the epicycle, and having its centre at a point on the line to the *Aux* of the equating circle, at such a distance that the centre of the equating circle lies midway between it and the centre of the zodiac. The motion of the centre of the deferent is the same as that given above for the centre of the epicycle, 59′ 8″ almost, daily, but in the opposite, westerly, direction, as seen in *Plate 65a*. It will be clear then, that when the centre of the epicycle cuts the vertical line leading to the *Aux* of the zodiac, *AB*, the centre of the deferent cuts the same line at the same time, since they have equal but contrary motions.

The third motion is that of the planet's centre around the circle of the epicycle, 3° 6′ 24″ a day.

When the centre of the deferent cuts the line *AB* at its high point, the four centres will be in line; when at its low point, the centres of the deferent and equating circles will coincide and the two circles will be of equal area.

While the centre of the deferent makes a complete revolution of the small circle, neither its *Aux* nor its *opposite Aux* traverse the whole of the equating circle, but are confined within two diameters of the zodiac tangential to the small circle. Further, no one point remains the *Aux* or the *opposite Aux*, but each point successively occupies those positions, for every part of the deferent goes round the zodiac, but the *Aux* and *opposite Aux* are confined within the limits just given.

Further, while the centre of the epicycle goes round the equating circle and the band of the zodiac once a year, in the same period it goes twice round the deferent.

Having thus summarised Dondi's explanation of Mercury's movements, let us see how he proposes to put them into effect. At the time that the clock was made, the *Aux* of the equating circle on the zodiac was 29° 2′ 14″ of Libra, according to the Alfonsine tables; a line is therefore drawn from the centre of the zodiac circle to this point, *Plate 65b*. On this line lie the four centres, *Plate 65a*.

The radius of the zodiac is divided into 33 parts, the centre of the equating circle and the centre of the circle of the centre of the deferent being 1/33rd and 2/33rds distant from the centre of the zodiac, respectively. The radius of the deferent is 20/33rds measured from the centre of the circle of the centre of the deferent, *Plate 65a*. The radius of the epicycle is 7½/33rds, measured from the circumference of the deferent.

The first two motions of Mercury are produced in the following way. The wheel *M* of 60 teeth, *Plate 65b*. carries behind it a broad pinion of 24 which engages the equating wheel of 146 teeth placed behind the dial. Thus each 365 days *M* turns $6\frac{1}{12}$ times, the pinion of 24 equally so, thus advancing the equating wheel of 146 teeth, which carries the arm marked 'Verus', i.e. the true position of the planet in the zodiac, one whole revolution.

In a slot in the arm of the deferent, that seen in the centre of the V (*Plate 65b* and again in *Plate 66c*) slides a pin fixed behind at the centre of the dial of the epicycle.

The pinion of 24 on *M* which meshes with the equating wheel, is sufficiently wide to engage simultaneously a pinion of 24 on the far end of the arbor of the pinion *L*, also of 24, *Plate 65b*. This latter meshes with the deferent wheel, having equally 146 teeth. This wheel is, therefore, turned equally through one revolution in 365 days but in the opposite direction. These two motions are slightly fast, as the revolution is completed in 365 instead of 365¼ days, but Dondi states that it is his intention that the clock should be stopped on leap year days, so that this error will be corrected when the clock is restarted.

The third motion, that of the epicycle of Mercury, is more complicated and cannot be reproduced by pure circles. Its *motus* is eastwards, i.e. 3° 6′ 24″ daily, but as we have seen, the centre of the deferent of Mercury is not fixed, but moving in a circle in the contrary sense. What has to be depicted is two uniform contrary motions one to the left due to the equating wheel, and one to the right due to the rotation of the circle of the deferent. These two motions begin together from the diameter of the *Aux* of the equating wheel and at the same moment on that diameter.

To do this Dondi constructs elliptical wheels in a most original manner. He takes a line, the length of the diameter of the equating circle and marks its centre *b*, *Plate 66b*. Above this he strikes off, in its correct position, the centre of the circle of the centre of the deferent *c*, and describes a circle of radius *cb* which will represent the circle of the centre of the deferent. From *c* he describes a semicircle to the right, and divides this into 12 equal parts. He then describes an

s

equal semicircle on the left from *b*, equally divided into 12 parts, producing the dividing lines beyond the circumference. The divisions on the left are those that the arm of the equating circle should traverse in equal periods of time, and with it the centre of the epicycle, represented by the pin sliding in the groove in the arm of the deferent, because these divisions contain equal angles at the centre of the equating circle. The 12 divisions on the right are the 12 arcs of the circle of the centre of the deferent that will be described in equal periods of time. The centre of the deferent and that of the equating circle meet on the *Aux* diameter of the equating circle, move away in opposite directions at equal speeds, meeting again at the *opposite Aux* diameter of the equating circle.

From the top of the small circle is struck off a point *e* at a distance equal to the radius of the deferent. Taking each of the divisions on the circumference of the small circle on the right-hand side in turn as centre, equidistant points *f*, *g*, *h*, etc., are struck off on the left. This gives the path the centre of the epicycle will travel from its *Aux* to its *opposite Aux* and back again. The twelve lines on the left are then reduced by 2/5ths of the radius of the deferent, to the points *a–n*, bisected and joined up to give the contour of the wheel on that side; the other side being made symmetrical. Two wheels are cut, one to be fixed and the other revolving around it. Each wheel has 24 fixed blunt nosed teeth cut in it, *Plate 66c*. These teeth will be of unequal size, but since the two wheels are symmetrical, the two wheels will mesh harmoniously. In *Plate 66c* these two wheels do not appear to be symmetrical, but they are so in the working sketches.

The wheel of the epicycle has 63 teeth cut internally and is driven by a pinion of 20, *Plate 66c*. The motion of the epicycle to the left should amount to 3° 6′ 24″ daily or three times round the zodiac, or 36 constellations, plus 54° 43′ 23″ each solar year.

The movable of the two wheels will be carried round by the arm of the equating circle once a year, so that the internal-toothed wheel of 63 teeth fixed to it, will equally turn once a year. This will turn the pinion of 20 carrying the epicycle wheel three times and 3 teeth over. Three times equals 36 constellations; each tooth equals 1/20th of 360, i.e. 18°, giving a total of 36 constellations 54°, being 43′ 23″ of arc too slow in the year. In *Plate 66c* will be seen a wheel with internally cut teeth. We have no other contemporary clocks with which to make comparison, but in view of the imaginative nature and complexity of Dondi's clock the writer feels justified in claiming a first appearance of an internally cut wheel or at any rate the earliest known example.

DIAL OF THE MOON

The astronomers of Dondi's day attributed to the moon four motions. First a daily *motus* westwards of 13° 11′ 39″ by the centre of the epicycle along the circumference of its eccentric deferent. This movement was not uniform along this circumference or about its centre, but was uniform about the centre of the earth and the zodiacal belt. Second, the centre of the deferent was taken as moving about the centre of the zodiac in a circle of radius of the distance between these two centres. Third, was the argument of the moon around the circumference of the epicycle of 13° 3′ 54″ daily in a contrary direction to that of the other planets. Fourth, the motion of the intersection of the two deferents of the sun and moon, known as the dragon's head and tail (the Nodes), of 3′ 11″ westwards daily.

The eccentricity of the centre of the moon's deferent, which is itself describing a circle, is 12½/90ths of the radius of the zodiac. The radius of the deferent is 2/3rds of that radius and the radius of the epicycle of the moon 6⅓/90ths.

The wheel of the equating circle, which is centred on the centre of the zodiac, has 164 teeth. To get this number of teeth Dondi divides by 11, then 3 and 5, getting 165ths. Then he divides the circumference plus 1/165th into 165, which gives him 164 virtually equal teeth, since one has been taken in twice over.

At the lowest point of the dial and on its face is fixed a pinion *A* of 12, meshing with the equating wheel of 164, *Plate 67a*. The arbor of the pinion *A* projects behind the dial and has squared on to it a pinion *b* of 16 affixed to the back of the dial and between it and the wheel of the *Aux* of the deferent of 257 teeth. A bridge, *Plate 68a* carries a wheel of 72 slightly oblique teeth, which is designed to revolve once in two days, having on its arbor a broad pinion *c* of 16 meshing simultaneously with *b* and the wheel of 257. The reason for the oblique teeth will be seen presently.

Thus when *E*, *Plate 67a*, makes half a turn, 36 teeth, to the East, or in the direction of the signs of the zodiac, the wheel of 257 moves westwards carrying with it the hub of the centre of the deferent. At the same time the wheel of the equating circle is moved eastwards 6 teeth, i.e., half a turn of pinion *A*, which is on the same arbor as pinion *b*.

In one day the wheel of 257 advances 8 teeth, therefore it makes a complete revolution in 32⅛ days, or 32 days 3 hrs., in which time the hub of the centre of the zodiac will have moved through the 12 signs. The *motus* of the *Aux* of the moon is actually 11° 12′ 18″

daily, or in 32⅛ days 11 signs 29° 57′ 15″, or only 2′ 45″ short of 12 signs.

As we have just seen, each day the equating wheel moves 6 teeth in the direction of the signs. This wheel of 164 teeth will, therefore, make a complete turn less two teeth in 27 days. The two teeth of *A* equal 1/3rd of half a rotation of *E*, or 8 hrs. Thus the centre of the epicycle of the moon will perform the circuit of the band of the zodiac in that time. In 27 days 8 hrs. the moon actually passes through 12 signs 0° 9′ 18″.

The main drive for this lunar wheel is not off the annual calendar wheel, as in the case of Venus and Mercury, but off the wheel of the *Primum Mobile* which, it will be recollected, has 365 teeth and turns through 366 teeth in a day. A wheel of 61, *Plate 68b*, meshes with the 366 teeth of the *Primum Mobile* and is thus turned 6 times a day. A long arbor stretching across the framework carries a pinion of 6, its teeth being cut somewhat obliquely, and meshing with the wheel *E*, which it will be remembered, also had slightly oblique teeth, and turns the wheel *E* of 72 teeth, one revolution every two days. Since Dondi had to deal with a seven-sided frame he could not get a straight drive and had to cut a skew gear. On the same basis as that given for the internally cut wheel, a first appearance is claimed for the skew gear.

In connexion with the argument of the moon in its epicycle, Dondi makes the following remarks. Firstly the moon moves west-wards in the upper part of its epicycle, while the other planets move eastwards. Their motion is equal about the centre of the equating circle, but that of the mean *Aux* of the moon is not measured in a line drawn from the centre of the epicycle to the centre of the equat-ing circle, but from a line drawn from the centre of the epicycle, passing through the centre of the circle of the deferent and terminat-ing on the far side of its circumference, *Plate 70a*.

With the other planets, the motion of the centre of the epicycle at times is less than that of the planet, so that the planet's motion be-comes retrograde, but with the moon, the centre of the epicycle dominates, so that the moon always moves to the east, albeit with irregular speeds.

As we have seen, the centre of the deferent of the moon takes a circular course, as was the case with Mercury, *Plate 65a*, but the motion of the centre of the moon's deferent and that of its *Aux* are slower than the centre of the epicycle, consequently they never coincide in the same place or position in the band of the zodiac. To portray this requires a different treatment from that of Mercury.

The means taken by Dondi to reproduce this motion are very elaborate, in fact he says 'it is suited to the intellect of the few only'. *Plate 70a* shows briefly the motion Dondi wishes to reproduce; *d* is the centre of the zodiac and *a* the centre about which the arm of the deferent turns clockwise, *b* is the centre of the epicycle, *m* is the moon at its *Aux*, *be* therefore is the line about which the angle formed by the radius of the moon in its epicycle will increase uniformly by 13° 3′ 54″ daily. The motions about the centres *a* and *b* have already been provided for.

In *Plate 70a de* is the diameter of the hub of the centre of the deferent, *ab* is the arm of the deferent, when the centre of the epicycle is at its *Aux* and *ac* when it is at its *opposite Aux*; the semi-circle represents half the hub of the centre of the deferent. This is divided into four parts and since the arbor of the epicycle is driven round uniformly about the centre *d*, the four points shown will be reached in equal periods of time. The lines drawn from *e*, through the centre of the epicycle and cutting its circumference on its outer edge, are those against which the angle formed with the radius of the moon will uniformly increase.

The working-out of the profiles of the fixed and mobile wheels, with blunt-nosed teeth, is long and complex. The centre of the mobile wheel is taken at *m*, *Plate 70b*; 1/3rd of *bd* is struck off at an equal distance from the zodiac on each of the other lines at *l*, *i*, *k* and *o*. From these points lines are drawn at 45°, 90° and 135° respectively, and down these lines are struck off *lx*, *ix* and *kx* respectively, equal to *dx* on the base, *x* being the centre of the fixed wheel, which for the moment is assumed to be circular. The corresponding points from *m* and *o* will lie on the base line and are not separately indicated. The point *x* on the base line is joined to the *x*'s of *lx*, *ix* and *kx* and the distances between these points and *x* on the base is bisected, giving five points of contact for the two wheels. These are joined up. They do not form a true semicircle, but the junction of two arcs passing through *syz* and *zgt*, the centres of which are very near to the centre of the true circle. To find the half-periphery of the mobile wheel one proceeds in a similar way, working from the points *l*, *i* and *k*.

The movable wheel has to turn 45° through each of the irregular intervals on the deferent, and this is not consistent with a rolling action. To effect this an equal number (five) of unequally sized teeth are cut in each section of the wheels, as shown in *Plate 70c*. Thus when turning round the fixed wheel the moving wheel will turn through equal angles in relation to the line running from the centre of the epicycle to the point *e*, *Plate 70a*, in equal periods of time.

During the period of lunation, that is from conjunction to conjunction occupying 29d 12 h 44' 3" the moon travels through 12 signs 25° 48' 59", during which time the centre of the epicycle travels the whole of the deferent twice, once from the mean conjunction of the moon with the sun to its mean opposition and once from the mean opposition to the mean conjunction.

Thus, while the movable wheel is making two turns round the fixed, *Plate 67a*, it carries the wheel *c* of 45 teeth round with it twice. This gears into the wheel of the epicycle of 84 and therefore turns it twice plus 6 teeth or $2\frac{1}{14}$th turns, which is equivalent to 12 signs 25° 42' 51" 26''', being slower than the theoretical given above by 6' 8", which may be corrected when it has accumulated.

DIAL OF SATURN

The planet Saturn has only two motions in longitude, one being the *motus* of the epicycle along the deferent and the other the argument of the planet along the circumference of the epicycle. The former, in the direction of the zodiac, is uniform about the equating circle which is eccentric to both the deferent and the zodiac; its eccentricity being double that of the deferent measured in a straight ine fro m the centre of the zodiac. The eccentricity of the equating circle is given as $6\frac{5}{8}$/8oths of the radius of the zodiac, and that of the deferent, half of that amount.

The second motion is eastward in the upper part of the epicycle and is uniform from its mean *Aux*.

In Saturn the first motion is 2' 0" 36''' which, when subtracted from that of the sun, viz. 59' 8" 20''', leaves 57' 7" 44'''. The line of the *Aux* of Saturn passes through the 12° of Sagittarius, and on this line lie also the centres of the deferent and equating circle.

The motion of the centre of the epicycle is governed by the annual calendar wheel through the wheel *M* with which it gears, as is the case with the other planets, except the moon. The wheel *M* of 60 teeth, *Plate 71a*, engages with the annual calendar wheel of 365 teeth, which is turned by it one tooth daily. Behind the dial on the arbor of *M* is a pinion of 6 *n*, *Plate 72a*, meshing with a wheel of 30, *L*, which will therefore make 1/5th of a turn i.e. 6 teeth in 60 days. *L* carries a pinion *g* of 10, which will therefore move the wheel *K* of 20, with which it meshes, 2 teeth or 1/10th of a turn. *K* carries on the front of the dial, *Plate 71a*, a pinion, *h*, of 10 which engages with the equating wheel of 180, which will, therefore, move 1 tooth or 2° in 60 days, or 2/60ths of 2°, i.e., 2′ daily, which is very close to the daily movement of the epicycle of Saturn.

The pin of the centre of the epicycle will travel upwards from *Aux* to *opposite Aux* and downwards from *opposite Aux* to *Aux*, because the centre of the equating circle is farther from the centre of the zodiac than the centre of the deferent.

The second motion, that of the planet in its epicycle, is faster than the first, being in a non-leap year 11 signs 17° 32′ 4″, this being the result of the subtraction of the planet's *motus* from that of the sun. Saturn, therefore, in a year goes round rather less than the whole epicycle by 12° 27′ 36″.

The first motion of Saturn, that is its mean *motus* for the passage of the whole ecliptic, is 29 years 5 months 4 days 8 hours nearly. During this period, while the centre of the epicycle is traversing the whole circumference of the deferent, the argument of Saturn, that is its motion in its epicycle, is 28 complete revolutions 5 signs 3° 3′ 24″.

In order to show this much accelerated motion, when compared with the first, Dondi proceeds as follows: he takes two equal-sized wheels of 30 teeth cut with blunt-nosed and spaced teeth as on the fixed and elliptical wheels of Mercury and the moon. One of these is fixed to the hub of the equating wheel and the movable one on to the cursor in one of the arms of the equating wheel; the diameter of the fixed wheel at right-angles to its two points of fixture being in line with the diameter of the moving wheel, both diameters being on the line to the *Aux*. All this train is placed on the front of the dial.

When the equating wheel is turned to the left, it will carry with it the movable wheel with blunt teeth around its fixed complement in a uniform motion about its arbor in relation to the centre of the equating circle. Since the equating circle has a uniform motion about its centre, the line just referred to will move through equal angles at that centre in equal periods of time. Similarly around the arbor in the centre of the movable wheel.

Then follows a somewhat complicated reasoning to demonstrate that the movement of the epicycle can be correctly derived from the movable wheel. The motion of the epicycle is as follows. As the movable blunt-toothed wheel turns, it carries wheel *T* of 60 teeth, *Plate 72b*, which is squared on to it. This turns the pinion *v* of 20 fixed to the arbor of the wheel *S* of 114 teeth, three times; which wheel now turns the pinion of 12 carrying the dial of the epicycle 28½ turns, or 28 revolutions 6 signs, which corresponds closely to the figure 28 revolutions 5 signs 3° 3′ 24″ quoted above.

In connexion with the dial of Saturn, Dondi says that he copied his calculations from elsewhere. Later in the MS he gives his own, somewhat simpler method. Was the calculation referred to one of his father's?

THE DIAL OF JUPITER

For Jupiter the *Aux* is given as 22° Virgo and on a line from this point to the centre of the zodiac will lie the centres of the deferent and equating circles. In this case, the wheel M, *Plate 73a*, meshing with the annual calendar wheel has 72 teeth and carries on its arbor in front of the dial a pinion of 4 which engages with the equating wheel of 240 teeth, so that one stud of this pinion drives the equating wheel through $1\frac{1}{2}°$ or 90′. Therefore with a forward motion of M of 1 tooth daily, it will take 18 days to move the pinion one stud, corresponding to 1 tooth in the equating wheel, in 18 days for 90″ or 5″ a day, which corresponds very nearly to the daily motion of the epicycle calculated as 4′ 59″ 16‴. Wheel T of 24 is fixed to the arbor of the movable wheel with blunt teeth. It meshes with a pinion of 12 on the arbor of wheel S of 65 teeth, which in turn meshes with the pinion of 12 of the epicycle. Thus for each turn of the equating wheel, S is turned twice or through 130 teeth, turning the epicycle through 10 complete revolutions plus 10 signs, which compare with a theoretical of 10 signs 8° 33′ 36″. This gives a daily motion of the epicycle very nearly equal to the theoretical of 74′ 9″ 4‴, the time for the centre of the epicycle to traverse the whole deferent being given as 11 years 10 months 9 days 17 hours 20 minutes.

The train depicted is an alternative train; another, which involved an internally toothed wheel as was used for Mercury, to drive the pinion of the epicycle, is described but not illustrated in the Bodleian copy.

THE DIAL OF MARS

This has to be constructed along the lines of those for Venus and Jupiter, with especial regard to that of Jupiter. The *Aux* is given as 14° of Leo. The wheel M, *Plate 74a*, taking up the drive from the annual calendar wheel, has 72 teeth with a pinion of 18 engaging with the equating wheel of 172 teeth. For the *motus* of Mars in its epicycle fixed and movable wheels with blunt teeth, the latter travelling on a cursor, as made for Jupiter and Saturn, are provided for. These can be seen in *Plates 73a* and *71a*.

The wheel, *T Plate 75*, has 53 teeth and the wheel of the epicycle 60 teeth. The teeth of these two wheels approach very closely, but do not engage. They are driven by a common pinion, *s*, of 15, which can follow them in their course up and down the cursor. The index arm is placed at the centre of the zodiac on a protuberance on the hub of the equating circle, owing to the greater eccentricity of Mars, *Plate 74a*. This arm will be carried round by the pin bearing the image of the planet, which is set at the commencement of the first sign of the epicycle, and which will slide up and down the groove in the arm.

Wheel *M* moves forward 4 teeth in 4 days, so that the pinion of 18 turns, in the same direction, eastwards, 1 tooth and consequently makes a complete revolution in 4 × 172, i.e. 688 days or 1 year 10 months 19 days, and the mean *motus* of Mars as given in the tables amounts to 12 signs in amost exactly this period of time.

In the same time the wheel *T* makes one complete revolution, whilst the movable wheel turns about that fixed, and since it has 53 teeth, by means of their common pinion, it will turn the wheel of the epicycle also through 53 teeth. As each tooth correspond to 6°, this equals 10 signs 18°. In the time taken for the centre of the epicycle to traverse the whole band of the zodiac, which is 1 year 10 months 17 days 22 hours 22 minutes, the mean *motus* of Mars is 12 signs as given in the tables, and its argument is 10 signs 14° 4' 26", the actual motion of 10 signs 18° being a little fast.

DIAL OF THE DRAGON'S HEAD AND TAIL (THE NODES)

This dial, *Plate 76a*, is situated in the fourth panel of the lower frame and, as may be supposed, is driven off the lunar dial, which is directly above it. The circle of the zodiac is inscribed on the dial and a hand affixed so that the left edge of the pointer is in line with the centre of the zodiac. The pointer is squared on to a wheel behind the dial having 204 teeth. This meshes with a pinion of 12 on its upper periphery, which pinion carries wheel *C* of 100 teeth. This in turn meshes with a pinion of 10 carrying on its arbor a wheel *F*, with 20 saw-like teeth. This wheel is driven, a tooth at a time, by a pin fixed at the back of the wheel *E* of 27 teeth in the lunar dial, *Plate 67a*.

Thus, since *E* turns once in two days, *F* takes 40 days to make one revolution, pinion *d* of 10 therefore takes 400 days to turn wheel *C* of 100. Hence the pinion of 12 will take 17 turns to turn once the wheel of 204 teeth carrying the indicating arm. Therefore the period of revolution for this arm is 400 × 17 days, 6,800 days or 18 years 7 months 14 days, including leap years, during which time the

Dragon's Head, or ascending Node, travels through 12 signs 0° 5′ 21″, as against the 12 signs exactly of the clock.

This concludes the description of the clock proper. It will be recollected that the slight irregularity in the *motus* of Venus was met by cutting unequal teeth in a circular wheel. Dondi now gives a train for providing the *motus* of Venus with a pair of fixed and moving blunt-toothed wheels and a common pinion for the latter and the wheel of the epicycle, as provided for in the dial, of Mars, *Plate 75*. Taking the lettering of this *Plate 75*, the wheel of the epicycle has 48 teeth, wheel T has 30 teeth; these two nearly touch but do not mesh. Their common pinion, s, has 12 teeth. Then, while the moving blunt-toothed wheel is turning round the fixed by the equating circle, T is turning the wheel of the epicycle through 30 of its 48 teeth, which equals $7\frac{1}{2}$ signs; this is the same result as is given in the description of the dial of Venus.

The remaining 28 pages of the MS contain three chapters devoted to the detailed descriptions as to how to set the various dials, how to read them and how to correct the various errors that creep in by reason of the inability of the various trains to portray exactly the motions of the various planets.

Dondi first deals with the general maintenance of the 'common clock', its regular winding and with the daily setting of the hour dial which in accordance with the then Italian custom, was to be set daily at sunset, although Dondi states it is far more correct to set the clock right daily when the sun crosses the meridian, as that point never varies and can be ascertained accurately by instruments or from a sundial.

Then there follow very detailed instructions as how to free various keyed wheels in the different trains, to liberate them for the setting of the dials, and details of how this should be done.

The second chapter deals with the reading of the various dials, the ordinary 24-hour dial, the number of hours left in the 24-hour day as shown by the scales for the rising and setting of the sun, *Plate 58a*, the calendar dials, etc.

In the dial of the *Primum Mobile*, in addition to the motion of the sun, can be read through the rete of the astrolabe at every hour of the day or night, the four cardinal points of the heavens, the degrees of the ascendant, descendant, zenith, nadir; from which four corners can be ascertained, at any hour, the beginnings of the 12 celestial houses, be it by day or by night, 'which cannot be learnt from any other instrument so far as known'. In view of the importance of astrology in the lives of the people at this time, such an easy and continuous method of indication must have been considered a great asset. Dondi then gives detailed instructions for the reading of the astrolabe, rising and setting of the moon and the planets, the altitude of the sun, the temporal hours, etc.

For the three 'higher planets', i.e., Mars, Saturn and Jupiter, as well as for Venus, the mean centre is obtained by noting the position of the arm of the equating circle (that which carries the centre of the epicyclic dial) in the scale of signs of that circle; the extent to which that arm has traversed the signs from the opposition of the *Aux* of the equating circle, indicates the mean centre of the planet. To get the mean *motus* you read the distance of the *Aux* of the equating circle from the 1st point of Aries on the zodiacal circle and add this to the mean centre; if the result exceeds 12, you subtract that number, leaving the mean *motus*.

The argument of the planet is the extent to which the planet has moved in its epicyclic dial to the left of the line through the mean *Aux*. The true position of the planet in the zodiac is seen from the image of the planet as it slides in the slotted arm. (The calculations for Mercury are slightly different.)

The direction, retrogression and stations of the four planets, and for Mercury as well, is found as follows. If a line drawn from the 1st and 7th signs of the epicyclic dial is at right-angles to the arm marked 'Verus', the planet is stationary. If when this happens the planet is on the left of the epicyclic dial, i.e. on the east, the planet is in the 1st station, and if on the right, i.e. the west, the planet is in the 2nd station. But if this diameter cuts the pointer at an acute angle, or if the angle be obtuse, or if the line and the pointer coincide, with the planet being opposite the *Aux* of the epicycle, then the planet's motion is retrograde.

As regards the Moon, since this has no stations, direction or retrogression, the motion of the moon is medium in its course when the indication would be stationary for a planet, slow when the indication for a planet would be 1st or 2nd station, and fast when the indication for a planet would be retrograde.

The third chapter deals with the various corrections to be made. In dealing with the clock proper, if it be slow additional weight is to be added, and although the illustration shows a balance, if the clock be fast, small weights are to be added to the balance, which 'when they hang are tossed by its beat and which are inserted, as it were in its motion'. Dondi recommends that a supply of these small weights be kept handy.

As already stated, the annual calendar wheel is to be corrected by stopping the clock for 24 hours on February 24th in leap year.

The different lengths of the day due to the eccentric course of the sun are referred to, the sun taking nearly 186 days to traverse from the 1st point of Aries to the beginning of Libra and 179 days from that point back to Aries. Dondi naturally does not know of the influence of gravity in this connexion; he states that the part of the circle of the zodiac corresponding to the orbit of the sun in the deferent is smaller at the zenith, which is at the beginning of Cancer, and is greater at the part opposite to the zenith, but that these inequalities equalise in 182½ days as between the semi-orbit of the sun from *Aux* to *opposition Aux* to the *Aux* and back again.

He then deals with the equation of time and with the varying daily differences between sun and mean time, giving the days of equality as the beginning of Capricorn, December 23rd, the beginning of Cancer, June 14th, early September and at an unspecified date in October. As far as can be ascertained from the somewhat verbose text, these dates are those where approximate equality will be reached as a result of the somewhat rough and ready corrections he advises, viz: set the dial of the *Primum Mobile* one tooth forward on the 1st of January, February, November and December and one tooth back on the 1st of May, June, July and August.

Provision is also made for the dial of the *Primum Mobile* for the correction of the annual deficit of 5 h 50 m according to the Alfonsine tables. Dondi proposes a correction of 6 hours, leaving an overplus of 10 m. 25 secs. p.a. This he reckons to be equal to 15″ arc or 6 hours in 35 years; the correction is therefore to be omitted in the 36th years.

For the dial of Venus the annual error of 5 h 50 m will be met by stopping the clock in leap year. The residual error is to be met by setting the wheel *M* one tooth forward in the 46th year.

There is deficit in the period of the argument of Venus; this should be 7 signs 15° 10′ 41″, but the clock is 10′ 41″ slow p.a. In 6 years this will amount to 1° 4′ 6″. The plate of the epicycle should be freed by loosening the keys in the slots and the dial advanced 1° every 6 years, the residual error being corrected after 90 years by advancing the dial additional 1°.

For Mercury there is, beyond the correction at leap year, provision for a secondary correction after 144 years by setting the wheel *M* forward 1 tooth. In the argument of Mercury there is an annual deficit of 42′ 5″, so that the dial should be set forward 2/3° annually with a residual correction of 1° in 29 years.

For the moon Dondi calculates about 2 hours in the moon's mean *motus* in 7 revolutions of the moon's epicycle, i.e. 19 d. 8 hrs. The wheel *E* of 72 teeth which turns once in 2 days, should be set forward 3 teeth. There is a residual error of 27″ of arc, which after 28 years equals 21′ 56″ of arc or 40 m. of the moon's mean *motus*. Therefore after 27 adjustments, on the 28th, i.e. after 5,357 days: 14 years, 8 months after the first setting, the wheel *E* should be advanced by only 2 teeth instead of 3. This adjustment will upset the wheel of the *Aux*, which should be set back on the pinion *c* every third adjustment of the wheel *E*.

There is a deficit in the moon's argument of about 6′ 8″ each lunar month; the dial of the epicycle is to be set forward 1° every 9 months 22 days 7 hours. This will leave a residual error of 1° every 44 years, therefore after 45 corrections, the plate of the epicycle should be set forward 2: instead of 1:, and so the argument of the moon will be entirely corrected.

Similarly corrections are given for the dials of Saturn, Jupiter, Mars and the Nodes.

Having seen the 'long-term' view taken by Dondi for the care of his clock, it is not surprising to find in the summing-up of the various corrections to be made, a strong emphasis laid on the necessity for a reliable clock-keeper who will note accurately the time at which the clock was started and those of subsequent corrections.

The thought may arise; why take all this trouble to get such accuracy in the astronomical trains when the errors inherent in the motive clock are so great? But we must remember that the astronomical trains, with the exception of that of the moon, were only moved on 1 tooth a day through the annual calendar wheel so that the errors of the clock, which were to be corrected daily, could accumulate for a long time before it became a day out.

Again one wonders what would be the effect of friction on such a vast assemblage of dials and complicated trains. True, Dondi provided a subsidiary drive sufficient to take from the annual calendar wheel the strain of moving the dials, also that the motions are very slow: one tooth of the calendar wheel a day at the most. It is this slow motion that makes workable his dynamically bad elliptical wheels.

Perhaps Dondi's long-term policy was justified, for we hear that about 70 years after it was made, in 1440, Michele Savonarola wrote of the difficulty of getting the clock repaired. Eventually a French astronomer was found capable of doing this. According to Baillie it was still working in 1470 just 100 years after it was made but in another half-century, in 1529, it was again out of order. Von Basserman-Jordan in his *Alte Uhren und ihre Meister*, Leipzig, 1926, said that Charles V had Dondi's clock repaired, which it very badly needed, by one Juanelo Torriani, subsequently taking the clock and Torriani with him to Spain when he abdicated, where it remained at the monastery of San Juste until the building was burned by the orders of Marshall Soult on August 9th, 1809.

This version has been contradicted by Bedini[1] who states that no reference has been found to Dondi's clock after 1529–30, Torriani is believed to have made another astronomical clock with eight dials and a globe, which went to Spain with Torriani and Charles V.[2]

Of the ultimate fate of Dondi's clock nothing certain is known.

How fortunate we are Dondi left us this rich legacy, so revealing of the state of the knowledge of the sciences of horology and astronomy at this early period. The writer has had completed the translation of that part of the MS omitted by Baillie, this now runs to some 130,000 words with about 180 drawings and working sketches. Together with Mr. Drover he hopes some day to be able to publish the whole translation. Mr. Drover also has a translation of the Astrarium which it is hoped also to publish.

One can only regret that the MSS Richard of Wallingford is believed to have written, dealing with his great astronomical clock, made about 1320, some 35 years before Dondi, has not survived.[3] A comparison between the two would be most enlightening.

Those of my readers who have had the interest and the patience to collate the printed descriptions with Dondi's drawings cannot fail to have been impressed with the accurate state of knowledge of astronomy at the middle of the fourteenth century and the magnitude of the genius of this great savant. The more he reflects, the greater his gratitude that it was possible for him to rescue in the 50's the result of Baillie's researches of the 30's after twenty years of neglect and relegation to oblivion by an unappreciative horological world in general. In this expression of gratitude he must include the names of Mr. Geoffrey Buggins, Managing Director of Messrs Thwaites and Reed, London, who had the courage to take the risk

---

[1] *Mechanical Universe*, op. cit., p. 39.

[2] *Morpurgo Tractus Astrarii*, p. 41.

[3] Since this was written, a Richard of Wallingford MS has in fact been discovered by Dr. J. G. North of Oxford.

of quoting for building the clock where others were not willing and to Mr. Peter Haward, his co-Director and senior Clockmaker who actually carried out the work. Mr. F. N. Fryer, an instructor at the Sir John Cass Technical College, London, for engraving a faithful reproduction of contemporary script.

This first hurdle over, remained the problem of disposing of the clock when made. A disappointing lack of appreciation of the importance of Dondi's work in the evolution of the horological and engineering fields, was encountered in the museums of England, Italy and Germany; only in the U.S.A. was this appreciation found, resulting in the clock now being in the Smithsonian Institution in Washington D.C.

Whilst the work of Messrs Haward and Fryer whose names are engraved at the bottom of the Dial of Venus rightly acclaims them as Masters of their Crafts, we have to admit that they had detailed instructions before them, whereas Dondi had to work *ab initio* Planning, Calculating and Designing.

Dondi, whose manuscripts have ceased to be copied and referred to horologically since about the middle of the sixteenth century now lives in the minds of horologists in all the principal countries of the world and this the writer feels is his most important contribution to Horology; but according to reports the visitor to Washington will look in vain for any reference to this.

The Original Greenwich Clocks

UP TO THE PRESENT very little has been known regarding these two clocks except from Baily's *Life of Flamsteed*, London 1835, from which we learn that these clocks had 14-ft. pendulums beating two seconds and that one had a spring suspension and the other a pivot suspension. These two clocks are seen to the left of the door in the well-known engraving of the Octagon Room at Greenwich which is believed to date about 1676. *Plate 77*.

In the absence of further details it was assumed that these long pendulums hung down the stair well to the left of the door until, when restoring the Octagon Room to its original state in 1959, the Ministry of Works established that the floor below the clocks had never been disturbed, but that the beams above the clocks had been hollowed out to allow the passage of a weight suspended by a single cord. *Plate 78a*. The object of the small windows above the clocks in *Plate 77* had always been a mystery since the windows were behind the clock dials and so could not be used for illumination, until a replica of the British Museum original Greenwich clock was made (*Plate 79a*) and fitted with a 14-ft. pendulum above it when it was found that the pendulum bob appeared exactly behind the window. A temporary position of this clock and pendulum seen in *Plates 78b & 79b* shows the method of connecting pendulum and escapement. The excursion of this pendulum is so small that it is often necessary to watch the seconds hand to be sure that the clock is going.

In the absence of any further information the assumption was made that Tompion recalled Hooke's experiment recorded in the Minutes of the Royal Society dated 28.10.1669 where he showed that a freely-suspended pendulum 14 ft. long with a heavy bob could be kept in motion by a pin set in the rim of the balance wheel of a pocket watch threaded to a wire loop fixed below the pendulum. This gave the desired combination of a long period of swing and a small arc, but it must be noted that the pendulum was freely suspended and that the escapement actuating it was below the bob and was a verge, the only type of escapement in a pocket watch at that time.[1]

[1] *Horological Journal*, April 1962.

Some horological writers have wrongly taken this combination of long period and small arc to connect Hooke's name with the invention of the anchor escapement.

Recent researches by Lieut.-Commander Howse of the National Maritime Museum, Greenwich have revealed quite a different state of affairs and he has kindly given the author permission to use this information.

He unearthed an extensive correspondence between a Mr. Richard Towneley, a landowner of Towneley Hall, Towneley, a village near Preston in Lancashire, and a friend of Sir Jonas Moore, who in 1676 ordered these two clocks to be made by Tompion, as is seen from the inscriptions on them (*Plate 79c*). Towneley was well known at the Royal Society, but was not a Fellow, possibly as he was a Catholic.

Towneley's end of the correspondence, i.e. Flamsteed's letters to him, is in the files of the Royal Society who have kindly given permission for it to be drawn upon. The whereabouts of Towneley's letters to Flamsteed, if they still exist, is not known.

In a letter dated January 22nd, 1676, mention is made of the Octagon Room being 20 ft. high which would allow a long pendulum to be hung above the clock. Tompion's two clocks presented by Sir Jonas Moore were not delivered until July 7th, 1676 (letter July 6th, 1676). Flamsteed notes in this letter that the clocks had 'pallets partly after, your (Towneley's) manner'.

Whether the height of the room was decided upon to accommodate the long pendulums or the long telescopes is an open question, probably the latter as the long pendulums above the clock were an innovation and long telescopes were in current use.

Heretofore the writer has given Tompion the credit for adapting Hooke's experiment of 27.10.1669 and applying it to these two clocks, but it would seem this may not be the case. In a letter dated February 11th, 1676, to Towneley Flamsteed writes: 'I cannot hope to have it go perfectly well till I have got a bigger weight on the swing and a room to get it in that may permit it to be hung, as in yours, above the clock, which is doubtless the only way to make them move regularly [this cannot be one of the two clocks delivered 7 July 1676] and after which contrivance, that that Mr. Tompion fits for us, will be made up' – i.e. the two Jonas Moore clocks. Thus it will be seen that Towneley's use of a long pendulum with a heavy bob hanging above the clock probably had an influence on Tompion in designing the two clocks made for Sir Jonas Moore.

Another interesting point that has emerged is that the two original clocks do not appear to have been delivered with standard anchor escapements, those now existing being presumably substituted when

T

the clcoks left Greenwich and had the existing 39″ one seconds pendulums fitted.

In a letter dated March 2nd, 1675, Flamsteed writes: 'I have a pendulum (clock) making by Mr Tompion' and on December 11th, 1675: 'the Pallets of my watch (clock) are in the old form', presumably standard anchor escapement.

Something quite new in horological history is a drawing of a semi-dead-beat escapement by Tompion which is now revealed for the first time. Flamsteed relates in a letter dated December 11th, 1675, how he removed it from a clock in Sir Jonas Moore's dining-room, took a paper impression of it, measured it and sketched it (*Plate 8oa*).

He writes: 'the pallets are applied and play upon it with the true chamfer given to the teeth and by this way Sir Jonas thinks there is little check given to the second finger.' The date of this escapement is about 40 years before 1715, the date always taken about that of Graham's introduction of his dead-beat escapement, but as Graham did not join Tompion until 1695, it is possible that this escapement was dropped. Towneley had evidently here designed an escapement of this type since Flamsteed continues: 'but he thinks your pallets may do better and therefore intends to write to you to get us a movement made . . . with pallets after your way'. This clock did not need a high room, a pendulum 6 ft. 7$\frac{7}{10}$ inches is suggested, 44 beats to the minute, period a week or more. Flamsteed adds: 'Sir Jonas desires only the bare movement, for the face and fingers made to be added here (Greenwich) without further troubling you.'

Another unknown Tompion invention is described in a letter dated February 9th, 1678. Tompion changes the two part-Towneley pallets in the two 'great' clocks for an escapement of his own (*Plate 8oc*) It will be seen that this escapement is a forerunner by about three-quarters of a century of Amant's pin-wheel escapement of c. 1749, modified by Lepaute a few years later. Flamsteed writes: 'The pendulums vibrate now not much more than half as much as formerly. The form of the pallets I have sent you coarsely deliniated.'

'*a a b* are in the same plane, but the pallets *p p* are curved backwards and stand slipping from each other as in yours (Towneley's). Perhaps the less vibrations and easier escaping in this way may have contributed something to the extraordinary acceleration before mentioned.'

On February 15th, 1678, Flamsteed fulfils a belated promise to give details of the trains of the two 'great clocks' (*Plate 8ob*).

.   .   .   .   .

The diameter of the barrel on the axis of the last wheel on which the cord is wrapped is $1\frac{7}{8}''$ bore. I forgot to count how many times it was wound round it but you will find it an easy calculation.[1]

[1] Pendulum wheel A teeth 30 diameter $\frac{3}{8}''$ cogga 8

B	48	$1\frac{1}{2}''$	8
C	80	$2\frac{7}{8}''$	8
D	96	$3\frac{7}{8}''$	8
E	112	$6\frac{3}{4}''$	8

Thus we see much new light is thrown on to this question of the design, making and supply of these two original Greenwich Clocks. Perhaps Towneley's letters to Flamsteed may some day be uncovered at Herstmonceaux to fill in the present gaps in our knowledge.

Note on Symbols of Measure in Horology

Of time
OhO′ O″ = hours, minutes, seconds

Of arcs and angles
O° O′ O″ = degrees, minutes, seconds

Of watch movement diameter
″ ′ = ligne = one-twelfth of an inch

Of large clock movement
‴   = one-sixtieth
′ ″ ‴   = minutes, seconds, sixtieth parts of seconds

Glossary

ALMACANTARS   Parallels of altitude.

APOGEE   The point where an orbiting body is farthest from the earth.

ARGUMENT   The angular distance travelled by a planet in its epicycle.

AUX   That point on the zodiac struck by a line drawn from the earth through a planet when the latter is farthest from the earth.

AUX, OPPOSITE   A point at 180° from the Aux.

AZIMUTH   Vertical arc of sky from the zenith to the horizon; the angular distance of this from a meridian.

BALANCE   An oscillating wheel, which is controlled by the balance spring and regulates the going of a watch, or of a clock.

CELESTIAL HOUSES   The astrological term for the twelve signs of the Zodiac.

CHRYSTALINEUM   A sphere in the Ptolemaic system that represented the year of $365\frac{1}{4}$ days.

COLLET   A dome-shaped washer used to render firm the hands of a clock.

COLURES   The two principal meridians of the celestial sphere which pass through the solstices and equinoxes respectively. They are therefore at 90° to each other.

COPERNICAN THEORY   The heliocentric (i.e. with a central sun) theory as developed by Copernicus.

COUNT WHEEL   *See* Locking plate.

CROWN WHEEL   The escape wheel in a verge escapement.

CYCLOIDAL CURVE   The curve traced by a point on the circumference of a circle that is rolling along a straight line. It is the isochronous curve developed by Christiaan Huygens.

DAY
Mean: The day of 24 equal hours.
Sidereal: The period between two successive passages of a star across the meridian.
Solar: The period between two successive passages of the sun across the meridian.

DECLINATION   The angular distance of a star, or the sun, north or south of the equator.

DEFERENT   The radius of a circle whose centre is placed outside the earth, to account for the departure of the planetary orbit from the true circle.

DOMINICAL LETTER   January 1–7 are allotted the letters A–G. The letter for the first Sunday for January is the Dominical Letter for the year. In leap years two letters are required, one up to February 29th and the next preceding letter for the rest of the year. The Dominical Letter is used in connexion with the ascertaining of the date of Easter Sunday.

DUTCH STRIKING   The repetition of either the past or coming hour at the half hour, on a different toned bell.

ECLIPTIC   The sun's apparent orbit.

EPACT   The age of the moon on January 1st.

EPICYCLE   The supposed circular course of a planet, the centre of which travelled round the circle of the deferent.

EQUANT   An adjusting circle to provide equal angular motion at its centre for a planet, to be combined with its eccentric motion.

EQUATION OF TIME   The difference between mean time and solar time, as shown on a sundial.

EQUATORIUM   An instrument for computing geometrically the position of the planets.

ESCAPEMENT   The means of control over the driving force of a clock or watch. It is an alternating motion allowing one tooth of the wheel to escape at a time.

FOLIOT   An early form of controller for a clock, an alternative to the balance.

GOLDEN NUMBER   *See* Metonic Cycle.

GRANDE SONNERIE   Where, in a quarter striking clock, the hour is also repeated at each quarter.

GREGORIAN CALENDAR   The amended calendar introduced by Pope Gregory XIII in 1582 whereby leap years are omitted in three out of every four centennial years. This was not adopted in England until 1752 when the correction amounted to eleven days, the omission of which caused the financial year to end on April 5th instead of March 25th.

INDICTION   A Roman period of 15 years for taxation purpose. It is used in ecclesiastical contracts.

LEAVES   Pinions have leaves, not teeth.

LONG-CASE   Another term for 'Grandfather Clock'.

LOCKING PLATE   A wheel with notches at increasing intervals which allows a clock to strike the necessary number of blows at each hour before an arm falls into a notch and stops the striking.

LUNAR CYCLE   *See* Metonic Cycle.

MAINTAINING POWER   A subsidiary force that comes into action for a few minutes when the driving force of the clock is nullified during winding.

MERIDIAN   A circle passing through a place and the north and south poles.

METONIC CYCLE   The Greek astronomer, Meton, discovered that the days of full moon are repeated in a cycle of nineteen years. The Greeks considered this so wonderful that they had it carved on stone in letters of gold, hence the term Golden Number.

MOTUS (MEAN)   The angular distance, measured from the 1st Point of Aries, travelled by a planet round the ecliptic.

NODES   Two points of intersection 180° apart where the apparent orbit of the sun intersects that of the moon, to which it is inclined by about 5°. When the sun, moon, earth and a node are in line an eclipse of the sun or moon will occur.

PERIGEE   The position of an orbiting body when it is nearest to the earth.

PTOLEMAIC THEORY   The ancient theory of the Universe evolved by the Greek astronomer Ptolemy on the geocentric principle, i.e. with the earth in the centre.

RATING NUT   A nut below the pendulum bob for regulation.

REGULATOR   An extra accurate clock, usually a timepiece fitted with a compensated pendulum, jewels, &c.

RIGHT ASCENSION   The co-ordinate of a heavenly body as measured by the angle the meridian passing through it makes with the prime meridian through the vernal equinox.

RISE AND FALL   A device for regulating the length of a pendulum.

ROMAN STRIKING   A method using two different toned bells, one for the I and one for the V as used in roman notation.

SHEEPSHEAD   A late form of lantern clock in which the dial protrudes materially beyond the clock body.

SOLAR CYCLE   A period of twenty-eight years, after which the days of the month fall on the same days of the week.

SOLSTICES   Those two points where the sun reaches its greatest declination North and South of the celestial equator, June 21st and December 21st. The solstices are mid-way between the equinoxes, and so at 90° to them.

SOUTHING   The passage of a body, say the moon, across the meridian.

SPANDRELS   Decorative cornerpieces found on clocks.

SPOON LOCKING   A hook with a flattened tail fixed inside a long case so that when the door was closed, it pressed in the flattened tail causing the hooked end to go forward and catch the hood frame, so preventing it being raised.

TEETH   Wheels have teeth, but pinions have leaves.

TIME

   Equation of: The difference between mean time and solar time, as shown on a sun-dial.

   Mean: The artificial division of the day into exactly twenty-four hours.

   Sidereal: The measurement of time by the successive passage of stars across the meridian. The sidereal day is 3 minutes 56 seconds shorter than the mean day.

   Solar: The time as calculated by successive passages of the sun across the meridian, as shown on a sundial. (*See* Time, *Equation of*)

TRAIN   A series of wheels and pinions geared together in a clock, e.g. going train, striking train.

ZODIAC   A belt in the heavens, about 18° wide, outside which the sun, moon and planets do not pass. It is divided into twelve signs, each of 30°. Aries (The Ram), Taurus (The Bull), Gemini (The Twins), Cancer (The Crab), Leo (The Lion), Virgo (The Virgin), Libra (The Balance), Scorpio (The Scorpion), Sagittarius (The Archer), Capricornus (The Goat), Aquarius (The Water Carrier) and Pisces (The Fishes).

Index

Ahlden, Duchess of, 92
Ahaz, Dial of, 18
Albertis, Jo. Baptiste, 65
Alfonso X, the Learned, 176
Aman, Jost, *Book of Trades*, 27
Amant:
his pin-wheel escapement, 204
Amenemhe't, 155
Anne, Queen, 56, 106, 117, 147
Antram, Joseph, 91
Apogee, 19
Archeian, 171
Armagh Observatory, 137
Arnold, John, 65, 85, 138
makes watch in ring, 139
Artificial Clockmaker, 38
Arts Decoratifs, Musee des, 46
Aske, Henry, 90
Astrology in daily life, 48, 180, 196
Astronomical trains, 172–99
Atkins and Downs, 165
Aureliano, clockmaker, 174
Aux, 184, 185, 186, 187, 188, 189, 190,
191, 192, 193, 194, 197, 198, 199
opposite Aux, 185, 186, 188, 191,
193, 198

Baillie, G. H., 171, 173, 200
Baker, Edward, 124
Baldewin, clockmaker, 173
Banff Museum, 55
Barbados, 137
Barker, Wigan, 134
Barlow, Edward, 87, 88, 153
Bartlett, 157
Barwise, 139
Bassermann-Jordan, Ernst von,
Alte Uhren und ihre Meister, 200
Bath City, 107, 134
Beaux Arts, Musee des, Antwerp, 31
Bedini, Silvio, 156, 173, 200
Beeson, Dr. C. F., 78
Behind My Library Door, 68
Benevuto della Volpasia, 60
Benson, John, 131, 149
Bertele, Dr. H. von, 50
Bibliographie Universelle, 1814, 172
Big Ben, 27
Blacksmiths' Guild, 29, 40
Blind men's watches, 27
Blundell, Richard, case maker, 101
Bodleian Library, and MS 620, 171

Bogardus, Edward, 159
Boston, 159
Boulle, 121
Boxer Rebellion, 125
Braganza, Catherine of, 73
Brahe, Tycho, 29, 30
Brass, Thomas, 122
Brass, use of, 29
Breuget, A. L., 139
Brewster and Ingraham, 166
Bristol, Conn., 159
Clock Museum, 165
British Museum, 66
Brown, J. C., 167
Brown, Thomas, 133
Brunswick Museum, 50, 63
Bruton, Thomas, 134
Buckingham, Duke of, 117
Budgen:
Thomas, 127
William, 127
Bull, Randolf, 54
Burgi, Jobst, 29, 30, 50, 51, 63, 78
Burnap, Daniel, 159, 160
Burt, Edwin, 168
Buschmann, Johannes, 63

Cajetano, David A., of Vienna, 173–4
Camerini, 59, 60
Campini, P. T., 157
Cape of Good Hope, 137
Caroli, Christian, 63
Cases:
Adam style, 131
Arched, 122, 124
Chippendale style, 131, 132, 136, 161
Curled pediment, 131
Double Steeple, 166
Gothic ripple, 166
Lancastrian made, 134
Mahogany, 115
Phyfe-type, 166
Sheraton style, 131, 136, 161
wooden, introduced, 27
Cayenne, 137
Celestial Houses, 144
Centre of oscillation, 42
Charles I, 58, 69
Charles II, 8, 69, 73, 75, 83, 94, 120
Charles IV, Emperor, 173
Charles V, Emperor, 200
du Chesne, Claude, 153

211

Printed in Great Britain by
Cox & Wyman Limited
London, Fakenham and Reading

FLASHBACK

A teen gang drives into peaceful Murphy's Harbour and commits mayhem. When a stolen car is found in the lake with a woman's body in the trunk, police chief Reid Bennett suspects they may also have committed murder. But the car owner identifies the dead woman not as his wife but as his wife's friend. And *her* husband seems to have disappeared...

FLASHBACK

Ted Wood

CHIVERS LARGE PRINT
BATH

Library of Congress Cataloging-in-Publication Data

Wood, Ted
  Flashback / Ted Wood.
    p.   cm.
  ISBN 0–7927–1819–4 (hardcover)
  ISBN 0–7927–1818–6 (softcover)
  1. Bennett, Reid (Fictitious character)—Fiction.
2. Police—Ontario—Fiction.   I. Title.
[PR9199.3.W57F54   1994]   93–27287
813'.54—dc20   CIP

British Library Cataloguing in Publication Data available

This Large Print edition is published by Chivers Press, England, and by
Curley Large Print, an imprint of Chivers North America, 1994.

Published in the U.K. by arrangement with HarperCollins Publishers Ltd
and in the U.S. with Charles Scribner's Sons, a division of Macmillan
Publishing Co.

U.K. Hardcover ISBN 0 7451 2070 9
U.K. Softcover   ISBN 0 7451 2082 2
U.S. Hardcover ISBN 0 7927 1819 4
U.S. Softcover   ISBN 0 7927 1818 6

Printed in Great Britain

For Bill, Beryl and all the rest of the Aussie Woods

FLASHBACK

CHAPTER ONE

Five kids were standing around an old Ford Fairlane on Main Street. I weighed them up as I jogged out of the trees on to the dusty road surface of Main Street. After three years as police chief in Murphy's Harbour I know every one of the locals by sight, and most of the regular visitors. This bunch was out of tune with the town and I jogged over to the wall of the grocery store in my running shorts and T-shirt and pretended to stretch against the wall while I weighed them up.

They weren't sporting any gang regalia, colours or the same baseball caps worn backwards but the way they lounged on the fenders of the car, smoking, showed they had something to prove.

Only one was an individual threat, the biggest, he could have been twenty or even older, the same height as me, six one, about 175 useful pounds, boxer's muscles although his face was unmarked.

One of the others was carrying a baseball bat and he looked the most knotted up. He was around sixteen, fair hair and a neat little rat tail tickling his neck. One of the smokers said something to him and he said something hard and flat in return and they all laughed, yukking it up like actors. Then he made his

1

move, along the front street in my direction towards a mongrel dog tied by its leash to a post at the other end of the store.

He picked up speed and cocked the bat and I sprang. He was five yards from the dog, I was ten but I covered the ground in four strides. The kid stopped when he saw me coming but drew the bat back and stood ready to swing. He figured I would halt, out of range, and use my silver tongue. Instead I took the two extra steps and straight-armed him in the upraised elbow.

He sprawled backwards, dropping the bat. I grabbed it before one of the others could. They were on the move, springing away from the car, closing on me, shouting. Then the big one held his hand up and they stopped.

'Pretty tough, shovin' people around?' He was doing his best to sound rough but he had an educated voice.

'I'm the chief of police here. What's your name?'

He ignored the question, cocking his head to his claque. 'Some pussy town you got here, chiefy, if that's how you dress.'

The rest of them had surrounded me, sniggering. I was glad I'd picked up the bat. I had to keep control or be swarmed.

I reversed it in my hands, holding it like a rifle and bayonet, butt towards him, and moved in on him, fast. He backed off, which gave me whatever psychological advantage

2

there was but the others were still around me. 'In the car, son, and head out.' I told him, not raising my voice.

'Or what?' he sneered, but he licked his lips.

'I'm counting three.'

He looked around at his guys and nodded and they started inching in again.

'One,' I said clearly. They were four feet from me now, all around.

'Two.' He stood his ground.

'Three.' I reversed the bat and slammed the handle down on his toe. Not a recommended move. It did no more than embarrass him, making him swear and hop on one toe. But it worked, making it look like I didn't need to do more than humiliate him. I whirled, to face the next biggest. 'Get him in the car and out of town or you're next.'

He tried to stare me down for a moment, then took the other guy's elbow. 'Come on, Eric, the hell with this place.'

The guy shook him off and hobbled to the car and I watched as he got into the passenger seat and sat there, glaring at me.

The other three scrambled into the rear of the car, one of them saying, 'You ain't seen the last of us.' Then the driver spurted away, spinning the car in a U-turn that tore a rut in the unpaved roadway and left a plume of dust as they roared back down the road towards the highway.

3

I heard a woman's voice saying, 'They were going to kill Ragamuffin.' It was one of our regular summer people bending over the dog which had roused itself at last and was standing, shaking off the dust it had gathered.

'Maybe not,' I said. Why sow anxieties? 'They're just kids.'

She's a fussy little woman, a widow in her seventies. 'Well, you sure showed them, Chief. Thank you.' She hoisted her grocery bag tighter under her arm and unwound the dog's leash from the post. 'Come on, Ragamuffin, let's go home.'

I glanced around the street. The usual crowd of youngsters was standing on the patch of dusty grass against the end of the bridge. It's the gathering place for teenagers, where the girls can giggle and the boys arm-wrestle and swear at one another in their newly broken voices. Occasionally I have to ask them to keep the music down to a dull roar, other than that they're harmless.

I went over to them and asked, 'Hi, did you know any of those guys?'

They didn't. Even the boys were glad to tell me that. Usually they're too cool to talk, letting the girls do it for them, but they were against the gang, strangers on their turf.

I nodded and left them, cutting my run short to go down to the police station which is south of the bridge, instead of crossing

4

over and making my usual five-mile circuit of the water, both sides, both bridges. I wanted to let the other police know what was happening. Most of the towns hereabouts don't have police of their own, they depend on the Ontario Provincial Police, the OPP.

I called the Parry Sound detachment and alerted them, giving the licence of the Ford and a rough description of the kids. Then I checked the car's ownership. It belonged to a Walter Patton at an East Toronto address. I knew that Toronto has teen-gang problems so that didn't surprise me, but I wondered what they were doing this far north. Setting up a branch plant?

I hung up and sat for a moment glancing around my domain. Pretty good by the standards of cottage country. The office has a counter between me and the front door with a bench for the few people who linger long enough to sit down. There's the usual clutter of police posters and a rack of public information brochures on things like road safety and child abuse that nobody ever comes in to pick up. My side of the fence contains a desk with the original muscle-powered typewriter that was new when the office was built in the 'sixties. Behind the desk there's a stool that was once used by our civilian employee, the 'mister' in police slang. But he was let go a couple of years back when he got into trouble and the

5

town's been too cheap to replace him since, so its seat is getting dull. Then there are a couple of grey filing cabinets, a teletype machine and, new this month, a Fax.

There were a couple of messages on the teletype. A wide load would be heading up the highway the following night. If possible, I should be at the highway entrance when it passed, routine. But the second one stopped me. George Kershaw, white male, forty-two years old, five-ten, had eluded the guard who had been sent with him on a day pass from Joyceville, a medium security jail. He'd skipped from Toronto, at the Skydome where he had been attending a baseball game. He was wearing a blue shirt and slacks, was unarmed but should be considered dangerous.

I tore the message off and clipped it on the board I keep for special news. I knew he was dangerous. I'd been the guy who locked him away, five years ago, in Toronto, where he had held up a bank, shooting the manager and taking a female hostage. My partner and I cornered him half an hour later. He'd used the woman as a shield, threatening to blow her away, his words, until I told him I'd shoot him through the mouth and he'd be dead before he could react. Then he shoved her away and dived, shooting at me but I hit him first, taking the fight out of him. He'd sworn at his trial that he would get me. A lot

6

of them do that but I had a hunch he meant it. And I've put a few guys in jail since I've been here, so I was sure he knew where to come looking.

That did it. I stuck the baseball bat under the counter, on a ledge that contained a pile of accident forms and a six-pack of empty pop bottles. Then I locked the station, shoved the key back in the pouch on my shoe and headed home.

Freda was watering the garden when I got back. Wearing a big hat and the striped dress she had made for her pregnancy and usually referred to as 'the tent'. She was full term now and had been flagging for the last couple of weeks as the July heat picked up, but today she was full of energy, spraying the tomato plants.

'You're back early. Have a good run?'

'OK, as far as it went, but there was a hassle in town. Nothing serious, but I figured I should hold off on the exercise until later.' I put my arm around her shoulder and she gave me a quick kiss, buckling the brim of her hat against my forehead. Sam, my big German shepherd, got up from the porch and came down to greet me, looking a little aggrieved. He figures he's my shadow and was until Freda and I got together. With my wife vulnerable, I felt more protective than usual. That's why I'd left Sam with Fred when I went out. Fred? It's her own joking diminutive of Freda. Not many women could carry off a name like that without having cynics raise their eyebrows, but she's a charmer and the name fits her like the men's hats some girls wear.

She patted me on the shoulder. 'Right now a shower is a pretty high priority, old sport. Go for it. I'll make us a salad with some of this abundance here.'

'I'm in danger of ending up healthy,' I said, 'if this marriage lasts,' and ducked as she turned the hose on me.

We were eating lunch when the phone rang. I wondered if it would be one of our storekeepers to report the boys were back in town but it was a citizen with another problem. There was a car in the lake on the far shore. He'd noticed it while he was fishing off a rock.

Fred said she was going to read for a while, so I left Sam on watch in case Kershaw intended keeping his promise. I figured his presence would be enough to keep her safe and she didn't have to know I was worried for her. She had enough on her mind anyway. Then I drove off over the bridge at the north lock and down the west shore of the waterway, our section of the Derwent River system although this stretch is really a narrow lake.

I saw a crowd on the rock the fisherman had told me about. They were staring down

8

and when I joined them I saw the car's rear end, a couple of feet underwater.

I asked, 'Is Tom Fielding here?'

A lean young guy with an expensive graphite fishing-rod said, 'I'm Fielding.'

'Thank you for calling in. When did you see the car?'

'About half an hour before I called you. I ran back home and telephoned. Is it stolen?'

'Can't say without seeing the licence plate, but it shouldn't be in there, that's certain. There's a car missing from Parry Sound.' I looked around at the crowd. Most of them would have been in bed before the car was even stolen, I figured, we get only a couple of TV channels locally. There's not much to do after dark but slap mosquitoes.

'Does any of you live close by?'

A woman nodded, she was about my age, late thirties. A looker but not working at it, lean, self-possessed, a cool, managerial type, I knew her by sight. 'That's my place over there.' She pointed to a white-painted cottage on the far side of the road.

'You're Ms Tracy, right?'

'Right.'

'Did you hear anything last night, Ms Tracy?'

She shook her head. 'No, but I was out until around twelve-thirty.'

As we spoke I was weighing up the terrain. The rock we were on sloped towards the water. One man could have pushed it into the lake unassisted. The splash would have been loud, but splashes aren't uncommon. My radio squawked and I held up one finger, 'Excuse me a minute, please.' I went back to the car and picked up the mike. 'Police chief.'

It was Gilles Perrault, the guy who runs the bait store on Main Street, reaching me through the phone line which kicks into my radio link. 'Reid. Gilles Perrault. Come quick. Kids been in, pushed the tank over, stole all kinds of stuff.'

'Be right there.' I took a moment to tell the crowd I'd be back with a tow truck. Then I told Ms Tracy, 'I have an emergency to attend to, could I come and talk to you later, please?'

'Of course. I'll be around until six.' She wanted to say more and I gave her a half-second before she blurted, 'I heard the radio. A swarming? Does that mean there are teen gangs in town?'

'I'm about to find out.' I inclined my head to her and left. On the way I called Fred and had her patch me through to Kinski's Garage. When they answered I told Paul about the submerged car and asked him to bring his tow truck up and start hauling it out. He swore when he heard it was under water, then grunted, so I guessed he'd find some way to get a chain on it. Then I put my

10

foot down and picked up speed to Main Street.

The gang had really done a job on Perrault's store. His floor was awash with water and minnows wriggling every which way and muddy with a mixture of worms and moss. Gilles and an elderly customer were struggling to set the fish tank back on its base. It was a galvanized cattle trough but lined with bricks on the bottom and heavy.

He was swearing rapidly in French as he worked and he didn't stop until we had the tank back in place and he had run a hose into it. Then he thanked us and set about scooping up his stock. I hooked a pail off the wall and helped him. Sightseers crowded around the doorway, but none came in to help, they stood there drinking up the sight. It's the same at every kind of calamity. Some help, most watch.

It took us about five minutes to get most of the shiners back in the tank which was filling slowly. While Gilles hunted down the last of his minnows off the floor I asked him what had happened.

'Was kids. Couple big, maybe seventeen, eighteen. The rest younger. They came in, one came up to the counter an' then the rest ran wild, grabbin' stuff, tippin' the tank. I try to stop dem an' one big one push me over. Two, t'ree others was throwin' worms out of the fridge.'

11

'Did you see the bunch I had the heyrube with earlier?'

'No. I was busy an' it was over quick. Some customer tol' me. Said they was gonna kill a dog. But I never seen these kids before.' He found a dustpan and started sweeping up the worms, swearing again in his guttural Québecois French.

It sounded like the return of the dog-bashers, looking to pay me back for chasing them off earlier, but I dug for details. 'Were they wearing any kind of uniform? The same baseball caps maybe or a handkerchief hanging out of their pockets, anything?'

'I never seen nothin',' Gilles said miserably. 'They took lures, couple rods, anythin' they could grab.'

I asked the customer, 'Were you in here, sir, when this happened?'

'No. I got here as they were running out of the place. About knocked me over.'

I washed my fishy hands, took the customer's name and address and told Gilles to make a list of what had been stolen while I tried to trace the kids, then I went outside, leaving the customer beating Gilles down on his bait purchase, claiming that the minnows were shocked and would go belly up in no time.

A couple of people claimed to have seen the kids leaving but no two of their descriptions jibed so I had nothing to go on. I gave up, going into each of the stores and telling each of the clerks to phone the moment they recognized any of the kids or if a bunch of youths came in at once, not to wait until they swarmed the place. Then I saw Kinski's tow truck heading north up the other side of the lake and I got back in the car and followed it up.

It turned off the roadway and backed down the rock through the crowd which had swelled since I left. When it stopped, just as I arrived, I saw it was Kinski himself, one of the hard-working Poles who got out of their country a year or two ago when Solidarity was making waves, and he had his son with him, a lean blond boy in jeans and a T-shirt which he shucked as soon as he got out of the car, revealing a swimsuit.

Paul waited for me to walk over, then said, 'Peter swims good. He come with me to put on the chain.'

'Good thinking. Don't try anything tricky, Peter, like getting yourself underneath the car, duck down and reach under, that's all.'

'No worries.' He grinned cheerfully while his father unhitched the hook and loosened the tow cable.

As we waited I asked him, 'Tell me, Pete, have you heard anything about any gangs around here?'

'Gangs?' I could tell he hadn't.

13

'Yeah, any bunch of losers hanging around together, maybe wearing something the same, same belt, same cap, same coloured shoe-laces, anything like that?'

He shrugged. 'I been workin' with Dad all summer, running the pumps an' that.'

'OK, thanks. If you hear anything, see a bunch of kids in a car together, make a note of the number, would you, and call me.'

'No worries,' he said again, then took the hook from his father and snapped on a scuba mask. He clambered down the rock and dropped neatly into the water, holding his mask on. His father let the hook loose and let it run down to water level where Peter took it. Then he took a couple of deep breaths and sank under the water. He came up once for more air, then the second time he gave us a thumbs-up.

'Out the way,' Paul called, and put the crane in gear. The truck lurched once, then locked, and the car came backwards out of the water with Peter treading water, clear of it. I saw that the driver's window was open. That was good. It probably meant the driver hadn't drowned. But I went to the left side of the car and checked anyway as the car cleared the water's edge. I'd already noted that it was the Honda that had been stolen from Parry Sound, a town half an hour north of here up the highway.

The crowd swarmed around it as it came

14

out of the water and I had to tell them to back off, missing Sam; one hiss from me and he would have kept them back with no trouble.

When Paul had it up on the rock I took a better look inside. It was empty and the radio was missing and the seats had been slashed with a knife. Another act of gang mischief. Three in one day. If there was any truth to the old superstition, that was our quota for a while.

I opened the door to let the water out. The key was in the ignition, I noticed, a single key, not ring. Odd. Just about everybody keeps their keys together on a ring. Having it separated out like that looked deliberate.

Paul got down from the cab of his truck and came to tie off the wheel. He saw the slashed unholstery and spat angrily. 'Punks. Big tough guys with a knife, yeah?'

'Gutless,' I said automatically. 'Can you take it to your yard? I'd like to look it over before the owner has it picked up.'

He agreed and waited for Peter, who was towelling himself off and slipping his T-shirt back on, then drove off with the Honda trailing.

I took ten minutes to check with the neighbours, making sure nobody had heard anything. Nobody had. The only help I got was that there had been a ballgame on TV until close to eleven, after that all the

15

residents had been asleep, except for Ms Tracy who had not got home-until after twelve and had read for an hour or so before turning off the lights.

'You're sure you heard nothing?' I was a bit surprised that the noise hadn't woken her up. The splash would have been loud enough to have startled people. And if kids had done this, there could have been some yelling going on.

'I have an air-conditioner in the bedroom window,' she explained. 'It's pretty noisy.' Then, surprisingly, she added, 'Come and see for yourself.'

'OK.' I walked with her, weighing up the facts. Allowing that the noise might have reached her before she went to sleep, there were two windows of time in which someone could have driven the car into the lake, just around midnight or after two in the morning. The only snag was that if everyone within a couple of hundred yards had air-conditioning they would all have been deaf to the noise. Ah well, no big deal, the car was intact, more or less, my job was over when I'd reported it found.

I had an odd feeling about Ms Tracy. She was cool to the point of rudeness and I wondered why. She had never crossed my path before and had no cause for resentment. Maybe she had some old militant attitude towards the police. A lot of people got that way in the 'sixties. All I knew was that she owned the cottage and came up here on and off all summer. There didn't seem to be any men, or women for that matter, in her life. She seemed to be one of those people who pass through life without touching the sides. Today she was wearing blue jeans and a cotton top knotted around her waist offering the occasional flash of firm brown belly. Not exactly erotic but attractive. And she wanted to help me. A minor mystery.

I followed her to the back of her cottage, the kind of winterized place that a lot of our long-time visitors build with plans for retiring here. Most don't. They stay in Toronto where the stores and their grandchildren make the winters more congenial.

The only concession to country living was a big screened verandah with comfortable chairs and a radio tuned to a classical music station. She opened the door and ushered me in. I stepped up on the porch and waited while she opened the main door of the house and said, 'Come on in, see for yourself.'

That was when my cop's instincts began to tickle. This was above and beyond the call of good citizenship. But I followed, keeping my hat on to show this wasn't a social call.

Her bedroom was comfortable, a queen-sized bed and a good shelf of books.

17

There was a pile of bound typescripts on the side table. I'd seen my wife studying books like them. She's an actress.

The air-conditioner was running and it was as loud as she had suggested. She raised her voice slightly. 'See what I mean? I couldn't have heard a head-on crash.'

'True enough. Thank you.' I turned immediately and went back through to the porch. She followed. 'I love this heat, don't you?'

'It helps to make up for the winters.' I paused and she leaned on the doorjamb, on one foot, the other raised on tiptoe behind her, a dated pin-up shot. 'Would you like some iced tea?'

'No, thank you. I have to look in at home. My wife's expecting a baby just about any minute.' I smiled to show I wasn't being standoffish. 'Thanks anyway. The reason I came with you is that I thought you might have something you wanted to tell me without the neighbours hearing.'

'Oh?' she cocked her head. 'Like what, for instance?' She looked the way she might have done in her office in town, exercising good control of some subordinate.

I raised my hands. 'No idea. But people have funny ideas about the police. It's unfashionable to be any more helpful than is absolutely necessary.'

'And you have me pegged for a feminist,

lesbian maybe, because I'm Ms Tracy, not Mrs.'

'I've been a policeman too long to generalize about anybody.'

'This place is my hideaway,' she said softly. 'In Toronto I work like a dog. I'm a feature film producer and I deal with every variety of bastard. Rich creeps who want to put money into movies so they can get next to the actresses, actors with egos the size of Czechoslovakia, unions, bitchy gay beauticians, every kind of headache you can imagine. But here I can be alone, be myself.'

It was more impassioned than I needed and I wondered why she was telling me. 'Well, thanks for the help. Enjoy your stay. When are you going back to town?'

'Next week sometime. When's the baby due?' Tit for tat. If I'd been exploring the possibility of a little dalliance she was carrying the ball.

'Any moment.'

'*Mazel tov*,' she said and smiled as if she meant it. 'Let me know when it happens. I don't always drink tea. We'll wet the baby's head.'

I didn't answer, just smiled and left, with the ripe summer warmth on my bare arms, feeling aroused. Chill out, I told myself. She was playing games.

I called in on Fred who was sitting on a chaise-longue by the back door, knitting. She got up when I arrived. 'Hi, honey. Like some iced tea?'

'You should be resting.' I wagged a finger at her. 'All this energy is getting me nervous. Sit still. I'll make it.'

'I phoned my mother this morning. She tells me the energy means today's the day,' she said cheerfully. 'Can't be soon enough for me, I'm tired of looking like the side of a house.'

'It's still the nicest-looking house in the neighbourhood, even with the bay window,' I said. She threw a cushion at me.

She likes an instant tea mix, so I chopped up a lemon and threw in the ice cubes and had the whole thing ready in a couple of minutes. She put her knitting down when I carried the tray out to the back yard and poured. She laid the cold glass against her cheek. 'Mmmm,' she said happily.

'Just had a lady make a veiled pass at me,' I said.

'Not surprising. You're almost attractive in a roughcast sort of way.' She sipped her tea. 'Who was it?'

'Woman called Tracy. Don't know her first name. She lives, summers anyway, across the lake, about half a mile south of the bridge. Says she's in the film business in Toronto.'

Fred frowned. 'Not an actress?'

'Production, she said. Was telling me this

20

place is her hideaway, away from terrible people like actresses and people wishing to have their wicked way with them.'

Fred wrinkled her nose at me. 'Look where it gets us.' She patted her stomach. 'Would it be Marcia Tracy, I wonder? She's head honcho at Northland Productions in Toronto.'

'Thirty-fiveish, trim, not much make-up, blonde.'

'Did she have a mole on her left buttock?'

'Right,' I said and Fred laughed.

'She's a ballbreaker. Two ex-husbands and a string of hopeful young studs behind her.'

'Fear not. I retreated with my honour intact.'

'Good for you, dear,' she said. 'Not much longer and we can make the bedsprings sing their old sweet song.'

'You're having a private room at the hospital?'

'You're a terrible man, Bennett,' she said.

I finished my tea and kissed her before heading down to Kinski's to look at the car. We've got a good thing going and I guess I'm one of nature's monogamists. It's my second marriage. My first was a girl I met in college. I dropped out but she got a degree in math, which has led her into computer sales. I was probably grating on her from the time I joined the Toronto Police Department and it fell apart completely when I cancelled a couple of bikers who were raping a variety store clerk. I was arrested for manslaughter and even though the case was dropped, Amy was long gone. There had been other women before Fred but not since she came into my life a year ago. I guess I'm terminally married.

Paul Kinski had the Honda in his pound. He does the tow work for the Ontario Provincial Police in this area and his yard is half filled with wrecks he's scraped off the rocks and roadways for fifty miles each way, rusting gently while the insurance companies and the courts dispense their decisions. The Honda looked almost new among them.

I called the Parry Sound detachment and reported the car recovered. The dispatcher read me off the name and address of the owner, then stopped. 'Hey, here's a thing. He's from your neck of the woods, Reid. Says he's staying at Pickerel Point Lodge, Murphy's Harbour. Be there for a week.'

'Pickerel Point? I wonder why he reported it stolen to you guys? Did he come into the office or call in?'

'No idea. No sweat anyways, cross it off your worry list.'

I hung up and called Pickerel Point Lodge. The manager put me on hold while she went out to the tennis court and dragged the owner in. His name was John Waites and he

22

sounded like a yuppie.

'Mrs James said this was important.'

'Police chief here. We've recovered your car. It's at Kinski's Garage, Petro-Canada station on Highway 69, half a mile south of the Harbour.'

'What kind of condition is it in?' An unusual reaction.

'Well, it wasn't cracked up but it's been in the lake and somebody has ripped off the radio and slashed the seats.'

'Slashed the seats?' There was a flutter of sound as if he had changed hands on the receiver. 'Well, goddamn it,' he said. 'When did that happen? After it was pulled out?'

I didn't like him, I decided. 'It was done when the car was recovered from the lake.'

'Very well. I'll come down and look. Stay there.' He hung up before I could tell him it wasn't driveable. Serve him right, I thought, he sounded like a creep.

There was nothing else going on, so I accepted Paul's offer of a cup of coffee and went into his little diner to enjoy it. He makes good coffee and I was OD'd on iced tea. I sat and savoured it until a Mercedes pulled into the lot, avoiding the pumps, and a young guy got out of the passenger side. He was wearing tennis gear that revealed he had a good build and a tan. He was around five-nine and had neat, yuppie hair, dark and a little long but immaculately sculpted over

23

his round head.

He came to the door and I checked behind him, trying to recognize the driver of the car, a woman who left without looking back.

He spoke to Peter at the pumps and followed the boy's finger to the coffee shop. I sat and waited for the grand entrance. He came up to me. 'John Waites. You called me about my wife's car.'

'The blue Honda, licence MW?'

'Right. Where is it?'

I got up and led him out to the car. I saw Paul shaking his head. He has European manners and hates impoliteness. Waites wrenched the door open and swore. 'Look at that. Vandalism.'

I said nothing until he got in and turned the key. Nothing happened. 'You would have been smarter to hold your ride for a while,' I said.

He swore again and banged the wheel with his hand. It all seemed a little too keyed up. Most people who get their cars back are sullen but they don't explode. 'Was that your wife in the Mercedes?' I asked.

He glared at me. 'No, it wasn't. If it's any of your damn business my dear Moira walked out yesterday, taking this car with her.'

'And then she called you from Parry Sound and told you it was stolen?'

'No. I did that.' He got out of the car and

24

slammed the door. 'I was mad at her and I knew she was going up there. She has a friend there, some other dippy painter. The car is in my name and I was so angry when she left I reported it stolen, just to embarrass her.'

'That constitutes public mischief,' I said. 'You could be summonsed.' I was stretching it but only slightly, he had certainly bent the law although nothing would be done about it.

'I wonder what else they took,' he said. 'I had my golf clubs in the back.'

'You didn't take them out when she packed the car and left?'

'She did it while I was out. Left me a note.' He took the key out of the ignition and undid the trunk. I looked over his shoulder as he did it and then shoved him aside before he could reach in. A woman's body was coiled in the trunk, her fair hair pasted over her face with the water that had drowned her.

CHAPTER TWO

Waites reeled back, covering his face with both hands. I held him by the elbow until I was sure he wouldn't collapse and he stood rocking up and down from the waist. When I

25

was sure he wouldn't keel over I turned my attention to the dead woman, going by the book, checking for a pulse. There was none of course, and she had a slight froth around her mouth. She had drowned.

Waites came back to the car. There were tears in his eyes and he made as if to lean on the rim of the trunk but I didn't let him touch it, putting my hand on his shoulder, propping him. 'I'm sorry, Mr Waites. Your wife is gone. Come inside.'

He shambled beside me to the diner. Paul Kinski looked up in surprise. I raised one finger to him and he bit down his questions and waited while I sat Waites in a booth. 'Do you have any liquor, Paul? Vodka, something?'

'Rye I got.' He raised an eyebrow at me and I held up one hand where Waites couldn't see it.

'Rye'd be good, can you get a shot for Mr Waites, please. This is an emergency.'

He went back into the house and came out with a bottle of Black Velvet. I took it off him and sloshed an ounce or so in a coffee cup and took it over to Waites. 'She was alive yesterday,' he said in a puzzled tone. 'Then we had a fight. Over nothing at all, really. She wanted to paint, I wanted her to play golf. Stupid. And it got kind of nasty and I went out for a walk and she left. And now she's never coming back.'

26

Paul Kinski was trying hard to overhear. I looked across at him. 'Can you get Mr Waites a cup of coffee, please? And can I use your phone?'

'Sure, come in back.' He walked out from behind the counter and drew back the curtain that led to the private section of the house. I went through and he followed me, his Polish accent coming out in his anxiety. 'What's happening, Chief? He's upset about the seats so much?'

'His wife's body is in the trunk. Make sure nobody gets into your yard. I've got to call the doctor.'

We went into the kitchen, where Paul's wife was stirring something on the stove. She hasn't learned much English yet but young Peter has taught me a couple of words of Polish so I smiled and said 'Djen dobrie' and she smiled back, showing a European gold tooth.

I took the phone and called Dr McQuaig. Fortunately he was in and promised to come right over. Next I called Carl Simmonds, the local photographer. He was just heading out on a wedding shoot but he said he'd come to the garage first. Finally I called McKenney's funeral parlour and asked them to send a hearse.

Then I went back out to the front and sat down across from Waites in the booth. 'What are you going to do?' he asked in a

27

dull voice.

'There's going to be a full investigation. I have the doctor coming and the photographer. I'm going to fingerprint the car and the doctor will do what he has to.'

'You mean he'll see if she's been raped. Why don't you talk straight?' He was angry. There were no tears in his eyes.

'We'll want to talk to this person she was going to see. Do you have a name?'

'Carolyn Jeffries and her husband, of course. They run a framing gallery, sell paints and frames and crap in Parry Sound.'

'Did your wife tell you she was going to see them?'

'She goes there all the time. She and the woman were in Art College together. I think Moira has—He stopped and corrected himself. 'I think she had a soft spot for the husband. He's an American hippy, bearded pinko type.'

'You don't like these people?'

'What's that got to do with anything? They weren't my friends, were they? Anyway, what's not to like? Granola and sandals and all that 'sixties garbage.' His bereavement hadn't made him any more charitable.

'When did your wife leave? What time?'

'Four o'clock was the tee-off time.' He fixed me suddenly with a bleak stare. 'You can check that if you want to. At the Pines.'

'And you had a fight and she left. What

28

time was that, do you remember exactly?'

'It went on,' he said vaguely. 'I'm not sure when it finished except that it was too late for golf and anyway, by the time I came back she was gone and my clubs were missing.' He was wearing a Rolex and looked like the kind of guy who measured out his day in fifteen-second intervals. Why was he being vague!

'Sorry for asking but did you and your wife argue a lot?'

He snorted mirthlessly. 'The reason we came up here was we were trying to get something going again. Things have been rough. This holiday was kind of one last try before she went home and called her lawyer.'

'It was that bad?'

'I don't know why we ever got married except maybe she needed a meal ticket. All she cared about was painting and I was dumb enough to let her sit home doing it while I worked.'

'But it didn't work out?'

'No.' He pursed his lips. 'It didn't work out. I got tired of coming home at nine, ten o'clock at night and finding the breakfast dishes in the sink while she sat in front of one of her stupid bloody paintings with no thought of time in her head. No dinner ready, not even dressed tidily enough that we could eat out anywhere reasonable. She was a slob.'

'The clothes she's wearing now look tidy.'

He looked at me with something like a sneer. 'Up here she'd've fit in like feet into shoes. That was the best she ever dressed.'

'You say she left a note. Do you still have it?'

'No. I flushed it down the john. I was angry.' Disappointing but in character.

Dr McQuaig's station wagon pulled into the lot and I stood up. 'The doctor just got here. Excuse me a minute. If you need more coffee, another drink, Paul will bring it to you.' He shook his head. I could see he had barely tasted his rye.

McQuaig is a tall old Scot and he was wearing paint-stained grey slacks and a check shirt. He had a beat-up hat on with a small Mepps spinner hanging on the band.

'Hi, Reid. An odd place for a drowning? Did Mrs Kinski slip in the shower?'

'No, this one's a homicide, Doc. Found a woman's body in the trunk of a car that spent the night in the lake.'

'Well I'm damned.' He came with me and bent over the body to check the throat with his forefinger. 'No doubt about it.' He peered at the foam around the mouth. 'This is classic drowning, Reid. She was alive when she went into the water, although she wasna kicking.'

'That's what I thought. If she'd been concious at the time she would have been scrabbling at the catch or pressing at the lid, or something. But she just lay there and died.'

He tilted his hat back and scratched his head thoughtfully. 'Ay, that's how it looks. I'll know better when I've examined her.'

'I've got McKenney coming for the body shortly. First I want Carl to photograph everything.'

'Right. I'll be at McKenney's in an hour. First I'll try a few more casts at that bass beside my dock.'

'Try a Fireplug if you've got one,' I said and he sighed.

'I think you've shares in the company, Reid. You never recommend anything else these days.'

As he left Carl Simmonds pulled in. He's the only chronic bachelor in Murphy's Harbour, a sweet guy but with a toughness to him that has been a big help to me on a lot of cases. Today he was wearing his working gear, a safari jacket, pockets crammed with gadgets and spare film, and he was carrying his Leica.

We shook hands and he said, 'A drowning you said, Reid?'

'Yeah, Carl, a homicide. Woman was shut in the trunk of a car and the car was driven into the lake, just south of the lock on the west side.'

'Hmmm.' He took out his light-meter and

31

thrust it close to the face of the dead woman. 'Pleasant-looking girl,' he said. 'Madly Woodstock.'

'That's what the grieving husband says. Only he's more mad than grieving.'

'Sounds suspicious.' Carl's voice had a playful yodel.

'We'll see. Meantime, if you could get all the angles, please. And then take a few shots of the interior. The seats have been slashed pretty badly.'

He looked up from his viewfinder. 'Sounds like teenagers. I guess you heard about downtown this morning? Two incidents.'

'I was there for one of them. This could tie in.'

He took half a reel of film, including close-ups of the foam at the mouth and of the dead woman's limp left hand lying across her body. Then McKenney and his ghoul-in-training arrived and I let them remove the body. It had not stiffened much and they laid it on their gurney and we got our first look at her face. Pleasant, I thought. Carl had picked the right word. No make-up, a fresh-faced, natural-seeming blonde in her late twenties. She was wearing a pale blue cotton blouse and a printed peasant type skirt and sandals. Her clothes were still wet and I could see that she wasn't wearing a brassiere, nor in much need of one.

For once McKenney worked without questions. He's a pale man in his fifties with a set of false teeth that look like a row of Chiclets. He's also the world's worst gossip and I knew he wanted facts to go on, but I gave him only one. 'The husband's in the diner. I'll bring him in later on to tell you about the arrangements. I'd guess she'll have to go to Toronto. Meantime the doctor will be there in an hour, if you could be ready, please.'

'Of course, Chief.' He nodded slowly. 'Whatever you say.'

'Thanks, Les. I'd be sunk without you.' Manners cost nothing, my dad always said.

They drove off and Carl took a few more shots of the interior of the trunk, then said, 'Got to go. It's only half an hour to the wedding and the family will be screaming for blood.'

'Thanks, Carl, can you call me when you've printed these up?'

'For sure.' He drove away and I closed the lid and went back into the coffee shop. Waites was sitting with his shoulders slumped, gazing into his coffee cup. A couple of other customers had come in and were looking at him curiously.

'We can go now, Mr Waites. I'll drive you back to the lodge. Later I'll ask you to come down to the funeral parlour and make

33

arrangements for your wife. And just for my report, I'll have to ask you to identify her, formally.'

'You thrive on this, don't you?' he said angrily.

'It's my job, that's all. I wish it wasn't distressing but sometimes it is.'

I led him to the cruiser, dropping five bucks on the counter for Paul, who protested until I waved him off. Rye isn't cheap and he had been invaluable, keeping Waites there while I worked.

As I drove Waites back to his hotel I went over the case. Waites himself was the most likely suspect. There was only his word for it that his wife had driven away. A more probable suggestion was that he had driven off with her himself, bumped her on the head maybe, then slashed the seats of his car to make it look like vandalism and driven it into the lake. His hotel was only half a mile from the place the car had been found.

Against that was his claim that his golf clubs had been in the car. If they turned up in his possession I would know he had been lying to me although that still would not prove him guilty.

The only confusing fact was the time he had reported the car stolen. Six-thirty p.m., daylight. He wouldn't have reported it missing and then run the risk of being found driving it, with his wife's body in the trunk.

At the hotel I went up to his room with him and checked the closet, not telling him why. I wanted to see that his golf clubs weren't there and none of his wife's things. Then I went in for a word with Mrs James who runs the place. She was brisk but friendly. It turned out she had been doing her books the day before and had barely left the office. But she called in the waitress who had been on duty at dinner-time and the girl reported that Waites had been there from the time she came on duty. He had sat at the bar all evening, with a break for dinner, then back to the bar. 'You know, like a movie, like drowning his sorrows. Didn't talk, didn't do anything. Just sat and drank.'

'Was he on his own?'

'Yes. Usually his wife's with him but not last night.'

'You're sure of that? You know the guy I mean?'

'Positive. 'Scuse me, Mrs James, but like he's picky, eh. His wife's nice but he's always finding fault, sent his steak back one night, complained that the coffee was cold. You know.'

'You know his wife, do you?' She nodded and I asked, 'Did you see her drive away yesterday afternoon, around four, five o'clock?'

'I'm in the dining-room from four on,' she explained, 'Sorry.'

35

'Thanks anyway. There's one other thing. He says his golf clubs are missing. Have you seen them around anywhere?'

'Haven't seen any layin' around. I could ask Chuck.'

'Chuck's our handyman. He's here all day,' Mrs James explained.

'Good, could you talk to him, please?'

She left and Mrs James asked, 'What's going on, Chief? There's more to this than a set of golf clubs missing.'

'His wife has drowned in his car. He says she took off in it yesterday. I want to know if that's true.'

She puffed out her cheeks in a little gasp of surprise. 'Lord, that's terrible. I'll ask around, see if anybody heard anything.'

'Preciate that. Try not to say too much, please.'

She said, 'Count on it,' and picked up the phone. I left after talking to Chuck, who had been away from the lodge from five until six, taking garbage to the town dump. No help there.

Dr McQuaig arrived at the funeral parlour as I did and we walked in together. 'You're quick,' I told him. 'Thought you'd still be fighting that bass.'

'Three pound, smallmouth,' he said happily. 'Damn if you weren't right with the Fireplug. He came from under a lily-pad and nearly tore my arm off.'

36

'I'll make a fisherman of you yet.'

McKenney had the body waiting for us in his preparation room, a grim place with a stainless steel table with draining grooves on it. He wheeled the gurney out and stood back, hands folded in front of him, waiting for the revels to begin.

'I'd like to keep this in the family, Les,' McQuaig said, 'If you don't mind, please. This is Chief Bennett's investigation.'

McKenney nodded without speaking and left and the doctor pulled the sheet off the young woman's body and pulled up her eyelids to look at her eyes. 'Her pupils are different sizes. I think the wee thing had a concussion.'

He rolled the body over, gently and felt in her hair. 'Ah-ah.'

'What is it?'

'She's been hit on the temple.' He fingered the spot, stooping to peer at it. 'It was one hell of a smash, the wound itself is depressed, although there's some swelling around it.'

'Any guesses about the weapon, or the guy who did it?'

'It's a small wound, must have been done with something small but heavy, a small rock held in one hand maybe.'

'Could it have been done with a golf club?'

He looked up in surprise. 'Ay, it could. A driver maybe. All that power concentrated in

37

one spot. What makes you ask?'

I told him and he gave me the measurement of the wound and I made notes. Then he undressed the body and examined it thoroughly. Waites was right, I realized. She had been wearing the kind of simple clothing that had been popular in the hippy culture. Even her panties were plain white cotton, worn for comfort, not for any excitement they might generate, some kind of statement on a woman this young and attractive.

'You want me to check if she was sexually assaulted?'

'Yeah, please,' I said and looked out of the window while he made his examination. There are some things about police work that I don't want to learn. Then he cleared his throat and I turned back. 'I'd say she wasna touched sexually,' he decided. 'But I'll take some swabs to be sure.' He did so and I stored each one separately in its own plastic bag for shipment to the forensics centre in Toronto. 'I've a refrigerated flask in the car you can use to ship that,' he said. 'I'll bring it in while you finish.'

'One last thing. Any idea what time she died? It would help me know when the car went into the lake.'

He put one hand on his chin and thought about it. 'I dinna think anybody, even an experienced pathologist, could help you

38

much, Reid. The water temperature has retarded the rigor mortis. The best opinion you could get would be no better than mine.'

'Which is what?'

'Something between twelve and sixteen hours back, I'd say.'

'Thanks.' It was no real help, encompassing both of the windows of opportunity when nobody within earshot would have been awake. My best hope was to make a house to house canvass along both sides of the lake within half a mile of the site. The sound of the car going into the lake could have travelled across the water and been heard on my side almost as loud as it was at the scene.

'Thanks, Doc. You've been very helpful. If you could get that flask I'd appreciate it.' He left and I wrote up my notes and then the door opened on McKenney. 'Chief, the bereaved is here.'

'Thanks, Les, hold him a second while I cover her up, then I'll come out for him.'

He went back out and I folded the dead woman's wet clothes and put them at her feet, then covered the body with the sheet and went out to the reception room with its purple drapes and piped organ music. Waites was sitting there, grey-faced. He was fully dressed now in expensive casual wear with a monogrammed JS on the shirt pocket. He looked up bleakly.

'Thank you for coming in, Mr Waites. Could I ask you to come with me, please?'

He didn't speak but I could see he was holding himself together very hard. I went ahead of him into the preparation room, sensing his revulsion at the surroundings. He walked slowly up to the gurney and stood, hands at his side, fists clenched.

I was next to him, in case he fainted. It happens sometimes to even the toughest men. 'Mr Waites. I'm going to expose the face and I want you to identify her for me. She doesn't look dreadful, I promise you.' He nodded and I rolled the sheet down, studying his face as I did so. He was the prime suspect and I wanted to catch his reaction completely.

It startled me. He gasped and said, 'There must be some mistake. That's not Moira. That's her friend, Carolyn Jeffries.'

CHAPTER THREE

He turned away from the gurney and bent from the waist as if he'd been punched in the gut. 'Sit down,' I commanded, and pulled a chair over for him. He collapsed on to it, and sat with his shoulders hunched, face in his hands. Relieved? Horrified? It was impossible to tell. At last he whispered,

40

'That's not Moira. Moira's still alive.'

'You're absolutely sure this is Mrs Jeffries?' I was floundering. The neat little case I'd been building was in ruins.

'They look like sisters,' he said. 'In fact, that was their cutesy name for one another. They'd call one another "Sis".' He hissed the word and I realized he was angry at the memory.

'How close were they?'

He looked up at me, focusing slowly on my face. There were no tears in his eyes. 'Are you asking if my wife was straight?'

'I'm asking how close they were. Did they talk to each other every day, every week? How often did they get together?'

'Every couple of weeks they'd visit, either way. And they spoke to each other every day or two.' He shook his head impatiently. 'How should I know? I work every day just about.'

'Work at what?'

He stood up angrily. 'What difference does that make?'

'Look, Mr Waites, I've got a dead woman on my hands. You're one of the few people who can tell me how she fits into the world. Indulge me, could you, please?'

He reached into his back pocket and pulled out his billfold. He had a sheaf of business cards in there and he handed me one. I read it: John Waites, LL.B. of

41

Donnely, Waites, Egan.

'Thank you. Just a couple more questions. First, what's the name of this woman's husband?'

'Stu. Stu Jeffries. He's a failed MBA type.' He threw in the second sentence with an angry sneer.

'I'm not sure what that means.' MBA I understood but what did this man mean by failed? That could be important.

'Oh, he got the degree, Harvard no less. But he couldn't cut it in business, not in the real world.' Waites was almost hissing again and now I could read his jealousy of the husband and impatience with a lifestyle he could not understand. 'So he and, her—' he paused and waved vaguely at the dead woman—'they copped out. They came up here and opened up their starving artist hideaway.'

'Did they make a living at it?'

'Sure, enough to live on if you're into rolled oats and alfalfa sprouts and making your own clothes out of spiderwebs, you know the routine.'

'You said your wife was kind of taken with this Stu. Why did you think that?'

'He knows all the words to "The Red Flag", maybe.' Waites turned away from me towards the door. 'How in Hell would I know what she saw in him, goddamn loser.'

'Where are you going now?'

'Home.' He paused with one hand on the doorknob. 'To the lodge. I'm not going to let her ruin my vacation, I've worked too hard to run back to Toronto and say, "There there, poor thing." He pursed his lips angrily and left the room before I could say anything.

I did the necessary policework. There was a telephone in the corner of the room and I rang Parry Sound police detatchment and spoke to the inspector on duty. 'We have a homicide here, Inspector. The deceased is a Parry Sound resident. A Carolyn Jeffries, around thirty, slim, blonde, no make-up. Apparently she and her husband Stuart run some kind of art supply shop in town.'

I was lucky. They have two inspectors and I'd struck the one of them who had experience in detective work. He asked the right questions and I was able to fill him in within a couple of minutes. He said he would send a car to the store and break the news to the husband, as well as checking to see if Moira Waites had arrived. He would keep me posted on developments, and send his own crime team down to examine the car and take over the investigation.

Dr McQuaig came back with his flask and I put the plastic evidence bags into it and had McKenney fill it with ice. It could go to the Parry Sound detectives when they arrived, one less headache for me. Then I

43

headed out to make a house to house canvass around the lake to try and uncover any witnesses to the car's going into the water.

I started around the corner from the funeral home, in the town itself. Town is overstating it a little. Officially we're an incorporated village, the lowest form of urban life. We have a Main Street with the bank, bait store, grocery, liquor/beer store, a Chinese restaurant specializing in hamburgers and a cluster of houses, most of them taking in summer guests, and a couple of side-streets of houses which also rent rooms to tourists. The rest of the village is straggled around the shoreline of the lake, every fifty yards or so.

Main Street is wide with the Lakeside Hotel and Marina on the water and a bridge over the lock. It's an unmade street, dusty in summer and lined with parked cars and with a knot of kids listening to music and giggling together. Remembering the two hassles from the morning, I stopped to talk to the kids. This was the early teen crowd, at the age when self-confidence only comes with numbers, before they get to the pairing-off stage. The girls were more forthcoming than the boys who all acted supercool. A couple of them had seen the swarming at the bait store but they didn't know any of the kids involved in it.

'They're not from around here, Chief,'

Debby Vanderheyden told me. 'Like, we wouldn't do something like that.'

Her friends all giggled and said 'Oh no' with mocking innocence, all a joke. They wouldn't need to swarm a store, I thought, all of them already knew who they were. Gangs are made up of losers looking for a sense of belonging.

One of the bolder girls asked how my wife was and they all giggled again. It was hard for them to imagine how an old guy like me had caused a pregnancy.

I asked them to call the station if they saw any gangs of kids in town. It was good insurance, they would rather watch me tackling the situation than see another store ripped off. It wasn't that they were so very law-abiding, they just weren't sure what the cool reaction was when a gang came to town.

Gilles Perault was busy and I lingered with him until he had time to talk. He wanted to discuss his swarming but I slowly got him around to asking if he knew if anyone had been out fishing the night before. The occasional dedicated man will go out after dark for pickerel and there was a chance one of them might have seen the car go into the lake. Gilles told me he'd check and I left town to drive up the east shore, knocking on doors.

It was sleepy mid-afternoon time. The trees were buzzing with cicadas and the heat

45

was enough to soften the bones, sending most vacationing adults for a siesta.

I called at a dozen or so houses, talking to the occasional group of swimming children but getting no help and causing a little embarrassment at some places where guys came to the door yawning hugely and explaining that their wives were lying down at the moment. Nobody had heard any thing the night before.

Sam was on the verandah at my place and he bounded down to the car to greet me, wagging his tail and keening low in his throat. I took a moment to fuss him, then went in. Freda met me at the door.

'Time to go, old sport,' she said. 'My water broke about an hour ago. I called the doctor and he said I should head up to the hospital.' Her face was a little pale but she seemed confident and I put my arm around her.

'I'll get your bag.'

'It's in the kitchen, behind the door, ready for a flying start.' She sounded as cheerful as ever, but she doesn't panic easily so I didn't waste any time. I just grabbed her bag and led her out to the police car.

'Really? You're taking me in that?' she laughed. 'The nurses'll think I'm a charity case.'

'Not a chance.' I didn't feel much like joking. All I had to do was stand around while she did the work. 'This thing's got a siren. If the stork picks up speed, I can still get you there on time.'

I tossed her bag in the rear seat and put her in front, handing her the seat-belt which she put on carefully. Then I told Sam 'Keep' and left him in charge.

The same bunch of kids on Main Street saw us together and instantly worked out what was happening. Some of the noisier girls called out good wishes and Fred waved. Now we were on our way I asked her about the pains and she told me there weren't any. 'But my water's broken. That's why he wants me up there.'

'Is that normal?' I had been to Lamaze classes with her through the winter but I was too close to this birth to be objective.

'Later is better but it's no cause for alarm.'

She sounded relaxed and I reached out my hand to squeeze hers. 'Hang in there, have you there in half an hour. Just keep me posted on the pains.'

'It's a bit like your tooth stopping aching when you head for the dentist. Nothing's happening.'

'That's a comfort. I like leaving tricky jobs to the experts.'

She didn't say much and I concentrated on my driving, pushing the speed to the limits of safety, overtaking everything in front of me. One doddery old guy didn't look

47

in his mirror to check my flashing lights behind him and I gave him a quick squirt of the siren which scared him out of his coma. He pulled right on to the shoulder in a cloud of dust and sat there while I accelerated over the top of the hill in front and lost him.

We came into Parry Sound twenty minutes later and I eased into the last space in front of the Emergency door at the hospital. Fred wouldn't let me get a wheelchair and we walked in arm in arm. The nurse on duty glanced at us oddly, wondering if a mercy call had turned into a romance. 'My wife's water has broken, Dr Rosen is her doctor, he said to come in.'

She pushed a form at me. 'Fill this out, please.'

'Not until she's taken care of,' I said and the nurse shook her head pityingly and said, 'Fathers,' but she got a wheelchair and whisked Fred away. 'Your husband can come and see you when he's been a good boy and filled out the form.'

I squeezed Fred's shoulder and waited until the nurse came back, then filled in the form, thanking my stars that I'd moved back to Ontario after my service in the US Marines. I love the States but hospitals there cost an arm and leg. Here it's all paid for.

Twenty minutes later I was up in an examination room with Fred, waiting for her doctor to get in from the golf course, it was

48

Wednesday after all, his half day. He had spoken to her from the clubhouse, Fred told me, where he'd come in from the first tee to answer his pager. I guessed he'd lingered to hit a few balls but he was there in ten minutes, a small, young guy with round glasses and not much of a tan.

He whisked me out of the room to examine her, then came out to report. 'It may be some time,' he said and immediately went over my head with details of dilation. 'Are you attending the birth?'

'I've taken the classes but honestly the idea scares the hell out of me. I don't want to be in the way.'

'Thank God,' he said earnestly. 'Some of the fathers are a royal pain in the ass.' He gave an apologetic half-smile and went on, 'You won't be needed for a couple of hours anyway. Why don't you talk it over with your wife? Then, if you've got anything else to do come back at—' he checked his watch—'let's say six o'clock.'

'Thank you, Doctor.' I went back in to see Fred who was being moved out to a pre-natal room. I walked with her as far as the door. The nurse left us there for a moment to talk, tactfully heading off somewhere else.

'Look, Reid, you don't have to be here, you know,' Fred said.

I stopped and gave her a quick kiss. 'I'm

all trained up to help, wouldn't want to waste all that knowledge.'

'Yes, you would,' she said firmly. 'Why don't you head out for an hour or two anyway? If you come in with me now you'll have to gown up and you're stuck here for the rest of the time.'

I weakened, very easily. 'Well, I have to check with the local people. I didn't tell you before but a Parry Sound woman has drowned at the Harbour. I should talk to the police here.'

'*Vaya con Dios*,' she said and waved me away.

The nurse must have been hovering. She was back in a moment, all brisk. 'You can come inside but you'll have to change.'

'I'm coming back later.' Fred was with me on the decision, so why did I feel like I was retreating under fire?

The OPP constable on duty at the Parry Sound desk was a fishing buddy of mine and he stuck out his hand and asked after Fred. 'In the hospital, the doctor says to come back at supper-time. Figured I'd check on the Carolyn Jeffries investigation.'

'The inspector's in his office. Come on through.' He flipped up the hinged section of the desk and opened the gate.

'Thanks, Mike.' I went through and tapped on Inspector Dunn's door. It was open and he was on the phone. He waved

50

me in. 'Chief Bennett just walked in, I'll put him on,' he said. He handed me the phone. 'S'arnt Holland, he's at the Jeffries' store.'

'Thank you.' I took the phone. 'Hi, Bill, Reid Bennett. What did you find out?'

'Hi, Reid.' Bill Holland is a good detective although he hasn't had much homicide experience. 'I was just in the store. There's a kid working there, says she hasn't seen hide nor hair of the Jeffries since yesterday. She came in and opened up like always, nobody there. First time ever.'

'Do they live over the store?'

'No. Got a place on the water on the edge of town. The girl, her name's Peggy Lindhoff, says she's rung the house, no answer. First time she's ever had to open up on her own. She figures something's wrong.'

'Let me explain. The owner of the stolen car says his wife had big eyes for this Stu Jeffries guy. She was a good friend of the wife but her husband led me to believe that she liked the husband a lot.'

'You sayin' they might have killed the wife so they could be together?'

'It's possible, but according to the husband, who's a lawyer, his wife and the Jeffries couple were all kind of hippy. They'd have shacked up together or something like that if they had hankerings. Not the types for a crime of passion.'

'Well, it's strange. This clerk says the
51

Jeffries were always there ahead of her. She's not a partner or anything, only helps out in the summer, says they're nice people.'

'I don't know much about them, except that the other woman's husband doesn't like any of them, including his wife.'

There was a pause and Holland said, 'Guess I should drive down to their house, see if there's any sign of life or if the car's still there. No matter what anybody thinks, this Jeffries guy and the Waites woman could've offed the wife and left for parts unknown.'

'I'll come down there and meet you. Where is it?' He told me and gave directions and I hung up and spoke to the inspector. 'I'll go over there. I'll need the husband to identify his wife's body. It's at the funeral parlour in Murphy's Harbour.'

'OK.' Dunn stood up. 'On the face of it, it sounds like a triangle. Even hippies get jealous, least these days they do.'

The Jeffries house made Waites' description of their lifestyle seem appropriate. It was small and neat with artfully contrasting blue shutters and a big well-kept garden. There was a bright yellow VW beetle in the driveway.

Holland was waiting for me, in his car. He's a typical old-time copper, big, running to fat, wearing a neat suit that looked like it came with two pairs of pants. He got out and shook hands. 'Hi, Reid, how's the wife?'

I told him and we opened the gate and walked up to the gingerbread porch. There were potted geraniums all along the sill and a set of oriental windchimes hanging silent in the stillness.

The door had an old-fashioned ratchet bell and Holland cranked the handle on it a few times. Nobody answered. There was no sound from inside. A woman in a big sunhat was watering her flowers in the next yard and Holland sauntered over to talk to her. No, she hadn't seen the Jeffries that day. 'Are they in trouble?' she wanted to know.

'No, ma'am. This is a social call,' Holland lied easily. He came back to the verandah. 'This is a pain,' he said.

'There's a cagebird singing in the house,' I said. 'People like this would've set it out here this morning if they'd gone to their store.'

'Y'reckon?' He looked at me thoughtfully. 'Guess you're right. An' if they're not, they could be long gone while we're waiting around here for them to come back.'

I bent and flipped the doormat over. A key lay under it. 'How convenient,' Holland said. 'Lemme see that a minute.'

He took the key and tried the door. It opened and he stepped inside and called 'Hello, Mr Jeffries. Anybody home?'

The cagebird fell silent and I stepped in after him. The house was tiny inside but beautifully furnished, not expensively but

53

with real style, antique Ontario pine everywhere, contrasting with bold modern paintings and good prints. We glanced into the two rooms off the centre hall. One was a dining-room, the other a sitting-room with a big bookshelf and an expensive music system. The birdcage was hanging in the window and I could see from the door that the water container was empty. That seemed out of character with the rest of the house and I followed Holland through to the kitchen. There were unwashed dishes in the sink, dinner dishes, and a glass baking pan with some dried-out greenish stuff still in it. Holland looked at the mess. 'Two plates. They didn't all eat together.'

'Let's check upstairs.' I led now, up the polished stairs to the bedrooms. Both were empty and were neatly made. There was nobody there, even in the closets or the bathroom.

'Looks like they've been away all night,' Holland said. He scratched under his chin thoughtfully. 'But their car's still in the driveway.'

'The wife's body was in the Accord.' I thought out loud. 'And that bug of theirs stands out like a burning bush. If the other two were taking off somewhere maybe they rented another car.'

'I'll check that out,' Holland said. He was opening the drawers in the chest of the bigger bedroom. It was full of neatly folded men's socks and underclothes. 'If the husband was takin' off he was travellin' light. Did this Waites woman have a whole bunch of money maybe?'

'Didn't sound like it, to hear her husband talk. He said she married him because she needed a meal ticket.'

'Yeah, but maybe she's got a satchelful of his credit cards.' Holland was rolling the thoughts around in his mind.

'Could be. But she was a painter, not into shopping, according to the husband.'

'I'd like to talk to that sonofabitch,' Holland said. ''S he still at the Harbour?'

'Says he's leaving for Toronto when he can get a car. I've got his home address and phone if you want to call him.'

'Thanks.' Holland copied the information into his book, then closed it firmly. 'Come on, we're through here.'

We went downstairs and I unhooked the birdcage and took it with me as we left. 'Where you takin' that?' Holland asked.

'Leave it next door, give us a chance to talk to the neighbour.'

He grunted but we walked over to the fence and spoke to the woman who was still standing in the same place, obviously curious about us. 'The Jeffries have been called away,' Holland said. 'If you see anybody in there, could you give me a call, please,

55

Sergeant Holland. Don't go over there, please, just call. And could you take care of their bird for them?'

'Of course, Sergeant.' She took the cage happily, a mystery of her very own, right next door.

She wanted to talk at length but Holland just nodded and beamed and we walked back to our cars. I took a minute to talk to him about the dead woman, mentioning the wound on the temple.

'Golf clubs?' he said. 'Likely ended up in the lake somewhere but I'll flag it at the station, see if anybody comes in with a set they've found somewhere.'

'Good idea. What's next?'

He yawned. 'Guess I should print the car you got out of the lake. Where's it at?' I told him and he said, 'Better get it up here in our pound where it's secure, be easier to get at anyway.'

He slumped into his car. 'Thanks for the help. I'll call if I hear anything.'

'Fine. I'll head back to the hospital, see if anything's happening.'

'Yeah. Good luck, hope everything goes OK.' He waved and left and I got into my own car and drove back into the heart of town. It was only five o'clock so I pulled in at a diner and ordered a burger and coffee. I wasn't hungry but remembered what they'd told us at the Lamaze classes: eat normally or you'll pass out in the delivery room. This was a duty.

The place was half full but I got a seat by the window and sat there looking out as I waited. The place next door was one of the better eating spots in town and I watched the first of the evening's customers drifting in. Most were holiday-makers, young groups of men and women laughing together, but as I was eating I saw a Mercedes pull into the lot. It jangled my memory and I realized it was the same model and colour as the one that had dropped Waites at the gas station. I would check the licence when I left, I decided, to see if I was right. I watched it and as its doors opened I saw that Ms Tracy was driving. She had a young guy with her and when he turned to speak to her I realized he was the leader of the gang I'd chased out of Murphy's Harbour earlier.

He was talking animatedly, giving the impression that he was very much in control of himself, sophisticated even, not like the angry gang member he had been that morning. He seemed older, more mature and, most important of all, he seemed to be courting Ms Tracy, acting with the eager agreeableness of a man trying to win over a new conquest.

I considered my options. My authority doesn't extend beyond the limits of my own bailiwick. If I went up to the kid here and asked him questions he could tell me to go to hell. Then he and Ms Tracy would leave before I could get a local guy to do the asking for me. I had to get something on him without his knowing.

I paid and tipped the waitress and went out to the parking lot. First I checked the licence plate of the Mercedes. It was the same one that Waites had ridden in, so he and Ms Tracy were friends at least. With that done, I went through the back door of the hotel. The kitchen was busy but one of the cooks waved and made a drinking motion with his hands. Did I want a coffee, beer, something? 'I'd like to talk to the manager or one of the waiters, can you call them for me, please?'

He went to the door with its glass panel and waved through it. A moment later a trim young woman in a smart blouse and skirt came through the door. The cook pointed at me and she spoke, smiling formally. 'Yes, what's up?'

'I'm here to ask a favour, please. Can you help me?'

'Depends what it is.' She was intrigued.

'There's a couple who came in three or four minutes ago, a woman around thirty-five, wearing a green top and a gold chain. There's a man with her, a little younger.'

'They're at table fourteen.' She cocked her

58

head. 'You want to talk to them?'

'No, but I'd very much like to get the young man's glass or bottle if he orders a drink. Is that possible, do you think, please?'

I never majored in charm but I applied all I had. She frowned. 'Is this going to make me liable in some court case?'

'Nobody else will ever know, I promise, it'll help me in an investigation I'm conducting.'

'Stay here,' she commanded and clacked out of the kitchen on her high heels, skirt swinging to stir a man's heartstrings. I waited four or five minutes before she returned, wearing a white glove on her right hand, carrying a highball glass. 'I put white gloves on the waiter. The only prints on this are your guy's right hand.'

'Thank you very much. I appreciate this.'

I held out my left hand, flat, but she said, 'Hold on, we have plastic bags somewhere.' One of the kitchen staff brought her one and she slipped the glass into it and handed it to me. 'There. Hope it helps. If it helps your case any, he drinks Glenfiddich.'

'Glad he can afford it.' I hefted the bag with my left hand and touched the peak of my cap with the right. 'You've saved me a lot of work.'

'Your name's Bennett, isn't it?' she said.

'That's right. I'm from Murphy's Harbour.'

59

'I was down there visiting one time and my friend told me you were a tough cop, lived alone with a big dog.'

'That's Sam, my German shepherd. He's off duty tonight.'

'And you're working on a case?'

'Kind of. I'm also waiting for word from the hospital about my wife, she's having a baby.'

'Oh.' Her tone became brisker. 'Well, glad I could help.'

She tritch-tratched away and I left with my package, remembering how lonely it can be when you're single.

I debated whether to hand over the glass to Holland for comparison with the prints he found on Waites' car but decided against it. I would check them myself and let him have them later. Right now the fact that this kid had been a gang member might be completely irrelevant to the murder he was investigating. The only tie I could see was that both he and the husband knew the Tracy woman. I would call in on her later, I decided, and ask about the boy. Meantime I went back to the hospital, where I met Dr Rosen who shook his head at me. 'Your wife's fine. She hasn't started having contractions, but the baby's head is high so I'm keeping her in bed. If she's still hanging fire this evening I'll induce labour.'

'Is that normal?'

'I do it all the time,' he said. 'For now we've moved her to a ward. Why don't you go and see her?'

★   ★   ★

The hospital gift shop was open and they had flowers for sale, locally grown roses, bundled by volunteers with more enthusiasm than skill. I bought a bunch anyway and went up to Fred's room.

She was sitting up in bed, reading a magazine. There was another woman in the bed next to her, sleeping.

Fred greeted me excitedly and repeated what the doctor had said. I went back to the nurse's station for a vase and put the flowers in water while we discussed what to do.

'You should go home and give Sam his supper,' Fred said firmly. 'I'm stuck in neutral right now. Nothing's going to happen tonight, they tell me. You can check around town like you do every night and call up at midnight.'

'I should be here,' I argued feebly.

'Sam is family too,' Fred said. 'You can't do anything here and he needs you.'

She was firm about it and relaxed. 'This is the most natural business in the world. And anyway, all I have to do overnight is sleep.'

'Well, I have to feed Sam, that's certain.'

'And check your properties,' she said with

a smile. 'You know you always do, even on your day off.'

In the end that's what I did, thankful to be out of the hospital. My own stays have always been painful, both here and in 'Nam, recovering from wounds. I knew that Fred would be going through something just as hard, even though it was going to be great afterwards.

The light was fading and the kids had gone from Main Street and the village was settling down for a quiet night. There was music coming from the open windows of the Lakeside Hotel at the Marina and a crowd of cars filled the parking lot of the beer parlour below the bridge, where the blue collar drinking gets done, but there were no people on the street. They were home, eating supper and rubbing lotion on their sunburns.

*　　*　　*

Sam was off the verandah when I pulled in and he looked up and barked at me. He isn't excitable and I knew something had happened. I called him over and fussed him and then let him lead me back to where he had been standing. He took me to his find, a package in the red-brown coarse paper they use in butcher shops to wrap meat. This one had obviously hit the gravel of the drive and rolled a couple of times and I could see that it had been opened, the original brown tape torn, then refastened with scotch tape. I picked it up, feeling the squashiness that announced it had hamburg meat inside. There was barely enough light left to examine it so I clicked my tongue at Sam and went into the house with him, carrying the package with me. I laid it on the countertop and slit it open with my pocket-knife. There was hamburg inside right enough, but it had been laced with a coarse white powder.

I let it lie there while I bent down to pat Sam's head as he looked up at me. 'Good thing you remembered your training, old buddy. This stuff's been baited.'

CHAPTER FOUR

TV cops can identify poisons at a glance. I can't, I must have been away the day they covered it at the academy. But it figured to be nasty. If Sam had been less well trained it would have killed him. I wondered who had tried it on. The teen gang probably, getting even for their loss of face that morning. I saved the evidence in case I got the chance to prove anything, rewrapping the meat and marking it 'Evidence. Poison.' and drawing a skull and crossbones on the package. Then I bagged it and stuck it in the freezer to send to the forensics centre when I had a chance.

Sam watched me closely. Hovering over the meat until I came home had sharpened his appetite. But his training had stuck, and saved his life. So, as a special reward I defrosted a chunk of our own hamburger meat to give him with his chow.

When he'd finished I sat on the back porch and had a beer, trying to find a pattern to the day. So much had happened. A teen gang had come to town, then the car in the lake, looking like it had been stolen by kids, vandalized. And most important, the dead woman in the trunk.

Was there a thread to it all? I couldn't see one, except for Marcia Tracy. She had turned up in both the puzzles. There was no reason why she shouldn't know both John Waites and the kid from the gang. It was just the timing of her involvement that intrigued me. I would have to talk to her, especially about the gang leader. He'd looked very different up in Parry Sound, dressed neatly, acting confidently, not like a rebel. How could he be two completely different people in the course of a single day? I needed to talk to him, not the way I would have had to on the street in Parry Sound, he could have brushed me off there, knowing I had no jurisdiction. No, it had to be a formal interrogation.

When I finished my beer I walked Sam around the property, telling him to Seek, his order to check for people hiding. He ran everywhere in the darkness, under the willows along the edge of the lake, out along the dock and into my boat, and into the woods on the far side of the road from the house. I was concerned about Kershaw on top of my other worries, but when Sam found nothing we drove back to the police station.

It was as I'd left it, except for a long roll of messages peeling off the teletype. I tore them off and skimmed them to see if Kershaw had been re-arrested. He hadn't been, but there had been a break-in overnight at a cottage in Orillia, about half the distance from Toronto to Murphy's Harbour. Not a startling event, but the perp had stolen some clothing, something a fugitive might have done, and the place was on the way to the Harbour.

The only other message that stopped me was a report of another gang swarming up at Pointe au Baril. It lies north of us, the other side of Parry Sound. A nondescript bunch of teens had hit the grocery, taking stuff but not really stealing it, tossing it away contemptuously as they drove out of town. Routine teen-gang behaviour but the report made me frown. Why would a gang, possibly the same gang, hit two little resorts, fifty miles apart, and leave the big town in

65

between untouched? Where did they come from? Gang problems are usually local. It's your own doctor's and lawyer's sons who band together and raise hell. It's their way of letting the neighbours know how little they care for their parents. Hitting on total strangers in two widely separated places was not normal gang practice and that was puzzling.

Nothing on the list called for action, so I locked up and drove up to Carl Simmonds' place. He was out on the lawn, on a swing seat, nursing a drink, but he got up and came to the gate to greet me. 'I hear you took Freda to the hospital. Is everything OK?'

'Fine, thanks, no action yet. I'm heading back at midnight.' 'Don't worry, Reid. I know she's going to be fine,' he said. 'How about a beer while I get you the pictures?'

We went inside and he cracked a beer for both of us and pulled out an envelope of eight by tens. Like all his work, they were excellent, crisp and clear. They didn't reveal anything I'd missed, but I thanked him.

He kibitzed a little bow. 'I hope the Andersons are as happy with their wedding shots. It was very difficult to hide the bride's big tummy.'

We went back outside and sat, with Sam lying beside me on the grass while we drank our beer. My mind was still running around the events of the day and I needed to talk.

For a year now I've had Fred to discuss things with, getting the benefit of a non-police point of view. It prompted me to open up a little to Carl. I knew he wasn't a gossip, my information was safe.

'Do you know anything about a woman called Tracy? She has a place on the other side of the lake, where that car went into the water last night?'

'That would be Marcia Tracy, the movie producer from Toronto,' he said at once. 'A friend of mine in Toronto works as a hairdresser in her studio. Tough lady, he says.'

'She seems to have a strange mixture of friends.'

'Maybe not friends, according to Claude, but she'd have lots of courtiers. She's important in the film business in Toronto.'

I thought about it a moment and then said, 'Well, I saw her today with the owner of that Honda. She drove him to Kinski's.'

'The poor man whose wife was in the trunk?'

'It turned out it wasn't his wife, but that's a different story.'

Another man might have cut in, pressing for details but Carl didn't. He asked, 'And?'

'And I saw her up in Parry Sound with the kid who was running that gang this morning.'

'On the street? It might just have been a

casual contact of some kind?'

'No, they were having dinner at Pietro's.'

'You're sure it was the same kid?'

'Positive.'

Carl was excited now. 'Dinner at Pietro's. Very fancy. Was he trying to sweet-talk her, maybe?'

'A seduction? Could be, I guess. Fred says she's got a string of young guys behind her.'

'Actors, of course,' Carl said and suddenly I could see the connection.

'If this guy's an actor, maybe this gang thing is his way of auditioning.'

'With actors, anything's possible,' Carl said. 'If she was remaking *The Wild Bunch* he would have turned up on a big Harley. Perhaps she's doing something about youth gangs.'

'That makes sense.' I drained my beer and stood up, picking up the envelope of photographs. 'Thanks for the beer and the wisdom, Carl. You'll send your bill for these to the station, will you?'

'Plus sales tax,' he said happily. 'Glad to have helped. Give my love to Fred when you see her.'

'I will. But I've got a call to make first.'

Sam whisked into the car ahead of me and curled up on the passenger seat, then I drove off, around the lake to Ms Tracy's house. There were lights on and her car was in the driveway. I got out and went to the door.

The radio was playing soft rock, a song that had been big the year I joined the Marines.

Marcia Tracy came out of the living-room looking surprised. She was wearing a cotton housecoat, practical enough that I scratched the idea that she was entertaining a young lover. She was wearing half-glasses on her nose and carrying one of the typescripts I'd seen in her bedroom.

When she recognized me she took off her glasses and opened the door. 'Well, this is a surprise. Am I to congratulate you, Chief?'

'Nothing's happened yet, Ms Tracy. I wondered if I might ask you a couple of questions, if you don't mind.'

Her tone didn't change. 'Just like Peter Falk,' she said. 'Come in.'

She opened the door and I came in and stood on the porch, keeping my hat on.

'I was having a scotch. Could I get you something?'

'No, thank you. I won't keep you long.'

'Too bad,' she teased. She smelt of some light fragrance, outdoorsy but provocative. When I didn't speak she said, 'Well?'

'What's the name of your new picture? The one you're planning right now?'

'What an odd question from an officer of the law. Are you trying to get your wife a part? I understand she's very good.'

'She's hung up her skates,' I said, smiling to ease the tension I could feel building up in

69

me. 'No, I wondered if you were doing a picture about teen gangs?'

She was just as light but her eyes narrowed a fraction. 'Why do you ask that?'

'Well, I had a run-in with a gang this morning, in town. I was off duty at the time and the only way I could resolve it was to neutralize the leader, boy about twenty maybe, six-foot, dark hair, useful-looking build.'

'Sounds yummy.'

'I wondered if you'd tell me his name, please?'

'Me?' She must have done some acting herself, she was almost convincing.

'Yes. You had dinner with him in Parry Sound. I'd like to talk to him.'

'That boy's an actor. He drove up from Toronto to see me.'

'In an old Ford Fairlane with four other kids.'

'I don't know how he travelled.' She shrugged and I could see she was enjoying herself, playing the tycoon, keeping me at bay.

'I'd really like to talk to him. Could I ask you for his name, please?'

'Is he in some kind of trouble?'

'Not at all.' I shook my head, all hearty and friendly. 'But he might be able to help me, that's all.'

'Sit down,' she said. 'This is very

interesting.'

There was no reason not to, so I did, taking off my hat. She sat opposite, letting a flash of leg show, then adjusting her housecoat. 'You really think it's the same boy?'

She was playing games with me so I took another track.

'You have a lot of friends, Ms Tracy.'

'One does tend to, in my circle.' She reached out to the coffee table and set down her script. 'I don't see how it can interest a policeman.'

'At around one o'clock today you drove John Waites down to the gas station on the highway where his car had been recovered. Have you spoken to him since?'

'No, why?' She had hazel eyes and there were tiny flecks of gold in the pupils, she was almost beautiful, I realized, but too square in the face, too strong to be appealing to most men.

'Because there was a woman's body in the trunk.' I watched her and she gasped and almost dropped her glass. It looked genuine. She stared at me for a long moment, then took a quick gulp of her drink.

'She drowned when his car went into the lake. Waites thought it was his wife at first.'

'It wasn't?'

'No. It was another woman, similar in appearance. He identified her later as a friend of his wife's, a Carolyn Jeffries.'

Now her composure had gone. She set down her drink and stood up, hugging her arms around her. I sat and said nothing until she turned to speak to me. 'What are you trying to tell me?'

'Nothing that isn't public knowledge,' I said. 'It's just that I lead a quiet life here. Then, in one day there are two teen gang incidents and a homicide. The car with the body in it had been roughed up the way kids might have done it. That's all I have, but I see you in touch with all the players and I wondered if there was anything you wanted to tell me.'

'Like what?' There was a cigarette box on the coffee table and she opened it and took one out. She looked around for matches but couldn't see any. I stood up and took out a pack of Lakeside Tavern matches and lit for her. She cupped my hand as she took the light and I could feel that she was trembling.

'Like, is there some connection that I'm not seeing? Between Waites and this actor whose name you haven't told me yet.'

'I know them both,' she said softly. 'John Waites is my lawyer. Eric Hanson is an actor. I know both of them, professionally.'

'I'd like to talk to Hanson. Do you know where he is?'

'No.' She said it quickly, then took a quick drag on her cigarette and said, 'No, I'm sorry, I don't know. If you call my office in the morning they'll put you in touch with his agent. He'll tell you.'

'That would be helpful, Ms Tracy, and I'd appreciate it, but it would be even better if I could talk to him tonight. If you could tell me, for instance, whether he's here now. Then I could talk to him and get out of your life.'

'He's not. And I don't like your tone.' She was suddenly all angles, lean and rigid as she stubbed the cigarette and tugged her housecoat closer at the throat. 'Please leave.'

I stood up. 'Thank you for the help, Ms Tracy.' I was going by the book now, lots of formality, no rudeness, leaving right away. She would have no cause to complain about me to the village council or the Police Commission.

She said nothing and I put on my cap and left, clicking my tongue for Sam who had been waiting outside.

I drove slowly down the road around the lake, past Pickerel Point Lodge. It isn't big, by city standards, a couple of dozen rooms, two tennis courts and a beach and private dock with a row of good-sized cruisers tied up. By night it looks its best, the floodlights and the light at the end of the dock magnifying the importance of everything. I could see a fisherman on the dock, using a surface lure by the look of it, retrieving in

73

slow stages, hoping to prod a pickerel into action.

I debated going in to see if Waites had gone back to Toronto but decided against it. I had nothing specific to ask him and he was a lawyer, he'd brush me off like a fly and it might screw up Holland's investigation, whenever that happened. So I took one last spin through town, checking the locks on all the properties that were closed for the night, then headed up the highway. But I was still restless and I slowed as I passed each motel, checking the parking lot for the Ford that Eric Hanson had been driving. I wanted to know more about him, specifically if stealing the Accord had been part of the game he was playing with Marcia Tracy.

I recognized Hanson's Fairlane, ten miles north of the Harbour parked at the Northont Motel. It's a cheap place, individual cabins about fifteen feet square, white paint peeling off them. A new guy took it over last spring but he's going quietly broke. Now, in peak season, there were cars outside only three of the places.

I went to the office and stepped into a museum of despair. Everything needed paint and there was dust on the furniture and drapes and tired old folders and the few tatty souvenirs of the area. The owner, a sour man in a T-shirt, came through a bead curtain behind the office and nodded. 'Need a room,

74

Officer?'

'Not tonight, thanks. But I'm interested in the people whose car is outside unit three. Could I see who it's registered to?'

'You gotta warrant?'

'I don't need one. Haven't you read the Inn-keepers' Act?' I wasn't sure myself what it said but it figured he hadn't read it.

'I'm too goddamn busy to read everything I'm s'posed to,' he said and pulled out a box of cards. 'What unit was that?'

'Three. The car's a Ford.'

'Three. Yeah, Sidney Greenstreet, Niagara Falls.'

I didn't laugh but it looked like I'd found my actor. 'Thanks.'

He mumbled something but slapped the box shut and went back through the curtain. I paused outside to whistle Sam to my side, then walked over the unit. The light was on inside and rap music was jabbering away, loud, with lots of bass to it. Teen-gang opera.

I knocked but nobody answered so I used the heel of my hand, thumping even louder than the bass on the ghetto-blaster. Nobody came and I tried the door handle. The door swung open away from me and then a man hurled himself at me, screaming something.

Instinctively I stuck my left hand out, palm towards him catching him flat in the chest. He stumbled but recovered in a

75

moment and came at me again, flailing and kicking, his face contorted with fury. I tried to hold him but he was too strong, too quick, and I knew he was zonked on something dangerous. I told Sam 'Fight' and he snarled and grabbed at the man's arm but the guy was too far gone to take any notice. He lashed out with his other hand and his feet, screaming non-stop. He landed a good clunk on the side of my head and I staggered, then drew my stick and hit him hard on the collar-bone of his free arm. It connected and his arm fell limp but he kept on closing on me and kicking, totally ignoring Sam. I knew I had to put him down.

I slid my hand down the shaft of the stick until only four inches projected out of my fist and stabbed him in the gut. It would have stopped any normal man but he didn't pause and I had to do it again before the wind went out of him and he collapsed, still trying to kick, his legs moving feebly as he fought for breath.

'Easy,' I said and Sam released his arm and stood back, hovering over him as I rolled him on his face and cuffed his right wrist through his belt to his left ankle, bending him in half backwards.

'Keep,' I ordered and Sam stood, growling into the man's face as he struggled to breathe. I took a quick look around the cabin. There was nobody else there and from the single six-pack of Kronenbourg beer I figured he was alone. There was a plastic bag on the chest of drawers containing about three ounces of white powder. Angel dust, I figured, from the way he'd acted and I wondered if that was what he'd used to bait Sam, hoping he would turn on me and I'd have to shoot him.

In any case he was o.d.'d on something, and needed a hospital. It would take too long for an ambulance to reach us. I had to take him to Parry Sound.

I ran back to the office and reached over the desk to pick up the phone. The owner came blustering out of the back but I pulled out a dollar coin and tossed it to him. 'Police business.' I reached the Parry Sound police and told them what had happened. They were on the bit, they promised to have a man at the hospital by the time I got there and to send a narcotics guy to check the motel room.

'What's all this about?' The owner stretched up to his full five-foot-six and snarled at me. 'You can't come into my motel and start laying down the law. This is a free country.'

'You've got a kid in unit three who's o.d.'d. The OPP are sending a man. Don't disturb anything in there, please, or you're in deep trouble. I'm taking him to hospital.'

He had more to say but I didn't listen. I

77

drove over to the unit and opened the rear door of the car.

The kid was fighting fit again but almost helpless. He still tried punching up at me with his free hand, aiming for my groin but I got hold of his arm and levered him on to his free leg and hopped him out to the car. It was a tussle getting him into the seat and he lay there smashing at the door with his free foot as I locked him in. Sam jumped into the front seat and I pulled off the lot and out to the highway, laying rubber up to the hospital.

A doctor and a couple of uniformed policemen were waiting for me and we got the kid out and laid him on a gurney while the doctor checked his eyes and then sponged his neck and gave him a shot.

It didn't take at once but by the time we reached the treatment room he was drowsy.

'What's he taken?' the doctor demanded.

'PCP, judging by the way he's acting. This was in his room.' I took the plastic bag out of my shirt pocket and gave it to him. He glanced at it, narrowing his eyes.

'Hard to say but you could be right. I'll need at least one man to stay with him. There's no knowing when he'll start fighting again.'

'We'll stay.' One of the Parry Sound men unlocked my handcuffs and gave them back to me. 'Pretty neat,' he said approvingly.

'Hand and foot together through the belt. Never seen that done.'

The doctor was sounding the boy's chest with a stethoscope. 'His heart's going like sixty.' He unclipped the earpieces and looked at me. 'How did you stop him?'

'I hit him in the solar plexus with the butt of my stick. I hope I haven't ruptured anything.'

'I hope so too,' the doctor said. 'I'll run some tests. Who is he anyway?'

'Goes by the name Eric Hanson. I want to talk to him when he comes down. Would that be possible?'

'Six hours at least, I'd say.' The doctor picked up the phone. 'Doctor Syme, Treatment Room Two. Can I have a restraint trolley here, please.' He hung up and looked at me levelly. 'What can you tell me about him that might help?'

'He was in a motel room. Looked like he'd eaten fried chicken and been drinking beer. He was alone when I found him, listening to loud rap music. He came to the door and went berserk.'

The doctor nodded. 'OK. Is he under arrest for anything?'

'Yes, assault police, namely me. And possession of drugs, namely that white powder I showed you. On top of which I want to talk to him about a homicide that occurred at Murphy's Harbour.'

The doctor whistled. 'He's been a busy boy. OK. I'll check him out, see what he's taken, see if you injured him. Then I'll sedate him. Are you staying here?'

'My wife's upstairs waiting to deliver a baby. I'll be up with her until that happens.' He nodded at me and I finished up the story. 'I don't have jurisdiction in Parry Sound but these officers will handle the arrest for me.'

'Fine.' He nodded briskly. 'I'll know where to find you if anything happens.'

I thanked him and went outside to make sure Sam was comfortable, letting him out of the car to mark out a territory for him so he could get out of the car window as he wanted. Then I patted him on the head and said, 'Wish us luck,' and went upstairs to Fred's floor.

I was just in time. The nurse told me that she had been put on a Pit drip, which I knew meant they were inducing labour. 'She'll be fine,' she said cheerfully. 'Are you one of the Lamaze fathers?'

I confessed and she said, 'When did you eat last?'

'What's that got to do with anything?'

She shook her head and reached under the counter for a lunch bag. 'Here. I've got a sandwich. Eat it now, I don't want you passing out on me.'

Well, the instructor had warned me, so I thanked her and ate, gratefully. Then I washed up and changed into a hospital gown. They provided a locker so my gun was safe, but I took the bullets out anyway and put them in my left pocket. They were uncomfortable but a lot less so than they might have been fired into somebody from my Smith and Wesson.

Fred was in the delivery room, lying back, her face beaded up with sweat. I kissed her and made nice noises, as per instructions, then wiped her face with a damp cloth and fed her an ice chip to moisten her mouth.

The contractions were coming thick and fast and I wasn't able to do as much as I'd have liked because she had a pair of monitors attached to her abdomen but I did manage to turn her on her side and give her a back rub, which made me feel useful at least.

Every few minutes the nurse came in to check her drip and the monitors. After a while she started tuning in the baby's heartbeat on the Dopptone and we listened to the galloping noises that told us everything was all right so far.

About three o'clock the doctor turned up and things got hectic for Fred. She's got a lot of guts and she didn't make much fuss but it hurt me to see her in such distress. And then, at three-thirty, the miracle happened.

'A fine big girl,' Dr Rosen said happily. He turned the baby upside down and slapped her back gently and she cried. She wasn't alone in that.

Fred squeezed my hand very hard and I bent to hug her, and the room started to swim. The nurse grabbed me and steered me to a stool. 'Caught you,' she said brightly. 'Why is it always the big tough guys who fall apart.'

After a moment I felt better and moved the stool over beside the bed and took Fred's hand. 'Sorry about that.'

She squeezed my hand. Already she had her strength back, and her control. She pulled on my arm and I leant over and kissed her.

'You big suck,' she said gently. 'She's perfect. We did it.'

'You did,' I told her and sat there until she judged I was fit to hold the baby. She was red and wrinkled but I said, 'She reminds me of my kid sister.'

'We'll call her Louise. And Ann, for my mother,' Fred said.

After a while I was shooed away and I went and showered and got back into uniform and reloaded my gun again.

The same nurse was at her desk and she got me a cup of coffee, insisting on sugaring it but leaving it black. She found out which floor Hanson was on and I thanked her for everything and left.

My world had changed. Fred was well, and at thirty-eight I was a father for the first time. The nagging anxieties of the last few months were gone and I felt whole again. It was like coming back to the world from 'Nam.

One of the Parry Sound men was on duty at Hanson's bedside. Hanson was awake, his eyes wide. I saw the strap over his chest, buckled low to one side where he couldn't reach it. The cop yawned. 'How'd it go? Your wife OK?'

'Yeah, fine, thanks. Had a little girl.'

He shook my hand and congratulated me. 'They reckon the baby's the same sex as the bossiest parent,' he said. 'Look at me, I got three girls.'

In my euphoria I laughed with him and said, 'Why don't you take a break? I'll sit with this guy a few minutes.'

'Wouldn't mind,' he said. 'He's been quiet. The doctor says he's not damaged any.'

He left and I stood at the foot of the bed looking at Hanson. 'Hi, how're you feeling?'

'Sore,' he said. 'My gut hurts.' His voice was different from what I remembered. He had dropped the roughness of his accent and he was a quiet, well-spoken kid again. Well, maybe not a kid, in his twenties, perhaps close to thirty. Had he been wearing make-up that morning? I wasn't sure.

'Feel like talking?' I wasn't going to force him. After what had happened upstairs the milk of human kindness was overflowing in me.

'Why not? I'm wide awake.' He seemed in control of himself so I put the questions to him.

'What was that nonsense at Murphy's Harbour yesterday? You're not a gang member.'

'Didn't convince you, huh?'

'Not really. What were you doing?'

'Research.' He tried to smile.

'How much research did you do?'

'Look, are you charging me over that?'

'I don't have to.' A nice neutral answer.

'I'll compensate the Frenchman at the baitstore. I didn't mean them to make a mess like they did.'

So he had done the swarming. 'Compensation should end that problem,' I told him. 'But there are a couple of other things I want to know about.'

'Like what?' He was wary.

'Like who loaded you up with PCP?'

'I don't know.'

'You didn't recognize the guy? Or you didn't see him?'

'I don't know anything about it.' He was firm now. 'Drugs aren't my thing. The odd joint at a party but nothing else.'

'Right now you're charged with possession of around four ounces of angel dust that I found in your room. Are you aware of that?'

He nodded. 'Yes. The cop who was here before you told me. He read me a whole song and dance about rights.'

'Did he mention anything else to you?'

'Isn't that enough?' It sounded like he'd been rehearsing that line. It came out perfectly.

'Did you and your gang do anything else in your research project? Now's the time to tell me.'

'We swarmed the grocery at Pointe au Baril.' His pronunciation was perfect although the natives usually say Point-oh-Barrel.

'I know about that. What about the car?'

He frowned fleetingly. 'Car? You mean the Ford? I borrowed that from a friend of mine in Toronto.'

'What about the Accord you borrowed from Parry Sound?'

He was puzzled, or acting convincingly puzzled. 'Parry Sound? I didn't get up to anything in Parry Sound. The other stuff was research for a part I'm after. If I'd have come into Parry Sound it might have gotten ugly. I didn't need that.'

'Well, where did you get the Accord?'

'What Accord?' He tried to sit up, raising his shoulders as high as he could with the belt around his chest. 'I don't know what in Hell you're talking about.'

'Tell me about these other kids who were

with you.' I kept my voice conversational. A nurse who was passing the open door paused to look in and I acknowledged her with a little wave. She nodded and went on.

'I picked them up in Wasaga Beach. Saw them bumming around together and turned them into a gang.'

'Where are they now?'

He shrugged. 'I split hours ago.'

'Did any of the others get into the angel dust?'

It was hard to tell whether he was giving me a performance but he looked anguished and close to tears. 'I was alone and I don't know anything about any drugs and that's the truth.'

'OK then. I'll just ask you one more question. Answer that and I'm through with you. Deal?'

I knew he was lying by his answer. 'I don't care how many questions you ask. I don't know anything about any drugs.'

It was all I was going to get out of him but I put my question anyway. 'Who joined you, at the motel, when you were kicking back, drinking your beer?'

'Nobody did. I was on my own.'

'One last thing, then. What are the names of the other kids?'

He relaxed, lying back and giving a little sigh. 'Let me see. The big one's name is Chuck. I don't know any last names but the

86

other guys were Fred and Glenn and Phil.'

I took my notebook out of my shirt pocket and copied down all the names and the descriptions he gave me, then thanked him as if he'd been a help and went out to the door to wave the Parry Sound cop back in. 'Watch him. He's acting innocent but he figures he's smarter than we are. Don't let him out of your sight.'

The cop was young and handsome with a little moustache. He didn't like my suggesting he might goof. He just nodded and went back in to sit with the kid. I left, hoping he would stay alert. Hanson was tricky.

Sam jumped out of the car window and bounded to greet me, wagging his tail. He was none the worse for his vigil but I fussed him and told him he was an uncle and then put him in the car and drove down to the Parry Sound police station.

There was only a lone uniformed man on duty in the station but he knew me and let me look at the arrest report they had drawn up on Hanson. He was charged with assaulting me and possession of a restricted substance. There was a space left on the page for the chemical name to be added once their forensic people had checked out the powder. I thanked him and was about to leave when I saw a golf bag leaning against the wall in the corner of the office.

'Going golfing when you get off work?'

He looked around. 'Not me. That was there when I came on at twelve. The detectives found 'em at the motel where you caught the Hanson kid.'

I hadn't seen any clubs in the motel room but then, I hadn't looked in the closet. But I checked them out anyway. A fine-looking set including three different putters. And the monogram on the bag was JW, the same one I had noticed on Waites' shirt-front at the funeral parlour.

CHAPTER FIVE

The constable said, 'Don't touch it, it's tied in with that homicide this morning.'

'I know. And I'd be happier if it was out of the way until the detectives can fingerprint it. Could you put it somewhere?'

'Sure.' He picked the bag up carefully, putting both hands on the soft sides where his prints wouldn't blur any that already existed, and carried it into the inspector's office.

I thanked him and went back to the car and headed down the highway. Daylight was beginning to seep into the sky. It was almost fully light when I reached the Harbour and drove through town, slowing down to check from the car that no windows had been broken in any of the Main Street properties. Normally I did it on foot but I was tired and I didn't stop, just went up to my house and let Sam out to seek again around the property.

There was nobody around and I stopped on the dock for a minute or two, watching the night mist dispersing on the surfaces of the lake and listening to the redwing blackbirds in the reeds. I was one lucky man, I figured.

But I was still alert, so I sent Sam into the house ahead of me to check it was clear before I went through to the kitchen and put some coffee on while I made the phone calls I had planned.

I let the baby announcements wait until I'd called George Horn in Toronto. He's a one of a kind guy, an Ojibway from the local reserve. He saved my hide one time, using skills a non-Indian doesn't have. Since then he has out-performed a whole crowd of city-bred hopefuls by graduating high in his law class. Now he was articling in the Crown Attorney's office in Toronto, on a fast track to a judgeship, I reckon. A lot of guys would get swelled-headed to have done what he's done but there's not an ounce of arrogance in him. He's stayed the same as he was when he ran the gas pump as a kid at the marina. I reached him at his apartment.

'Hi, George, Reid Bennett. How are you?'

'Hey, Reid, good to hear from you. How's Fred?'

I told him about the baby and he congratulated me. Then I asked, 'Do you have any time to do me a favour?'

'I can make time. What's up?'

'Well, there's three people I'd like to know more about. One of them is in custody for drug trafficking. Should be simple to chase him up.'

'In custody where?' He doesn't waste words.

'Parry Sound. The detectives will be following up, I guess, but it would be faster for you, he's a Toronto resident.'

He wrote down Hanson's name and then I told him about the other two. 'This is a bit more complicated. First, a guy called John Waites. He's a lawyer.'

'Why are you interested?'

'His car was stolen and recovered with a dead woman in the trunk. She's a Parry Sound resident so they're following up, but this guy identified her as his wife at first, and now the dead woman's husband and Waites' wife are missing.'

We talked it over and he made notes. 'I've seen his name around the courts,' he said thoughtfully. 'He's a criminal lawyer. He's good. You think he killed this woman?'

I explained about the golf clubs and the

concussion and he was quiet a moment. 'This guy Hanson, he had the clubs, right?'

'In his room at the motel. Only the driver was missing and that could have been the murder weapon.'

George was thoughtful. 'You'd think he'd have enough moxie to get rid of them if he'd killed that woman.'

'That's the way I see it. The other thing is, he claims, naturally, that he doesn't know anything about the PCP in his room. There could be a case that whoever dosed him up with the stuff also left the clubs there to incriminate him.'

'That's what a good lawyer would claim. You'd never get a jury to convict on a case like that.'

'Yeah, well, that's why I want to know about Waites. If he's a criminal lawyer he knows his share of rounders, guys who might off his wife for him and stick the blame on this dumb kid.'

'But you said it was a woman from Parry Sound killed.'

'She and the dead woman are very much alike to look at. If my theory is right, a contract guy may have goofed.'

He digested that in a moment's silence, then asked, 'So where does this Marcia Tracy fit in?'

'She knows both men. No law against that. But she knows Waites well enough to drive him out to the highway when his car was recovered and she had dinner with the Hanson kid the same night.'

He was silent again, recalling his days at the marina, trying to recall Marcia Tracy. 'She the woman who owns the old Dalton place on the west side of the lake, half a mile down from the lock?'

'That's where she lives when she's here. I don't know anything about any Dalton.'

'Before you came to the Harbour, Reid. He was a banker. He was widowed and married again. He died in Toronto around ten years back. I remember it involved pills and there was some discussion about did he fall or was he pushed. I guess Marcia Tracy is his widow.'

'Different name,' I objected.

'She's a big F feminist, in case you hadn't noticed. Likely that's her maiden name.'

'Apparently she's big in the film business in Toronto. A producer. Fred says she's well known, a ballbreaker with a couple of husbands behind her.'

'What's the name of her company?'

'Northlands Productions, I don't have an address.'

'OK. I'll look into it. Some of it I can do myself but I'll get Bill Serrel to do any legwork. Remember him?'

'Hell, yes.' Serrel was a sixtyish ex-cop. On retirement he had gone to work for the

Crown Attorney's office. He was a quiet, thorough man, inclined to spend too much of his lunch-hour in the beer parlour, but aside from that a sound guy. 'Tell him hi,' I said.

'Will do. I'm coming to the Harbour tonight. It's my mom's birthday tomorrow so I've begged a day off to add to the weekend. I'll bring what I can find out with me, unless I hit something vital. Then I'll call.'

'Thanks, George. I owe you one.'

'*De nada*. See you tonight, and give my best to Fred.'

I hung up and called my sister in Toronto. She was just heading out to her job as creative director at an advertising agency but she cheered with delight at news of the baby and put her husband on to say hello. He's a Toronto homicide detective by the name of Elmer Svensen. I played Cupid for them a couple of years ago when Elmer and I worked on a case together in Toronto and he met Lou, who was divorced. He made all the usual noises about the baby and then I had a word of shop with him.

'Ever run into a lawyer name of John Waites?'

'Yeah. Tough sonofabitch in court. You've seen him there.'

'Don't remember him. It's been three years, remember.'

'He's been around longer than that. I
93

recall he was in on a case of yours two, three years before then. Junior counsel representing that bank robber you shot.'

'Kershaw?'

'Yeah, that's the guy. Took a woman hostage. You got your picture in the papers over that one.'

'That's the guy who skipped his guard on a day pass from the pen, right?'

'The same one. Crazy, eh? We lock the bastards up and the parole board says they can go to ball games with some dopey baby-sitter.'

'And Waites was his lawyer.'

Elmer picked up my tone. 'What's he been up to, Waites?'

I filled him in on the homicide and he clicked his tongue. 'You know, from this end, it sounds to me like Waites could've been paying somebody to off his wife only they got the wrong girl.'

'That's what I'm thinking, too. Any chance you could do a little checking for me, Elmer, see if she was rich or if he had a big insurance policy on her.'

'I can do that. Although you've already got a motive. A guy like Waites wouldn't want a divorce. Under Ontario family law he'd have to give her half of everything if they'd've split up. He's a high liver. He wouldn't want her cutting into that.'

'Well, he's not exactly living high, taking

94

his vacation at Pickerel Point Lodge. It's pretty fancy by our standards up here but the Côte d'Azur it ain't.'

'I'll ask around,' Elmer said. 'Gotta go. Louise has got her hand on the doorknob.'

'Thanks, Elmer. 'Preciate it.'

The next call I made was to Fred's parents. They live in the interior of British Columbia, which is three hours behind us on the clock. But her mother answered, sleepily.

'Good morning, Ann. It's Reid. I wouldn't have woken you up at four-thirty but there's great news. You're the grandmother of a beautiful little girl.'

'Oh Reid, that's wonderful.' Her soft West of England accent still persists after forty years in Canada. 'How's Fred?'

I gave her all the details and she asked all the right questions. Then I asked the ugly one. 'How's Harry today?'

'Still asleep, he had a bad night, Reid. God forgive me, I sometimes wish for his sake that it was over.'

'Maybe the good news will give him fresh heart.'

'I hope so. Look, it's impossible to travel right now. But as soon as you can, I hope you'll come out and see us. He'd love that.'

'Week after next unless something unforeseen crops up. Take care of yourself.'

'Bless you, Reid. I'll send Fred some flowers as soon as the store opens.'

95

That reminded me what I had to do: order some flowers and put an announcement in the paper. But it was too early to do either for another hour so I took my coffee into the living-room and sat on the couch. An hour later I was waking up, the full cup still in front of me. I got another cup and showered again and changed, then called and ordered roses at the Parry Sound florist's. I also placed an announcement in the paper. After that I put Sam in the scout car and drove down to Main Street.

Things move slowly in a resort town. The bait shop was open, of course. Gilles gets there at first light to be on hand for the early fishermen, but the grocery was just opening and the bank and liquor store employees were arriving for their ten o'clock starts. I stopped in to chat to Gilles, telling him that Hanson wanted to compensate him.

'I lost four rods an' five reels is all. I'll make up a bill,' he said angrily. 'But y'know, Chief, that young guy 'e should do community service, 'im. Make 'im clean up in some place messy.'

'It could come to that. He's up on a couple other charges.' I was going to leave but he remembered Fred and I shared the news with him, which was a faster way of getting it around town than taking an ad in the newspaper.

It worked that way. I had trouble getting

out of the station where I went to check the teletype. There was nothing on it about Kershaw. He was still at large but the phone rang continually with well-wishers. I managed to call Fred, who sounded strong and happy. I told her I'd be in at two o'clock and when I'd hung up I put the phone on the answering box, asking people to ring Parry Sound OPP if they couldn't reach me. I didn't want the air filled with congratulations and I'd be in touch with Parry Sound myself to pick up anything worthwhile. Next I took a quick run to the Northont Motel to see if the owner remembered any visitors to Hanson's cabin. He didn't and seemed glad of the fact. The cabin was locked and sealed with an OPP sticker, which had angered the owner even further.

I went back to the station and called Parry Sound to talk to Sergeant Holland. 'He's headed down your way, Reid,' the constable told me. 'He's going to get a statement from this Waites guy whose car was stolen.'

'Waites is still here?'

'Guess he must be. That's where Bill's headed.'

'Thanks. I'll join him there.'

Pickerel Point Lodge was busy. Four couples were out playing tennis and other people were getting ready to take their boats out but they were all comfortable Mom and Pop types, not like Waites. A yuppie like him would have been as out of place here as an ocelot at a kid's pet show. Coming here had been a real concession on his part. Maybe he really had been trying to please his wife. And maybe she had been genuinely difficult to get along with. But had he set her up for a killing?

There was no police car outside, so I parked and got out, taking Sam with me. It was going to be Holland's investigation. I would just wait and work with him, making sure Waites didn't leave.

Mrs James was in the lobby and she told me that Waites hadn't been down for breakfast. There was a 'do not disturb' sign on his doorknob. I asked her to head him off and call me if he came down, then walked through the lounge and out to the back of the building. The lounge gave on to a broad deck with recliner chairs on it and a sandy beach in front. A couple of pleasant-looking young mothers were sitting on the deck watching their children play at the water's edge. To the right was the long wall of the building, cut off from the deck by a five-foot wooden fence. To fill time while I waited for Holland I went down the steps in front of the deck and walked around the building the long way. That was when I noticed the rope.

It was the primitive fire-escape from an upstairs room, a two-inch rope with knots every few feet. Normally it should have been

98

coiled under the window of the room but in one case it was hanging down, reaching almost to the ground.

The bedroom window from which it hung was open wide. All the others were open part way with a fly screen in the open section. That meant that somebody had come down the rope. I guess I should have gone around to the front desk and asked whose room it was but I didn't take the time. Calling on old boot-camp skills, I grabbed the rope and walked myself up the wall to the room above. At window-sill level I paused, raising my head cautiously to look inside. Nothing seemed out of place but the bed had not been slept in. I grabbed the window-sill and heaved myself inside.

From the window I could see that the closet door was open and there was a man's suit lying on the floor next to it, the pockets inside out. I took out my gun and advanced towards the door of the bathroom which was ajar.

The door opened at a push of my toe and I saw, in the mirror facing me that there was nobody hiding behind it. Still with the gun in my hand I moved into the bathroom, looking down around the door to check nobody was crouched there. Nobody was. But John Waites was lying face down in the empty tub, still dressed in the clothes he had worn to the funeral parlour. And spreading out beneath him was the rusting stain of day-old blood.

I holstered my gun and felt his throat automatically for a pulse. There was none and the body was already stiff.

The security chain was in place on the door so I unhooked it, then, carefully not touching anything else, I went back to the window and slipped back down the rope. A couple of kids were walking by towards the beach and one of them said, 'Hey. Neat-oh. I'm gonna do that.'

He headed towards me but I told him, 'Stay down, please. That's dangerous.' And as a safeguard I told Sam 'Keep' and left him there while I ran back to the deck and up into the lodge.

Holland had just arrived. He was talking to Mrs James and he looked up in surprise. 'Hell, Reid. I figured you'd still be in bed, you were up all night.'

'Waites is dead,' I said.

Mrs James gasped but Holland made to go out the way I had entered. 'No, he's up in his room. Somebody got out down the fire-escape rope. I climbed up to check and he's dead.'

'The key, please.' Holland held out his hand to Mrs James, who pulled a key from the pocket of her skirt.

'This is the master. What are you going to do?'

'We're going to check. Then I'll need to

100

talk to your staff. Don't let any of them go anywhere before I've done that, please.' Holland was polite even in his urgency. 'Which room is it?'

'Two-oh-six. Come on.' I led the way and we ran upstairs and Holland unlocked the door.

'Did you take the chain off?'

'Yes. Whoever it was went down the rope.'

We went into the bathroom and looked at the body. Holland didn't even touch it. 'The blood's good and dry. I'd say he was killed last night sometime.'

'Looks right to me,' I said. 'How'd you want to handle this? There's a doctor in town but he's not a forensics expert. You want to call your own people?'

'This is your turf.' He was grinning. 'Like, fair's fair, huh? I wanted to talk to this guy but Murphy's Harbour isn't my jurisdiction.'

'Fair trade. You took the Jeffries woman off my hands yesterday. I'll take care of this one. But I could use some help.'

'OK. Compromise.' He straightened up and looked at me. 'I'll help you for a while, call our crime scene guy in, then you take over.'

I guess it was ironic, two cops more or less tossing a coin to see who investigated a homicide, but places like Murphy's Harbour fall between the cracks of the police system. I'm fine with most things but a homicide

101

investigation takes a team and there was just Sam and me. If we were going to find whoever had killed Waites, I'd need support.

We started by calling for help, Holland phoned his office to send the crime-scene team. They're a small detachment and their team consisted of one man, a jack of all trades. He would take the photographs, then dust for prints and, if necessary, vacuum the room for samples of lint that might have come from the murderer's clothing, although that would be hard to prove in court. Hotel rooms have so many people through them that a good lawyer can usually sway a jury on peripheral evidence like that.

To fill in the time until he arrived, we interviewed the staff. Nobody had seen or heard anything unusual but we established that Waites had ordered room service, an unusual request in such a small establishment as Pickerel Point Lodge. That had been at nine-thirty. He had ordered a bottle of Scotch, asking for Glenfiddich, but had settled for their bar brand, J. & B. The dining-room waitress who had taken the bottle and ice up was off duty until noon but Mrs James called her house. She was out but would come in to work as soon as she returned.

The Scotch order made me think, on two counts. To start with, Glenfiddich was Hanson's drink. Second, there had been no bottle in sight in the room. Perhaps the murderer had taken it with him. That suggested Kershaw as the murderer. He was on the run, cautious about going into public places like a liquor store, even if he had money. He would have taken the whisky without thinking.

After we'd talked to the staff we canvassed the other guests. The guy who had the room on one side of Waites was out fishing but the man the other side had heard nothing. He had gone up to his room and hit the sack early, around ten. Maybe by that time Waites was already dead.

And that was as far as we could go on a first sweep. Mrs James said she would have the other man call me when he came in from fishing, and that was it.

We went back up to the room and looked around, without touching anything, while we waited for the crime-scene expert. Two glasses had been used but the bottle of Scotch was gone. 'Should be some prints on these glasses anyway,' Holland said with satisfaction. 'Might be able to name the guy right off.'

'It could be this Kershaw who skipped on his day pass in Toronto,' I said. 'I found out this morning that Waites was his lawyer when he was sent up.'

'Getting even for the lousy defence?' Holland laughed.

'It's not that simple. If he'd been looking for Waites he would have stayed in Toronto, not come here. And if someone in Toronto had told him where Waites had gone, how did he know which room? Yet nobody downstairs saw anybody strange in here last night.'

Holland frowned, creasing his solid, single eyebrow. He looked like a puzzled chimpanzee. 'I thought his wife might've gone back home. If she had, she could have told the killer, but I've got the Toronto police checking his address. She didn't come back overnight, I know that.'

We stood there, looking at one another blankly, trying to see if there was some connection we'd missed. My own early theory had died with Waites. I had seen a possibility that he had set up his wife to be murdered. The man had seemed angry enough for it. And then the man who did the job had gotten the wrong woman. The idea made sense right up until somebody knifed Waites. But there was a second possibility.

'How about this? Waites set somebody up to kill his wife. My guess is it's this Kershaw. As a lawyer, Waites could have known in advance when Kershaw would be getting a day pass. He arranged to set him up with a car parked somewhere close to the ballpark in Toronto. So Kershaw, or whoever it was, comes up here and kills the wrong woman.

Then the guy turns up here to collect whatever Waites had promised to pay him. Waites gets angry and tells him he's killed the wrong woman and he's not going to pay. So the guy knifes him.'

Holland unfurled his eyebrow and nodded. 'Some kind of sense in that. We'll know for sure when Dave Stinson gets down here and fingerprints those glasses.'

'Guy like Kershaw would know enough to wipe the glass,' I said and Holland shrugged. 'For now, I like your idea. I'm going to get it on the air, see if we can round the sonofabitch up. He oughta be inside anyway.'

'OK. I'll wait here while you go use the phone.' He left and I stood at the door, looking over the room. There was a dent on the neatly made bed, as if someone had sat there with his back to the headboard, and the only chair in the room was facing it. Aside from that the only thing out of place was the suit on the floor with the pockets inside out. That didn't make sense to me. A professional criminal, even a bank robber, wouldn't have turned the pockets inside out. You do that only if somebody is wearing the pants. With a suit on a hanger you could check the pockets by scrunching up the fabric in one hand.

I checked the closet, pushing the door open wider with the back of my fingernails to

105

avoid putting extra prints on it. It was empty except for a pair of golf shoes with trees in them. Waites had obviously been a perfectionist.

The missing clothes made me wonder more about the suit. If the killer had taken everything else, why had he left this? Maybe he'd been rushed and had grabbed the bag and left, or maybe it was a red-herring, that he wanted to show us that he'd gone through the pockets. Or maybe the suit was intended to lead us off track some way.

I was standing there when Holland appeared at the doorway, he was out of breath. 'Listen, they told me on the radio. You've got a problem in town. Somebody called in. There's a bunch of kids swarming the grocery.'

CHAPTER SIX

He offered to come with me but that would have meant a delay while he sealed the room. I didn't need him anyway, not with Sam. I ran down and out the front door, whistling for Sam who bounded around the corner of the building and leapt into the front seat.

I spun away towards the lock, knowing I'd be too late but that somebody would probably have got the number of the car they'd left in. After yesterday's incident the kids around Main Street would have their eyes wide open.

I was right. The kids had all gathered at the door of the store. I wheeled up alongside. 'Did anybody get the number of their car?'

Two of them had taken it, and a description. This one was different, a newer car, a Chrysler Magic Wagon. Mommy's car for one of the little darlings, I guessed. 'Which way did they go?'

They had headed out straight along the side road to the south entrance to the highway. It figured from that they would be heading south, back to the anonymity of their own communities. 'Phone the OPP in Parry Sound and give them the car number. OK?'

'Right.' One of the girls dug into her shoulder-bag for a quarter and I spurted away down the highway.

The Magic Wagon was gone. I pushed the police car to the limit but there was no sign of them. By the time I was ten miles south I knew they had pulled off down one of the little side roads that led to enclaves of cottages on the beach. They would park there and giggle, maybe smoke up a while, then come out later in the day when the heat was off and they could get home without being stopped. By that time the local police would have called on the owner of the car and been told what a good boy little Johnny was and that he couldn't possibly have been mixed up in a swarming. We would be too late to do anything about it. The kids would disperse and the owner's son would have an alibi that put him fifty miles from the Harbour at the time.

Discouraged, I turned and drove back to Murphy's Harbour. The crowd had started to break down into little groups and they watched me as I went into the grocery. Mrs Horn, George's mother, was sitting on a hard chair at the entrance. She's a handsome, dignified woman and she was composed as she always is, but quietly angry. Behind her, the store owner was working along the shelves, picking things up and putting them back in place. When he saw me and pointed to Mrs Horn, I touched my cap to her. 'Hello, Jean. Were you here when it happened?'

'They killed my dog,' she said quietly.

'Where is he?'

'Jack put him in the back of my truck. I was just coming out of the store with my bags and they got out of their van and walked over and one of them hit Muskie on the head with a baseball bat. I tried to grab the boy but he pushed me over and they ran in here. Before I could do anything they were out and gone.'

'Did you see which of them killed

Muskie?'

'Yes. I'll know him next time.'

'Good. We have the licence number, we'll have him arrested.' It was fine for me, an open and shut case, but it was a tragedy for her. That old hound of theirs had been a fixture in her life.

'Why would they do that, Reid?' She looked up at me, calm but angry, the way a lot of Indians have been with a lot of white men for a long time.

'I'm sorry it happened,' I said. 'It's some kind of initiation stunt they pull. To get into the gang a kid has to do something illegal. A lot of the time they go for dogs. One of them tried to bait Sam last night.'

'You'll get him, Reid.' It wasn't a question.

I had two homicides and an escaped con to worry about but this one was personal. 'I'll get him,' I promised.

She stood up slowly. 'Thank you.'

'Can you describe the kid who did it?'

'He was about eighteen, I think, dark hair, a little rat tail at the back. 'Bout three inches taller than me.' Five-nine, I registered. It sounded like the kid I'd picked out the day before as the number two in the gang.

'What was he wearing?'

'A T-shirt and jeans. On his T-shirt it said 'Hermann's Gym.' It was spelt with two ens.'

109

'Thank you. Would you like a cup of tea at the restaurant before you go home?'

'No, thank you, Reid.' She picked up her purse. 'Oh, and George phoned me. Congratulations on the baby.'

I thanked her and we shook hands and I put her into her pickup. Then I went back in and got the details of the swarming. Nothing much had been stolen, but they had ripped down a couple of pyramids of cans and used one big pop bottle to smash a bunch of others. I made soothing noises and got the owner to make a list of his losses and damage. Then I went back out to talk to the kids outside. One of them had seen the dog being killed and they confirmed the description Mrs Horn had given me. Yesterday's events had turned them all into good witnesses. I thanked them and made a note of the girl's name in my book against the time the case came to court, then I went to the station and reset the telephone to cut directly into my radio if it wasn't picked up.

I stood there for a moment, thinking what to do next. There was nothing much I could do until I'd traced the registration of the van and a policeman had spoken to the owners. But before I called the registry I called George Horn's office in Toronto. He was in court, his secretary told me so I gave her the message that his mother's dog had been killed, not saying how, and suggesting that a new puppy might make a good birthday present.

Then I rang the licence bureau and gave them the name of the gang's Magic Wagon, 382 HHD. The operator was back within fifteen seconds. 'Yeah, it's registered to a company, called Painters' Nook, 331 Main Street, Parry Sound.'

'Thank you,' I said and hung up. The long arm of coincidence had overreached itself again. Painters' Nook was the store run by the Jeffries.

That information sent me back up to see Holland at Pickerel Point Lodge. He was standing outside Waites' room, smoking a cigarette. 'Tryin' to stop but it's impossible when you're working,' he apologized. 'How'd it go?'

'The gang was driving a wagon registered to Painter's Nook. That's the Jeffries' place, right?'

'Yeah.' He stubbed his cigarette on the sole of his shoe and put the butt in his pocket. 'How in hell did they get their hands on that thing?'

'Maybe they stole it. But if so, where from? It wasn't at the store yesterday when you were there, was it?'

'No. I checked with the girl at the store yesterday, after we wondered how Jeffries had got away without taking his VW or the Waites woman's Accord. I meant to mention

111

it to you, but with this killing it slipped my mind. Didn't seem that important anyway.'

'Maybe it's not. It could be coincidence, like winning the lottery the same day you're struck by lightning,' I said. 'Think about it. The Waites' Accord is stolen by what looks like a gang. The Jeffries woman is dead in the trunk. Then a gang, the same gang we had in town yesterday, turns up in Jeffries' other car. It sounds to me like Jeffries is behind this whole thing.'

'I've already broadcast a description of him as a missing person,' Holland said. 'Him and Moira Waites. I'll have it reissued, with the note that we want to talk to them about two homicides.'

'Did you check if this Jeffries has a record?'

'Yeah, he's clean. He's an American, from Milwaukee.'

'From the description I got the Jeffries are a crunchy granola kind of couple but I'm starting to doubt it. This gang using his car is just too much of a coincidence. Maybe it was him who put his wife in that car trunk and let the gang kids drive it into the lake. Maybe he and Moira Waites are off somewhere now, playing Mom and Pop.'

Holland swore softly. 'Hold on here, please, Reid. I'll phone the office, put out a stolen car call on that Magic Wagon, and get Jeffries posted as a homicide suspect.'

112

He pattered off downstairs and I went into the bedroom where Stinson was putting his camera away. He's a thin, balding guy, in his early thirties, looking more like an accountant than a cop. He stopped to shake hands with me. 'I hear tell you're a mother, congratulations.'

'Thanks, Dave. Yeah. Fine big girl, three point six kilograms.'

'Which is what? Close to eight pounds? Your wife OK?'

'Fine, thanks. I'm going up to see her later.' I wanted to talk about the case but you can't rush courtesies and he was genuinely concerned for Fred, so I let him get back to business.

'Well, I'm through taking pretty pictures. We turned the guy over. He's been stabbed in the chest, and then his throat was cut. Whoever did it wasn't fooling. They wanted the guy dead.'

'You going to print the glasses?'

'Thought I'd take them with me. I'm going to print the surfaces in here and seal the room. I'll do the glasses back at the office, I prefer working there.'

'Before you go, I've got a present for you. It's a glass used by a guy called Hanson. I arrested him last night for possession of drugs so I guess they've printed him now, anyway. If you get some prints maybe you can compare them with these.'

'Thanks, I guess,' he said. 'Means more work but what the hell.'

'What'd you make of the suit?'

He scratched the dome of his head and frowned. 'Been thinking about that. Whoever killed him took everything else but his golf shoes and the suit. And those pockets being turned inside out. Why would somebody do that?'

'That's what I was thinking. The only thing I came up with was that they wanted to draw attention to the suit, which means away from something else. Only I don't have any idea what else that could be.'

'Nor me.' He bent and picked up the suit jacket. He squeezed it in his fingerprints. 'Feels like silk. Waites had money, that's for sure.' Then he frowned. 'You'd figure he'd take better care to keep it pressed.'

'It's rumpled all right,' I said, and fingered the fabric. 'Shouldn't have got in that shape just from being dropped on the floor.'

Stinson gave a little chuckle. 'Looks like he's been swimming in it.'

'That's it,' I said. 'That's what must have happened.'

He looked puzzled so I explained about the car in the lake, with the dead woman in the trunk. 'This could be the suit he was wearing when he drove off that rock.'

'Why would he do that?' Stinson looked at me disbelievingly.

'Maybe he was planning suicide but chickened out.'

Stinson cocked his head suspiciously and took the suit from me. 'Could be. Anyway, I don't know if the Forensic lab can prove that it's been in the lake, but I'll ask them to check.'

'Good. Put it in a bag right away. There might be weed or something on it. Will you get a sample of lake water to compare?'

'Sure. There's one chance in a zillion it'll help, but those guys are good. They're using the OPP lab as an example in textbooks in the States these days.' He sounded wistful and I guessed he was sick of working in the sticks and wanted to get to Microscope Central in Toronto, where the miracles were performed.

'The other thing he left was the golf shoes.'

'Overlooked them, is my bet.' Stinson picked them up.

'Dinky little feet for a guy Waites' height.'

'Are they too small to be his?'

'Naah.' He shook his head cheerfully. 'Typical yuppie lawyer. Small hands, small feet, neat. And fussy as well. Lookit, shoe trees in his golf shoes.'

He snapped the little triggers on the trees and pulled them out. Surprisingly, they weren't normal shape. Instead of being pointed as the interior of the shoe would

115

have been, both were cut away at the ends. We looked at one another without speaking, and Stinson tilted the shoes and gave them a shake. Inside each one was a small bag of clear, very strong plastic. And inside each bag were two neatly folded bindles of the kind street dealers use to package cocaine.

'Well, well,' Stinson said happily. 'So the late lamented had a hungry nose.'

'You sure it's coke?' I was thinking of Hanson and his own stash of powder, together with the evidence of his behaviour. He hadn't been using coke.

'I can't tell.' Stinson opened one package carefully, not breaking the neatness of the folds. 'I'll have forensics take a look at it. Why'd you ask?'

'The kid I pulled in was high on angel dust.'

Stinson refolded the bindle and put it back in its plastic bag. 'Wouldn't expect a guy like this to be on that kind of crap. Coke, yeah, seems like half the guys in his bracket are.'

'I'd appreciate knowing, please, Dave. Right now I've got a call to make.'

'OK, I'll give you a ding when I find out, OK?'

'Thanks.' I went back to my car and got the bag containing Hanson's Scotch glass out of the glove box. A bunch of little kids had gathered around the car, trying to get Sam's attention. I let him out so they could pet him and they did, happily, while I went back into the lodge to find Holland. He was using the telephone in Mrs James's office and I waited until he'd finished, then gave him the glass, with the news of where I'd got it.

'OK, thanks.' He took it. 'Where're you headed?'

'I'm going to break the news about Waites to Marcia Tracy. She knew him and she knows this Hanson, the kid who was leading the teen gang yesterday. She's got to know something I don't. If I find anything out I'll let you know.'

'Thanks. When will that be?'

'I'm coming up to see my wife in the hospital. See you after, say around four this afternoon.'

His single eyebrow came down gloomily. 'Yeah, may's well. I'm supposed to be off at three but I don't see that happening today.'

I put Sam back in the car and drove up to Marcia Tracy's cottage. Her Mercedes was parked in the shade and she was lying on a blanket in the sun, wearing a one-piece swimsuit without straps. She had a good body, lean and well-shaped. She was an attractive sight and I felt the normal male excitement. Her radio was beside her, playing what sounded like Mozart.

Her eyes were closed but she turned her head when I opened the car door, then sat up, hugging her arms around her knees. She looked relaxed and languorous and I got the feeling that she had no idea of the big things that had happened since we had spoken last.

'What is it now?' she asked, snapping off the radio.

'I'm afraid I have some disturbing news, Ms Tracy.'

'Oh?' She cocked her head, surprised by my formality. 'What happened to Colombo and "just one more thing, ma'am"?'

'Mr Waites was killed last night. At the hotel in town here.'

She gave a half shriek. 'What are you saying?'

'I'm sorry to have to tell you but I've just come from there. Somebody stabbed him.'

She stood up in one fluid movement, holding one hand over her mouth. 'Oh my God.'

She was genuinely shocked but there were no tears in her eyes. A very contained woman. 'Who did it?'

'We're trying to find out. So far we don't have any idea, but there are some fingerprints in his room. We're hoping they'll help.'

She took a deep breath, then another. 'Come inside,' she commanded and led me to the verandah. 'Sit down.'

We both sat and she composed herself for a further few seconds, then asked, 'Why did

118

you come to see me?'

'I knew you were friends with him. You drove him to the gas station yesterday. I wondered if you knew anything about him that might help us.'

'He was my lawyer,' she said tightly.

'Yes. You said that before. But I find he's a criminal lawyer. Do you have call for a criminal lawyer in your business?'

Her face tightened even further. 'And just what do you know about my business?'

'Not much. Just what you've told me, but I don't know of any business outside of crime that needs a criminal lawyer.'

She glared at me, her lips pursed, a study in anger. 'I was charged with a driving offence. He represented me.'

'When was that?' It kept it conversational, I didn't believe her.

'How should I know? A while back. He got me off.'

'And that's it? He acted for you and you remained friendly and when he ended up in Murphy's Harbour, you knew he was here and gave him a hand when his wife walked out and her girlfriend was murdered?'

'What are you saying?' It was a hiss.

'I'm asking, not saying. I've got a murder to investigate and I don't know much about the guy except that he knew you. So I came to see you.'

'I've told you all I know about him.'

'Then why did you ask me in? You could have told me to go away without inviting me in.'

She shuddered suddenly and I saw that the skin on her arms was drawn up in tiny goosebumps. 'I'm frightened.'

'It's unlikely anyone else locally is in danger.'

'How can you say that? You don't know who killed him.'

I played my second card. 'Might have been his dealer.'

Her eyes flashed. 'Are you saying John used drugs?'

'Yes.'

She didn't reply and I let her sit for a few seconds longer. 'So does that guy Hanson we talked about yesterday. I found him high and murderous on something, probably PCP.'

She stood up, taut and tanned. If Fred hadn't been part of my life I would have wanted to get to know her a lot better. 'How many more bombs are you going to drop on me?'

'I was hoping you could help me a little. You didn't tell me a lot that was useful last time we talked.'

'I know very little about Eric Hanson.' She waved one hand airily. I got the feeling she was happier talking about Hanson than about the dead lawyer. 'Oh, his work, of course. He's more intelligent than the usual

120

run of actors. Most of them are unbelievably dumb.'

'I gather he was doing some kind of research yesterday, when he rode with that gang. When I saw you together I assumed that he was auditioning or whatever for some movie you were making.'

She was in control of herself now. She bent to the cigarette box and took one out. I'd left my matchbook on the table and there was one last match in it. She lit her cigarette and dropped the burnt match in the ashtray as she drew smoke deep into her lungs. 'You mentioned something like that last night. If Hanson's in trouble I guess I'll level with you. Yes, I'm trying to get a new movie together. It's about teen gangs. He's a little old for the lead but he's good. He could handle it.'

'You'll have to scratch him now. He could do a couple of years for what he's charged with.' I was fishing, but she made no answer and I had a new insight. 'Is that why you retained Waites? To keep people out of jail when they were working on a movie of yours?'

She struck a pose, perhaps unconsciously but very stagey, jutting one hip and cupping her right elbow in her left hand, holding her cigarette up next to her face, looking at me quizzically. 'There's some of that goes on,' she said. 'Especially with drugs. There's too

121

much drug use today and sometimes people get caught. If it shuts down a production a lot of people stand to lose money.'

'Has Waites ever represented Hanson?'

'I don't know. Hanson has never worked for me.'

The conversation was headed for another stalemate so I changed my tack, making it more personal. 'I have no right to ask you this but I've got a lot of things breaking at the same time. Can I ask you to help me, please?'

'Ah-ah. Humility.' She sounded triumphant. I just smiled. I'd been polite throughout all my talks with her but apparently I hadn't tugged my forelock often enough.

'Well, yes, I guess you'd say that. I wondered if John Waites ever discussed his private life with you.'

She drew on her cigarette and resumed her pose. 'Not in detail. Why d'you ask?'

'From talking to him yesterday I got the impression that he was pretty annoyed with his wife. He's—was—a button-down yuppie lawyer. She's kind of a bohemian, lets everything go to hell while she paints. That's what he said. On top of which, he didn't seem too broken up when he thought she was dead.'

She looked at me without saying anything, then suddenly stubbed her cigarette. 'It's early, but I'm going to have a drink. Would you like something?'

'No, thank you. I'm working.'

'Suit yourself.' She padded off into the house and I heard ice cubes clinking and she returned with a deep, dark drink. She sat down and raised the glass. 'To his memory.'

I nodded and waited, there was more to her grief than friendship. I was starting to believe that Waites had been one of her lovers. He was in the right area, rich and important in his field, an equal of sorts. But her next words surprised me.

'I guess you'll find out some time so I might as well tell you. John was my second husband.'

CHAPTER SEVEN

If she was expecting me to reel back, slapping my forehead at the shocking revelation, she was disappointed. I'd already seen that she and Waites were close and Fred had told me she had a couple of exes. The news figured. But to humour her I showed polite surprise with a question. 'How come you got on so well? Most people stay away from their exes.'

'I'm not most people,' she said defiantly.

'I can see that, Ms Tracy. Tell me, please.

Did John Waites bring his wife up here because of you?'

'I happened to mention that the Lodge seemed like neutral ground for them, fancy enough for her, passable for him, that's all.'

'But both you and Mr Waites knew the other would be here?'

'Yes.' She was brisk again. 'This was to be business as well as pleasure. As always, I have a few problems with this new production and his advice was useful. We figured he could spend some time discussing things with me while his wife painted.'

'And did that happen?'

'He came over a couple of times. She'd promised him she would play golf but she forgot all about it once she got here. She had her goddamn easel and paints in the car and she set them up on the beach and that made her deaf and blind. He could have laid the cocktail waitress on the sand in front of her and she wouldn't have seen it.'

She was starting to loosen up now and I eased into the reason I'd come here. 'How badly did she bug him? I mean, he sounded really ticked off about her when I spoke to him yesterday.'

She answered as if it were a social question with nothing to do with the wife's disappearance. 'Her art was starting to get to him. I think he figured she would change when she married, that she'd relegate her painting to just a hobby. I guess he felt a bit like a guy who's married an alcoholic. She had him, what could she possibly want more than that? You know.' She waved one hand vaguely. 'He didn't realize that everything else, including him, came second to her paint-box.'

'Is she any good?'

She sipped her drink and gave a grudging nod. 'I guess. She's some kind of impressionist. Since she married John, her work brings big prices in Toronto.'

'Didn't that please him? He seemed like a man who wanted success.'

'He was. But it had to be his own success. That's what came between him and me. As long as I was hanging on by my fingernails he felt confident. When I made *Family Pride* and then *Bugaboo* and started making real money, things fell apart.'

'And where did he meet this girl? I imagine she's younger than he was.'

'Not a lot. She's thirty. And I know exactly where he met her. It was at the studio. At a wrap party for *Family Pride*. She came with the cameraman.'

'And John made the moves on her.'

She looked at me through narrowed eyes. 'I can tell you didn't like him. He wasn't your type, was he? Too sophisticated.'

'I only met him twice, both at bad times.' It wasn't the whole answer. Waites had not been a guy I wanted to spend time with.

'Women adored him,' she said softly. 'He didn't bother wooing, he was too confident. He radiated power. Without half trying he could seduce any woman he wanted.'

'And he worked his magic on this girl?'

'He didn't. Not at first, and it infuriated him. I saw him with her and kidded him about losing his touch.' She smiled, but not fondly. 'A dumb thing to do. He decided she was a challenge and he went to work on her the way she worked on her painting. In the end she said yes, not because she wanted him particularly, I never thought so anyway, but because he was always there.'

'And where were you while all this was going on?'

She gave a little jerk of her head and reached for the cigarette box. I recognized it as a defence mechanism. 'You could say I had plans of my own. And anyway, I was away a lot. We shot *Bugaboo* in the Rockies and I was out there on location for three months. I'm a producer, not a housewife.'

Listening to her made me glad that Fred had pretty well given up acting. A wife who disappears for three months at a time to the other end of the country is not my idea of the perfect mate. I'm a chauvinist, OK, but I hoped I'd never be sitting home with the baby while Fred was three thousand miles away smiling at a camera.

'And when you got home, what happened?'

'He'd moved out. He'd been living with her for a week. So I had a meeting with him, not her, I didn't want to see her, ever. And we agreed to a divorce.'

'Why did he marry her? If all he wanted to do was prove he was wonderful he could have moved on.'

She lit her cigarette and blew smoke thoughtfully. 'I asked him the same thing. He didn't have an answer, but I think I did. She made him feel incomplete. Not sexually or in a male sense, but intellectually. I guess she had the same kind of power that he did, in a different way. She never really surrendered to him. She slept with him but it wasn't as important as her painting. He wanted to possess her, the way he might have owned one of her paintings.'

'If she was making good money as an artist she didn't need him, surely?'

'She's been making good money only since her marriage to John. Before then she was making a couple of hundred dollars a time in some crummy gallery in Soho, that's in New York in case you didn't know.' I did, as it happened. Once on liberty I had spent a weekend with a girl a lot like this Marcia Tracy sounded, in her studio in Soho. But Ms Tracy was still explaining. 'He pulled some strings, lined up some buyers for her

127

and arranged for a fancy gallery to show her work. It sold out. Maybe it's a bubble that will burst now he's gone. Maybe she's good. I don't know. I don't understand pictures unless they move.'

This was all good background but it wasn't advancing my investigation, so I pressed a little harder. 'Is that where she came from, New York?'

'No. She was from Wisconsin or some deadly place like that. She studied in New York and moved there. From there she came up to Toronto with the cameraman I told you about.'

I'd been hoping for an address but obviously she didn't have one to give me, so I asked the next question, hoping it wouldn't stop her talking. 'Do you think maybe he wanted her dead?'

That blew it. She stood up, carefully setting down her cigarette first. 'John was not the ideal husband,' she said carefully. 'But he was no murderer, if that's what you're asking.'

'Did he talk about her to you these last few days while they were staying at the Lodge?'

'No.' She made a move towards the door. 'And this discussion is over. You're trying to get me to say he wanted to kill her. He didn't and I won't. Please go.'

'Sure. I have one last question, please. Did you know he had a cocaine habit?'

'No, I did not.' She was fierce now, angry enough that she might easily have been lying, but she wanted me out so I went.

'Thank you for your help. Will you be staying up here for a while?'

'Are you telling me not to leave town?'

'I thought I asked a polite question, Ms Tracy,' I said as I stepped down into the sunshine.

'I'll give you a polite answer. I haven't decided yet. How does that suit you?'

'It'll have to do. I'll be in touch.' I clicked my tongue to Sam who was lying in the shade, beside her car and walked out to my own car. She lay down on her blanket again and turned up the radio. She had not brought her drink with her, I noticed.

On my way back to the station I called in at the Lodge and spoke to Holland. He said he would supervise the movement of Waites' body to Toronto for forensic work and I was able to go back to the station to do the paperwork. I typed up the report on Waites' death and copies of the statements Holland and I had taken from the people in the Lodge. And after that I also recorded the gang swarming and the killing of Horn's dog.

I'm a better typist these days since Fred bought me a book and made me put masking tape on the keys so I had to follow the book to find them. It worked and I'm faster but this job still took me until one-thirty and

129

there was no time to go home and change before visiting the hospital.

By the time I'd picked up the roses and a box of candies for the nurses it was two-thirty and I reached Fred's room at feeding time. I've seen a lot of things in my life but nothing so far has topped the thrill of watching Fred with the baby.

In uniform I felt like a bull in a china shop but Fred put me at ease. She was over her ordeal, feeling strong and well. She would be coming home in two days, she told me. I said 'good' while I juggled my workload in my head. I had a lot to do and it wouldn't ease up until I had at least located Moira Waites.

'You're being very quiet about all this, dear,' Fred said as she gently put the baby over her shoulder and patted her back. 'What's been happening while I've been in here multiplying?'

I gave her a scaled-down version of events and she looked sober. 'Are the OPP going to help you on this? A murder involving a man from Toronto, you can't handle that on your own. You'll need help from a lot of people.'

'It's heavy right now, but it'll settle down soon.'

'While things are so busy for you maybe you should stay at the Harbour and work on it, rather than drive up here all the time.' She's a good woman, a real cop's wife, understanding that the job has to come first

130

sometimes.

'Maybe, if you don't mind, I'll put off coming again until tomorrow afternoon. We've had some gang trouble on Main Street and I'd like to show a little more presence for a day or two, people are getting spooked.'

The baby gave a tiny burp and Fred wiped her mouth and told her she was a clever girl. The woman in the next bed was watching us like a visitor to a zoo. I guess she hadn't realized that policemen procreate just like real people. After a while the nurse came and took the baby back to the nursery and Fred got up and walked around there with me to peer through the window and watch our firstborn yelling as lustily as the rest of them. 'The nurses tell me she's a screamer,' Fred said, hanging on to my arm. 'Can you handle that?'

'For you and her I could handle anything at all.'

At a quarter to four I left, after she'd made me promise to stay away until the next day at least. I was anxious to get on with my investigation so I didn't need any urging. I returned to the car and let Sam have a stretch, then drove up to the police station.

Holland was in the detective office with his feet on the desk and a cup of coffee. He told me where the machine was and I grabbed a cup for myself, remembering that I'd had no lunch so far. The way things were breaking and with Fred away I was going to lose weight. 'Coupla things,' he said, after he'd asked the expected questions about Fred and the baby. 'First off, Stinson found prints on the glasses from the room. One set was the deceased's. The other set isn't on record, so far as the computer in Toronto has been able to check. And they're not Hanson's either.'

'That's another theory shot to hell,' I said. 'I'd been hoping we'd find they belonged to Kershaw, that escaped con.'

Holland shook his head. 'No dice. The guy in Toronto checked Kershaw's prints individually. It's not him.'

'So what's the second thing?'

'Second thing is that a hotshot lawyer from Toronto came into town and sprung the kid you arrested last night, this Hanson.'

'What was his name?'

'Hers. A Ms Freund. Works for the same firm as this Waites guy. She gave me one of their cards and Waites is on the list as a partner.'

'I just found out that Waites' firm works for a movie producer, Marcia Tracy, she's staying at her own place in Murphy's Harbour. He was on a retainer to cover the company's butt if any of their people got in legal trouble.'

'This Hanson kid works for her?' Holland was only half interested, he hadn't been with

132

me to see the way all the strings in my caseload led back to Marcia Tracy.

'Not yet, apparently. She's considering him for a part in a movie but maybe he knew about Waites from that, talking to other actors, stuff like that.'

'Maybe.' Holland was looking smug, holding the most interesting news for last, I guessed. 'There's one more thing.'

'Helpful, I hope.'

'Could be. Could tie the both homicides together in a neat knot. We found prints on the car, that Honda Accord. No ID of course, because they're the same as the prints on the glass in Waites' room.'

We sat and sipped our coffee, staring at each other sightlessly. The whole thing was tying together. After a little thought I had an idea. 'Hey, have you checked the Jeffries' house for prints? Could be that he's the guy responsible. Just maybe he found out, say, that Waites was boffing his wife. He kills the wife and puts her in Waites' car so we figure Waites is behind it. Then, for whatever reason, he goes to see Waites and kills him.'

'Doesn't hold water,' Holland argued reasonably. 'If some guy came to my house after, God forbid, his wife had been murdered in my car, I wouldn't send out for drinks.'

'Waites was yuppie. Who knows how guys like him think?'

Holland was still unhappy. 'You know the rules of evidence as well as I do. I can't print Jeffries without arresting him or having his consent.'

'No sign of him anywhere?'

'Naah.' Holland finished his coffee and scrunched up the cup, tossing it at the garbage can. It missed and he grunted and picked it up. 'I've done everything I can but unless we go nationwide with this thing we can't stake out every car rental, every ticket agency, for him or the Waites broad to show.'

'And it's his car that the teen gang used to buzz Murphy's Harbour.' I thought out loud. 'Maybe we should concentrate on finding that car. It'll be a mass of fingerprints by now but we might find his in it somewhere.'

'It's an idea.' He swung his feet down. 'I'll put the car out as wanted for investigation in a homicide. That'll wake up the troops more than it just being stolen.'

'Good idea. Now, while I'm here, I have to file a statement about the Hanson arrest. Can you get me a typewriter?'

He sat me down with a machine and I did my thing and he witnessed it and I was on my own. By now it was six in the evening and I was hungry enough to take a bite out of Sam but I drove back to Murphy's Harbour to eat. The presence of the car on Main

134

Street would remind the good folks where their taxes were going.

It was good to be back at the Harbour in any case. I like the spot. It's been home for three years and they're good people. Right now, on a bright summer evening, it was at its best with the shadows lengthening across Main Street and everyone moving slowly in the warmth. I sat at the window of the restaurant and ate a good dinner. Yung Luk is a gourmet cook if you let him do things his way and I had his Thai soup and Szechuan beef while most of the other customers ate fish and chips. Then I paid and took Sam for a stroll around town.

I went into the grocery and the bait store. Both owners were glad to see me. They'd already heard about Waites' death so I didn't have to explain where I'd been all day, but I got the usual small-town feeling that they wished I'd give them more attention and quit showboating, which is the way people look at a murder investigation when they're not involved.

It was seven o'clock and night was coming down on the town. The two lights on Main Street were on already with their usual halo of mosquitoes, and so was the big light at the dock of the Marina.

All the berths at the Marina were full, and, as I always do, I started my evening patrol at their hotel, the Lakeside Tavern. I went in by the back door and ambled through the kitchen with Sam at my side. The cook had a hamburger someone had sent back as too well done and he gave it to me for Sam who crunched it down and wagged his tail.

Amy Vanderheyden was at the desk in the back and she greeted me happily and bent to pat Sam, the only dog allowed in there. She chirruped happily about Fred and the baby and tutted about Waites' death and I smiled and nodded and looked around. The usual crowd of boaters and cottagers were in for dinner and the trumpet, piano, drums band was playing 'Don't cry for me, Argentina' well enough that a couple of Moms and Pops were pushing one another around the dance floor. A typical Thursday night in Murphy's Harbour, except for the homicides I was working on.

The Vanderheydens' daughter, Beckie, was waiting table, flirting happily. She's a good-looking blonde of sixteen and like all smalltown girls she's waiting for someone from Hollywood to drive into town and discover her. But she has her Dutch parents' level-headedness and when she saw me she excused herself from the table and bustled over.

'Hi, Chief. Congratulations on the baby.'

'Thank you, Beckie. How's things with you?'

'Good,' she said, then put her hand on my

136

arm, which surprised me, she's not forward. 'Chief, you know those kids who ripped off the grocery today?'

'I wish I did. I'm looking for them.'

'I saw one of them a while back. Mom sent me to the store for some Parmesan cheese and I saw the biggest one, he was on his own and I think he was going into the Murphy's Arms.'

'That's the kid with the dark hair, around five-nine?'

'That's the one. I heard tell that he killed some Indian lady's dog. He's got some nerve, coming back to town after that.'

'He sure has. Thanks very much, Beckie.' I nodded to her mother and left the place quickly, getting back in my car for the short ride to the town's other hotel. It's below the lock, a standard beer joint with draught beer and no food facilities, the place our locals do their drinking.

Again I went in through the back door. No kitchen here, just a corridor with the beer storeroom to one side behind a solid steel door. I came out behind the bar where Eddie the barkeep was running the beer tap full steam, moving one glass after another under the spout without turning it off. He looked at me and made an offering gesture with a glass but I shook my head. 'Maybe later, thanks, Eddie. I'm looking for a kid in here.'

Eddie completed his order and turned off

the tap, wiping his hands on his apron as his waiter strode away. 'Under age, is he?'

'No sweat. That's not why I want him.' I looked around, recognizing most of the crowd. And then I saw the boy. He was sitting alone with a beer in front of him, smoking a cigarette. He had the pack stuck in the sleeve of his T-shirt, the same T-shirt he had worn when he killed the Horns' dog. I studied him for almost a minute. He seemed nervous, probably because he was under age but also because he was out of his element. These were real people around him, guys who worked hard and came home tired. He didn't. I could tell that from this distance. He had to buy his muscles at Hermann's Gym.

He was watching the door, and that worked in my favour as I moved towards him between the tables. I was half way there before he saw me and bolted for the door. I didn't give chase. Instead I told Sam 'Track' and he bounded after him, grabbing the heel of his right shoe so that he tripped and sprawled headlong. Before he could sit up Sam was over him, snarling an inch from his face.

Then noise in the bar stopped as if someone had switched off the sound on a TV. Then one guy shouted, 'Go get 'im, Sam,' and everyone cheered and I knew they were on my side, Sam's at least, and that was

138

just as good.

I've taken the same psychology courses as any policeman these days and I even took a couple at college when I came out of the Marines. So I knew the worst punishment for this kid was to hurt his pride.

I did it by pulling his arms behind him and snapping the cuffs on his wrists. He went scarlet with shame but I was glad. He'd caused a lot of distress for the Horns. Now it was his turn.

'You're under arrest for malicious damage, assault on a woman and for causing undue pain and suffering to an animal,' I told him. Then I pulled out the card from my notebook and read him the formal caution and the rest of the Charter of Rights ritual. I did it loudly enough that the beer drinkers all heard and the kid's eyes filled with tears of frustration. Then I eased him up on his feet and bent to fuss Sam and tell him he was a good dog. He does a lot of my work for me and earns me the biggest chunk of the respect our locals have for their law enforcement system. A couple of them cheered, and one of them, bolder than the others, dared to reach out and pat Sam's head.

'This the guy who killed that man at Pickerel Point?' he asked and I just smiled like the cat who swallowed the canary. 'He's in custody, I'm taking him in, if you'd get the door, please.'

'Yeah, sure.' He bustled ahead of me and I touched the boy between the shoulder-blades and sent him ahead. The crowd followed as I put him into the police car and drove off. I checked them in my mirror to see if they were going to follow down to the station but they just broke up again and went back in for another beer. Good. I didn't need an audience.

At the station I went in the back way, confronting my prisoner with the reality of law-breaking. The place isn't shocking, unless you're in handcuffs. There are four one-man cells along the back wall. Each one has solid walls and a cage front. They contain a bare plank platform, a toilet and a hand basin. That's it.

In the space in front of the cells there's a wooden desk and a chair. I unlocked the handcuffs and said, 'Sit.'

He sat, rubbing his wrists, not looking at me. His flush had gone now and he was pale under his tan.

'Turn your pockets inside out, lay all your possessions on the table.'

He sat there and said, 'I want to see a lawyer.'

'You'll get one phone call when we're through here.'

He didn't move. His face had drawn itself into a pout. He was frightened but proud.

I opened the top drawer of the desk and took out the arrests book and a pen. 'I'm just going to say this once more. Empty your pockets.'

'Or what? You gonna kick the shit out of me?' Even scared, his voice was schooled. He didn't say 'outa'.

I hissed at Sam and he snarled and thrust his muzzle an inch from the boy's knees. The kid licked his lips. 'I'm telling my lawyer you did this to me,' he said, but he was fumbling in his pockets as he spoke.

'Easy, boy,' I told Sam and he sat on his haunches while the kid stood up and turned his pockets inside out. All he had was a clasp knife and money, a few coins and a bundle of bills. I patted him down and checked there was nothing hidden in his socks or back pocket. 'Cigarettes too,' I said.

Angrily he took the pack from his sleeve and tossed them on the desk. 'Now take off your belt and shoelaces. And your watch, that goes with your other stuff.'

'Why are you taking my belt and laces?' he asked as he did it.

'So you won't hang yourself with them.'

'Why would I do that?'

'Happens all the time. What's your name?'

He looked at me and then away. 'I don't have to tell you.'

'It's all the same to me. Suit yourself.' I counted his money. 'You have twenty-eight dollars and fourteen cents. One Buck clasp knife. One yellow-metal wristwatch, Rolex on dial. One pack of Export A cigarettes.' I made the entry in my arrest book. *John Doe, 17–19 years old, 5ft 9ins., black hair, brown eyes. Wearing Levi jeans, Reebok running shoes. Charged with* ... I wrote in the charges and looked up, putting the top on the pen, looking as satisfied as I could manage. I wanted him cracked. 'Right. Now you wanted a phone call. Come with me.'

In the front of the office I sat him on a stool and picked up the phone. 'What number do you want to call?'

His mouth was working as he weighed his alternatives. No doubt he knew a little law, knew that he could wait until I called a bail hearing and then leave town. That would give him a chance to explain his problems to his parents face to face, to cut down on the shock they were going to experience if he rang them now. 'You got a pizza place in this town?' he asked.

'No. Is that the only call you want to make?'

'Yeah.' His decision made he was tough again. 'Yeah. So stick me in your slammer. See if I care.'

'First I'm going to get a statement from you,' I said easily. 'Sit down there.' I indicated the chair beside the desk.

He sat down, crossing his legs, folding his

arms, a closed book.

I ignored him and pulled out an occurrence form and started typing. He watched me, breathing very shallow.

'Right, now.' I lifted the top of the paper and read to him. 'John Doe, you are arrested on the following charges. You have been given the caution and advised of your rights under Canada's Charter of Rights and Freedoms. Now I'm going to ask you to make a statement. Name?'

He almost fell for it. 'Phil,' he said and then stopped, angry at himself. 'You've got it down there, John Doe.'

'Right, Phil. How did you come into town tonight?'

'I'm not saying. I was here, OK?'

'Dumb,' I said cheerfully. 'If you'd stayed out of town I might never have found you. You'd have been free to swarm more places, kill a couple more dogs maybe.'

'I don't know what you're talking about.'

'Listen, son. You're in deep trouble. Right now you're thinking that if you get out of here you can run away and I'll never find you. But here's a hot flash. I'm not letting you out until I know who you are and where you're from. So all you're doing is making your parents even angrier at you than they are now.'

'You don't know anything,' he said. 'In the morning you have to deliver me to a

143

court somewhere. When you do I'll be bailed out and you're left holding a bag of fresh air.'

'So your daddy's a lawyer, is he?'

That silenced him. It didn't break him down but he was starting to realize that he'd lost.

'You could get away with this still, you know. Or most of it. I know that Hanson set you up. Did he give you the car you came here in this afternoon?'

'I don't know any Hanson.'

'Fine. I'll ask you again later. Right now you're going in the cells.' I stood up, leaving the half-completed form in the typewriter. 'Let's go.'

He stood up. I could see that his confidence was evaporating. There was no audience for his bravery. It was just him and me, and Sam, a solemn, silent presence. He needed somebody there to appreciate what he was doing, otherwise he was going to lose confidence in himself entirely. I figured he'd be ready to talk to me in about an hour's time. It would seem like an eternity to him.

I put him in the cell furthest from the door, the most isolated-seeming in the place, clanked the door shut and locked it. Then I did the hardest thing yet. I left him, without finding out where he had found the Jeffries' car, and walked out of the back door, locking the deadbolt behind me.

I got back in the car and drove into town

again, trying to work out where the kid could have come from. I was surprised by the fact that he had not been carrying a driver's licence or any other ID. Probably he was under nineteen and had left his wallet in the car that brought him, not wanting to be embarrassed if he was asked for proof of age. It also meant that one of the vehicles in town was his. Maybe, if luck was on my side, it would be the Jeffries' Magic Wagon.

But I couldn't see it anywhere in town, so I took a slow drive up and around my whole patch, checking the cars parked at every cottage and the guest houses and our few lodges. It took me an hour and a half, counting a ten-minute stop at home to feed Sam and heat myself a cup of day-old coffee in the microwave I'd put in since marrying Fred.

At close to ten I was back in town again, shaking the door handles on all the lock-up premises. Everything was secure and I walked Sam back to the car just as a new Subaru four-wheel-drive pulled up. It stopped beside me and George Horn stuck his hand out of the window. 'Hi, Reid.'

We shook hands. 'Hi, George. Good to see you. Been home yet?'

'Yeah. My mom's pretty shaken up. The new puppy helped, thanks for the tip.'

'Welcome. She'll be glad to hear I've got the kid in the cells.'

'Good. What's his name?' He got out of the car, a slim tall man, neat in his dark city suit.

'He won't say but his first name is Phil.'

George was thoughtful. 'You'll have to release him tomorrow after a bail hearing.'

'Not if I don't get a name and address. He can't win.'

'Who did he call when you let him use the phone?'

I told him about the bravado and George shook his head. 'Watching too much TV.'

'Yeah. I wish he'd open up. When he came to town and hassled your mother he was driving a car belonging to the husband of the dead woman, Carolyn Jeffries. We've had another murder in town and I want that car badly. I want to trace Jeffries or Waites' wife. I think they're together and they left town in that car.'

'And the kid won't talk?'

'Not a word. Figures he's a hard man.'

George pursed his mouth, as angry as I've seen him. 'He's a little prick, killing poor old Muskie like that.'

'Well, I'm not about to give him the third degree but I want to crack him open. I plan on trying him again when I get back in.'

'Leave it with me,' George said. 'Give me fifteen minutes and I'll be at the station.'

'I can't let you take him apart, George, much as you'd like to.'

146

'I won't.' He looked at me very straight. In the harsh street light his face looked chiselled. 'You trust me, don't you?'

'You know that. You saved my ass last summer. I still owe you for that one.'

'Trust me,' he said. 'I won't do anything illegal, I promise. Borderline unethical but nothing that will get me thrown out of law. I don't want to end up back on the pumps at the Marina.'

'What are you going to do?'

'You'll see,' he said. 'And afterwards I'll come in and tell you what we found out in Toronto.'

He got back into his car and drove down over the bridge to the hotel where he parked and went into the phone-box. Then I put Sam in my car and drove back to the station.

This time I went in through the front door and spent a minute or so checking the teletype and generally advertising my presence. When I was sure my prisoner knew I was back I went through to the cells, carrying a pop can as if I was just enjoying a cold drink.

He was standing against the bars of his cell and he spoke at once. 'I want that phone call now.'

'You refused your chance.'

'I was confused, you didn't explain it to me properly.' He was tense but still acting tough. He would be an unpleasant adult, I figured, a bullying boss and a bastard around women.

'If you want to tell me your name and answer a few questions I'm prepared to let you make a call, even though I don't have to,' I said.

He slammed the bars with his hand. 'You go shove it,' he said. 'I've waited this long. I can wait all night.'

'Suit yourself.' I shut the door and returned to my desk where I sat and read the teletypes. Nothing on it was new to me. The OPP had reissued the description of Jeffries and Moira Waites and the Magic Wagon, specifying they were wanted in connection with a homicide, but there was nothing else of interest on the list. I finished it and waited a few minutes more until George came in.

He came the front way and called out 'Good evening, Chief,' loud enough that the prisoner could hear out back.

'Good evening, sir, what can I do for you?'

He winked at me and pushed a nine by ten envelope across the desk. 'Your info,' he mouthed. Then he said out loud. 'I'm visiting in the neighbourhood and I saw you arresting a man at the Murphy's Arms Hotel earlier.'

'Yes. I did.'

George's face was perfectly straight. He said, 'I happen to be an attorney and as you don't have one in this village of yours, I

148

thought perhaps he might need one.'

'I've heard of lawyers chasing ambulances but this is a new low, if you ask me.'

'Nobody asked you, Chief. Please keep your opinions to yourself and ask your prisoner if he wants to talk to a lawyer.'

I went to the back door and opened it with a slam. 'You, kid. There's a lawyer in town. He's asking if you want to talk to him.'

He had heard every word of our conversation and he was standing at the bars grinning a mile wide. 'Yeah. I do. Bring him in. Like I can't come out there, right?'

I turned and called George. 'He'll see you.'

George came through and I got a chance to see him move. He's about six feet tall, and lean. In his suit and white shirt he looked like authority on the move. He came in and pulled out a card which he handed to the boy. Then he turned to me. 'Please leave us alone and shut the door.' His tone was snooty and I glared at him for the kid's benefit but did it, slamming the door.

They were out there five minutes while I looked at the information George had brought me. It contained brief biographies of Marcia Tracy, Waites and Hanson. I read Tracy's first.

She was thirty-eight, formerly married to the banker Dalton, from whom she had inherited the cottage, then to Waites. That ended in divorce one year before. She had been arrested once, for impaired driving but had gotten off. Waites had defended her. She had been born in Toronto and had taken the television course at Ryerson, the big polytechnical institute in Toronto, and worked at a number of jobs before founding her own production company on the death of her first husband. A bracketed note said that his death had been investigated but eventually the inquest had declared it accidental. In George's neat handwriting was the note, 'I have more, will tell you.' At that point she had inherited his insurance and estate and used the money to open her business. She had married Waites six months after her husband's death. For five years she had struggled to keep her company afloat but had then had a couple of successes, *Family Pride* and *Bugaboo*.

Her divorce from Waites had been uncontested and there had been no division of family property.

At this point in my reading George came back to the doorway and spoke to me in the same loud voice, not his normal tone. 'Did you realize that my client is a juvenile?'

'I didn't realize he was your client?'

'Well, he is. And he is also seventeen years old and you've got him locked into an adult facility.'

'He's alone, in no danger.'

150

'At the moment, no. But if you get busy and these cells are filled, who knows what terrible things could happen. I want him released immediately into my charge.'

'I'm not letting him go until I have his name and address. I have to notify his parents and I want to make sure he returns here for a preliminary hearing tomorrow at noon.'

'I'll give you the name. That will have to be enough. I'll take responsibility for him after that.'

'I don't know you from a hole in the ground. How do I even know you're a lawyer, not some other rounder from that gang of his?'

'My card,' he said and handed it to me with the shadow of a wink. I read it. John Noble, insurance broker.

'OK, then. I'll have to let him go. Once I know his name.'

'Phillip Freund.' He spelt it for me. The name tickled my memory but nothing caught.

'And you'll have him back here tomorrow?'

'Yes. I'm going to drive him to where he's staying and I'll pick him up and deliver him back for a hearing. When will that be?'

'I can get the magistrate here for noon.'

'Right. Let him out.'

I took out the key and unlocked the cell.

151

Even with George working whatever he was doing I hated to let the kid go. He thanked me by saying, 'Still feel like a big-shot? Eh, copper?'

'This isn't over yet, Phil,' I told him. 'Wait for the last laugh.'

CHAPTER EIGHT

The kid couldn't resist giving me the finger as he reached the door. I ignored him and sat down, wondering just how George was planning to smarten him up. For a moment I almost went out after them and brought the boy back, but reason won. If I held him and got an investigation team down from Parry Sound the boy would just toughen up. He would know that the bigger the police department the less chance there was that anything physical would happen to him. And if they succeeded in opening him up by sweet talk, they would probably have their findings thrown out of court later. The lawyer his parents could afford to retain for him would argue that we hadn't observed the boy's rights.

I shook my head and hoped that George had seen a way around it all. It would be clean, even if the legality was a little rocky. I was confident of that. George had come a long way from the Reserve. He wouldn't blow it all. His personal loss would be unbearable, but even worse would be the way all his doubters would shake their heads and mutter about not being able to trust an Indian even when he'd been to college.

Slowly I sat down again and opened Waites' file. It didn't tell me a lot that was useful. He was a high profile guy, for a man in his early thirties. He had a way of swaying juries and had built a reputation for making the police look foolish, which delighted the newspapers but didn't endear him to me. It's always easy for a lawyer, with the advantages of hindsight and unlimited time, to examine an investigation and find some petty thing that a cop didn't consider in the half-second in which he had to decide before pulling his gun or breaking down a door. I'm not a vigilante but I'm more concerned with justice than law. In my view, lawyers mostly don't care about justice, they use the law as a fine-tooth comb to try to drag their clients out of trouble.

Waites' personal file was slim. He had graduated from Osgoode Hall, Canada's foremost law school, the one George Horn had aced, articled at his father's firm although Waites senior had been dead by that time. He had been admitted to the bar in '79. According to George's notes, the firm's best defence lawyer had suffered a

153

stroke the following year and Waites had been moved into the second spot, taking over as the firm's top criminal man in '86, the year after he'd lost to me over Kershaw. Since then he had won a number of shaky cases and had a good circle of satisfied clients, including a Colombian cocaine dealer and a couple of murderers, all of whom probably felt they owed him a lot more than the money he'd cost them. George had noted that he was known as a womanizer and had been married twice, the first time to Marcia Tracy.

Hanson's file had some surprises although nothing was helpful in the case. His real name was Eric Kowalski. His father was a garbageman in Toronto. He had appeared in a number of plays around Toronto and had studied with a woman called Poirier whom George described as the high priestess of The Method. His reviews had been good and he had appeared in a number of TV commercials. On two occasions he had worked for Marcia Tracy but according to George's notes, had been only an extra with no speaking part. He was twenty-eight years old and lived with a woman fifteen years his senior. She was a sound engineer for CBC, our national TV network. Her name was Hanson and no doubt he had taken it as his own because it sounded less ethnic.

I closed the file and was sitting with my

feet on my desk, thinking about it when a car drove up outside. I swung my feet down and waited. A moment later the car drove away and the front door of the office opened. George came in, smiling. 'Can you believe it?' he asked cheerfully. 'I stopped at Kinski's gas station on the highway, left the kid inside while I went in to buy some pop and some sonofabitch stole my car, with the kid in it.'

I played the game by his rules. 'Any idea who it was?'

'No. The guy on the pump said there were three Indian looking guys in a pickup truck. Two of them got out and got into my car and drove off, just like that.'

'Where's the kid?'

'That's the funny part. They took him with them.'

'They're not going to punch him out, are they?'

'No,' he said sincerely. 'They're Indian. They won't touch him.'

'I just hope the hell you know what you're doing, George. You want me to report your car missing?'

He looked at his watch and yawned. 'A bit late tonight,' he said. 'Why don't you make a note of it and we'll look for it when you drop me off at home. You know what Indians are like. They've probably gone back to the Reserve.'

'Does your mom know what you're

doing?'

'She's too busy making a fuss of her new dog. I got her a German short-hair. Pretty little guy but it'll grow big enough that kids with baseball bats won't take after it like they did with Muskie.'

'And your dad can train it for hunting. Good idea.' I wanted to talk about Freund, wanted to know where the Jeffries' Magic Wagon was, but that wasn't going to happen tonight. Instead of pushing it I asked him about the information he'd brought me.

'You made a note on the Tracy file, something about her first husband's death.'

'Yeah.' He sat down the other side of the desk and I put my feet back up. Like most North Americans I'm more comfortable that way. Like every Indian, he isn't. He sat back in his chair and said, 'One of the guys at the office remembered the case. It seems there was talk that his wife, this Marcia Tracy, was running around a lot, screwing actors and the owner of the production house where she was working. According to my source, there was some kind of scandal brewing and Dalton, that's the husband, had hired a private detective to follow her. Then one night he died. Just like that. The coroner said he'd had a couple of Scotches before going to bed and had taken sleeping pills. Seems his heart was a little touchy and the combination finished him.'

156

'You think she knocked him off?'

'The inquest ruled it accidental. There were some who thought it might have been a suicide, or even murder. According to the transcript, the housekeeper said there had been bad blood between the two of them and Dalton had been talking divorce to her, that's the housekeeper.'

'I guess Marcia would have been out on her ear if the old guy had divorced her.'

George shook his head. 'Not entirely. That was after the Family Law Reform Act. She was entitled to half the house and so on, but it wouldn't have been cut and dried. And the way it ended she got a cool half-mill in life insurance, on top of everything else.'

'Sounds to me like a hell of a good motive for feeding him a few drinks and some extra pills.'

'The jury didn't buy it. She came across as the grieving, misunderstood widow. She was young, by their standards anyway, around thirty, a career woman. The way the guy at the office remembers, that went over big with the jury, there were a couple of what he calls bra-burners on it. Anyway, they found it accidental and the whole thing was dropped.'

'And six months later she marries Waites.'

He nodded. 'Yeah. Then they divorce, he remarries, all three of them come up here and the wife vanishes and he winds up dead.

You've got to wonder if something from the past didn't crop up.' He paused, 'Oh, one thing more, from the present. I learned that she's got money troubles. She had a couple of big successes but her last few movies have been crap. Now she's trying to raise money for the next one and nobody's coming forward.'

'So she's strapped. That's interesting. And we already have the feeling that she killed her husband for money. I wonder how this ties together with what's happening here?'

George shrugged. 'Unless she's got insurance on the dead woman, I don't see how it can help her.'

'There must be something,' I said, 'but we won't know until we've got more. I have to talk to Moira Waites and her boyfriend. I guess he's her boyfriend, this guy Jeffries whose wife ended up dead in the lake.'

'You'll get your chance in the morning. The kid'll be back and he'll talk up a storm.'

'Nobody's going to rough him up, George? You know I can't sit still for that.'

'Nor can I.' He stood up. 'You may not want to hear it but the case I'm working on right now in Toronto is about a policeman who hammered some wife-beater. Good old frontier justice, right? Except that the reason the wife was being beaten up was because she was having an affair with the same copper. He's looking at five years and I'm

158

going to see he gets it.'

'That's the only way to play it. Right down the middle.'

He paid me a compliment. 'If every cop worked the same as you, Reid, life would be a lot nicer.'

I swung my feet down. 'So I guess the sweet talk is so you can get a ride home.'

' 'Preciate it, please.'

'OK. Come on, Sam.' I switched the lights off, except for the blue light over the door outside, and led Sam and George out to the police car.

It was after eleven by now and the Reserve was in darkness. George invited me in but I refused. I planned to spin down the highway a few miles each way, looking for the Magic Wagon. Then I'd take one last pass around the Harbour and hit the sack.

I did it all and found nothing and after midnight I pulled in at my house and let Sam out of the car to seek. He found nobody but he showed a lot of interest in the space around my house, so I went around it with him, flashing my light everywhere to see if someone had broken in. It looked intact so I opened the front door and let him go first. Again he found nothing and I fed him and let him out for a minute, then cleaned my teeth and went to bed.

The phone rang at four-thirty. I grabbed it on the first ring. 'Police, Murphy's Harbour.'

159

It was George. 'Sorry to drag you out so early, Reid. Our neighbour, Jim Buck, he says he was fishing last night up at Loon Lake. Says there's a car on the road looks like mine. Didn't get the number. I wondered if you wanted to give me a ride up, see if we could find it, scratch it off your stolen list.'

'I'll be over there in fifteen.' I hung up and went to the bathroom for the world's quickest shower and shave. Then I took Sam and drove to George's place. Everyone was up and his mother came to the door to see George off. She stood there under the porch light with the puppy under her arm and she waved at me and held the puppy up. I called out hi and drove away with George.

'I guess Jim Buck is resting up,' I said easily. 'His lights weren't on.'

'I guess. He's been up all night fishing,' George said. 'Got some nice pickerel, couple around four pound.'

'Was he with the kid all night?'

'He was fishing, but his brother's still up there,' George said.

'What happened?'

'I'm not sure. Why don't you ask Freund? My guess is he'll be talkative.' George flopped his head sideways, sleeping or pretending to.

Loon Lake is on a side-road to begin with and then a further eight or nine miles into

160

the bush on an overgrown logging road. At night, on foot, you would never find your way down there unless you were born here and knew every tree. I made no comment and a few miles in we came to a fork. My headlights played over George's car, covered with dew.

'Good as new,' he said happily. 'Isn't that lucky?'

I looked at him. 'Now I wonder which of these roads a man might try first, looking for the kid?'

'That one looks good.' George pointed.

'Did anybody stay with the boy?'

'Don't know what you mean,' he said, getting out. 'But, come to think of it, Jim said that his brother Jack wasn't home yet.'

'I'll call you later.' I drove off up the logging trail until a deadfall blocked it completely, then got out and turned Sam loose to seek. It was still dark and I carried a flashlight with me but didn't turn it on, letting my night vision develop on its own. It would be light within another hour and I could manage until then.

Sam ran in and out of the bush all the way, then he checked and looked up before bounding away again. It was jackpine here, low to the ground and tangled, second growth. I didn't try to penetrate it, knowing that the boy wouldn't have gone into the bush here, he must have blundered off the trail further up where the trees were better spaced and he lost the trail in the darkness. I went on, looking for a likely spot.

I found one, a couple of hundred yards further on and turned off in the direction Sam had taken. A moment later I heard his bark, about a quarter of a mile ahead among the trees. They were thicker here so I made sure to blaze myself a trail I could follow out, snapping off branches and leaving them hanging at eye level. It made more noise than I liked but I didn't think the boy would notice. The only thing he was hearing was Sam, who would be standing in front of him, giving tongue the way he's trained to. It would sound to a kid as if Sam were out for blood.

I reached him a few minutes later. He was up in a tree, sitting with his knees drawn up uncomfortably. I shone my light on him and saw his face was scratched with branches and he had been crying.

'Easy,' I told Sam. Then to the kid: 'What the hell happened to you?'

'Keep him away,' he sobbed.

'He's the one who found you. You ought to be grateful. Come on down, he won't bite.'

I kept my light on him, watching as he made a quick attempt to dry his eyes on the front of his T-shirt, then turned and shinned clumsily down. Most kids would have hung from a branch and dropped but he hadn't worked things out that far. He climbed all the way down and came over to me.

'Thank you,' he said and tried to shake my hand.

I didn't shake. 'What happened?'

'A bunch of Indians stole the car. They put me out here.'

'Here?' I played dumb. 'How in hell did they drive here?'

'Close,' he said. 'There was a trail. They were talking Indian. I couldn't understand. Then they opened the car door and shoved me out. I was lost. It was dark. And the mosquitoes. Oh my God.'

'No sweat. I found the car. This is a popular fishing spot, I've found stolen cars before up here. And I figured I'd take a look for you, in case you'd wandered off and got lost.'

'I heard a bear,' he said. 'There's bears here.'

'Yeah. Lots of them. Well, I can take you out now, or I can leave my dog keeping you up that tree and go away. Which would you like?'

'Take me out,' he said. 'You wouldn't leave me, would you?'

'Why should I help you? You haven't helped me.'

'I will. I promise I will.' He was almost wetting himself with fear.

163

'I'll think about it.' I sat down on a log, keeping my light on his face. 'Depends on you. Now tell me where you found the car you came to the Harbour in yesterday.'

'On a side-road, you know, off the highway. We were down there in that old heap of Eric's an' we knew you would recognize it if we came back. So we were looking for another car and we found one.'

'Unlocked with the keys in it?'

'No. It was locked. But Cy, that's one of the kids, he's done things with cars before. He said guys sometimes leave cars with the key hidden somewhere. It was up the tailpipe.'

That meant the car had been left for a second user.

'Could you show me the place where you found this car?'

'It was on Ellis Lane. I remember a signboard when we came out again.'

'And you left the car there?'

'No. Cy drove it away. He knew where he could sell it, he said.'

He continued to talk but I was thinking. I'd seen the car after supper at the motel where I'd found Hanson.

'What time did you find the car? The wagon?'

'Around noon. We used it to come back to your town for the swarming.'

I was working it out. Perhaps this Cy had

been in cahoots with Hanson, had been another plant, maybe another actor.

He had taken the car to get away from the gang and return it to Hanson. After all, I had seen the car at the motel late at night. In fact, maybe Cy knew in advance where the Magic Wagon would be hidden, knew that the keys would be with it. Which meant I had to find him and talk to him.

Freund was anxious to come clean. It was a good sign and I was still learning from him, so I let him continue.

'And Cy had gone by then?'

'Yeah. I told you. Like, most of us were just out for laughs. But he was looking to make some money. I mean, he's bad.'

'So are you. You killed a woman's dog, pushed her down, and then went and trashed a store. Is that your idea of a laugh?'

He bit his lip. I kept the flashlight on his face, even though it was starting to grow light around us. He probably wasn't aware of it in the glare. After a moment he spoke, in a trembly voice. 'I didn't want to. Really. But the kids were on my case. They said I shouldn't be the leader. Cy knew about cars. He had more guts'n me. When he came back he should take over. I had to do something heavy.'

'She'd had that dog twelve years. It was a member of the family just about, and you prove something by whacking it with a club.

165

I ought to walk out and leave you here.'

'Don't do that!' He almost screamed it. 'Don't leave me here! I'll make it up to her. I promise.'

'I can't let you off.'

He gave at that point and wept like a baby for about a minute. I turned the light off and stood up. George's treatment had worked, maybe better than it needed to. The kid had started out with a low opinion of himself and now he felt like a hole in the ground. But I was a half-inch further ahead in the case.

'Where's the wagon now? The one you drove to the Harbour in.'

'I don't know. The guys were going to pick me up later, like, after I'd had a beer. Like, even killing the dog didn't impress them. They dared me to go in the bar in Murphy's Harbour. They said I wouldn't have the guts to go into your town and break the law again. I had to do it. They went off somewhere. They were going to come back for me and then we were going home.'

'You keep saying "they". Who do you mean? Was Cy back by then?'

'Yes. He was driving. He said he'd pick me up after and we'd all go home.'

That gave me a first entry to my search for the mysterious Cy. 'So Cy set up a rendezvous with you, before he left?'

'Yes. He said to pick him up at the Honey Harbour road. He said he knew a guy there

166

who would buy the car.'

Honey Harbour is close to the motel where I'd found the old Ford. Probably he'd returned the car to Hanson and then walked the half mile back down the highway. I asked him, 'What does this Cy look like? What was he wearing?'

He gave me a pretty thorough description and I noted it and then asked my last question. 'Where's home?'

'I live in Toronto but I'm staying at Wasaga Beach. That's where we were all from. What must've happened is the guys came back and found out about you busting me and they took off there with the car.'

'Let's go.' I stood up and moved out, using the light for the first part of the way to check on the trail I'd left. Within a couple of minutes we were back at the roadway and I left the light off and marched briskly back to the car.

He kept up with me, taking the occasional little extra step to stay alongside. I threw him a question. 'What does your dad do?'

'He doesn't live with us. My mom's a lawyer. She's gonna kill me.' He was calm again now but frightened down to the soles of his feet. 'She's big on animal rights. Always talking about fur coats and experiments and stuff like that. When she hears what I did, she'll hit the roof.'

'And then you'll feel almost as bad as Mrs

Horn did yesterday. That's almost fair. Add in a couple of hundred hours of community work and you'll be close to paying back what you owe.'

'Oh God,' he said and then nothing.

We reached the car and this time I sat him in the front. He didn't need any further humiliation. He'd grown up overnight.

He showed me where they had found the wagon. It was a lonely section of road, half a mile from the lake shore and with no cottages around it. I knew there was a cluster of them at the bottom end but this wasn't in my jurisdiction and it was still too early to stir up a bunch of holidaymakers. I decided I'd tell Holland and let the OPP men make a canvass to see if Jeffries and the woman had been down there. Probably not. Jeffries and Moira Waites had most likely changed cars here. And that meant they could be anywhere at all.

As I headed back to Murphy's Harbour I thought about Freund. He needed help. He wasn't going to get it from his mother. She'd provide expensive legal counsel for him to hide behind but he'd never be free in his own head unless he stood up for himself now.

'Listen,' I said at last. 'I know the woman you hurt. She's a good person. I figure if you went to her and apologized she'd drop the charges against you.'

'Go and see her?' His mother had done a

job on him. He sounded terrified.

'If you face up to her you're facing up to what you've done. It'll be over. Otherwise you're going to feel like a dork every time you look in the mirror.'

He didn't speak for a long time. Then he said, 'All right. Could you take me there, please?'

'Sure. She lives on the Reserve.'

His head whipped around. 'You mean she's an Indian?'

'Didn't you notice when you were shoving her over?'

'No. I mean, she looked just like anybody else.'

'Right.' I said. He had a lot to learn and Jean Horn would be a good teacher. I said nothing else until we pulled up in front of their neat little bungalow. It's not fancy by city standards but it's tidy and Jean has as much garden as she can squeeze out of the sandy soil. It was full of tomatoes and corn and cucumbers and Jean was out there weeding, the puppy gambolling around her feet.

She stopped and looked up as I drove in. 'Recognize her?' I asked and Freund nodded, gulping quietly.

'Her name is Mrs Horn. Go and talk to her.'

I sat there while he got out and went up to the gate, moving slowly, gathering his courage. She straightened up and looked at him without speaking. He went over to her, inching carefully between the rows of vegetables, watching his feet at every step. Then he stood in front of her, his back to me so I couldn't see his face. I watched Jean. She said nothing for a long time then bent down to pick up the puppy and I saw Freund make a swipe at his eyes with his sleeve. She handed the puppy to him and he stood stroking it, letting it lick his face.

After a minute or so Jean took the dog back and set it down, then came over to the car. I got out. "Morning, Jean. Whaddya think? About the charges?'

'If I charge him, he's got a record,' she said. 'Forget it.'

I stuck my hand out to her. 'Thanks, Jean. I know where George gets his heart from.'

She shrugged and shook hands. 'He says he wants to make it up to me. I don' want his mother's money.'

'Looks to me like the house could use some painting,' I said. 'And I know Peter would sooner be fishing.'

She laughed out loud. 'Guess where he is now?'

'Have the kid do it. He'll feel better for it.'

'I'll ask him,' she said. 'I got some coffee on. Had breakfast?'

'Not yet.'

'Come on,' she said. 'An' let Sam out, if

the puppy won't rag him too bad.'

I let Sam out and she put the puppy down and it went crazy with delight, circling and yapping at Sam, trying to get a game started. I rubbed Sam behind the ear. 'Go on,' I said and he knew he was off duty and played with the puppy as if it were his kid brother.

Freund had come out of the vegetable patch and he came up to us. He looked a little more comfortable but without any of the smugness he'd shown the night before.

I looked him in the eye. 'Mrs Horn has agreed to drop all charges,' I said. 'But there's a condition attached.'

'I don' mind,' he said eagerly, then, 'Thank you, Mrs Horn. I was a jerk.'

'Yeah. Well how are you with a paintbrush?' I asked him.

'Never tried,' he said, surprised.

'This is where you learn. The house needs painting.'

'I'll get the paint,' Jean said. 'I don't want money off you.'

'When can I start?' He looked as if he'd just won the Oscar.

'After breakfast,' she said. 'Come on. You need to wash up as well an' I'll put some alcohol on those scratches.'

He turned his head away for a moment, composing himself. 'Thank you,' he said.

I went in after them and Jean brought the puppy inside so that Sam could get a rest.

He needed it. A puppy will wear out any full-grown dog the way a toddler can wear out an adult, I thought, and pondered my own future. Life was going to be busy.

We washed up and Jean painted the kid's scratches with rubbing alcohol and she made a big breakfast. It was a treat for me as well. Fred had been watching her weight the last month or so and meals had become fairly spartan around our place. She had offered to cook me other things but I'd said no, and hadn't done it myself because I know she's got a good appetite of her own and I couldn't expect her to stay on a diet if I was living it up.

At around seven I drove back to town, leaving the kid with Jean Horn who was going to start him scraping the house before painting. He had a couple of days' work ahead of him and he looked very pleased with the prospect. He said he was going to ring his mother first, before she left for her office. Apparently he was supposed to be staying with friends at Wasaga Beach. The friend was some college kid whose own parents commuted to the cottage at the weekend, so there had been no panic about his being away overnight. But now it was time to check in and let his mother know what was happening. He wasn't too pleased with the protest but I figured it would be easier than it had been to confront Jean

172

Horn.

The bait store was open and I had a word with Perrault, then checked the rest of my properties, looking for break-ins. We don't get many, even in summer when the town is swollen to five times its size with holiday-makers, but this morning we had.

The back door of the grocery was open. It hadn't taken much. The door must have been the same age as the rest of the building and was dried out and brittle. Somebody had put their shoulder into it and forced the rusty old hinge screws out of their sockets.

I told Sam 'seek' and sent him in ahead of me, knowing it was an unnecessary precaution. The break-in had been done overnight no doubt and the guy was long gone.

Sure enough, the place was empty. The cash register had its drawer hanging out, as it was always left overnight and the safe in the front window was in place. Nothing seemed disturbed but I rang the owner and waited until he showed up five minutes later.

He looked around and swore, then checked to see if anything was missing. 'If it's candy it was kids,' he told me. 'But I don't see kids busting the door in. They just shoplift.'

'How about food?' I asked him. 'Any of that gone?'

He looked at me, eyes narrowed. 'I'll

check. Hold on.' I followed him as he went around the food section, a tiny deli counter and a display of cheeses in the dairy case.

'Yeah,' he said at last. 'There's a coupla salami and a box of good Cheddar gone. And some bread. How did you guess that?'

'There's an inmate on the run from Joyceville,' I told him. 'I've got an idea he's up around here somewhere. It could be him.'

It was Kershaw, I figured. He had found his way to Murphy's Harbour and I wondered when he would find his way to me.

CHAPTER NINE

There wasn't much to go on. The store has so many people through it that there was no way Sam could pick out the shop-breaker's scent. I tried it anyway, letting him sniff where the man must have stood to rifle the two food counters and he did it, then led me to the owner who was standing at the back door, checking the damage. I tried Sam again at the back door but he couldn't pick up a scent, so I gave up.

The owner was angry. 'Sonofabitch. Twice in two days. My insurance is gonna go crazy,' he said. 'Look it. Forced the door right off the goddamn hinges.'

'Get a steel door put in,' I advised him.

174

'I'll try to find this guy and if and when I do you can go after him for damages. But he won't have any money or he wouldn't have been stealing food.'

'You're right. Dammit. I'd sell this place if anybody'd buy it off me. Hell, Chief. This is too much. You gotta keep a better lid on things. Two losses in one day. That's not why we pay a police chief.'

'If it makes you feel any better, I've caught the kid who did the swarming yesterday. He's over at Horns', painting their house. He said he'll make the damage good.'

'Well, I guess that's something,' he said grumpily. 'Sorry I sounded off.'

'Sorry about the crime wave. But I know who I'm looking for. If I find him I'll get him to pay for the damage.'

'Yeah. OK.' He waved me off. 'I know you do a good job. It's just I'm thinkin' why me? OK?'

'OK. See you later, Jack.'

I called Sam and went out to check the rest of the properties. Nothing had been touched. I was especially careful around the liquor store. Kershaw hadn't been the one who got the bottle of Scotch the night before and after five years inside he would want a drink. But the locks were all in place, so I drove down to the station and went in.

The phone rang almost immediately and I picked it up. 'Murphy's Harbour Police.'

'My name is Mrs Freund, may I speak to an Officer Bennett?' No please.

'I'm Bennett, Mrs Freund.'

'My son just phoned. I find he's been coerced into doing manual labour for some family of Indians.'

There were so many things to argue with that I didn't bother. 'Did he tell you why?' I asked politely.

'He said he'd got himself into trouble and the woman was letting him do this for her instead of preferring charges.'

'Did he tell you the nature of the trouble?'

'Nothing she wants to prosecute him for, so it can't be much. I feel this is some ruse to obtain his labour. Why should a boy be permitted to demean himself in this manner? That's what I want to know.'

'You think work is demeaning?' Two can be as snooty as one.

'In case you haven't heard about it in your township, Canadians have certain civil liberties.'

'And in case you haven't heard about it in Toronto, assault of a woman, plus other offences, is enough to get even a first offender a criminal record.'

She shouted now. 'I want to speak to your superior.'

'I'm the Chief, Mrs Freund. What's your complaint?'

'My complaint is that my son has

176

apparently been tried and found guilty without a hearing.'

'If you'd like a hearing I'll be glad to arrange one. Come on up to the police station at Murphy's Harbour and you can conduct your own. Unless you persist in your attitude, Philip will get off without a criminal record. How does that sound?'

There was a long silence. Her pride was all banged up but she was an intelligent woman. 'What are the precise charges?'

'Didn't your son tell you?'

'His exact words were "I pushed a lady over and did some other things".' Her voice became lower. 'What kind of things? Were they sexual?'

'No. They were not directed at any person. But they were criminal. The plaintiff has very generously agreed to drop the charges. She doesn't even want money. Instead she has agreed to let him work out his indebtedness. He's glad of the chance. I know him fairly well by now. Maybe better than you do in some ways.'

That didn't sit well but she swallowed her anger. 'I'll be up there at noon. Will you be there?'

'I'll try, but I'm in the middle of a homicide investigation. I'd prefer it, and so would your son, if you just stayed where you were and let him work things out. He'll be a better man for it.'

'He's just a boy,' she almost screamed.

'Today. Tomorrow he'll be a man, a better man if he does what he's set out to do.'

'That's a matter of opinion.'

She was weakening but she sounded like a reasonable person. 'This has to be your call, whether or not to let him continue. I hope you'll consider your actions very carefully and bear in mind that he's got feelings of his own.'

She put the phone down without speaking and I hung up and called Parry Sound. Sergeant Holland was in his office and I filled him in on the location where the Magic Wagon had been found. We mulled things over carefully for a while and decided that we needed to speak to Cy, the gang member who had known about cars. 'I wish we hadn't let that Hanson guy go so fast,' Holland said. 'No choice, of course, but it's starting to look like he knows something about the Jeffries woman. I'll ring Toronto, have one of their detectives chase up Hanson there. And we'll look for this Cy.'

'I've given you the description. It matches one of the kids I saw in town first time the gang came here. The Freund boy may be able to give you something more. He's over at the Reservation, painting the house for the woman whose dog he killed.'

'You figure you can trust him?'

'Yeah.' I hadn't given him any details, the

fewer people knew about it, the safer George's reputation would be in future. None of the Indians would say anything, that left the secret with me. I wanted to keep it that way.

'Well, I'll send a couple of guys down to Ellis Lane to talk to the locals. On the way down there they can talk to Freund.'

Hearing him speak the name triggered my memory with a click. 'Freund? Isn't that the lawyer who sprung Hanson yesterday?'

'Yes. Dammit, I must be asleep. How can I get in touch with her? You got her number?'

'No. But she's coming here at noon. And you can call the Horns and get her number off her son.'

'I'll take care of it,' he said. 'I want to talk to Hanson. Should have kept him in custody but we couldn't.'

'OK. I'll leave it with you. I've got a lot on my own plate here. We've got a shop-breaker in town and I figure it has to be a fugitive. Seems to me we may have that guy Kershaw up here. Plus I'm still waiting for the guy in the next room to Waites to make a statement. I'll head up to Pickerel Point Lodge and talk to him.'

'OK. I'll keep you posted when we hear from forensics in Toronto or if we round up this Cy kid, or Hanson.'

I thanked him and hung up feeling useless.

Detective work is largely a matter of sifting reports, of questioning dozens, even hundreds of people and looking for patterns of similarity in their stories. It's easiest when you have dozens of men asking the questions and a computer to compare their findings. Alone, I was going to be lucky to find anything useful in the Waites case. And I was starting to worry about Kershaw. I had a feeling he was my shop-breaker and that he was holed up in the bush close to town, waiting for a chance to get even with me. By now he might have picked up a gun somewhere so he could stay back out of sight and drop me when I wasn't expecting it.

The prospect was scary but I spent two whole years in Vietnam under the same threat and had come out intact except for busted-up arms from the booby-trap that had killed the guy ahead of me on the trail. I'd also been shot since, the last time a year ago. But now I had a family to consider. That made it different.

I spent a while on the telephone, first calling Joyceville for a current picture of Kershaw. The only one they had was his admission photograph, five years out of date at least but they promised to fax it to me. I could photocopy it and spread it around town, that might help a little. I also phoned Fred in the hospital. She was waiting for the baby to be brought around for her morning feed. She sounded bright and cheerful but admitted that she didn't feel quite as energetic this morning as she had the day before. I arranged to visit her in the afternoon, then left the station, turning the phone to the radio.

I drove around the town first. It was a picture-postcard morning. The sunlight was lying over everything like gilt on antique furniture and people were moving slowly, muscles slackened by the warmth. The kids were rambunctious, of course, a bunch of them were running and swimming on the tiny beach beside the marina and the usual teens were impressing one another beside the bridge. I drove over and up to Pickerel Point.

The guest I'd wanted to talk to was in the lounge. He asked me to come outside and I thought he might have something to say that would be important. He had not called me, he admitted, because he was embarrassed. I had to reassure him that what he said would be kept in confidence before he allowed that he had not been in his own room at all that evening. He had been elsewhere.

I looked at him, a lean city-dweller in his late fifties, brown from his week of fishing but nervous. He was going through a divorce, he explained. He had come to the lodge to fish, nothing more, but he had struck up a friendship with a lady, he used the word with care, he was obviously smitten

181

and wanted to keep her out of any hint of scandal. She was divorced, younger than he by some considerable amount, etc, etc. It's one of the older stories in the world but he figured he'd written it for the first time so I went along, then quietly checked with his date.

She wasn't a bombshell, a quiet, pleasant woman in her forties, a birdwatcher, she said, who had come here for a few days' birding. Everything checked out so I thanked her and wished her luck and left, driving idly around the lake road, examining all the empty cottages. There are a number, even in the height of the season, which stand empty all week. This was Friday morning and the owners would be coming up from Toronto after the rush-hour for their weekends. In the meantime I wanted to be sure that nobody had broken into any of them, especially now that we had a shop-breaker in town. It would have been ideal for him, the perfect place to lie low for a couple of days. He would be on the move by now, ahead of the owners' return, but if luck ran my way, I might find where he had stayed and track him with Sam's help.

There were only a few. I'd covered them all earlier in the week but I tried the doors and checked around again. There were no broken windows or signs of any forcing having been done so I went on until I came to Ms Tracy's place.

Her car had gone. She might have retreated to Toronto, I thought, or perhaps just gone out for a while but I parked the car and got out, bringing Sam with me.

The air-conditioning was still humming in the back window so it seemed as if she was still in residence. The verandah was open but the front door was locked and there were no signs of anything having been forced. I would have headed back to the car except that Sam began to growl. Most owners immediately shush their dogs, but that's a civilian reaction. I just stood back and watched him for a moment. It might have been a skunk or porcupine under the house, that would have triggered him, but he didn't make an approach. He growled low in his throat for about a half minute, under the rear window where the air-conditioner kept humming. And then he slowly tilted his head and howled, so softly that it was almost imperceptible but it made the hair stand up on the back of my neck. It was his response to something I wasn't hearing or seeing. And whatever it was, it was inside the cottage.

I told him 'Good boy' and went around the place again, checking the doors. They were locked and I stood for a moment sniffing for smoke. Fire would have upset him. Or perhaps Marcia Tracy had left her radio on and they were playing some song that had high-pitched tones in it. If that was the case, it would end in a little while and so would Sam's reaction.

I went back and checked him. He was still howling. Then he stopped and barked sharply. And that was the deciding factor. I'd seen him howl at music before, but nothing had ever made him bark. He was hearing something that his training told him was trouble.

I didn't wait any longer. The back door had a glass pane in it and I took out my stick and knocked it in. The noise was shocking but Sam did not react. He continued to howl, and then bark. I stood at the broken window and looked in. I was looking into the kitchen. Nothing seemed out of place and I stood and listened carefully, hearing nothing at first, and then, very faint, a human noise, a moan.

I whistled Sam and reached through to unlatch the door. There were bolts in it, in addition to the lock and I had to lean in over the broken glass and tap them open with my stick. Then I let Sam in and followed as he bounded out through the kitchen door and straight to the back bedroom.

He bounced on stiff legs, barking furiously. I was a second behind him and saw what had distressed him. Marcia Tracy was lying naked across the bed, unconscious and bleeding, her face a swollen mask.

'Easy,' I told Sam. 'Good boy.' He relaxed and I gathered the woman's arms to her sides and wrapped her up in the bedclothes. She made no sign of awareness so I left her and called Dr McQuaig. He was out, at the hospital in Parry Sound, but his wife was home and she's a nurse. She said she would come right over and warned me not to try to give the woman anything to drink or to move her. I was to call the ambulance at once. I know enough about first aid for her advice to be redundant but I said OK and dialled the ambulance number. The dispatcher told me they would be there in half an hour. Next I phoned the Parry Sound OPP and gave them the licence number of the missing Mercedes which I had in my notebook from two days before. The driver should be approached with care and should be held, I told them. Also the arresting officer should take a good look at the man's knuckles and check for blood on his clothing. The corporal said he would put it on the air and I hung up and went to look in on Ms Tracy and see if she was moving.

She wasn't conscious but she was breathing and I bathed her face with cold water, hoping she would come around. She didn't and I knelt there, hopelessly, sponging her face and waiting for Mrs McQuaig. She arrived in five minutes, a rangy, capable Scotswoman who swept in and knelt beside me.

'The poor wee thing's taken a pounding,' she said. 'Was she like this when you found her?'

'Out cold. She's naked under the bedding.'

'Had she been raped?'

'I've no idea. I covered her up right away to keep her warm.'

'That was guid,' she said in her soft Highland voice. 'She was punched,' she said firmly. 'I've seen the same injuries at Glasgow Royal on a Saturday night often enough. The man who did it has marks on his knuckles, most like. Any idea who it is?'

'There was nobody here. If you'll stay with her I'll look around, see if he left anything that Sam can get a scent from. But her car's gone. He likely took that.'

'Do it,' she said. 'If she comes to I'll call you.'

I left her and looked around carefully. Not much seemed to have been touched in the place. Ms Tracy's robe and a nightdress were lying on the floor at the entrance to the bedroom. The nightdress was a practical-looking item of flowered cotton. She had not been expecting an assignation, I judged. It was torn at the throat, the way a man might have ripped at it in his haste. On the kitchen table I found the remains of her breakfast, a coffee cup and half a grapefruit. There was no second cup and the kitchen was neat. It looked as if she had been finishing breakfast when the man arrived. It had not been a social call or she would have taken down another cup, the percolator was full.

I checked her purse. It was turned upside down on the couch in the living-room, the contents, cosmetics and her cheque-book, lying there. Her keys were gone and there was no money or credit cards. Whoever had attacked her had robbed her and gone. He may have raped her first, we wouldn't know unless the doctor at Parry Sound took a swab, but judging by the torn nightdress I figured the attack must have had a sexual content.

I led Sam back into the bedroom and let him sniff around the rug and the end of the bedclothes, then turned him loose with the command 'Track'. He ran to the front door and when I let him out he went directly to the point where I had last seen her car parked. Then he stopped and began casting around. I watched, wondering if he would find the man's arrival track. If he had come out of the woods I would follow him back to see where he had come from, probably the place he had spent the night. There might be something there that was useful. But he only went a few yards further down the driveway and then doubled back to the front porch.

I put him over it again and he repeated the

performance, step for step. It meant that the man's track began and ended on the driveway, which meant he had come in a car, which again meant that he had not been alone, someone must have driven off after leaving him here. In my eyes that meant that Kershaw had not been the guy.

As I stood there I heard the wail of the ambulance siren coming up the road and I waited and waved them in. The paramedics jumped out and got their gurney and a board. One of them was a big serious-looking woman and she led the way, bossing the other one with a succession of curt commands. He was an older man, around fifty, and he followed her without a word, rolling his eyes at me helplessly.

'In the bedroom,' I told them and they trotted in and took over from Mrs McQuaig.

'Did you find her?' the woman asked her.

'No, Chief Bennett did.' Mrs McQuaig narrowed her eyes. She was used to respect and this woman wasn't giving any out.

'Was she like this?' The woman asked as she strapped an oxygen mask on Ms Tracy's face.

'I wrapped her up and wiped her face. I have the swab here.'

The woman unwrapped Ms Tracy and she and her assistant carefully got the board in place, supporting Ms Tracy's neck and wrapping her carefully in their own blankets.

'Are you coming with us?' the woman asked. So far her assistant hadn't uttered a word.

'Yes. I'll follow in the police car. Use your siren and get her up there pronto.'

'We'll do our job. Just do yours,' she said.

I picked up the swab, a bundle of paper towels I had used to wipe Ms Tracy's face with, and went into the kitchen for a plastic bag. 'You won't need that,' the woman said bossily.

'You do your job and leave mine to me,' I said.

She snorted. 'Come on, George, we haven't got all day.' She led the way with the gurney.

I turned to Mrs McQuaig. 'I want to be there when she comes around. Could you do me a favour please and wait here until I get back? I want to fingerprint this place later and I don't want anyone else in here.'

'What if the guy comes back?' She asked the question without fear, the way she might have asked for a weather forecast.

'Wait in your car on the road. If anyone drives in, get the licence number and drive to Pickerel Point and call me on the phone. Same thing if anyone goes into the bush behind the house. If there's no answer, call the Parry Sound OPP. I'll be back in about an hour. It's a lot to ask, but could you take it on, please? I don't have anybody else.'

'Sure,' she said grimly.

'Thank you, Alice.' I touched her on the shoulder and left with my plastic bag in my hand, and took off after the ambulance.

The man was driving, taking out his frustration, I guessed, wailing his siren and winding the ambulance up pretty good for such a narrow road. But speed was important, I had a lot to do once I'd spoken to the doctors and installed an OPP man at the hospital to speak to Ms Tracy when she came to.

We sped up the highway and reached the hospital within twenty minutes, faster than I'd driven it with Fred on her way to Emergency. There was a doctor waiting for us and he took charge at once. I followed him into the examining room, carrying my plastic bag.

He worked quickly, checking her vital signs, then sending her in for a head X-ray. While we waited for the plate I had a chance to speak to him. 'These are the paper towels I used to wash her face. If the man who did this cut his knuckles, his blood may be here as well. Is there any way of checking the group?'

He was young and had the oddly cropped beard that you usually see only on Mennonites, an earnest guy. He took the bag in one hand and looked at the bloody mess inside. 'It won't be simple but I'll try. I'll only use part of it for my test. If I don't get anything we can send the rest to the forensics place in Toronto.'

'Thank you, Doctor. Also, I want to speak to her as soon as she comes to.'

'Right.' The X-ray technician brought in the plate she had just exposed and he nodded thanks and clipped it on to a light board. He looked at it for a long time, then shook his head, puzzled. 'I'm not a neurologist but I can't see anything wrong, structurally.'

'What does that mean?'

He looked at me, tapping his teeth with his right thumbnail. 'It means that the wounds are superficial. And in every case like that I've ever seen that means she should be conscious by now.'

'You think she should be able to talk to us now?'

He nodded thoughtfully. 'I think maybe there's something else, like, say, she's ingested something that's anaesthetized her.'

'Like what?'

He pondered some more. 'It's impossible to say. She doesn't smell of alcohol but other than that it could be any kind of depressant, an illegal drug of some kind, maybe heroin.'

I thought about that for a moment, remembering how reluctant she had been to talk to me. 'Is there a chance that she's just acting unconscious so I can't talk to her?'

'Is that likely?' He frowned now. In a rural hospital like this he wouldn't have treated many crime victims, he wouldn't know how suspicious a cop can be.

'It's a possibility. There's a lot going on down on my patch, her ex-husband was murdered there and she's involved in a couple of things that make me suspicious.'

'Well then—' he straightened up and flicked off the light on the panel—'we'd better check that out.'

CHAPTER TEN

As a former hockey player I'd thought the doctor might have used smelling salts under her nose to bring her around, but he wasn't about to do anything so rough and ready. Instead he went back to her and leaned over, close to her ear, and said loudly, 'Can you hear me?' He repeated it a couple of times, then glanced up at me and said, 'I don't think she's conscious,' and to her, 'I'm going to take a sample of your blood to test for drugs. You'll feel a little jab.' He swabbed her arm and took a vial of blood, wiped her arm again and put a Band-Aid on the mark.

A nurse came in and took the blood sample away. I told him, 'There were signs of a scufffle at the scene, Doctor. I think she
192

might have been sexually assaulted. Can you examine her for that, please?'

'If you like. Turn your back,' he said primly. When the nurse returned he told her, 'Betty, I have to make a test to see if this woman has been assaulted. Get a swab, will you, please. In fact, get three of them, we'll do this right.'

I turned and stared at a blood pressure machine on the wall until he said, 'All right, Officer.'

I turned back and he nodded. 'There are signs of recent sexual activity. It doesn't necessarily signify violence but it may.'

'Can you label the swabs for me, please? I'll have to send them to forensics.'

'Right.' He sent the nurse for plastic bags and he marked each swab and I initialled and sealed them in his presence and hung on to them. He said, 'I'm sure she would never have allowed me to take those swabs if she were conscious. That's good enough for me.'

I held up one hand. 'You're the expert, Doctor. I'll ask the Parry Sound guys to leave a policeman with her. When she comes around she can talk to him.'

'Good. In that case I'll get her assigned a bed. She'll probably be in the intensive care unit if you want to leave now.'

'A detective from the Parry Sound unit is going to meet me here. I'll stay with her until then.'

193

There was a tap at the door and he called, 'Come in.'

Holland came in. ''Morning, Dr Baer, 'mornin', Betty. I'm here to talk to Chief Bennett, can I take him away a while?'

'Of course.' The doctor seemed relieved.

The nurse smiled and said, 'Chief Bennett. You're our new father, aren't you?'

'Yes. I'd like to visit my wife after I've spoken to Sergeant Holland, if that's OK.'

'I'm sure it will be.' She didn't seem hung up about visiting hours.

Holland led me outside. 'Let me get this straight. That woman's the ex-wife of this Waites guy?'

'Right. Someone beat her up, raped her probably, then locked her place and took the car.'

'Could be this Kershaw guy who's on the lam from Joyceville. He's not been picked up yet.'

'If it is, he's with someone else. Sam tracked him to the driveway and lost him. He must have arrived by car.'

He scratched his chin, making a rasping noise where he'd missed a few whiskers that morning. 'You sure set a lot of store by that dog's nose.'

'He does a good job, never been wrong yet.'

'Yeah, well. We've got the car on the air. When'd you think this happened?'

'She'd had breakfast but hadn't washed up yet. So the guy hasn't had more than a couple of hours.'

'That's a hundred, maybe a hundred and fifty miles. Hell, he could be half way to the States now.'

'The guys at the border would find him if he tries to cross. I specified that in my call. Also I've mentioned that her credit cards are missing.'

'Have you reported that?'

'No. I came right up here as soon as the ambulance arrived. I'll take a minute and do it next.'

'Good. That could get us somewhere. If the guy's dumb enough to use the card.'

We talked a little longer and he promised to have a uniformed man detailed to sit with Ms Tracy and take a statement when she came around. In the meantime there was nothing else to do but notify the credit card companies that her cards had been stolen by a man we wanted on a major felony charge. With their computer working for us we would soon have a location if the thief tried to use one of the cards.

The companies were easier to deal with than the government. But not by much. I wasn't sure which cards she had and I was forced to do some bullying before the clerks at the other end of the line would tell me whether she was a customer. And then I had to speak to supervisors before I could get them to promise cooperation if the cards were used. It took half an hour before I was free to go upstairs to visit Fred.

She was dozing when I got to the room and I sat by her bed for about ten minutes before she opened her eyes with a start and saw me. She wasn't so limber today but she was just as cheerful as ever and we went around to the nursery and looked at the baby, who was asleep. It was pleasant, feeling like a civilian for a few minutes, and I tried to keep my mind off the case I was working on but Fred soon saw through me.

'You've got a lot on your mind, haven't you?' she said as I took her back to her room.

'Yes, there's a whole complicated case going on right now at the Harbour and I'm up to my rear end,' I admitted.

'First things first,' she said. 'Why don't you go back down there and get on with your job? I'm fine here. I'll be out tomorrow and we can take it from there.'

I found out what time I could pick her up and she kissed me gently and I left, dropping in on Ms Tracy's room on the way out. She was still unconscious but there was a policeman with her, reading a paperback book. He had a tape-recorder with him and he seemed a capable guy. I chatted with him for a minute, giving him a few details that would help him to talk to her, then left and drove back to the Tracy place to relieve Mrs McQuaig.

She was sitting in her car across the road from the Tracy place, listening to classical music. Nobody had come back, she told me and I thanked her and she left.

I took the fingerprint kit out of my car and went inside, leaving Sam to 'keep' outside. He picked himself a shady spot under a tree and sat there, watchfully.

Now I had time I examined the house properly, seeking anything I might have missed in my haste to get Ms Tracy to hospital. First I checked the kitchen. She had probably been here when the man arrived, eating her grapefruit. I tried to put myself in her place. She had been alone, otherwise two coffee cups would have been in use, so she must have heard the car drive up and gone to the front door. Then she must have recognized the caller. Otherwise she would not have let him in. She was alone, in her housecoat. After the things that had happened at Murphy's Harbour in the last couple of days most women would either have ignored a stranger until they had got dressed or else spoken to him through the closed door. That meant her attacker was no stranger to her.

That much was good news. When she recovered consciousness she could give us a name. Dandy. I could issue a warrant for the guy and when we got him it might even help in my search for Waites' killer, or the man who had beaned Mrs Jeffries and stuffed her into the trunk of the Waites Honda. Maybe.

In the meantime I did the job thoroughly. First I examined her housecoat and nightgown for blood traces. There were none. So the attacker had stripped her first, possibly raped her first, before he beat her up. On that thought I examined the bedding. There was blood on the pillows and the top of the sheet but it was only smears, there was no spotting as there might have been if the attack had taken place as she lay there. So I looked all around the room, and then I found bloodstains on the wall beside the door. I checked the height, remembering how tall Ms Tracy was, about five-eight. The marks were an inch or two lower, as if someone had rammed her head into the wall.

I thought about that for a long time, putting the fact together with the placement of the injuries on her face. It made sense. The upper part of her face had the worst damage, mostly around the eyes.

There didn't seem much for it but to wait until she woke up and gave us a statement, but in the meantime I dug out a few flakes of bloodstained plaster board and put them in an evidence bag. I also made detailed notes of the location of the bloodstains and entered them in my notebook, together with a sketch of their appearance. Then I examined the bed again and this time found bloodstains on the heavy old alarm clock on the bedside table. There was a fingerprint on the glass, clearly delineated in blood. I got my kit out and lifted it on tape, then dusted the rest of the clock, finding another print on the back.

Next I checked the bathroom and the kitchen for signs that the man had washed his hands there after the attack. Unless he had been crazy that would have been his logical move before leaving the house. I found nothing visible.

Perhaps a forensics team might, in the sludge of the U-trap under the sink, but that was out of my league so I concentrated on trying to pick up other prints. I lifted a set off her coffee cup and then her lipstick cartridge and then had to admit I was stumped. There was nothing else I could do on my own.

Before I left I called the hardware store on the highway and had them send a guy up with a sheet of glass to fix the back door. I also asked him to bring a padlock and hasp for the front door. Without Ms Tracy's keys I would have had to leave the place open if I was to look in here again before she returned.

He came right up, a chatty kid of about nineteen who tried to find out what happened. I told him the place had been broken into and the owner had asked me to install a lock. That satisfied his curiosity. Break-ins don't happen often but he just muttered about goddamn kids while he quickly and efficiently closed the place up. By the time he had finished it was noon and I drove back to the police station with Sam.

There was a Cadillac parked outside with a woman in it. Mrs Freund, I remembered. I got out and went over to her. 'Sorry if I've kept you waiting. I had another emergency this morning.'

She didn't acknowledge my answer. 'Where's Phillip?' she asked.

'He's up at the house he's painting. Does he know you're coming?'

'I thought you would have brought him here as you promised.' She was glad of the chance to attack me, but my shoulders are broad. If you want popularity you join a rock group, not a police department. I looked her over. She was forty-fiveish, smartly dressed in a linen suit, carrying a briefcase. She was handsome rather than pretty, a brunette, heavier than she might have been for her height but attractive for all that. Her appearance shouted 'money'.

'I've just been investigating an assault case. It took precedence over our rendezvous. Come inside, please.'

I unlocked the station and led her inside. She looked around contemptuously but said nothing. I let her through the counter and offered her a chair. She shook her head but I sat down anyway. I was in charge here.

'What, precisely, is my son charged with?'

'At the moment, thanks to the generosity of the woman he assaulted, there are no charges outstanding. However, if you choose to open all this up again, he faces a slate of charges.'

'What are they?'

'Assault, first, as mentioned. He pushed a middle-aged woman down on the ground. Secondly, drinking under age. Thirdly, theft and public mischief. Fourth, having a weapon dangerous to the public peace. Fifth, and this one won't sit well with you he tells me, causing unnecessary pain and suffering to a dog.'

She went pale under her tan. 'What happened, Officer?'

'Why don't you sit down, Mrs Freund?' I suggested again. 'Would you like a glass of water?'

'No, thank you. I don't need water,' she said but she sat, holding her briefcase on her lap.

'Your son got mixed up with a youth gang,' I told her. 'It's a gang I very much want to track down because it's involved with another case. The leader of the gang is Eric Hanson, the man you represented in Parry Sound yesterday.'

She was startled. 'Hanson works for a

client of my firm. He's in his twenties, far too old to be involved in some kid stuff gang business.'

'He's dropped out of sight. I want to talk to him. Do you know where he was going when you had him released?'

'No. But the Parry Sound police have his Toronto address. That's good enough, surely.'

'He's not there, we're told. I wondered if you knew where he might have gone.'

She shook her head. 'I represented him at the bail hearing. Acting on the facts as I saw them, I was able to get him released on his own recognizance. He's to show up again for a court appearance on Monday next. I expect he'll be there. In the meantime I imagine he's taking some time to think things over.'

'I hope you're right. But in addition to the charges against him he's the guy behind your own son's trouble.'

'How so?' Her face was grim. She would be a tough opponent in court, I imagined.

'He's auditioning for some film part. He put together a gang of disaffected kids. Twice over the last two days they swarmed properties on Main Street here. On the second occasion, your son was carrying a baseball bat with which he killed a dog. The owner tried to hold him but he pushed her over and assisted in the swarming of the store before she could get up to help. He got away. Then later he came back into town and went into the beverage room where he was drinking beer when I arrested him.'

She pursed her lips, breathing heavily. I waited for her to speak. When she did it was so low I could hardly hear her. 'This would never have happened if he had a real father.'

'It would never have happened if your son had not been ripe for recruiting. And what makes it all the more complex is that the film this Hanson is trying to get into is one your client, Ms Tracy, is producing.'

'I know nothing of her work. She was John Waites' client. I merely acted for him as he was on vacation.'

'You know he's been murdered?'

'I learned that yesterday at the police station in Parry Sound. It was a shock to me.'

'I think maybe Hanson can help us understand what's going on. And just to complicate things further, Ms Tracy was assaulted this morning. She's unconscious in Parry Sound hospital.'

'Good God.' She shook her head as if the information had wedged itself somehow in her receptors. 'This all makes Phillip's problems seen very small.'

'They can be small. If you just let him go on the way he's going today. He's making amends and building some self-confidence.'

'You know these people well, do you?'

'Very well. Their son's a lawyer with the Crown Attorney's office in Toronto. They're exceptional people. I'd trust them with anything.'

Surprisingly her next comment wasn't about the tangle of problems around us. She spoke very softly. 'It hasn't been easy, bringing him up on my own.'

I wanted her help. Maybe she could find Hanson for us, or get Ms Tracy to fill us in on whatever was going on. I chose my words carefully. 'I think you'll be comforted to know that he's changed from the first time I met him. I think he was trying on the rebellion thing and he's found it doesn't suit him. He's a changed boy.'

Without warning she started to sob. It was so out of character with her businesslike clothes and manner that I was startled. I got up and handed her the office box of tissues and then went out to the cells and ran her a glass of cold water. By the time I brought it back to her she was in control of herself and she took the glass gratefully and sipped. I sat and waited until she set it down and spoke again.

'I've been on my own with Phillip since he was twelve,' she said. 'I do what I can but there's no male example in his life. I know it's not healthy but what can I do?'

'What happened to your husband?' I

didn't really care but it seemed like a humane question. I figured she would chat for a few minutes and then I could shoo her back where she'd come from so that her son could keep on painting and growing himself some backbone.

Her answer shocked me. 'He was a criminal,' she said. 'He was sent to prison for ten years.'

'Does Phillip know this?'

'No. I told him his father had left me and we moved away from the area where we'd been living before. None of our neighbours knows any more than I've told them.'

'That's five years ago. Your husband should be getting out soon.' I wondered what he'd done. Ten years is a savage sentence for anything less than murder. He must be a hard case. Maybe her concern was for the fact that he would be back on the street in the near future.

'We're divorced now.'

'Then your only concern has to be your son.' Way to go, Dear Abby. 'If you like I can take you up to see him, but if you want my honest opinion, it would be better if he stayed there until he's finished his job. A couple of days should do it.'

She blinked a couple of times before speaking but her voice had regained its strength. 'You seem like a very sensible man. If you believe this is best for him, I'll go

205

along with you.' She stood up. 'Thank you for being so considerate. I take it that you personally have dropped the drinking under age charge?'

'Yes. It's trivial, most kids try it.'

She held out her hand and I shook it as she went on. 'I'd like to compensate the woman. What do you suggest?'

'She told me that she didn't want your money. She's pleased that Phillip came and apologized to her and she's happy to have her house painted. I'd leave it at that.'

'Perhaps I might pay for the paint?' She badly wanted to do something tangible but I knew Jean Horn better than she did. 'I think the best thing you could do is write to her. Thank her for dropping charges and for giving your son a chance to make amends.'

She considered that for a moment and then nodded. 'Yes, that sounds best. Now, what about the stores my son swarmed?'

'They don't want to press charges but they're business people and they lost money.'

'Where are they?' She was toughening up again now, facing the fact that she would look bad over the next little while, the mother of a delinquent.

I told her and she said, 'Will you tell Phillip that I came to see you? Tell him to call when he's finished his work and I'll pick him up.'

'Will do. And might I ask you a favour in return?'

She was at the door. 'I think I can guess. You want me to let you know if I learn the whereabouts of Hanson.'

'Right. And if you should talk to Ms Tracy, perhaps you could ask her to be more helpful. She knows personally now that this business is serious.'

'I won't be seeing her, I have to go back to court this afternoon. But if I can help, I promise I will.'

'Thanks very much, Mrs Freund.'

She paused with one hand on the doorknob. 'It's not Mrs. It's Ms Freund. I dropped my husband's name when he went to prison.'

'Good idea,' I said. She seemed like a sensible woman, obviously successful, in charge of herself. She didn't need the handle some criminal had hung on her.

'I thought so,' she said. 'And I never liked the name Kershaw anyway.'

It knocked the wind out of me. 'Kershaw? You mean George Kershaw, the guy who was sent down for bank robbery in nineteen eighty-five?'

'Yes.' She looked at me very hard. 'And I did follow the case even then, Officer. And I know he was arrested by a man called Bennett. Was that you?'

'It's a small world,' I said and thought that

207

it was getting smaller by the hour.

'I understand he made a break from a day pass,' she said.

'We'll get him and he'll be back inside for the rest of his sentence.'

She didn't answer right away and I wondered if I'd offended her, but at last she said, 'I hope so,' and left.

After she was gone I sat down to think about the case. Something more than coincidence was at work here. I pulled out a piece of paper and drew a bunch of circles, one for each of the names involved in the case, Waites, Tracy, Hanson, Cy, Freund/Kershaw jr, Kershaw sr. Each of them was linked to at least one of the others. Then there were Mrs Waites, the vanished woman, Mrs Jeffries, the first victim, and her husband the store-keeper. They were all part of another, secondary group, tied to the first by the presence of Waites.

It was tantalizing but it proved nothing. What we needed was to sit down with one of the principals and ask questions. So far that wasn't possible. Waites was dead. Marcia Tracy was dead to the world. Hanson and the other kid, Cy, had vanished. The case was cold and getting colder.

It's four years since I worked in Toronto, I quit after the scuffle with a bunch of bikers that saw me arrested for manslaughter and cost me my marriage, but I've maintained contact with some of the detectives I used to deal with and now seemed a good time to renew auld lang syne.

I tried Elmer Svenson first but he was out of his office so I rang my old partner, Irv Goodman. He works in the fraud squad and spends a lot of time in his office, going over the books of companies suspected of some kind of scam. He answered the phone cheerfully and asked how things were. 'Must be nice, sitting around in the sunshine. How's Fred? She had the baby yet?'

I filled him in and he wished me *mazel tov* and after I'd inquired about Dianne and the kids we got down to business. 'I've had two homicides here and they're tied in with a kid in Toronto, an actor.'

'Name?' Irv doesn't waste time.

'Eric Hanson, born Kowalski. He lives with a woman called Hanson who works at CBC. The address is Apartment 3065, 413 Delaney, do you know it? Seems to me that used to be a parking lot.'

'Not the last two years, it's a chi-chi condo now, lake views and all that good stuff. What's he done?'

I filled him in and he asked a few questions, until he had the facts shuffled in his own way. Then he said, 'What are you doing?'

'I'm waiting for the Tracy woman to come round. She might be able to tell us something, although there's no guarantee that the guy who beat her up has anything to do with the case. I just figure he might.'

'Anything else about Hanson might be useful?'

'Yeah, he was driving an old Ford, licence number 197 HKH, registered to a guy called Patton, in Scarborough. That might help.'

Irv noted the number and then said, 'Even if you find him it still sounds like a long shot. What are the OPP doing?'

'They're trying to trace Jeffries and Waites' wife, widow now, I guess. But from what I make of it, those two're holed up somewhere, could be they've got the blinds drawn and they're jumping on one another's bones, not knowing what's going on, or maybe they're part of this and they're hiding out.'

'And what do you want out of Hanson? Haven't the OPP called out detectives to check him out?'

'Maybe. But I want to know how come he roped in the Kershaw kid for his gang. That can't be pure coincidence.'

'You think Kershaw did the killings?'

'It's a good bet. Waites could have sprung Kershaw and asked him to kill his wife. Kershaw killed the wrong woman. Then somebody, maybe Kershaw, killed Waites. All that would make its own kind of sense, but I can't understand why this Hanson kid would drum up a gang that just happened to include Kershaw's son, and use the gang to make trouble in Murphy's Harbour.'

Irv was silent for a long time but I didn't add anything. At last he said, 'So it figures that Hanson is part of the scam, whatever it is, maybe a trick to keep you occupied while Kershaw does his thing.'

'Sounds screwy, I know, but there has to be a pattern here.' I hadn't mentioned Kershaw's old threat to me but Irv has a long memory.

'What I remember of Kershaw, he was planning to get even with you when he got out, that right?'

'They all say that.'

'Yeah.' Irv was thoughtful. 'But they don't all walk away from day passes at the same time that a whole other thing is going down where you live. I'd watch your back for a while, old buddy.'

'Sam does that for me, but thanks for the warning.'

'Yeah, well, I haven't had lunch yet so I'll grab a couple hours, go talk to this Hanson, or his lady if I can't find him.'

'Thanks, Irv. There's times I miss having a load of other guys on the team.'

'You wouldn't miss this bullshit,' he said devoutly. 'I haven't seen the sun all week, been hanging over a bunch of books since last Friday, that's eight days nonstop.'

'Your own fault for getting an education,' I kidded and he laughed and hung up.

I was busy for the next hour, parcelling up my evidence, the swabs and fingerprints from the Tracy case, and arranging to ship them to the forensics centre in Toronto. Then I drove out to Kinski's gas station from which George's car had been stolen the night before. Paul said he would hand the package to the express company driver and asked if I'd found George's car. I told him yes and he shook his head. 'Goddamn Indians. Ask me, you can't trust any of 'em.'

'No harm done,' I said. 'I found the car, not a scratch on it. Those kids yesterday ripped up the seats and stole the tape-player, this wasn't touched.'

He'd been expecting a full agreement but he grunted and left it at that. I went from there to the Horns' house. George's car was in the driveway but I could see Phillip painting the house, doing a neat job on it, not slopping the paint or getting himself messy. And the house was growing brighter by the minute.

He stopped when he saw me and waved with his brush. 'Hi, Chief, whaddya think?'

'Looks good,' I said. Sam had come with me and Phillip came down the ladder and patted him on the head. Then he looked up at me and asked the hard question. 'I just found out that my lawyer is Mrs Horn's son.

212

Did you know that?'

'Yes.' Tell the truth and shame the devil my father used to say.

He shook his head ruefully. 'Jeez. Am I dumb! I thought he was doing me a favour.'

'He was. All the charges have been dropped. I was just talking to your mother.'

'What did she say?' He was nervous again now, his acne blooming.

'It's all over. She isn't going to interfere. She said she'd pick you up when you called that the job was finished.'

'I don't think I'll get it done today,' he said. 'Mrs Horn says I can stay here tonight.'

'How do you feel about that?'

He was angry now, at himself. 'I feel like a jerk. That's how. These people are nice.'

I laughed. 'You're not the first guy to feel that way. I was a hell-raiser myself at your age.'

'Yeah?' He seemed relieved. 'Like, what did you do?'

'I took my dad's car on a joyride when I was fifteen. Went off the road and dinged the hell out of it.'

Now it was his turn to laugh. 'What happened?'

I shook my head. 'The old man was one of a kind. He was madder'n a snake but he didn't hit me. He made me work with him until we'd got it back into shape. Then he picked up some parts from God knows where and helped me build a dirtbike to ride until I was old enough to drive.'

'He sounds like a great guy.' The boy looked wistful. 'You still see a lot of him?'

'He was a miner. The stope collapsed on him and his partner the year I turned eighteen.'

The boy's eyes filled with tears. 'Aaah, hell,' he said.

'Listen, I wanted to ask you a couple of questions, about these other kids you were with. You mind talking?'

'No. I already spoke to the OPP guys.'

'OK. I've found out that Eric, the sparkplug of the gang, he's an actor, he's older than he looks, twenty-eight. I figure he's trying out for a part in a movie and he put the gang together for some kind of experience, research, whatever.'

He thought about this without speaking for a while. 'I'm trying to remember how it was,' he said at last. 'Like, I was hanging around the beach, scoping out the girls, you know. Only none of them would talk to me. I was from somewhere else. They were all local. You know how it is.'

I nodded and he went on, 'So anyway, there were three of us guys, I guess I was the oldest. We hung around together and then this Cy kind of tagged on.'

'Had you seen him around before?'

'No. He just turned up one day and hung

214

around. He made us laugh. Said the broads were all a bunch of dogs, we'd likely get AIDS or herpes if we went with them.'

The police text on the genesis of gangs came back to me. A company of rejects. Bull's-eye. 'So how long was it before Eric showed up?'

Phillip thought for a moment. 'Not long. Next day, I guess. He drove up in an old clunker, that Ford we were driving, remember? Cy started calling him names and Eric karate-kicked him, knocked him over. Then he picked him up and asked if we'd like a beer. So we said sure and he took us in his car and bought a two-four and we all had a couple bottles. That was the first day.'

'Then what happened?' It sounded more and more as if Cy had been an accomplice. The karate kick could have been an actor's trick, delivered on cue, with no force but seen as terrible if the guy on the other end fell over. I didn't think Hanson knew martial arts. He hadn't seemed competent on either of the occasions I had tangled with him.

'That was two days before we came up here. The next day we kibitzed around on the beach at Wasaga, like, we broke up the volleyball game and just generally acted like goofs. Then Eric said this was boring. Why didn't we head off somewhere and have some fun.'

'And that was when you drove up to

Murphy's Harbour? Did you stop anywhere else on the way?'

'No, except to buy some beer. Like, I was bored with the drive. There's all kinds of places we could have stopped but Eric said he was looking for the perfect place. And he pulled in here.'

'Did he say why Murphy's Harbour was perfect?'

'Yeah. He said there was just one cop here, we wouldn't have any fuss with police.'

So he'd done his homework. 'Was Cy his number two man?'

'No.' Phillip ducked his head. 'No, like, Eric said I should be his lieutenant. He said I was smart and Cy was dumb.'

'And what did Cy say about that?'

'He kinda sulked but the other kids called him crybaby so he just shrugged and said, OK, go on, see if he cared.'

'Did it ever occur to you that the two of them, Eric and Cy, had set this thing up between them?'

Phillip thought hard about it, rolling his lower jaw forward the way some people do when they're concentrating. 'Come to think of it, yeah. The day after Eric kicked him, Cy took his shirt off and there was no bruise on his chest, where the kick landed. The kids saw it and they all said he was—' he hesitated and said—'you know, a pussy, that Eric hadn't hurt him at all. But now you say

216

it, maybe Eric really hadn't hurt him, maybe it was all some kind of show they were putting on.'

'Eric is an actor,' I told him. 'He's a professional. He gets paid to make people believe he's telling the truth when he says things.'

'Then maybe it was all a show,' Phillip said bitterly. 'And I fell for it and killed poor old Muskie for a coupla goddamn phonies.'

'I went and killed people in a war for a bunch of goddamn phonies,' I told him. 'But you can see why I want to find Eric, or Cy.'

'I'll think about it,' he promised. 'If I think of anything that can help you I'll let you know.'

'Good. It's important, Phil. I'm counting on you.'

It was one-thirty when I left him and I drove back into town and had a hamburger and Coke at the restaurant, then went back to the office to check the Fax machine.

The authorities at the prison had sent the photograph of Kershaw. It was less than perfect but it gave an idea of the general look of the man, together with a physical description. I pasted it down on a sheet of paper and typed, '*Wanted for escaping from custody and for theft. Believed to be in this area. If seen, do not approach, ring the police station at Murphy's Harbour or the OPP at Parry Sound,*' and put both phone numbers below.

The bank has a photocopier so I went in and made a couple of dozen copies. The manager took one and taped it to the wall where customers would see it and didn't charge me for the other copies. Then I made a circuit of town, leaving one in at the stores and bars and the marina and campsites and the two locks.

Around four o'clock I was finished and came back to the office and telephoned Holland. He told me Ms Tracy was still out but he had some results from forensics in Toronto. Waites had a trace of cocaine in his blood and an alcohol level that suggested he'd taken about two drinks. Death had been caused by the stab wound to the chest which had severed his aorta. The cut to his throat had been made first. It was bad but, given immediate treatment, he might have survived it.

'Anything on the fingerprints?'

'Nothing helpful. Whoever used the glass in his room is not on record. The only thing they'll say is that the guy who made the prints has smallish hands.'

'Does that fit with what you know about this Jeffries character?'

'I hear he's around five-nine and kinda scrawny. No idea of his hand size.'

'I'd sure like to talk to him. I wonder where in hell he's got to?'

'Well, he's not been seen down Ellis Lane.

218

My guys turned it over down there. A couple of people had seen the grey car there, the wagon. It was seen eight a.m. yesterday morning and was gone by two in the afternoon.'

'I wonder if he went down there as soon as he left Parry Sound? Maybe had a rendezvous with another car and changed it there.'

'Yeah, well, how would the other driver have left? You figure someone would deliver a car and then walk away? The grey wagon was left there, remember.'

We both had ideas at the same time. I said, 'Maybe I could bring Sam up to the Jeffries house and pick up something with his scent on it. Then I'll have Sam track around at Ellis Lane. He might be able to show something we've missed.'

'Worth a try, I guess,' Holland said without enthusiasm. 'I was thinkin' maybe those kids have switched the licence plate on the grey wagon. I'm going to put it on the air that guys should check the licence of every wagon they see.'

'Right. Might be worth doing the same thing with Ms Tracy's Mercedes. If Kershaw took it, he'll change the plates for sure.'

'I'll get on it,' he said.

'Good. Meanwhile I've got a Metro Toronto detective checking on this Hanson character, see if he can shed a little light on

219

what's happening.'

'Oh, that was the other thing,' Holland concluded. 'The package in his room was PCP, angel dust, and the same thing was found in his blood.'

We thought about it some more and promised to call each other if we got anything new. He also promised to send a man down to the Jeffries place and bring a pair of his shoes to the station in Parry Sound so I could get Sam looking for him.

When we'd finished the call I hung up and called Irv Goodman. He was pressed for time. 'The inspector wants my findings on these books by the morning, that's why I didn't call back. I was going to call around eight, when I'm done here. But I did find out two things.'

'Good, what were they?'

'Well, first, he and this Hanson woman split up a coupla weeks back. She doesn't know where he is. That's the big thing, so we're lost for a way to find him.'

'Pity, but OK, what was the second thing?'

'The reason they split up,' Irv said. 'Seems his lady found out he was having a fling with some other woman, a film producer. She, that's the girlfriend, figures it's just a professional thing. The producer is older than him, although that doesn't mean much, hell, this Hanson woman is forty-five if she's a day.'

'Professional—you mean he was sleeping with the producer to get a job?'

'Wait, I didn't tell you the best bit.' Irv chuckled. 'The job he's after is something about being the honcho of a street gang.'

'And the producer is Marcia Tracy of Northlands Productions.'

'Absolutely,' Irv said happily. 'How d'ya like that?'

'It's tying up tighter and tighter,' I said.

'There's one other thing, something I dug out of her accountant, guy I did a favour for one time. And this could be vital. It seems this Tracy woman is in financial trouble. She had a coupla successes, but that was a year or two back. Now she's had four stinkers in a row and she can't get backing for her new movie.'

I didn't mention George's version of the same story. 'So she's in trouble?'

'Big trouble. She's mortgaged everything to get this new movie off the ground. If it doesn't go through, she's in a hole.'

'I don't see how it fits exactly. But it's a damn good motive for what's going on up here.'

We jawed a while longer and I thanked him, then hung up and the phone rang again. 'Hello, is that Chief Bennett?'

'Yes, go ahead, please.'

'This is Dr Baer. The woman has come round. Can you come in and talk to the

221

Parry Sound officer, please.'

'Be there right away. Thank you, Doctor.'

I ran for the car and wailed up the highway. At the hospital I went straight up to Ms Tracy's room. The doctor was there, and the constable, who nodded to me. 'She knows the guy,' he said. 'His name's Hanson.'

CHAPTER ELEVEN

I took my hat off and went over to the bed. Ms Tracy looked at me, moving her head painfully. 'I understand you found me.'

'My dog. He heard you over the noise of your air-conditioner.'

'Thank you,' she said.

'How are you feeling?' I wanted her to see me as the good guy, not the hardnose she had thought me earlier.

'I feel like death warmed over,' she said, and tried to smile.

'Nothing permanent's been done. The doctor will fix you up so there isn't a mark within a week.'

I sat down on the chair beside the bed and winked at the doctor. He took the hint and left. 'I'd like to catch the guy who did this to you. He belongs inside.'

'It was Eric Hanson.' She said it angrily.

'He raped me and beat me up.'

'We'll get him, I promise you. Tell me what happened.'

'I was just finishing my breakfast when he knocked on the door.'

'Was he alone?'

That made her frown. 'Yes, why do you ask that?'

'Did you hear a car drive up before he knocked? Or did you get the impression he'd walked?'

'I didn't hear a car.' The question had confused her. I wondered whether she had rehearsed her story or was still not functioning properly. 'Why do you think he came in a car?'

'It might have helped if I knew, that's all. Go on, please.'

'Well, he came in and I asked if he'd like a cup of coffee but he said no. He wanted to know if I'd finished casting my movie.'

'And what did you say?'

'I told him yes and he asked if he'd got the part he was angling for. And I told him I still hadn't made up my mind.'

'Were you telling him he hadn't got the job?'

She frowned and the effort tugged at the plasters on her face, making her gasp with the shock. I waited and at last she said, 'He's too old. There's an American boy, a dancer, if I can get him he'll be perfect for it.'

'And what happened then?'

She turned her head away on the pillow for a moment and when she looked at me again there were tears in her eyes. 'He got angry. He started to shout at me and I told him to leave.'

'And then what?' I asked the question gently, as if I believed those tears in her eyes were real. Her story was coming out too well, as if she had rehearsed it. Tears might have been part of the rehearsal. Drama was her life's work, after all.

'And he attacked you.'

She nodded dumbly, then wiped her eyes on the edge of the sheet. 'He and I had been close before. He'd always seemed so courteous.'

'What did he do?'

'He grabbed at me and called me a bitch. He said I'd only wanted him for sex.' She sniffled. 'He said I was too old to get a man for myself, that I used my position to take advantage of young men who would never bother with me otherwise.'

'And then what?'

'Then he tore my nightgown off and pushed me down on the floor and raped me. He kept on asking how I liked being used, the way I'd used him.'

It was possible but she was telling it too well. I've talked to a lot of women who've been assaulted. They don't lay things out as

224

straight as this usually.

I played along anyway. 'Nice guy. And did he beat you up then?'

'Yes. While he was, you know, on top of me, he was hitting me.'

'Did you hit him back? Is his face marked?'

'I tried but he held my hands. He's very strong.'

I heard a movement behind me but I didn't turn, I wanted her to think that her story had my whole attention. Then Holland came and stood the other side of the bed. He said nothing and she ignored him and went on.

'And what happened then? Did you pass out?'

'I guess so,' she said, she looked away, at Holland, and then back. 'I'm not sure. I was hurt. I think he picked me up and kind of dragged me through to the bedroom. I don't remember.'

'Did he hit you with anything other than his fists?'

She shook her head regretfully. 'He hit me again but I was numb, I don't know whether he used anything else. Is it important? Look what he did to me.'

Holland was anxious. I could feel his excitement across the space between us but he didn't speak, he's a professional, this was my investigation.

'Did you know he took your car and rifled your purse, took whatever money you had and your credit cards?'

'I passed out,' she said and then, 'Look, I'm thirty-seven years old. I've been through a lot in my life but I've never had anything like this happen to me before. I was in shock.'

'OK. Thank you for your help, Ms Tracy. We've already put out a description of your car as being stolen. We'll circulate Hanson's picture. Do you have one at your house?'

'No.' She seemed sure of that. 'There's one in the file in my office in Toronto. Or you can get one from his agent. I gave you his name yesterday.'

'I'll get right on to it,' I said. 'You'd better rest now. We'll leave the policeman here so you'll feel safe. Then tomorrow, when you're rested, maybe we could talk about this some more.'

'Oh God,' she groaned. 'Oh well, I guess so, if you must. I just want you to catch him.'

'So do we, Ms Tracy. Thank you for your help.' I stood up and smiled at her, then nodded to Holland who took the hint and came out of the room with me.

'Got the bastard dead to rights,' he said happily. 'Description, complaint, hell, we can even get a photograph.'

'She's lying,' I said.

That stopped him cold. 'Lying? Don't

226

look to me like she's lying.'

'That's not the way the attack happened. If it was an attack.'

'What are you smokin'?' He was angry. 'What makes you so all-fired sure she's not telling it like it was?'

'Couple of things. First her story. It's hard to believe a guy could hold both her hands and rape her at the same time he's punching her in the face like that.'

'It's possible,' Holland said. 'He's a big kid. I saw him. He's six feet anyway, one seventy-five.'

'Sure it's possible. But I've seen the room where it happened. There are no bloodstains on the floor where she says she was attacked, but there's blood on the wall at face height. Whoever attacked her rammed her head into the wall a few times. She'd have remembered that. And there's blood on the alarm clock next to her bed. Somebody hit her a few licks with that for good measure.'

'But like she said. She was dazed, she doesn't remember.'

'Ask the doctor, if you like. He said he couldn't see any clinical reason why she should have been unconscious when she came in. She may be faking this whole thing. There's a chance that Hanson did call on her, that he did even drive away in her car. He may even have screwed her but I don't think a few clumps in the head in the middle of all the sexual activity would account for her being so dazed that she didn't remember having her head banged into the wall later.'

Holland wasn't convinced. He cocked his head thoughtfully. 'What's your version, then?'

'I think she's lying. I'm not sure why. Could be that Hanson got snaky when she told him he hadn't got the part he was after in her movie. He may even have raped her, although a lawyer would get him off. According to my latest update, he's split up with his steady girlfriend over his affair with this woman.'

'So he's her boyfriend.' Now Holland understood what I was saying. 'They had an argument. He threatened to get nasty so she wants to get him sent down, just to punish him.'

'Exactly. It's even possible she banged her own face on the wall a few times, maybe even hit herself in the face with her clock.'

'But then what? You say the house was all locked up. Would she have locked herself in, where nobody would find her? That doesn't make sense to me.'

That was a fact which had bothered me as well and I turned my full attention to it. 'Maybe she didn't intend for me to find her,' I thought out loud. 'Maybe she was expecting some other guy, someone who would have found her banged up and gotten mad and taken after the guy she said had done it to her.'

'Yeah, but what about her car and keys being missing?' Holland was coasting now, shooting down my theory with cold hard facts. 'You mean she drove her car off somewhere, dumped her keys and money and then came back to her house and banged herself around so some strange guy, some Mr X, would feel sorry for her and climb on his white horse and go out to set things right? Come on, Reid. That's not the way it works.'

'I've sent the clock and some prints I found to Toronto for comparison. I'll know better when I hear back. Meantime we should find Hanson. He's tied up in this whole thing, the Jeffries killing, this assault, recruiting the Freund kid into a gang. I want him.'

'Put him on the air, then,' Holland said. 'And chase up this agent of his, get a photograph.'

'Right.' I recalled my reason for driving up here. 'Did you get something from Jeffries' place for my dog to track from?'

'Yeah. There's a pair of running shoes in my car. You want 'em now?'

'May's well. I'll make the calls. Could you leave them for me, please?'

Holland chuckled indulgently. 'This is a good scam you got goin', Reid. Whenever nothing's breaking, call in the dog and take a nice long walk in the fresh air.'

'He earns his keep,' I said. Sam had done more for me than the entire OPP in my years at the Harbour.

'OK. Call from the front desk. I'll see you there.'

We went out to the front and I made my calls. First to the OPP office to circulate Hanson's description and then to Toronto to ask the Headquarters detectives to pick up his photograph from his agent and get it out to all police departments on the Fax. Holland came back while I was calling and dropped a pair of running shoes in front of me in a plastic grocery store bag. They were pretty funky and I figured Sam would have no trouble picking up Jeffries' scent from them.

I glanced outside and noticed that the sun was low. I had only about an hour left before dark but I didn't leave right away. I went upstairs quickly to have a word with Fred. It didn't seem right to leave without doing that. She was lying back on the bed, but she sat up happily when I came in. I kissed her. 'Hi, love. How are you feeling?'

'Can't wait to come home,' she said. 'The nurse tells me I'll feel weak for a day or two but I can do that at home, can't I, just as easily as I can here.'

'What time can I spring you?'

'Any time after nine. Can you make it?'

'Hey, no sweat. I've even cleaned the place up.'

'Made our bed, I guess you mean.' She smiled. 'You need to make up the crib and all the other things. There's three of us now.'

'Bossy,' I said. 'You rest up and I'll be here at nine.'

She winked at me and I left and went out to the car, carrying Jeffries' running shoes.

By the time I reached Ellis Lane and found the spot where the grey wagon had been parked it was dropping dark. But I took my flashlight out of the glove box and then gave Sam a good whiff of the shoes and set him loose. He ran back and forth with his nose to the ground and finally came to a point about twenty yards off, where he stopped. It was as I'd thought. Jeffries had left his car there and driven away in something else. So that was one good theory proven, to no advantage. I fussed him and let him try again but he just covered the same ground, so I called him off and drove back to Murphy's Harbour with him on the front seat and the bag with the running shoes in it between us.

As I drove I found thoughts coming at me from every angle. I was responding to the road at one level and at another I could see Fred. And on another plane I was thinking about the case and realized suddenly that the running shoes next to me were small, no more than an eight or nine. The man who had killed Waites had small hands. The fingerprint guy had been sure of that. Maybe it had been Jeffries.

I headed for the second entrance to the Harbour and drove straight to the Lodge. Mrs James was surprised to see me but she opened the door to Waites' room and left me there with Sam and the pair of running shoes. I shut the door and took out one of the shoes. I gave it to Sam to sniff and then told him, 'Track.'

He put his nose down and began to run around the room. He went into the bathroom and barked at the edge of the tub and then he ran to the bedside where the depression in the pillows still showed where a man had sat, and barked again. And finally he checked and went over to the fire-escape rope that lay coiled in the corner, anchored to a bolt in the window-frame and barked again.

I called him off and fussed him as if he were a puppy, rubbing his great head and telling him he was a good boy while he whined happily. 'You're a better cop than I am, Sam,' I whispered. 'You've told me who killed John Waites. Now all we have to do is find him.'

CHAPTER TWELVE

I took Sam downstairs and checked under the window. The scent hadn't lasted as well in the open air but eventually he tracked around the blind side of the building and out to the parking lot. Jeffries must have driven away from that point.

Mrs James was still working and she told me that nobody of Jeffries' description had rented the room that she could remember, nor had she seen him visiting. She would check with her staff.

It was a downer but I got a similar response when I phoned the OPP with my news. Holland was off duty and I had to talk to another detective. He wasn't excited. He was working on a break-in at a local gas station. It was small potatoes but he had a good chance of solving it. He promised to put my message on the air. It might help, he said, without enthusiasm. Reminding me that we didn't know where the guy was or what he was driving.

That thought sent me back to Ms Tracy's house. She had known Waites and his wife and the story of their marriage, maybe she also knew the Jeffries in person. It was a slim chance but I was grasping at straws by now.

She was away so I gave up and drove

downtown to check on the Friday evening activities. It was warm and the air was full of a smalltown charm that made you think of summer nights long ago when there would have been women in long white dresses enjoying the evening air and the sound of a mandolin ringing across the water. That night there were only the usual teenagers with a radio playing something by Reba McIntyre. I made my rounds of the properties, then drove home for supper.

I let Sam check around the place first and when he found nothing I went in and foraged. There wasn't a lot in the fridge but I made a sandwich and a pot of coffee and called the hospital. Fred was feeling good and we chatted while the coffee perked. She was excited about coming home and gave me a shopping list.

We said good night and I sat with my coffee, thinking about the case. There were four people who could tell us useful things. One of them would turn up soon, I hoped. The odds were good on Hanson. It was his ambition in life to be well known. He would show up somewhere. And Moira Waites would be back painting, trying to sell. Jeffries might be different. If he'd killed Waites he would be keeping his head down and might already have left the country.

That left Kershaw. I didn't know much about him beyond the facts of his arrest.

He'd sworn to get even but that was talk. Now he was out he would put freedom above revenge, I figured. He could find work. As long as he didn't work for anybody who needed his Social Insurance Number for the payroll he could give himself a new identity and disappear.

But would he? I thought back to the arrest. He had been high on cocaine, his lawyer had insisted. Previously he had been of good character. I remember the smiles exchanged between the cops involved when his lawyer came up with that chestnut. But he had looked respectable enough, had come to court in a good suit and tie, looking more like a banker than the raving gunman I had been obliged to shoot. And his wife was a lawyer. What had driven him to holding up a bank? Cocaine was the easy answer but it didn't satisfy me.

On impulse I called my sister's house. She was in but Elmer was still working. He had a new shooting to investigate, some Vietnamese had shot down the owner of a restaurant in front of his customers that afternoon. She sighed at that and wondered what kind of city Toronto was turning into.

'World-class. Isn't that what the politicians keep boasting? Now you've got world-class crime to go along with the theatre and all the cultural stuff,' I suggested.

'I figure I'm too young to be pining for the old days, but I can't help it,' she said. 'Anyway, how's Fred and the baby?'

I told her they were coming home next day and she made approving noises and then Elmer came in. She put him on and he told me about the case. 'The witnesses swear the kid was no more than fifteen, sixteen. I'm telling you, Reid, it's the pits these days.'

'How about taking your mind off it for a minute or two?'

'You need some help,' he said. ''S long's I don't have to go out of that door again tonight, that's fine.'

'Just from memory, maybe. Remember this guy Kershaw, the bank robber on the lam from Joyceville?'

'Yeah, he's still out. What about him?'

'Well, he seems to be tied in to what's happening up here and I was trying to work out any connection. I know he held up a bank, shot the manager and took a hostage. I'm wondering why.'

'He was a cokehead, wasn't he?'

'Yeah, but he had a lot going for him. He was wealthy. He wasn't the kind of guy who would rob banks to support his habit. He would have pulled some white-collar scam, mortgaged the house, something.'

Elmer was quiet for a moment, then he said, 'Chuck Grady was in the detective office back then. I'll give him a call, see if he can remember anything.'

'That'd be good of you, Elmer. It would help if Chuck knew what Kershaw did for a living in those days, anything to give me a line on why he was robbing banks.'

'If I can get him tonight, I will; otherwise tomorrow morning, that be OK?'

'That'd be great. Hope it doesn't mess up your evening, what's left of it?'

'I don't have anything on. There's an AA meeting at nine but I'm too late now. I've started painting, ya'know. I never had a hobby in the old days and a lot of the guys say you need something to do, otherwise you start getting itchy without a drink.'

'That's not a problem any more, is it?'

'Been dry for three years by the grace of God,' he said 'But it helps take my mind off work. I'm just a dauber.'

'Then get daubing. And take care, OK?'

'You too,' he said and hung up.

As I was washing the dishes, the phone rang. It was Jean Horn. 'Hi, Reid, I wondered how Fred was, when she's coming home.'

I told her and she said, 'That's why I called. I was wondering if you'd like me to come over and smarten the place up before she gets back?'

'I've kept it pretty good, thanks, Jean.'

She laughed. 'I'm not talking about having the dishes washed. You need food and flowers. I'll bet you've got nothing in the fridge but a couple of cans of beer, am I right?'

'Well, I must admit, except for half a head of lettuce, yes. But Fred's given me a list.'

'You've got enough to do without going grocery shopping,' she said. 'How about I come by in the morning, around nine?'

'That would be very kind of you. I'll drop you off a key and some cash.'

'Good. Come by any time before ten and we'll be up.'

It was nine-fifteen so I drove over there right away. George and Phil Freund were outside under the porch light, filleting a couple of big bass. The kid was beside himself with excitement. 'Look at that, Chief,' he said. 'Three pounds. I caught him.'

'With a Fireplug, I bet.'

George laughed. 'You an' your plugs, Reid. I'm Indian, I don't use plugs.'

'Used a little frog,' Freund said happily. 'Caught the bait, then caught the fish. We're having it for breakfast.'

'Nice going,' I said. It was starting to look as if Eric Hanson had done this kid a favour when he brought him into the gang. 'I've come to see your mother, George.'

'Go on in. They're watching TV,' he said, still working with his knife. I tapped on the door and Jean called me in. She was in front

238

of the television, knitting. The puppy was asleep by her feet. Her husband was across from her in his chair, head lolling as he dozed.

I gave her my spare housekey and some cash which she resisted at first, and then asked her about Freund. 'He's a good kid, Reid. I don't know why he did what he did yesterday.'

'His mother came up to see me today. She's been raising the boy on her own. His father's gone. She's not short of a buck, she's a lawyer, but there's been no man around to set the boy an example.'

'Him and George get on just fine,' she said. 'And he learns real well. He caught that bass out there.'

'His mother appreciates what you're doing,' I told her. 'And so do I.'

'Yeah. Well,' she said. 'You want some coffee?'

'No, thanks, I just had supper. I'm going to check around town again and then hit the sack, more coffee would keep me awake.'

She laughed. 'Better get all the sleep you can before Fred gets home with the baby. Then you'll know about losing sleep.'

'You're a big comfort. But thanks for the help. I know Fred will be grateful.'

I left, still worrying about the case. There was so much to do. Somebody should be canvassing every motel, every lodge and rooming-house for a hundred miles around, but the OPP didn't have enough men. The best they could do was a telephone canvass, missing half of the places for sure. We needed real manpower like I'd been part of in Toronto. There we could put a team of guys together to check everything, witnesses, past addresses, parking tickets, all the hundreds of tricks needed to come up with a lead. On my own I was like an ant trying to measure the pyramids.

I was glooming quietly when the break came, a phone call, switched to my radio. I took the mike. 'Murphy's Harbour Police.'

'Parry Sound OPP. Got something for you. A woman's been abducted from a motel on Sideline 12, the Bonanza.'

'I know it. When?'

''Bout five minutes ago. The owner says a man grabbed her and pulled her into a car.'

'On my way. Are your guys coming?'

'Yes. Be on the lookout for a small blue car. Driver around six feet, one-ninety, dark hair, that's all she had.'

'She?' If this was the missing woman's car the registration should have been on the check-in card.

'The owner. Says it looked expensive.'

'I wonder if it's the missing Mercedes?' I said. 'On my way.'

I hung up and hammered out along the side-road and back to the highway, heading
240

south five miles to Sideline 12. It was too dark to check the colour of cars coming the other way. Maybe one of them was the car I wanted but I concentrated on getting to the Waterfall.

It was a middlebrow place, a long, low building set hopefully in a spot cleared of trees but otherwise devoid of attractions. A good place to go bankrupt.

A woman was standing in the middle of the lot, beside a suitcase which was lying as if it had just been dropped there. She ran towards me when she saw the flashing lights.

'Officer, he went that way.' She pointed back the way I had come. Nothing had passed me as I drove the side-road so I asked, 'What happened?'

'I was in the office and I saw a car parked out here. Then I saw a man running to it, carrying this.' She tapped the suitcase with her foot.

'Did he drop it and take off? What about the woman?'

'She ran after him, screaming. I couldn't make out what she was saying but she caught up with him and he dropped the case and hit her in the head.'

'Then what? Did you shout?'

Now she stopped, licking her lips nervously. 'Well, not exactly.'

'What did you do?'

'Well, I was robbed once, so I keep a

shotgun under the counter. I pulled it out and fired it.'

I frowned inwardly. This isn't Dodge City, people don't use shotguns to keep the peace, but I was glad she had.

'Then what happened?'

'He just pulled her into the car.'

'Did he try to pick up his case?'

She cut the story to its bare bones. 'I shot again and he took off like a bat outa hell.'

She had broken the law but I wasn't going to cast the first stone. She might also have broken our case open.

'Did you see the licence? Any part of it, just one or two numbers?'

'He had his lights off, I couldn't see anything.'

'Did you recognize the woman?'

'It looked like Ms Baker from unit nine.'

'Let's look inside. Do you have a key?'

'Yes.' She pulled it out. 'What about this?' She nudged the suitcase.

'I'll put it back in the room. It figures he's stolen it from there.'

I picked it up with the flat of my hands. It was full and heavy but I managed and took it to the door of unit nine.

She tried the door. It was ajar. 'Don't touch it, please, and stay outside, if you would,' I told her and whistled for Sam. He was at my side in an instant and I shoved the door with the back of my hand and told him

'Seek'.

He snaked by me and around the bed, which was unmade. On the far side he checked and began barking, his head low to the ground.

I followed him in, taking a moment to shove the bathroom door open and glance in. There was no light but the room was small and I could see that it was empty. Then I turned to Sam and saw what he was barking at. Beside the bed lay the body of a small, bearded man, head lolling on a broken neck.

CHAPTER THIRTEEN

The owner asked, 'What is it?' in a nervous voice.

I whirled to her. 'Don't touch anything. Stay there, please.'

'What's going on?' Her voice was shaky with fear. 'Something smells bad.'

'There's a body here, it's a man. Stand outside, please.'

She gave a low, frightened wail and stepped out, holding on to the doorjamb for support. I crouched and felt for a pulse in the man's neck. There wasn't one, of course, but the body was still warm. I hushed Sam and stood up, looking around at the room. The bed was unmade. There were a few personal things, women's lotions and a hairbrush, on the chest of drawers. A brown grip with the lid flopped down stood on the canvas stand in the corner. I looked in and saw it was full of women's clothing. That reminded me of the other case and I went outside and brought it in, again lifting it with the flat of my hands on either side so as not to get prints on it. I stood it beside the door.

'Can I use your phone?'

'It's at the office.' She was breathing fast and shallow, hyperventilating. But I needed answers. 'What did he look like?'

'Big. Your size. I couldn't see his clothes except that he had dark pants and a light shirt. He wasn't wearing a jacket. And I think he had dark hair.'

'Thank you. Now relax. Hold your breath for a while if you can.'

She drew in a big breath and held it as she led me to the office. I ran ahead of her and dialled the Parry Sound OPP.

The man on the desk told me they had two cars on the way. One of them a patrol car, should be there any moment, the other had the inspector in it. That was good news. It meant they had jumped the same mental hurdle I had and suspected that the affair was tied in with our homicide investigations. 'Get on the horn. Tell him there's a dead man here, looks as if it could be Jeffries. And the guy who did it is around six-one, one-ninety. He has dark hair, a light shirt, dark pants, no jacket.'

'Will do,' he said.

I looked up at the owner. 'Can you remember anything at all about the car?'

'It was blue, I think. But it was too dark to tell properly.'

'Dark blue, light blue?'

'Dark. A small sedan, looked foreign.'

I passed the information on to the dispatcher and hung up. The owner had settled down again now, here in her own familiar surroundings. I put her more at ease. 'Play down the shotgun when you talk to the OPP. You're not supposed to use it, but I'm glad you did.'

'It didn't stop him taking her,' she said ruefully.

'The case he left behind will be useful. We'll find him. Now, could you tell me your name, please?'

'Joyce,' she said, 'Joyce Graham. What do you want to know?'

'OK, Joyce. What did the woman look like?'

She hadn't seen the woman herself but remembered from her daughter who had registered her that she had arrived alone, without a car, saying a friend had dropped her off and that her husband would be in later. That had been the previous day.

'Can I talk to your daughter, please?'

'She's at a party, I'll call her.' She picked up the telephone.

'Don't say anything about the body. We don't want a crowd of people here cluttering the place up.'

'Right.' She dialled and when the phone was picked up I could hear the music through the phone from four feet away. She had a tense little conversation with the daughter, who didn't want to come home, but eventually she agreed and Mrs Graham hung up. 'She's on her way.'

'Fine. Now tell me, have you been into the room at all since yesterday?'

'No. I offered to clean up this morning but they told me they didn't want it, so I left them alone.'

'Them. Did you see the man?'

'Yes, a little guy with a beard. He said his wife was in the shower. Polite but not friendly if you know what I mean.'

'Did he sound American?'

'Yes, Michigan or some place, I thought.'

'And did they have a car here?'

'No. I wondered how he'd got here but they'd paid for two days in cash so I didn't push it.'

I stood a moment, thinking. It was no use rushing back down to the highway. The car had a twenty-minute start. It was up to the OPP to stop it. Maybe they'd put roadblocks out if they could spare the manpower, but even if they did, he'd probably turn off when he saw the line-up and vanish down some side-road. In daylight it might be possible to find it from their helicopter but until then he was lost to us.

'I'm going back to the room,' I told her. 'There's a couple of cars coming. Show them the room, and let me know when your daughter gets here.'

'Right.' She nodded. 'I'll put some coffee on.'

I went back to the room and looked at the body. Whoever had killed him had been strong; aside from that, no clues. But the suitcase drew me. Jeffries, if this was Jeffries, had been killed for the case. What was in it?

I heard a car siren and went to the door of the room. The car pulled up in front of me and a woman officer got out. I could see that a number of the doors had opened now and anxious-looking people were poking their heads out.

The policewoman came over. I knew her slightly and said, 'Hi, Elaine, step in.'

She came in. 'I heard there's a body.'

'Over here. Mind where you step.'

'Right.' She followed me and looked down at the body. 'That's Stu Jeffries,' she said. 'I was in his store once to get a picture framed.'

'The woman with him was taken away. The guy was after that suitcase.'

'Wonder what's in it?' She looked over at it, glad to look away from the body.

'When the inspector comes we'll open it. For now, the best thing we can do is canvass the other units, see if any of them saw anything.'

'Right. I'll start at the far end. Can you secure this place and take the other end?'

'Yeah.' I stepped out after her and placed Sam in front of the door, telling him to keep.

I went to the other end of the building and checked with all the occupants. They were all anxious to help but in the end they had nothing new to contribute. They all mentioned hearing shots and one of them said that there had not been a car parked in front of unit nine. So Jeffries and the woman had been stranded here. It made me wonder who had dropped them off. Had someone picked them up from where they had left their Magic Wagon and brought them here? Another mystery.

Elaine and I met to compare notes, just as the inspector arrived, a guy called Dupuy, a good copper. He was driving the car and he had the crime scene man with him. Stinson looked as if he'd been dragged out of a party somewhere and there was a smell of beer on the night air, but the inspector wasn't commenting.

Elaine and I were briefing them on what we'd found when a car pulled in and a young woman got out. The motel owner was standing in the shadows and she scurried out and brought the woman over to us. 'This is my daughter, Aileen, she was here when Ms Baker checked in yesterday.'

Dupuy took over. 'Thank you for coming to see us, Aileen. What can you tell us about Ms Baker? What did she look like? Did you see anybody with her, any visitors?'

It turned out that the girl didn't know much more than her mother had already told me. She had a description of the woman, who sounded like a twin for the body I'd found in the car trunk. The only thing she could add was that she had an American accent. That gibed with what I'd heard about Moira Waites.

Dupuy left Stinson to talk to the woman and we went to the room. He wrinkled his nose. 'Smells like his bowels gave out.'

'His neck's been broken. It happens, I guess.'

We went and looked at the body. Dupuy crouched and checked the angle of the neck. 'It would take a strong man to do that.'

'Kershaw, the guy on the lam from Joyceville, I'm sure he's up here. His name has come up in my inquiries. This could have been him.'

'What makes you think that?' Dupuy asked, not looking at me, his eyes flicking around the room.

I told him about Waites having been his lawyer and very tentatively aired my theory that Waites might have arranged for Kershaw to kill his wife.

'Sounds farfetched,' Dupuy said, but not dismissively. 'We need more than a theory. Does his description match the guy the owner saw?'

'As far as it goes, yes.'

'Well, that's something. We'll know when we've printed everything in here.'

'He was trying to steal this suitcase,' I said. 'I lifted it back in, by the sides, flat-handed. Other than that it's untouched.'

'I'll get Stinson to open it for us and we'll search it.' He left the room and came back with his assistant, who was pulling on a pair of surgical gloves.

'Might be best if we searched the room first, Inspector. If this thing's locked, maybe the key's in the deceased's pockets.'

'OK, dust the outside while we look around,' Dupuy ordered and Stinson set to work while we started investigating the scene. We chalkmarked the location of the body and had Stinson take all the essential shots. Then we rolled the body over and examined it closely. Aside from the broken neck there were no apparent wounds. The hair was pulled up from the scalp as if the killer had grabbed him by the hair. 'How did he break the neck that way?' Dupuy wondered.

'That's an unarmed combat trick, left arm around the throat, then roll the head forward, using the left elbow as a fulcrum under the jaw to snap the neck,' I said. 'It's quick and quiet.'

'Where would a guy learn that?' Dupuy asked. 'That's not the kind of trick you learn at a storefront karate class.'

'It's standard unarmed combat training. Maybe he learned it in jail from some ex-soldier.'

'What was he in for, refresh me.' Dupuy frowned.

'Bank robbery, took a hostage.'

'He sounds like a real rounder. This could be his work,' Dupuy said. 'We're going to need guys. I'll make a call. You look around but don't move anything.'

He went to the phone and I started checking the floor and all the exposed places. There wasn't anything unusual. In the bathroom I found an electric razor but aside from that everything was feminine, shampoos and lotions. There was a purse on the night table. I was holding it when Dupuy came back.

'What a time for this to happen,' he said angrily. 'A third of my people are on leave. I've had to call guys in from days off, the Midland detachment is setting up road blocks to the south, I've got one guy
251

blocking Highway 69 outside Parry Sound and I've sent Elaine up to help him. I've been on to Toronto and they're putting a team together but they won't be here until morning. And I've called Holland. He's getting back to the office.'

'You can count on me as long as it takes, Inspector.'

'Thank you. What did you find so far?'

'Not much, except for this purse.'

'OK, take a look in it,' he said.

It was a big, practical purse, some kind of woven raffia construction, and inside it was the usual jumble. But there were two wallets. I took them out one at a time. The first had ID and cards in the name of Carolyn Jeffries, along with a few dollars. The second one belonged to Moira Waites. It had three hundred and forty-six dollars in Canadian cash and a US hundred-dollar bill.

I showed them silently to Dupuy. He shook his head. 'Why would she keep both sets of ID?' He looked at the drivers' licences side by side. 'They look near enough alike that she could have used the Jeffries women's credit cards, I guess.'

'That must have been it,' I agreed. 'But she must have known it would have made her the prime suspect for killing Mrs Jeffries if we found her with both IDs.'

Dupuy had been a cop long enough to see the argument with that. 'She could have

252

pleaded ignorance, just keeping the wallet for her friend when she saw her. It wouldn't have put her away, would it?'

'I guess not.' I finished searching the purse but found nothing that helped.

At last Dupuy said, 'You go ahead and search the rest of the room. Dave and I will search the body.'

He waved me on and I opened all the drawers. There was nothing much in any of them but under the sink in the bathroom I found a bottle of J. & B. Scotch, half consumed.

'Can we get some prints off this bottle?' I asked. 'It could be the one from Waites' room.'

Dupuy looked at it. 'That's the brand that was taken from Waites' room, right?'

'Right. And the suitcase has Waites' monogram on it as well. So we've wrapped up one homicide.'

'Yeah, the one that's not on my duty sheet,' he said ruefully. 'Big deal.' He called Stinson in to print the bottle and while he did that, Dupuy and I stripped the bed, finding nothing hidden. Then we looked into the closets and the open suitcase. It was filled with women's clothes. 'Did you notice that Jeffries doesn't have anything of his own here,' I said. 'The suitcase Dave's working on was taken from Waites' room. That's Waites' monogram.'

'You're saying that this guy didn't know he was going to be away overnight?' Dupuy asked, pointing a toe at the body.

'Seems that way. And I wonder why? What was he involved with the first day that stopped him going home again?'

'He didn't have to,' Dupuy said. 'He's about the same size as Waites. Maybe that's why he stole the suitcase when he killed the guy. Gave him a whole new wardrobe. Yet the woman had clothes. She was expecting to be away from home for a while, he wasn't. Maybe she knew something he didn't when they left.'

'The woman who was abducted isn't his wife. His wife was killed in that drowned car. This woman is Moira Waites. She was away from home when she left Waites,' I explained. 'Waites told me that she took everything when she left in his car, the one her friend was found dead in.'

'Is this everything she took?' Dupuy asked. 'One suitcase?'

'No, I don't think it is. She's a painter. She would have had cavases, paints, all that stuff, but it's not here.'

'Must be in her car,' he said.

'But there's no car. And the owner of this place says she came on foot.'

'I wonder if she left it up at the Jeffries place?'

'I didn't notice it yesterday but it's worth
254

looking at again. And it's also worth watching the house, see if she heads back there.'

'It's a long shot but I'll get Holland on to that,' Dupuy said, and scratched his head wearily. 'I can't find any pattern at all in this. Three people who know one another, including a husband and wife, all killed, and clues left all over the goddamn province. Waites' golf clubs up near Honey Harbour. Waites' suitcase here. Waites' car used in the first woman's death. And this guy—' he flipped a hand at the corpse—'flitting around out of sight for two days, then turning up dead in a motel with Waites' widow. What's goin' down?'

'I can't work it out. But there's more to it than that, even. The Tracy woman and the Hanson kid are all part of the same daisy chain. She was married to Waites. The actor was working for her, or trying to. She gets beaten up, says Hanson did it. Hanson disappears.'

'Is there something we're missing there?' Dupuy asked. He was tired and out of his depth. Although he had been a cop longer than I and held a good rank, he didn't have the same experience with homicide and was wary about making moves that might look dumb.

I wasn't out to carve him so I said, 'Don't forget Kershaw. Waites was his lawyer. I still figure that Waites sprung him to kill his wife. And on top of that, it's Kershaw's son who ended up in the gang that Hanson put together. This isn't just random. There's a pattern OK, even if we don't see it.'

'I think I'll have Holland go talk to this Tracy woman in hospital. Maybe she can tell us something new.'

'Good idea. You want me to go ahead in here while you call?'

'Yeah, sure.' Dupuy nodded and walked out. I worked on for another five minutes before he came back. 'Caught him at the station, he's going over there now,' he said, then added, 'She couldn't have done this, she's in hospital.'

'No, she didn't do it, Inspector. But she crops up everywhere we look.'

'You're right. We'll finish up here.' Dupuy waved his hand at the half-unpacked suitcase. 'There's not much more and I'll bring the cases with me when I come back to the station.'

We went back to the suitcases, sorting through the woman's case first. It had nothing useful in it, just a variety of simple but colourful clothing that reminded me of Waites' description of his wife's wardrobe. An arty type.

We took everything out and searched all the internal pockets and compartments but there was nothing there. An innocent piece of luggage that had belonged to a woman with nothing to hide. It gave us no clue.

We repacked the case and checked the dresses hanging in the closet. There was nothing in them but the labels from some womens' store in Toronto. I folded them into the suitcase and we searched the body. It proved once and for all that he had killed Waites. In the pockets we found ID in the names of Jeffries along with six hundred and eighty dollars cash and then, in another pocket, all Waites' credit cards. We looked at one another without speaking when we pulled these out. Waites' murder was solved, but I wasn't going to quit looking until I found Moira Waites and knew who had driven Carolyn Jeffries off the rock into the lake.

In the bottom of his right-hand pocket we found the suitcase key and we opened it up. It had an immediate bonus for us, a neat little zippered briefcase inside on top of the clothes. Dupuy took it out and looked at me knowingly. 'Maybe now we'll have something.'

I was anxious to examine it but he played the senior officer, opening it and taking out a manilla folder. He frowned at the cover. 'Street boy,' he read. 'What the hell does that mean?'

'It's likely the name of Ms Tracy's movie.'

He looked at me disbelievingly and

opened the file. I was trying to read over his shoulder and he tilted the paper towards me a fraction to make it easier. I saw that the top sheet was a financial statement of some kind, columns of figures and names.

'Breakdown of projected costs,' Dupuy said. 'Jesus, how much does it cost to make a movie?'

I wanted him to hurry up. Maybe he knew more about figures than I did, most people do, but I was deeper into the case than he was, I would see something important faster than he. But he read it through with painful thoroughness, then passed it to me. I sat on the bed and re-read it. The various cost projections were itemized. Script, lead actors, a million dollars allotted there, no wonder Hanson had been so anxious to get the part, balance of cast, location costs, wardrobe and on and on. Nothing useful. A total cost of 6.3 million.

Then Dupuy handed me the second page. This was a summary of the fund-raising efforts. She had assembled only five million dollars, including a promise from the Canadian Film Development Corporation, which had a question-mark pencilled against it. There was also a pencilled note at the bottom. 'I mill. possible on delivery.'

'What's that mean?' Dupuy asked.

'Beats me. Maybe it's a film term of some kind, or maybe it means she has to deliver something to get the million.' I was baffled, as he was. None of the people or companies listed had any significance to me. 'I'd just say that if she can't find another one million three hundred thousand dollars, the project's off.'

Dupuy had spent his career in small towns but he was not a dull man. 'They raise this kind of money routinely, don't they?'

'My wife's the expert. She says it's always a struggle and Ms Tracy told me she's having problems with the production. That means money, I guess.'

'Still doesn't tell us anything,' he said. 'This is just business, this guy Waites was a lawyer, it figures he would have business stuff with him.'

'What are the other papers?'

He leafed through them. 'Names, presumably of people she plans to hit up for the money. List of actors. Then there's some kind of story, says "treatment" on it.'

He took his time reading through the papers, passing them to me very slowly. None of the names rang a bell. They were mostly individual names, together with their companies which were again simply collections of names, no indication what the companies did, although I could tell from the addresses in Toronto's Bay and King Streets business area that they were all prestigious outfits.

Then he handed me the next sheet, a production summary. It had a listing which began with the director and the technical people and most of these slots had names inked in. Then came the cast and the first inked in name was Eric Hanson.

'This doesn't gibe with what she told me in hospital today,' I said. 'Hanson's name is inked in. She said he wasn't getting the part and that's why he attacked her.'

'She could have changed her mind,' Dupuy said tentatively.

'Sure, she could. But when you figure he's been acting out the part of bad boy in my jurisdiction, you wonder whether he was paying her off for the part.'

'Does that make sense?' Dupuy shook his head. 'Do guys go to that kind of length to get parts in movies?'

'Anything short of killing, if the part's big enough.'

'Well—' he breathed a long sigh—'your wife's the actress, not mine. Maybe you know. Anyway, read this.'

He handed me the last item, the treatment. I read it through quickly. It involved a teenager who got tangled up in a gang, starting with a disaffected group of kids in a high school. They carried out swarmings and a couple of beatings and then graduated to drug sales. The boy started having second thoughts and when he was told to commit a murder he tried to get out. With the gang after him, he hid out in an apartment belonging to a woman in her thirties. She and he have an affair and she straightens him out and he moves in with her.

'Pretty kinky stuff,' Dupuy said.

'It could appeal to women without a guy in their lives.'

'Are there enough of them to make a picture sell?' His small town background was showing now.

'Toronto is down by the head with single women. It's a good idea, they can enjoy watching someone their age end up with a young stud with a heart of gold. I figure this Tracy woman is pretty smart.'

'If she's so smart, how come she hasn't raised the money she needs?'

'Beats the hell out of me,' I admitted. 'But it's routine as far as I know. What interests me more is that the plot kind of matches up with the actor, Eric Hanson, and the way he moved in on Ms Tracy. That much is true to the script.'

'You think he killed this guy?' he flipped his hand at the body that we had been walking around as if it were some piece of furniture.

'My bet is Kershaw, but Hanson is big enough.'

'I'll call Holland and get him to ask Tracy

about all this,' Dupuy said. 'And I'll have them collect the body, then we can finish looking at this stuff and close up until the morning.'

'Right. You want me to go on looking through the case?'

'May's well.' He left with the folder and I crouched by the case and dug deeper into it. It was full of clothes, all of them casual but expensive, but I remembered the cocaine we had found in Waites' room and I shook out each item to make sure it didn't have a package concealed inside it. None of them did and I got to the bottom of the case without finding anything.

I crouched there for a while longer, looking at the case blankly. Nothing useful, except maybe the file on Tracy's movie. And yet I had a feeling that there was more. There had to be. A man had been killed for this case. It had to contain something important. There was only one angle we hadn't checked, and one quick way to find out if I was right.

I went outside and called Sam. He bounded over to me and I fussed him, then calmed him and led him into the room. He looked over at the body but gave no reaction and I played the last card I had. I've trained him to be a one-man police department. Even though I don't get many drug cases I worked with the OPP dog trainer on developing his nose for drugs. Normally he doesn't react to anything he's not told to, but now I gave him his cue.

'It has to be a good solid hint,' the trainer had advised me. 'Like, normally we put a different collar on a dog when he's sniffing drugs, that alerts him. But you can do it with a command word. But make it unusual. Don't say anything ordinary.' So I held up one finger to Sam and used the code word, a memory of my own past. 'Mei Kong.'

He stiffened and turned away, searching. He sniffed the body on the floor, then left it and turned his attention to the pile of clothing, beginning to growl low in his throat. Finally he reached the suitcase and began to bark, furious now, scratching at the bottom of the case with his front feet as if he were trying to dig a hole through it.

Behind me I heard the door open and I turned to see Dupuy in the doorway. 'What the hell's going on here?' he shouted angrily.

'A new twist,' I told him. 'My dog has just shown me there's a stash of drugs hidden in this suitcase.'

CHAPTER FOURTEEN

I told Sam 'Easy' and bent down to rub his head and let him know I was proud of him. It

263

had been months since I'd tested his drug-sniffing skills, but he had performed as if he did it every day and given us something new to go on.

Dupuy was unconvinced. 'You sure about this?' He was examining the case. 'This thing looks perfectly normal.'

'Must be a hidden compartment,' I told him. 'It needs examining by the drug squad.'

He picked the case up and shook it, holding it up by his ear, an instinctive, useless test. 'Doesn't look like it,' he said again. I took out my pocket knife and probed the bottom of the case. It was lined with a paisley cloth and the surface underneath was firm, aluminium probably. 'Want me to cut it?'

'Why not? The owner won't complain.'

I put the case on the floor and pressed on the tip of the knife blade. It gave, easing through the thin metal. I started sawing back on it, cutting a slit on the inside of the lid. White powder leaked through the crack. 'Here it is.' I showed him and he shook his head in disbelief.

'How in hell did they pack that thing? It looks like it went in there when the case was made.'

'Maybe it did. I don't know. But it's there. What do you want to do now?'

'I figure we wrap up here and I'll take this back to the station'.

264

'We should watch this place tonight,' I said. 'The guy who killed Jeffries may come back to get this.'

'I know,' Dupuy said impatiently. 'I'm going to leave a man here. Can you hold on until he arrives?'

'Sure. Soon's the body's gone I'll lock up, turn out the lights and sit out of sight somewhere, watching.'

Dupuy bent over the case. 'The guy who was chased off must have known this was full of dope.'

'Which means he must have been tight with Waites.'

'Maybe your idea is good after all,' Dupuy said carefully. 'Maybe Waites' wife knew about the dope as well and was going to blow the whistle.'

'That's a solid motive for killing her.'

'Maybe.' We looked at one another, thinking hard. He was beginning to see the case the way I did. Like me, he felt flooded with useless information. We had everything except answers.

I thought for a moment. 'Sergeant Holland should be told about this now, while he's having a talk with the Tracy woman.'

'I guess I'll go see if he's there yet,' Dupuy said. 'The meat wagon's on its way. Can you stay here till then?'

'No problem. Then I'll wait for your man to arrive. Tell him to flick his lights twice so

265

I'll know it's him.'

'I will. And thanks.' He left Waites' clothes piled where I had folded them and took the suitcase with him, closing it carefully first. 'Talk to my guy before you leave.'

'Right.'

He walked out and I sat on the edge of the bed, stroking Sam's head absently. There were so many connections staring us in the face. But how did they fit? This latest angle, for instance, the drugs. Dupuy was right, the way the case was filled made it very professional. But who was behind it? The suitcase belonged to Waites. Had he known about the drugs? Or had they been put in there before he bought it? And when had he bought it? And why was it with him in Murphy's Harbour? And why had Jeffries taken it when he killed Waites? Had he taken it just for the clothes it contained, or had he known it was packed with dope? And where had Waites been taking it in the first place?

I thought about that aspect for a while. We're further from Montreal than from Toronto, so he couldn't have been intending to ship it there. On the other hand, we're closer to Sault Ste Marie where there's a crossing into the States. Perhaps Waites had intended to send it over the border there. But why hadn't he done so already? He'd been in Murphy's Harbour almost a week.

And that was when I had another idea, the reciprocal course. Maybe he had arrived here with a clean suitcase and someone had filled it for him. Maybe he had to sell it in Toronto. Maybe the stash in his golf shoes had been some kind of advance payment for his involvement.

That raised the question of who his supplier had been. He was tight with Ms Tracy. But if she were the source, surely her contacts would have been in Toronto. That was where she spent ninety-nine per cent of her time.

I was roused by the sound of a vehicle outside and then a tap on the door. I called, 'Come in,' and the door opened to admit a couple of ambulance men. 'We're here for the body,' one of them said. He was young and elaborately casual, his hair cut bowl fashion, long on top, almost shaved at the sides, out of character with the formality of his uniform.

'He's here.' I pointed and they brought in their stretcher and stood looking down at the dead man. 'Well, thank God he ain't heavy,' the other one said. He was older, with the red face and explosive skin of a heavy drinker. 'Last call we got was this heavy old broad up three flights of stairs. Goddamn near killed me getting her down.'

'You're lucky this time,' I told him. 'Try not to scuff up the chalk mark.'

'No problem,' the young one said. He wrinkled his nose. 'Jeez. How can you guys work in a stink like this?' I said nothing and they rolled the body on to the stretcher and left, joking back and forth to show what hard nuts they were.

I switched off the light and left the room, driving my car around the back of the unit, out of sight of the road, then took Sam and went out to the front of the unit, close to the entrance. I made myself comfortable with Sam beside me, waiting. No cars passed. At this time of night the side-road was used only by the locals and they were in bed. At last a car approached, from the direction of the highway. As he pulled in he flicked his lights and he pulled in at a vacant spot down the front of the unit.

The driver turned and wound his window down as I approached. There was enough starlight for me to see that he looked young. A uniformed man, I guessed, press-ganged into plainclothes stakeout work in his own car. He spoke first. 'How're you tonight?' the tough-guy mask of a green copper.

'Good. You? You know what's on?'

'Yeah. The inspector briefed me.'

'Good. We want this guy, if he comes back.'

He looked at me contemptuously, without speaking. Who the hell was I to tell him anything? He was chewing gum, I noticed, and I hoped he could handle the job. The man we wanted might come back on foot and if this guy got bored and turned on his radio Kershaw or whoever it was would be spooked.

I asked him to call his office and let them know I'd left, then collected the car and drove back up to the harbour. It was after midnight but there were still cars parked in front of both drinking spots so I looked into both places. The crowd had thinned in each of them but there was no sign of Kershaw or Hanson. I checked all my properties one last time and waited in the car for half an hour, until the bars both closed and the last customers drove out then took one last trip to the station to check for messages.

There were a couple of Faxes and about a yard of entries on the teletype which I read first. Nothing new. More details of the case, the descriptions of Kershaw and Moira Waites and Hanson and the make and number of Ms Tracy's Mercedes, all issued by the Parry Sound dispatcher.

I went over to the phone to check the Fax machine and while I picked up the messages I pressed the preprogrammed button to get the OPP. The desk man told me that Sergeant Holland was talking to the inspector and put me through. I glanced at the Fax messages as I waited. The top one was a circular, inviting me to save big bucks on a new Chevrolet. I crumpled it up as Dupuy answered.

'Bennett?'

'Right, Inspector. I wondered what Bill learned from Tracy.'

'Nothing,' he said. 'Let me put him on.' There was a rustle as the phone changed hands, the distant burble of voices in the room and then Holland said, 'She'd gone, Reid. Signed herself out.'

'Dressed in what? She was naked when we brought her in.'

'She called the Salvation Army. They brought her in some clothes.' Holland was thinking now. He obviously hadn't analysed the details before this.

'Where did she go? She didn't have either money or a car.'

'The Sally Ann captain gave her a few bucks. She took a cab from the hospital. We're following up on it now but she's gone like a wild goose in winter.'

'There's a bus for Toronto at midnight. Gets to the highway here around quarter to one. I guess you checked that. Other than that she must have taken a room someplace.'

'We're checking but we've only got one man on patrol, the other guys are on the road block.'

'Did the doctor have anything to say about her condition?'

'Just one thing. Apparently you'd asked

270

him to take a blood test for drugs. He didn't find anything.'

'Did he say she was faking the coma?'

'Wouldn't commit himself on that one.' Holland humphed tiredly. 'Gave me the usual medical double-talk, that the degree of loss of consciousness did not tally with his experience of her kind of injuries. Nothing we could take to court.'

'You need me to come up and help? I'll check her house first.'

There was a muffled consultation and then Holland said, 'No. The inspector says we all need a break. She's not a suspect. I was just going to talk to her for background. He says the hell with it, we'll chase her up tomorrow.'

'Suits me, it's been a long day. I'll take a ride by her house on my way home, though.' I realized how tired I was, finding to my surprise that I had sat down without thinking about it and was leafing through the other Fax sheets as I talked, hardly seeing what I was reading.

Holland made some answer but a word in the next Fax sheet caught my eye and I missed his comment. The word was 'Kershaw'. I said, 'Hold on a second, there's a Fax here might help.'

I read it quickly. It was from my sister's house. She had installed a machine so she could work at home sometimes when the

271

kids were off-school. The message was from Elmer Svensen.

Reid. Talked to Chuck about Kershaw. He says K. was running an investment brokerage, small stuff. He thinks K. had dipped into the money, $2–3 hundred thou. His bet went sour and he tried the bank caper. Seems there was a shipment of negotiables coming in that day and he knew about it. Not a standard robbery. Also, Chuck says the investment that failed was a movie. Does this help? There was no charge laid on the scam, his wife made the losses good.

'Listen to this,' I told Holland. 'The circle keeps on getting smaller and smaller.' I read him the Fax and waited.

He said, 'Yeah. Could tie in, I guess, if it was Tracy's movie.' He didn't sound enthusiastic and I knew why when he went on. 'Alla this stuff's older'n hell. I don't see how it helps to know what happened six, seven years back. We got three warm corpses to worry about. We've got reporters up the yin-yang here. Everyone's wantin' to know when we're gonna make an arrest and we keep comin' up with stale stuff.'

I took a moment to get my excitement down to his speed. He didn't see the connections the way I did. It all seemed academic to him with media people chasing him for action. By the morning the media would be down here, bugging me when they realized that the OPP didn't have any sexy

272

answers. Then I might feel like he did.

'It ties in,' I said slowly. 'From where I sit, and I'm sitting because I'm just as pooped as the rest of you, we've got some kind of reunion of rounders. First one of them we can get hold of, including the Tracy woman, and this thing's gonna come to pieces in our hand. You'll be promoted, Dupuy will get to be Prime Minister and I'll get my week's pay.'

He knew I was right but his agreement was feeble. 'I know, Reid, but we got three people, four if you count this Kershaw guy, all of them can untie this thing for us and one or other of 'em's gonna turn up soon. I say we call it a night.'

I could imagine Dupuy sitting across from him, nodding agreement. An arrest would profit them. They belonged to an organization with room to move ahead. But they were weary.

'OK. It's a night,' I said.

'Yeah. Good idea. Get back at it first thing. Meantime we'll check all the motels, see if they've got the Tracy woman staying there. Shouldn't be hard to track her down if she's in town.'

Not if she was dumb enough to take a motel, I thought, but she wasn't. Either she would rendezvous with somebody and drive away or else she would check in at some guest house run by a widow who would have

273

the lights out by now and wouldn't be checked.

'I'll look in on her house on my way home,' I said. 'Talk to you tomorrow.'

'Right, thanks. Oh, and the inspector says, can you send us a copy of the Fax, together with the source.'

'Will do, but don't call them, he's a cop too, working on a homicide in Toronto. He needs his sleep as well. Besides, he's my brother-in-law.'

'Small world,' Holland said and hung up.

I sent them the message, along with Elmer's name and rank in the Metro department, then closed up the station and drove back to Main Street, over the bridge and up the side of the lake to Ms Tracy's house. It was in darkness and there was no car outside but I was wary and drove by without slowing and stopped around the next bend in the road. Then I took Sam and walked back down there and checked the house. The padlock was in place in front and the back door was shut and didn't look as if it had been forced. I'd bolted it when I closed the house up and had not yet given Ms Tracy the key. She was still away.

I stood there and thought for a while, wondering what to do next. I hadn't thought to ask Holland the time she had checked out. Maybe she was still on her way down here. Maybe. And in the meantime I had nothing

274

to do but sleep till morning.

That decided me. I've slept out a lot. Camping with my family as a kid, and most of the nights I spent in Vietnam. And I had Sam with me, he'd wake me if anyone showed. I would rest here. I moved out into the bush beside the house, close to the road, took off my cap and stretched out on the dry duff of needles and debris from the pine trees overhead. Sam settled beside me and I lay there and relaxed in the warm night, glad that the mosquitoes had given up, as they do after midnight. Pretty soon I was asleep.

Sam woke me, stirring slightly, and I opened my eyes and sat up, wide awake, the way you are in the boonies when the guy on watch nudges you. A car was coming up the road towards us. I checked my watch, it was three-eighteen.

I crouched up as it pulled into Ms Tracy's driveway.

Someone got out of the passenger side. Her car! And she was not alone! I had them!

I pulled my gun and stepped out on the driveway with Sam beside me. I was thirty yards from the car and edging closer when I heard Ms Tracy swear. 'There's a goddamn padlock on here. Help me.'

I stopped as the driver got out of the car. There were two other people inside I saw, and then, outlined against the glare of the headlights I saw that the man was carrying a long gun. 'Police. Drop the gun,' I shouted.

He whirled towards me, levelling the gun and I fired twice and dived sideways into the trees as the orange muzzle flash from the shotgun bloomed towards me, round and bright as the sun.

Shot crashed into the branches over my head and I heard Ms Tracy scream. Then the car roared back towards me and past, the driver's door open with the driver craning up over the roof. He fired again, too high and I fired back, emptying my pistol at the tyres, but he wheeled back and slammed the door as he raced off up the side-road, back towards the highway.

I shouted 'Fight' at Sam and he bounded to the step where Ms Tracy was still screaming, his barking blending with her voice.

'Guard,' I shouted and he fell silent, crouching in front of her, baring his teeth as I sprinted for the scout car.

I was almost a minute behind them but I roared after them, staying in second gear, siren blaring, hoping one of my good citizens would hear and phone the OPP. There was no sign of the car ahead but I drove flat out, pushing the car to the limit of my skill. Back I raced, to the north side of the bridge opposite Main Street, alone in the darkness. And then, far ahead at the edge of the highway, I caught the flash of their headlights in the trees as they slowed there before turning north. I followed, driving one-handed now, frantically adjusting the wavelength on my radio to the OPP frequency. It was hard at the limit of the car's speed, watching for oncoming traffic, trying to catch a smaller, faster car screaming down the middle of the road, but at last I got close and bellowed into the microphone.

'Bennett, proceeding north from Murphy's Harbour. Hot pursuit of a blue Mercedes. Shots fired. Do you read?'

There was a squawk, broken up. I was far enough off frequency to be unreadable, I guessed, and gave the knob a tiny flick. I repeated my message three times, flicking the frequency each way, bracketing the OPP wavelength the best I could. Then I came over a hill to look down at a mile-long slope on the highway ahead and saw no car. I'd lost them.

I kept on, adjusting the set again until finally the OPP man answered. 'Bennett, location please? Location, over.'

'Seven kilometres north of the Harbour. No sign of the car ahead. Car may have pulled off into Honey Harbour or along side-road 513. Have my dog holding Ms Tracy at her house. Send a PW down for the interrogation. Will proceed as far as Wildhaven Lodge and then return to the Harbour.'

'Roger, hold, Bennett,' the dispatcher said anxiously. 'Here's the inspector.'

It was Dupuy. I briefed him in two sentences and he told me to return and hold Tracy at her house. A policewoman would join me in twenty minutes.

So I killed the siren and turned back, taking time now to check a few hundred yards into the Honey Harbour exit from the highway, finding it as peaceful as my own community was, on good nights. No Mercedes. Then I sped back to the Tracy house.

She was standing on the porch, motionless, Sam in front of her. I shone my flashlight over her and saw the terror in her eyes. I told Sam, 'Easy boy. Good boy,' and made a fuss of him before telling her, 'Sit down, Ms Tracy. I have a policewoman coming and then we'll take you to the station. You're under arrest.'

I hadn't worked out what the charges would be and she didn't cut me any slack. 'What for, for God's sake? I get a ride home from Parry Sound with some people and you come out of the bushes shooting at them. What's going on? Tell me that.'

'Who were they?'

'I never saw them before.' Her voice was clear and confident. She was going to lie. I gritted my teeth and hoped the OPP would trace the other car. She was only a minor part of the mystery. She hadn't done any of the killings and it was the killers I wanted.

'Make yourself comfortable. We have about ten minutes to wait,' I said.

'I need to use the bathroom, you bastard.'

'Ten minutes,' I repeated.

'I can't wait that long. I was terrorized by your goddamn dog.'

'Then step down into the side somewhere. He'll come with you. I'll wait here.'

She swore angrily and sat down, her back against the door with its padlock still in place. I ignored her, reloading my revolver and glancing around. There were maybe half a dozen places within a couple of hundred yards each way but there were no lights showing. People were asleep or didn't want to get involved, which was good.

'Who was in the car with you?' I asked.

'How would I know?' she said angrily. 'I got out of the hospital and as I was walking down the street in Parry Sound they gave me a lift.'

It was too early to lean on her. I needed a woman there to remove any chance of her claiming I'd molested her. Tough as she was, she would do it automatically to discredit me and any evidence I got from her. But maybe I could trap her into something. 'How many people were in the car?'

She thought that was innocent. 'Three. Besides me.'

'Two men and a woman?' That had been my reading, although I hadn't had time to concentrate on the others once I saw the driver had a gun.

'They didn't talk, I don't know.'

'You're lying,' I said. 'That was your own car.'

She didn't answer for a moment, then sneered. 'I thought it seemed familiar. Small world, isn't it?'

'Either you help us or you're going to be in jail for aiding and abetting an escaped prisoner in the commission of a murder,' I told her. 'Now you sit there and think about that for a few minutes until my partner arrives.'

'I've got nothing to say, now or later. This is all ridiculous,' she said but there was fear in her voice. I said nothing, just stood and waited for ten long minutes until I heard a car coming.

It was an OPP cruiser and Elaine Harper got out and walked up to us. I did everything formally. 'Officer Harper, this is Ms Tracy. She is under arrest for aiding and abetting an escaped prisoner in the commission of a homicide.'

'Sounds like you're in a whole lot of trouble, ma'am,' Elaine said cheerfully. 'Where d'you want to do this, Chief, here or at your office?'

'At the station, please. Will you take Ms

Tracy in your car?' Thank the Lord they're allowing women into the OPP. There would be no chance for our prisoner to allege misconduct.

'Fine. Come with me, please.' Elaine made an 'up' gesture with her finger and Ms Tracy stood slowly. 'Do you have any cigarettes?' she asked.

'Don't use 'em,' Elaine said.

'Then may I open my house and get some?'

'What do you think, Chief?' Elaine turned to me.

'If we go in there I'm going to conduct a search for drugs,' I said. 'Do you still want to open your house, ma'am?'

'Where's your warrant?' Ms Tracy demanded. Her voice was strong but it had a nervous tremor.

'I'm going to apply for one as soon as we reach the station. It will be issued while you're in the cells. This way I save time. What would save more time is for you to admit that you have drugs in there, if you do, and I won't have to turn my dog loose.'

In the starlight I could see the policewoman looking at me strangely. She hadn't heard about what the suitcase contained. She thought this was a fishing trip.

Ms Tracy said nothing for about half a minute. Then as Elaine reached out to bring her along she spoke. 'The hell with it, I need a smoke. Do you have the key for this padlock?'

I undid the padlock and she produced the front door key. 'Where did that come from? You had nothing with you when you left here?'

'It was under the mat,' she said angrily. 'Even with your dog after me I picked it up.'

Not an honest answer, but credible. We followed her through the verandah and she unlocked the inner door with the same key. 'I have to use the bathroom,' she said, switching on the light.

'I'll have to come with you,' Elaine said. I watched the tension between them. Elaine was smaller, only around five-six and slight, with the bulk of her gun incongruous on her slim waist. Ms Tracy was taller and older and her contempt was enormous.

'Afraid I'll hurt myself?' she sneered.

'Maybe. Or flush your dope down the john,' Elaine said. 'Let's go.'

They went into the bathroom and I looked around, wondering where drugs would be hidden if she had any. There were a thousand hiding-places but I knew Sam would find anything so I relaxed and waited.

When they came out again I asked Tracy, 'Do you have any drugs here, ma'am?'

'It's not ma'am. It's Ms,' she hissed. 'And no. I don't have any goddamn drugs. But I

282

have friends who use this place from time to time. Maybe one of them has put something somewhere that I don't know about.'

I smiled. 'There. Now you're golden. I'll get my dog to check.' I bent to fondle Sam, holding his head between both hands to get his attention. Then I told him Mei Kong and stood up.

The women watched, fascinated, as he stiffened and turned his head slowly, sniffing the air. Then he sniffed the couch and one of the chairs, growling softly. Someone had used dope in this room, sitting there. And at last he went over to the bookcase and sniffed up high, then stood on his back legs to claw at a shelf of books about four feet off the ground.

'Easy,' I told him and lifted the books down. There was nothing behind them but his head sank to one of the books and he barked again, scratching at its cover with one foot. I picked it up. It was old, red leather bound. *Supreme Court of Ontario Decisions 1899.* I read and opened it up. The centre of the pages had been hollowed out and there was a plastic bag of white powder inside.

'Is this your book?' I held it up to Ms Tracy.

'That belongs to John Waites. He left it here. Said he might have to consult it occasionally,' she said. 'Happy now?'

'Happier,' I admitted. 'Take your

cigarettes and let's go.'

Elaine took her arm and we left, me carrying the book with its white cargo. It might prove something, I thought. She would get off a charge of possession by blaming Waites, but if the chemists could prove it was identical to the contents of his suitcase we might be able to find out more about its source. And the find put more pressure on her. Now, she might volunteer some help.

I watched Elaine put her in the cage of the patrol car and then whistled Sam and checked the driveway where the man with the shotgun had been standing. I couldn't see any evidence that I'd hit him but I found his shotgun shell, and then, lower down the driveway, where he had fired as he backed out, I found two more. I picked them up on the end of my fingers and put them into the windshield of the cruiser. Once we found the gun I could have ballistics check the cases and see if they matched. Then I'd have attempted murder to add to the charges. Good additional material if it got down to a plea bargaining situation.

Wearily now I drove around and over the bridge to the police station. All I could think of was that I should have shot out the back tyre before I challenged the gunman. That way I would have stopped the car. Dammit, Bennett, you're getting slow, I told myself.

Elaine was waiting at the station and when I unlocked the back door she got Ms Tracy out and led her inside. We booked her formally, Elaine charging her and reading her rights. Then I stepped out into my office while Elaine searched her. She opened the door a couple of minutes later. 'She's clean. Nothing but some cash and her cigarettes.'

'OK. Let's call the inspector, see if he can join us and we'll talk to her,' I said. 'And I'll put some coffee on. I can hardly stay awake.'

'Getting old.' She grinned. 'Let's put her in a cell and do it.'

We went back out to the cells and Elaine ushered Ms Tracy into the cell farthest from the door, the most isolated and therefore the most frightening. She said nothing and we left her there and came out to the telephone. Elaine phoned Parry Sound and the dispatcher told us that Inspector Dupuy was out, supervising the search for the Mercedes. He would try to raise him on the radio.

Elaine took over the coffee-making chores, laughing that she had tasted my coffee and wasn't going to set me loose with a pot ever again. It took a while to perc and we had some and offered a cup to Ms Tracy. 'Ready to talk yet?' Elaine asked.

'I want a lawyer,' she said. 'I get a phone call, don't I?'

'Sure. You said "no" earlier. Have you changed your mind?' They might have been

285

college buddies, kidding, from Elaine's tone, no threat, no tension.

'I want to call,' Ms Tracy said and Elaine led her through to the office. I went with them and watched as Ms Tracy dialled, wondering how many people around know their lawyer's phone number without looking it up. She waited for about ten seconds, then said, 'This is Marcia Tracy. I've been arrested at Murphy's Harbour. It's now—' she glanced up at the clock—'four-fifty, Saturday morning. Can you help?'

She hung up and we led her back to her cell where she sat on the wooden board bunk and sipped her coffee. 'You haven't got long to plea bargain,' Elaine said quietly. 'Did you think of that? We're going to find that car, come daylight. And when we do, your help won't be worth spit. Act now and we might be able to bargain with the Crown Attorney.'

Ms Tracy set down her coffee cup and lit a cigarette from the little pile beside her. 'This has been the worst day of my life. I've been raped, beaten up, knocked unconscious, terrorized by a slavering dog and arrested. What can I say?'

'You lied about the rape,' I said. 'We found Waites' suitcase. It contained some interesting things, including your production file.'

'What's that got to do with my being

286

raped?' She flung the question at me furiously.

'You told me this morning that Hanson did it when you turned him down for the part in your movie. But you've got him inked in.'

She looked at me grimly, holding a mouthful of smoke for a long time, then releasing it as she spoke. 'I was confused when you talked to me. You have to remember, I'd been knocked out. I didn't know what I was saying.'

'But now you're clear-headed. And here's a clear proposition for you. I will do my level best to have all the charges against you so far—' I held up my hand—'all the charges that have been read to you, dismissed, if you tell us who was in the car with you and where they were going.'

She looked at me for a long time. The she stubbed her smoke on the bowl of the toilet and tossed the butt into the water. 'You heard what he said.' She pointed at Elaine who nodded, not speaking.

Now she dusted her knees, looking down primly as if she were wearing a long skirt. 'Very well. They were going to snatch the kid and hold him to ransom.'

I knew who she meant but Elaine blurted, 'Which kid?'

Ms Tracy looked at her levelly. 'Phillip Freund,' she said.

287

CHAPTER FIFTEEN

I ran to the phone and dialled George Horn's number. It rang three times and Jean Horn answered. 'Hello?' She sounded alert. Good, she was already up.

'Reid Bennett, Jean. I've heard that some guys are coming to grab young Phil. Is he there?'

'Still in bed. I was just getting up.'

'Is Peter there?'

'No. George and him went fishing.'

'You have a shotgun?'

'Sure. You know that.'

'Load it. I'll be there as soon as I can, ten minutes. If you see a blue Mercedes pull up, poke the gun out of the window and fire over their heads. Don't go out, they're armed.'

'Jesus Christ,' she said, startling me. She's a good Catholic.

'Be right there.' I whistled Sam and unlocked the chain on the firearms, grabbing the Remington pump shotgun and a box of double-O buckshot and ran out.

Sam sat beside me and I raced back through town to the bridge, and up the side-road past Ms Tracy's house. The Reserve has an unmade road of its own, leading from their little private marina. I put the siren on and flew along it, juddering over the washboard surface, slipping on the corners as I jammed on every bit of speed the road would handle.

I saw no cars and there was no telltale cloud of dust in the air ahead of me, that much was good but I didn't slacken speed until I reached the Horns' house and cut the siren.

Jean came to the door. She seemed calm but her voice was a little higher pitched than usual. 'You sure about this, Reid?'

'We have a woman in custody. She told us.'

'Come in.' She stood aside and I came in. She had an old pump shotgun behind the door. I picked it up and unloaded it, working the mechanism four times, ejecting three shells and then nothing.

'You won't need this now.'

'Well, that's good,' she said easily. 'I leave the hunting to Peter. Want some coffee?'

I had an idea and I put it to her. 'Where could I hide the scout car?'

'Jim Buck's garage is empty. You could put it there.' She looked at me. 'You planning on staking us out here?'

'Yes. The OPP are in charge of the case. I've got an officer at the station and more are on the way.'

She gave a faint grin. 'So you're gonna lie in the weeds like a big old muskie waiting for a pickerel.'

'Makes sense,' I said. 'Call Jim, tell him I want to use his garage for a couple of hours. Could you do that?'

'He's out with the guys,' she said. 'Jus' do it.'

'Right. I'll be right back.'

I went out again into the first tinge of daylight and drove the extra hundred yards to the Buck house. Jim is a widower and lives alone. The place is run down but he has an old clapboard garage that houses his snowmobile. There was room alongside to squeeze the scout car in. I did it and shut the door, then took Sam and the shotgun and shells and walked back to Horns'.

Phil Freund was up and washed. He looked a little sleepy yet but was glad to see me. 'Hi, Chief. Mrs Horn says you're staying here a while.'

'Yes. We got word that a couple of guys were looking for you. I'd like to talk to them.'

'Talk?' He smiled crookedly. 'Never thought you'd need a shotgun to talk to someone.'

'One of the guys is on the lam from jail,' I explained. 'He may not want to listen.'

He was holding the puppy which was squirming in his arms, trying to get down and play with Sam. 'Easy, munchkin,' he said and tried to stroke it.

'I'll set Sam outside the back door,' I said.

290

Nobody would see him there from the road and I was certain that if they came it would be by car.

'Shall I take Blue outside, Mrs Horn?' he asked. 'He didn't wet in the night, he needs to go.'

'I'll take him,' she said. 'It's best if you stay in until this is sorted out.'

'Can I use your phone, please, Jean?' I asked and she nodded.

'Help yourself.'

She took her dog outside and I set Sam on the back step and then phoned the OPP. The dispatcher told me that all hell had broken loose. The helicopter was taking off at first light to search for the Mercedes, the inspector and every available officer in the area were down in my vicinity looking for the car, and a special team of investigators, with a superintendent no less, were heading up from headquarters in Toronto to talk to Ms Tracy.

I filled him in on my plans and gave him the Horns' phone number, then hung up. Jean was back in, putting a skillet on the stove.

'Pancakes and bacon,' she said. 'How's that sound?'

'Not for me, thanks, Jean. I'm going to hole up across the road where they won't look.'

'Take this with you,' she said firmly and

gave me a cup of coffee, adding, 'You don't eat right.'

'Later,' I said. 'Thank you. When Phil's had his breakfast, let him work outside. Phil. I want you to hang loose, try and stay in front of the house where I can see you. Nothing's going to happen but I want them to see you if they show up.'

He laughed nervously. 'Hey, no problem.'

I gave him a wink, then took my coffee to oblige Jean, and crossed the road quickly. I found a rock to sit on, behind a birch tree. When I was installed I whistled Sam and he ran across after me and lay down at my side as I sipped the coffee, nursing the loaded shotgun in my right hand.

Morning came, grey first, then bright, burning off the dew and waking up a few late mosquitoes who buzzed around me hopefully. I hadn't thought to bring fly dope so I amused myself by keeping count of those I killed before they bit me. The score was mosquitoes seventeen, Bennett thirty-two by the time a car came down the road, moving slowly.

Phil Freund was in the front of the Horn house, repainting a window-sill. He looked up when the car passed but went on painting. A cool kid, I thought. He was going to be all right.

The car wasn't a Mercedes but I wasn't really expecting one any more. They would know it was hot and would have stolen something fresh, probably from a marina in Honey Harbour, knowing the owner would be away and not report it missing for a couple of days at least. This one was a Chev, old enough that it didn't have an automatic lock on the steering. They had chosen well.

I watched as they tooled by. The sun was low and behind them so I couldn't see faces, but I picked out two people, both in front. They cruised on up the road a couple of hundred yards, then turned in a driveway and came back, on the same side as the Horn house.

They stopped and got out, both of them. The driver was short and trim, the passenger taller. Neither one looked heavy enough to be Kershaw but I couldn't have told anyway. They were wearing stockings over their faces.

They went through the gate and over to Phillip. He came down from the stepladder in a rush when he saw them but they grabbed him, the smaller one putting a hand over his mouth to muffle his yell. The puppy was yapping under their feet and the small one kicked it aside, sending it yelping for the door.

I let them reach the gate and come through on to the road, then stepped out, pointing the shotgun. 'You two. Down on your faces.'

They let him go and split, one going each

way. I paused a moment to point at the big one and yell, 'Track' and Sam bounded after him. Then I took off after the small one. He was thirty yards ahead, making for a bare rock on the side of the road. From there he could break in any direction into the bushes. I shouted 'Halt,' then fired the shotgun, high over his head.

He took a couple more steps, then ran down like a broken toy and turned back, hands high. 'Don't shoot,' he screamed.

I trotted up to him and cuffed his hands behind his back, then called Phillip. 'Come and hold this one, Phil.'

He came forward nervously and I jogged down the road the other way to Sam who was standing over the second guy, snarling into his face.

'On your feet and take that mask off.' I kept the gun pointed at his legs, looking businesslike.

'Don't shoot. I can explain,' he said and I recognized the voice, even before he pulled the stocking from his head and his features sprang back into their usual shape. It was Hanson.

'Hands on your head, walk back to your buddy.' I waved the gun muzzle and he came, moving as carefully as if he thought the road was mined.

Phil Freund was walking back, one hand on the other prisoner's arm. 'I know him. It's

Cy,' he said excitedly. 'Why were they trying to grab me?'

'That's what I'm about to find out.' I took a moment to peel the stocking back from the prisoner's face and recognized him as one of the gang members I had seen in the first encounter. 'You're in a mess of trouble,' I told him, unlocking his left handcuff. I snapped it on to Hanson's right wrist, right hand to right so that they couldn't run freely. 'Stay here,' I said, and told Sam, 'Guard.'

He sank low in front of them, baring his teeth, and I went to Buck's garage and drove the scout car back to the prisoners. I put them both in the cage and told Sam 'Easy'. 'I'd like you to come with me, Phil. I'll just tell Jean what's going on.'

She was already at the gate and she waited for me to come up. 'Nice work,' she said. 'They never knew you were there.'

'I've been taking Indian lessons from George.'

She laughed. 'You get good marks.'

'Listen, I'm going to take Phillip with me. The OPP detectives will want to talk to him and I'd like to have him at the station anyway, keep him on ice until this is wrapped up. I'll bring him back later to finish up.'

'No problem,' she said. 'He's about done anyway. I'll clean the brush.'

I nodded to her and left, calling Sam to sit

next to me, with Phil the other side of him. The boy was quiet, embarrassed, I guessed, at seeing what kind of guys he'd been associating with.

'It's just about over,' I told him. He looked at me, full of questions but I just winked. I didn't want to tip my hand to the guys in the back.

There were three more cars at the station, but they were unmarked. If they were police cars, I didn't recognize them. I let my prisoners out and led them to the back door. As I put the key in the lock the door was opened from inside by an OPP detective I knew, Walker, all the way from Toronto head office.

'Hi, Reid. Looks like you struck oil.'

'Yeah. Now we've only got two unaccounted for, Kershaw and Moira Waites.'

'Well, bring these guys in to join the party,' Walker said. 'Ms Tracy's lawyer just showed.'

'What's he saying to her?'

'It's a woman,' Walker said.

He stood back so I could bring the prisoners in. They were silent, frightened. Phillip followed them and as I stepped up through the door I heard him say, 'Mom!'

His mother was sitting at the desk in front of the cells, writing in a notebook. When she saw him she sprang up and hugged him, tears running down her cheeks. 'Darling. They wouldn't let me come and get you.'

'I'm OK, honest.' He was close to tears but gruff with teenage machismo. 'The Chief caught the pair of them.'

She let go of him, staring at the prisoners. Then she sprang like a tiger, slapping at them furiously. 'You rotten little bastards!' she screamed.

Walker grabbed at her and Elaine the policewoman took her hands. 'Take it easy, ma'am. They're in custody. Your son's OK.'

Ms Freund went on shouting but I was watching the prisoners. Hanson handled it better. He looked at the floor, not blinking. I could see tears starting down his cheeks. An actor to the end. The other kid was angrier. 'Keep her off. We didn't do anything.'

'You tried to kidnap this boy,' Walker said. 'I'm going to read you the charge and tell you all the wonderful things you can do to get off them, then you can talk all you want.'

'I want a lawyer,' Cy shouted. 'I'm not saying a thing until I see a lawyer.'

'Not me.' Ms Freund was composing herself. 'I'm removing myself from this case. You find somebody else.' She turned and shouted back at the rear cell, where I could see Ms Tracy's hands through the bars. 'You too, Marcia Tracy. You're on your own.'

I spoke to Hanson. 'One question,' I said.

'Where's Kershaw and the woman? Answer that and I'll do whatever I can for you.'

'Thank you, Chief,' Hanson said. 'I don't need a caution. I'll tell you everything I know.'

'Where are they?'

'We left them at the cottage in Honey Harbour,' he said. 'I'll take you there.'

'Fine. We'll go in your car. Elaine, can you come with me to pick it up?'

She was about to answer when the door to my office opened and the superintendent walked through. 'Pick what up?' he asked.

I knew him, a stickler for the book but a good copper. 'The kidnap car. This prisoner is going to take me to where the other two are staying. I want to go in his car.'

'Is that necessary? Why don't we head over there in force and take them? Are they armed?'

'Yes. Kershaw's got a shotgun and he's not afraid to use it.'

'OK. You and Walker go with the witness and take the car. We'll have back-up two hundred yards behind you.'

'Good.' I unlocked the cuff from Cy and snapped it over Hanson's other wrist. 'Let's move.'

Walker came with me, checking the load on his gun as we walked out to my scout car. I took the shotgun out of it and called Sam and we drove Walker's unmarked police car over to the Reserve and collected the Chev. I stuck Hanson in the passenger seat and Walker and Sam took the rear. By the time we got back to the bridge the other police car was waiting for us and we headed out up the highway to Honey Harbour.

'It's in about two hundred yards,' Hanson said. 'We rented it this morning.'

'That was dumb,' I told him. 'Why didn't you just run when you got a new car?'

'Kershaw wanted to pick up the boy. He said his ex-wife had money. He said she'd pay to get the kid back.'

'How come you got sucked into a dumb plan like that?'

'I had no choice,' he said carefully. 'They had enough on me that I couldn't get out.'

'That doesn't wash, Eric. He had no clout. And he was the guy who loaded you up with angel dust, right?'

'Yeah. We were both staying at the motel. I joined him there after I went to dinner with Ms Tracy. We had a party, celebrating the shit I'd created at your town, and he told me he had some good stuff. So I took some. But there's more to it than that.'

'You mean you were running drugs?' It was the logical question. Drugs had to be at the bottom of the whole case, I couldn't see any other explanation.

'Not me,' he said miserably. 'John Waites and Tracy and the Jeffries were all running drugs. They used to bring them in at Sault Ste Marie. They had a deal with one of the Customs guys. They used a special suitcase. Moira Waites would pick the case up when she came to visit and carry it back to Toronto.'

'And were you involved?'

'No.' He said it fervently. 'I've only been involved in this gang stuff as a favour to Ms Tracy. She said she would give me the part if I did it, to keep you busy. And to pick up Phil, get him involved.'

We were approaching the turn-off for Honey Harbour and I slowed and turned on the indicator. 'We'll talk some more later. When we get there, you run up to the door in a panic and tell them the kid's out cold, you had to hit him. Can he come and help carry him inside.'

'Right,' he said, then drew a deep breath, the way I've seen Fred do when she was rehearsing a part. I knew he was going over his business and said nothing as we pulled up at the door.

I got out quickly and pretended to be digging into the rear seat with the open door between me and the house. Walker took his cue and dropped down out of sight. He had his gun drawn and he was resting his head on Sam, who was looking at me expectantly. I waited thirty seconds and then Hanson came running out. 'He's gone,' he shouted. 'He's left the woman here tied up.'

'I'll check.' I called Sam and sent him ahead through the open door. He bounded in, barking. A woman was lying on the floor, her hands tied behind her, a tea-towel wrapped around her mouth. I left her there a moment longer while Sam checked each of the tiny bedrooms. They were empty. Then I holstered my gun and took out my pocket knife and cut her hands free. She fumbled with the cloth around her mouth and I checked her hands and undid the knot.

She was gasping with fright and anger. 'That bastard!' she screamed. 'He didn't have to do that to me.'

'Who didn't?' I knew but I wanted her confirmation.

'Kershaw,' she said, gasping, out of breath but becoming calmer. 'George Kershaw. He's the man who killed Moira.'

'You're not Moira Waites?' Now she had surprised me.

'No. I'm Carolyn Jeffries. Kershaw killed Moira and put her in the trunk of her car.'

CHAPTER SIXTEEN

I looked at her stupidly. 'Waites told me that the woman in the trunk of his car was Carolyn Jeffries.'

'I'm Carolyn Jeffries,' she sobbed. 'They told you I was dead so that nobody would know Moira was dead. Waites would have said she ran away with Stu.'

'Well, why did you run away? And who helped you when you left your car up that side-road?'

'Questions,' she said bitterly. 'I've been terrorized and abused in every kind of way by an animal since last night and you ask me questions.' She was weeping uncontrollably. 'A man has been in prison for six years. Can't you see how horrible it's been?'

'I'm sorry. I'll get you to a doctor.'

She would talk later, she would tell us everything, but this wasn't the time to ask questions. I went to the kitchen for water and as I returned, Walker came in, breathless. 'I've looked all around outside. He's gone,' he said.

'Meet Mrs Jeffries. She's just telling me what's going on.' It was his cue to nod and say nothing while she talked.

Now, with a glass of water in her hands and the knowledge that the worst was over, she did. 'Waites got Kershaw out of prison. I don't know how. He brought him up here to kill Moira. Then we got a phone call, Stu did. We were just finishing dinner. And he said we had to leave right away. I wanted to know why but he just said we were in terrible danger. So we left. Then some woman lent

302

us a car and checked us into a motel. And that's where that bastard found us.'

'But what were you scared of? Why didn't you just go to the police?' I knew the answer but I wanted confirmation. Walker and I listened intently wanting to hear and remember every word she said.

'Drugs,' she said bitterly. 'Waites and Stu had cooked up this scheme to bring in cocaine over the border at the Soo. I never realized until the last time Moira visited. She had begun to wonder why her husband encouraged her to come and see us so often. Then, last time, I found Stu repacking her case, putting her clothes into the duplicate case he had in his closet, the one he used when he crossed the border.'

That was enough for a start. It was time to do the difficult thing. 'Mrs Jeffries, I'm afraid I have some bad news for you,' I said.

She turned and picked up the tea-towel she had been gagged with and wiped her eyes angrily. 'Not news,' she said. 'I was there, wasn't I? I saw him doing it, killing Stu for that goddamn suitcase.'

She sat on the couch, sobbing. Walker looked at me. 'I'll get the superintendent. He can take over.'

The superintendent wasn't much bothered about public relations. He came into the room and spoke to Mrs Jeffries. 'We'll find this guy, he can't have got far.'

303

Not a word of sympathy for her loss or for the ordeal she had been through. Just business. It rang as clumsily as the old gag about 'Are you widow Jeffries?' but she took no notice and it reminded me that I had personal priorities of my own. I checked my watch. It was nine o'clock. I was supposed to be at the hospital, collecting Fred.

I spoke up. 'I've got to pick up my wife from hospital, sir. I'd like to leave my dog guarding my place in case Kershaw is after me. He threatened to try.'

'No need for that.' The superintendent was playing by the rules now, his rules. 'I'll send an officer to watch your place until you get home.'

'There's a neighbour woman coming in to tidy up for me. That's why I can't leave the dog on watch. Can you get someone over there right away?'

'I said I'd do it.' He was imperious now. I was nominally a chief but if I'd been in the OPP I would have been at best a sergeant. He didn't want discussions he wanted obedience.

'Fine. Thank you. I have to get her. When she's settled in, I'll come down to the station and we can tidy things up. Right now I need a ride back to my car.'

'Good.' He nodded to Walker. 'We'll take these people back to Murphy's Harbour for now. You look after Mr Bennett.'

So that was me, a mere citizen in his eyes. Walker said, 'We'll take the detective car, Reid,' and we went out to it and got in, with Sam in the back seat.

'Make sure he sends somebody,' I told Walker. 'This guy Kershaw swore he was going to get me and I don't want my wife and kid in danger.'

'It'll be done,' Walker said. 'I'll make sure of it if it should slip his busy mind.' Sarcasm dripped off the word 'busy'. I was glad once again that I didn't work for a big department. The politics are endless.

He let me off at the Horn house. Jean had already gone so I couldn't turn Sam over to her, which would have been the perfect answer. Instead I stuck him in the front seat and set off for Parry Sound.

Fred was dressed and waiting, with the baby asleep in her arms. She beamed when she saw me. 'I thought you'd forgotten us.'

'Sorry, love, it's been a busy morning but we've wrapped things up now, we can relax.' The OPP would soon find Kershaw, I thought, no need to alarm her.

She kissed my stubbly cheek. 'You're looking kind of lived-in, old thing,' she said. 'Been up all night carousing?'

'You're half right,' I kidded. 'Except the carousing part.'

She wrapped the baby a little tighter in her shawl and I went for a nurse. That meant we had to take a wheelchair which made Fred a little impatient. 'I'm going to have to walk when I get home,' she protested cheerfully.

'All the more reason to sit while you can,' the nurse said and we all went out to the front door.

The nurse laughed when she saw the scout car. 'Hey, wonderful limousine service you've got.'

The one thing I'd forgotten was a car seat for the baby, so I took five minutes to drive into town and buy one. Then we strapped it in place and set the baby in it, her head close to the shotgun in its front seat bracket. Fred smiled. 'I'll tell her about this when she's older. Her very first ride was in a police car.'

I strapped Fred in neatly and set off down the highway, travelling at the limit, scaring a whole line of drivers into unusually good driving manners. It was a beautiful morning, blue skies, warm, perfect high summer and I tried to relax. The only missing link in the chain was Kershaw and he wouldn't stay loose for very long. But his threat still bothered me. And he was in striking distance of the house. It made me cautious as I drove up the last half mile from Murphy's Harbour to the house. Fred was sitting up, bright and talkative. If she sensed I was on edge she said nothing about it. And then we reached the house and I saw Elaine Harper's OPP cruiser in the yard, next to Horn's pickup.

'Company so early?' Fred said. 'What's the occasion?'

'Jean Horn offered to come over and freshen the place up,' I said. 'And the OPP car is Elaine Harper's, you've met her. I guess she's stopped off to see the baby.'

I pulled in on the far side of the other cars, still cautious.

'Stay here a moment, I'll get the camera,' I lied. Something wasn't right. Two women in the house and a baby arriving on the doorstep. One of them should have come to the door.

'We can get pictures later,' Fred said, but I said, 'Please, I want to catch this moment.'

She leaned over and kissed me. 'You're a sentimental s.o.b., Bennett, and I love you.'

I patted her hand and got out, letting Sam out of the car. I whispered 'Seek' and pretended to tie my shoe lace as he ran around through the bushes, finding nothing.

I straigtened up then and headed for the house. Nobody came to the door and I felt my skin draw tight with tension. Something was wrong, I was sure of it.

At the door I hesitated. If Kershaw was inside, threatening the women with his shotgun he would kill me the moment I opened the door. If he wasn't, I was being a fool. But I had to be sure.

I thought for a moment, then pretended to fumble in my pocket for keys. I turned to look at Fred who was craning down to see through the window of the other cars to the door. I made a turning motion with my hand and mouthed, 'Forgot my key.'

Then I stopped off to one side of the door and reached across to tap it with my knuckles, withdrawing my hand at once.

Instantly the door blew apart, the shotgun load shredding it in a shocking burst of sound. I gave a shout and slammed both feet hard on the floor, like a flamenco dancer, still standing off to one side.

It seemed like a year and then the muzzle of the gun stuck out through the hole in the door, pointing down to where my body should have been lying.

I grabbed the muzzle, feeling it hot in my palm, and snatched it towards me. He hung on but I wrenched him against the inside of the door and I had the muzzle turned from me. Still holding it with all my strength, I threw my weight against the broken door and it gave, sending the door back against the wall. He was in there but not trapped. He let go of the gun and tried to get out. I didn't hesitate. I drew my revolver and reached around the door to shoot him through the body. He gave a grunting cry and went slack. I hooked the door away from him with one foot and stood over him, gun trained on the middle of his chest.

It was Kershaw. His hair was greyer than

in his photograph but unmistakable. He was holding his side and blood was oozing through his fingers.

'Jean! Elaine!' I shouted, and heard a muffled half scream. I stepped away from Kershaw, carrying his shotgun in one hand, my service revolver in the other, and crouched to look around the door jamb into the kitchen.

Both women were lying face down on the floor, hands and mouths tied with strips of tea-towels. Elaine looked up at me. 'Is there anyone else?' I shouted it, in case the shots had deafened her. She shook her head and I took a quick look back at Kershaw. He hadn't moved and I pulled a knife off the magnetic strip and cut her hands free, then Jean Horn's.

'He's down. Watch him,' I said as they untied their gags. I grabbed the phone and rang the station. Walker answered and I filled him in. I was trembling with tension and fury. 'The bastard could have killed my family,' I shouted.

'Be right there. Take care of the women.'

Walker hung up and I turned to the women. 'Did he hurt you?'

Jean spoke first. 'No. He said he was going to have some fun when you were dead. He didn't want to take the time until then.' She was calm but pale.

'Sit down,' I told her. 'You too, Elaine.'

Elaine sat, weeping. 'I'm sorry, Reid. I was sitting having a coffee with Jean and he just walked in on us with that gun. I should have been doing my job.'

'Forget it. Sit down. I'll get my wife and baby in.'

Elaine stayed where she was but Jean came out to the living-room where Kershaw was sitting, blank-faced, pressing his hands uselessly against the wound in his side. 'He's hurt bad,' Jean said. 'Leave him. Get Fred. Take her in the back way.'

I touched her on the shoulder in gratitude and ran back out to Fred. She was in the front seat of the car, the baby in her arms, talking softly to her. 'It's over,' I said. 'You can come in now.'

She looked up at me, rocking gently with the baby, her face chalk white. 'I can't take this,' she said softly. 'I love you. You know that. But I saw that door explode. You could be lying there now, dead.'

She began to weep, tears spouting from her open eyes. I bent and held her very close and she forced her head into my shoulder, wiping her eyes to and fro against my shirt front. 'It's over,' I told her. 'I'll quit this job if you want.'

'It's never over,' she sobbed. And then Jean Horn came out of the house. She came over and touched me on the back and I let go of Fred and stood up.

Jean knelt beside her. 'What a beautiful baby.' She held out her hands and slowly Fred gave up Louise and Jean took her, crooning to her in Ojibway.

Fred wiped her eyes on her sleeve and got to her feet. 'Let's get inside,' she said.

Jean straightened up, carrying the baby, and I took Fred's arm and led her to the back door. Elaine Harper opened it without speaking and Fred stepped up inside. 'Where is he?' she asked me.

'In the front, by the door. Stay with Elaine, please.'

Elaine steered her to a chair and I went to Kershaw. His head had slumped forward and his jaw had dropped. I knew he was dead.

I was crouching there and I heard a car pull up outside. Walker and the other detective came up the steps, the superintendent behind them. Walker bent and felt Kershaw's throat. 'Well, he won't make any more trouble,' he said softly.

The superintendent was puffing. 'What the hell happened here?'

'I'll tell you in a minute. Right now I've got to look after my family.'

The superintendent looked at me sharply. 'You can't just walk away,' he began.

'Watch me,' I told him.

I went back to the kitchen. It was empty. Fred and Elaine were standing outside with

311

Jean Horn who was still holding the baby. 'You can't take her into the house with that thing in the door,' Jean said. 'I'll take them home with me until it's cleared up.'

Fred protested but Jean clung to the baby, crooning. 'It's better,' she said.

I took Fred's arm. 'It really is, dear. I won't be long here. Then I'll pack us a bag and we'll take right off for your folks.'

'Maybe,' she said and I was happy to see the first of the steel coming back into her voice.

I drove them over in the scout car and came back to find the ambulance crew taking Kershaw's body out of the house. The superintendent was talking to Elaine Harper and he looked at me as I came in.

'I hear you were too smart for him.'

'Seems that way. I hope you've got all the pictures you need. I'm going to scrub that blood out of the walls and get a new door put in.'

'We don't need pictures. We have first-hand evidence from PW Harper,' he said. 'Go ahead.'

And so I did it, changing the cleaning water four times before every trace of the blood was gone. Then I called the lumber yard and got them to send a new door right away, and a handyman. After that I sat down and made a formal statement to the OPP.

'You're free and clear,' Walker said. 'Clear

312

case of self-defence.'

'Good.' I was still not talking much. 'Now I want you to take the prisoners away. I'm through. Right now I'm hanging up my skates.'

'For keeps?' he asked in surprise. 'Hell, Reid, don't be too hasty on this. You've got a good little place here.'

'If my wife wants me out, I'm quitting. Right now I'm taking time off.'

'Good idea.' The superintendent had come out of the house and was listening. 'We'll tidy up the ends.'

And take whatever credit was around, I thought without bitterness. 'We got statements from everybody,' Walker said. 'What a bunch of whiners, they were all so eager to get off, that they've incriminated the hell out of one another.'

'What did they do about a lawyer?'

'Hell, shysters came down like flies on honey,' Walker laughed. 'Two from Parry Sound, three from Midland, phone calls from as far away as Toronto.'

'But the suspects all talked?'

'Yeah. Sang like birds,' Walker said happily. 'We got everything. Bill Holland came down with Inspector Dupuy from Parry Sound. He says you called the whole shot on it.'

'Walk me through it,' I said and the superintendent stepped in. 'You're still in shock,' he said. 'Do you have a drink in the house?'

'Yes. Good idea. I'm off duty now.'

I got my bottle of Black Velvet rye and after a little polite headshaking they all joined me. I poured myself a solid double, the others took them lighter and Walker relaxed with his drink on his knee.

'Waites was at the bottom of everything. Him and Jeffries. They were running coke over the border at the Soo and down to Toronto. They were working for some sleazebucket Waites defended one time in court. Jeffries was the pipeline. He'd pick it up and bring it this far, then Waites' wife would bring it down. Only she didn't know what was going on until a couple of weeks ago when her friend Carolyn found Jeffries changing the suitcase Moira had brought up for a new one, full of junk. The women talked about it and Moira Waites was going to blow the whistle.'

That all made sense and I nodded. 'And Waites sprung Kershaw to kill her?'

'Right. He set her up, Kershaw killed her and put the car in the lake, slashing the seats so you'd think it was a gang thing. Then Waites rang the Jeffries and told them what had happened. They panicked and ran. Ms Tracy met them on a side-road and put them into a motel. Kershaw and Hanson were already staying at the other place, where you found Hanson.'

'What was Tracy's angle? Money for her movie, what?'

'Yes. Waites promised to get her the money she needed if and when the murder came off as planned. Her end was to create a disturbance and take care of Kershaw. That's why she organized young Hanson to fake this gang crap.'

'What went wrong?' They'd all got what they wanted, I thought.

'Kershaw wanted more money. He'd been paid ten grand but he knew he had Waites over a barrel. He went after more. And at the same time Jeffries made trouble. He had money in a safety deposit box in the bank but he couldn't get it. So he went to Pickerel Point to have it out with Waites and they fought and he killed him and took the case, knowing it was loaded with coke and he could get money on that.'

'And Kershaw went after the case.'

'Right. Ms Tracy helped him, told him where the Jeffries were hiding and lent him her car. Only she acted too fast. She realized you'd come asking questions when you saw her car was missing. That's why she banged her face up and said she'd been assaulted.' Walker raised his glass triumphantly. 'But we got 'em.'

The superintendent sipped his rye slowly. 'Kershaw's been up here ever since he got away from Toronto. When you found Hanson at the motel he got out of the back window and ran. That night he hid out, stole food from the grocery. He didn't want to kill you until he'd got more money to get away. He figured he'd get more from Waites, he was counting on it. He didn't know Waites was going to be killed.'

'And Ms Tracy set him up to kill me?'

'Yeah,' the superintendent said. He didn't like telling this part of the story, but maybe the drink had loosened him up a little. 'She figured by then that you were pretty good at your job. That's why she'd had Hanson pull this gang caper. But when you were right behind her, stepping on her heels every move she made, she figured you had to go.'

It was as close to a compliment as I would ever get from this man. I changed the subject. 'Why did she involve young Freund?'

Walker explained it. 'She had Hanson pick up Kershaw's kid in the beginning, so she would have something to hold over Kershaw's head. Apparently he wanted to see the boy, despite the divorce.'

'But in the end he tried to have him kidnapped,' I protested.

'When he didn't get the coke and didn't get any of the money Waites had promised him, yeah. He figured, kill two birds with one stone: spend time with his kid, have his

316

ex-wife pay him as well.'

There was a tap on the door and I went out to find the guys from the lumber yard there. No carpenter. They were sorry but he was sick.

That did it for me. I shoved the OPP guys out and spent an hour hanging the door and fitting a new lock. Then I drove over to the Horns' place. Fred came to the door when I got there. She said nothing for about half a minute, we stood and looked at one another and then she kissed me, gently. 'Let's go home,' she said. 'I'll get Louise.'

So I thanked Jean and drove my wife and baby back to the house. She looked at the new door. 'Pretty neat. Ever think of taking up carpentry as a career?'

'I can do,' I said carefully. 'I'm off now and I'm not going back.'

She undid the straps around our daughter. 'Not for a month anyway,' she said. 'We'll go out west first, think things over from a distance.'

'OK.' I put my arm around her shoulders and we walked slowly up the steps to the house, feeling my way back into my life, wondering if anything would be the same from here on.